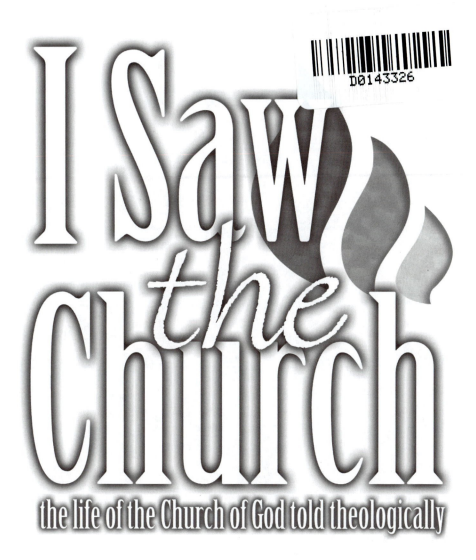

I Saw the Church

the life of the Church of God told theologically

by

Merle D. Strege

Arthur M. Kelly, Editor
Arthur M. Kelly, Publication Coordinator
Cover and Layout by Curtis Corzine and Virginia L. Wachenschwanz

Contents

For

Robert H. Reardon

Friend of God and Servant of the Church

I am praising God tonight for salvation in Jesus, for his saving, keeping, and healing power. I was saved and sanctified seven years ago and have not grown tired. The way gets brighter all the time. When I accepted this truth, I declared myself free from sectism, having prior to that time joined three denominations, the first when I was about twelve years of age. The first time I heard a saint preach, I discerned the body of Christ, which is his church.

Mrs. W. B. Steele
Pounding Mill, Virginia

I was converted a number of years ago, and enjoyed many blessings, God witnessing to my soul that he was with me. I lived in sectism all those years, but about six years ago I heard the whole truth preached. I saw the one body and obeyed God's command and came out, rejoicing in Jesus.

D. H. Akers
Hooker, Oklahoma

This morning finds me with victory in my soul, brought about by two works of grace. In my heart is great rejoicing that the church, the church that is the bride of Christ is being robed in garments to meet the bridegroom.

Juletta Jordan
Phoenix, Arizona

I write this to encourage dear ones to trust in the Lord. I have found his word true where he says he will do more for us than we can think or ask for. I thank God for the church of God, the pillar and ground of the truth.

S. J. Brown
Florida

Foreword

An ancient Greek philosopher spoke to the tension between theory and practice when he wrote "history is philosophy teaching by example."[1] A current-day church historian has tweaked that aphorism to suggest that the history of the Church of God is its theology worked out by practice. For those more accustomed to reading theology from a systematized, sometimes esoteric, text, this may be a rather striking claim. In Merle Strege's telling, however, the stories of the significant people and events in the life of the Church of God constitute not only that movement's history but also the formation of its doctrines.

Certainly others have addressed both the history and the theology of the Church of God. From the days of its late nineteenth-century founding, leaders of the movement published a magazine and eventually books chronicling their activities and the development of their beliefs. In the last two generations particularly, scholars examined the broad sweep of the movement as well as some of the nuances of its doctrines. Specifically, John W. V. Smith's *The Quest for Holiness and Unity* provides a comprehensive history of the first century of the movement. Barry Callen's *Contours of a Cause* and *It's God's Church* and Gilbert Stafford's *Theology for Disciples* and *Church of God at the Crossroads* provide insights into components of the movement's theology. And Strege's previous work, particularly in *Tell Me the Tale* and *Tell Me Another Tale* and a chapter in his edited work *Baptism and Church*, explores myriad connections between the movement's participants and its beliefs.

The current work by Professor Strege is somewhat different than these, though, and this difference adds crucial insights into how a church movement first casts then institutionalizes its theology. Equally well educated as a historian and a theologian, the author avoids the temptation to deal with these two elements separately by emphasizing the narrative quality of theological formation within the church. Strege's work demonstrates that he is well informed both in history and theology of the power and complexity of the study of narrative. In such work, the story of the subject becomes preeminent over theoretical models or abstract debates. In the case of the Church of God, Strege argues that the theology of the movement emerged as the people, both leaders and followers, lived out what they thought it meant

i

to be a church. Beyond origins, Strege describes crucial turning points in the life of the movement that contributed to the unfolding of the story, bringing it through crises and prosperity and into the twenty-first century. Often these points also led to a recasting of the previous stories into useable models for present circumstances.

In his artful narrative, Strege serves at least three types of audiences. First, those who consider themselves to be a part of the Church of God reformation movement will find rich retellings of the heritage of the movement, its leaders, and its foundation. For relative newcomers to the movement, this work will explain such features as why there is no creed, confession, or formal membership. Longtime followers will likely know the works of Smith, Callen, Stafford, and Strege, and will recognize in this volume not repetition but a grand synthetic weaving of threads contained in the previous works. Likely, the narrative casting of the development of church doctrine will also be enlightening to those within the movement. Invariably, there will be those who, upon reading the "original doctrinal intent" of the founders, will want to return to that vision of the church. Others will see the progression through the decades and understand afresh Stafford's reasons for describing the Church of God at a "crossroads" in his latest work. The dialectic posed by these views is but the latest version of the process described in this volume. In this sense, Strege's work is an invitation to dialogue within the church on the function of theology of any stripe for the people of the Church of God.

A second audience, those rooted in similar church backgrounds, will find in Strege's work a strong model for analysis of their own settings. Several holiness churches founded in the nineteenth-century struggled with questions of identity and purpose, especially in the decades following the Second World War. Some moved squarely into the ranks of Evangelical Protestantism; others gravitated toward mainline denominations; still others faded entirely from the ecclesiastical horizon. At their inception, each of these groups also "saw the church." Reading the story of the Church of God's theological development provides useful handles for understanding how groups with such a strong narrative core confronted challenges from within and from the outside. Recognizing that a group's path sometimes depends as much on a casual comment, an impromptu meeting, or an untimely illness as it does on the work of the Holy Spirit places that group's past, present, and future in clearer perspective. Strege's clear-eyed analysis provides hope and a path for those who seek understanding of similar stories.

Still a third audience, that of professional scholars in the fields of history and theology, will be delighted to find a volume with a strong analytical thesis, extensive and thorough documentation, and innovative interpretative approach. Not only in his blending of history and theology, but also particularly in Strege's application of insights from narrative theory, serious students will find a significant contribution to techniques for the study of religious groups. His endnotes and bibliography will serve those who follow as a powerful beacon. Strege steps confidently into the middle of a lively debate among historians about the differences between and the relative merits of "telling stories" and interpreting events.[2] Historians and theologians will eagerly read Strege's blending of these elements.

Strege's contributions at these levels testify to his intent both to serve and educate through his work. This volume, as well as his previous work, manifests a deep concern for his subject. But he does not allow that personal attachment to cloud his obligation to scholarship. It is not an easy task to explain how a people who disavow denominationalism create a church or how an organization and body of teaching emerge from those who decry established order and are suspicious of authority. In that sense, contemplating the implications of Strege's work will be both challenging and rewarding for his readers.

1. Dionysius of Halicarnassus.
2. For more on this discussion, see Allan Megill, "Recounting the Past: Description, Explanation, and Narrative in Historiography." *American Historical Review* 94 (June 1989), 627–653.

Cole P. Dawson
Professor of History
Warner Pacific College
Portland, Oregon

Acknowledgements

Some people possess a remarkable ability to write independently of the aid and assistance of others. I am not such a writer. The list of people to whom I have become indebted in the course of writing this book is long indeed. Some of my debts are of recent origin, but others reach back more than half a century. To attempt to acknowledge all the people who in one way or another have helped me with this project raises the fear that I will fail to mention all who deserve recognition here; to any who are unintentionally slighted I offer my sincerest apologies. You know the help that you gave, and that knowledge will unfortunately have to suffice.

This book has been in gestation for more than twenty years, ever since I first offered a course in the history of the Church of God at Anderson University's School of Theology. Before I taught that course, I had to learn something about the Church of God myself. The man who first introduced me to that subject was the late John W. V. Smith, who carried around in his head a knowledge of the movement more comprehensive than any other person I have known. Any list of acknowledgements must begin with "John W. V." After my seminary study came graduate school and three professors in particular who guided my development and gave me opportunities to try my wings as a fledgling scholar and teacher. Thanks to Eldon Ernst, Joe Chinnici, and John von Rohr of the Graduate Theological Union for their encouragement and investment in me.

Once I began teaching the history of the Church of God, scores of students were subjected to my ideas and interpretations. The great majority listened carefully, most of the time quite patiently but sometimes not, and had both the interest and good sense to question me—often, in the process, immeasurably improving my understanding. I have also lectured in many different church settings: ministers meetings, anniversary celebrations, state and national conventions, and so forth. Listeners there have always granted me a fair and courteous hearing before asking questions or commenting out of their knowledge in ways that also have contributed to my understanding of the movement's history. I owe a debt of thanks to all those who have listened, commented, and questioned over the last twenty years and more.

Several individuals contributed the kind of assistance on which scholars depend if they are to write on the basis of adequate research. Archivists and librarians at Asbury Theological Seminary and Winebrenner Theological

Seminary aided my research into the origins of some of the earliest theological ideas and connections of the Church of God. And I could not have written this book at all without the generous assistance of Douglas Welch, Director of the Archives of the Church of God, who without complaint or murmur speedily answered my request for another obscure document, record, or photograph. A research grant from the Faculty Development Fund at Anderson University also directly benefited my work by underwriting the expenses for a summer research assistant, Todd Faulkner. Justin Kauffman prepared the indices. Much of the first draft of this book was completed during a sabbatical leave from Anderson University, for which I am also appreciative. Other portions were written during time that I stole from some of my responsibilities as a committee member and department chairperson. From my dean, Blake Janutolo, I nevertheless heard only expressions of support for this project.

My work has also benefited from discussions with several friends of many years' acquaintance. For more than twenty years Anderson University has been my academic home, and I am privileged to work there with colleagues who I also count among my friends. Their interest in this study and concern for me, especially in its final stages, has been a source of great encouragement and strength. Conversations with Spencer Spaulding, Fred Shively, James Lewis, and Barry Callen pointed me in new directions. James Christoph, Cole Dawson, James Lewis, Robert Reardon, and Gilbert Stafford read the manuscript either in whole or in part and offered valuable criticisms that markedly improved my writing. Other friends—Gene Newberry, Harold Phillips, and Gene Sterner—offered suggestions as enlightening as they were crucial in saving me from serious errors. Any that remain in this book are mine alone; the contributions of my friends have only strengthened it. My three weekly breakfast companions, Rich Willowby, Bill Soetenga, and Arthur Kelly, improved my work as their friendship improves me. The last named of those three also edited the manuscript. I cannot say what a gift it is to have in the same person a highly skilled editor and a particular friend of many years who often understands better than I what it is I want to say.

Then there is my wife of nearly thirty-three years, Fran, a daughter of the Church of God who loves it dearly. The persistence of her questions about its life and thought were matched by her patient toleration of my early evening sleepiness at the end of yet another day when I had started writing at an hour of the morning that she considers impossible. My oldest debt is to the people of Park Church of God in St. Paul Park, Minnesota. Most of those sensible, decent, God-fearing men and women who contributed so much to my early religious formation are now gone. Had they not been the saints they were, I suspect that my enthusiasm for the church that held their vision would be far less than it is.

Lastly, and by way of explaining this volume's dedication, I wish to acknowledge the intellectual and spiritual debts that I owe Robert H. Reardon, Anderson University President Emeritus since 1982. It is said that contemporary college presidents differ from their predecessors in that the latter read history and philosophy whereas the former contemplate financial statements. It was my good fortune that Dr. Reardon's presidency was in some respects a throwback to the nineteenth-century American evangelical college. The clergymen-presidents of that era typically taught moral philosophy, the capstone course of the undergraduate curriculum. By the time I arrived on the Anderson campus as a freshman in the autumn of 1965, he no longer taught courses, but Dr. Reardon used the undergraduate chapel pulpit to similar effect. An able preacher who routinely took his turn in a rich and varied program of speakers and artists, he proved the quintessential model of a Christian disciple's pursuit of the life of the mind. The dedication of this book means to recognize and thank him for that example.

Merle D. Strege
Lent, 2002

Prologue

In the mind of C. W. Naylor all was not well with the Church of God movement as it approached seventy years of age. The time had come for honest reflection and a critical assessment of the movement's theology and its stance among the churches of North America. A veteran minister of the Church of God, Naylor believed that he had earned the right to offer this criticism in the hope that it would clarify ideas about the movement's mission, enabling it to achieve a sense of its own identity in the process. At the middle of the twentieth century Naylor was one of a handful of surviving ministers who could say that they knew D. S. Warner, whose labors were crucial to the movement's beginning. His ministry overlapped Warner's for three and a half years before the latter's death in 1895. Naylor was a witness and participant in many of the sweeping changes that had occurred in the Church of God from its earliest decades to the beginning of the post World War II era. Yet he did not rest his criticism on the authority of an eyewitness and one who had personally known Warner at that. He also was a careful student of the books and articles published by Church of God ministers and writers all the way back to the movement's beginning days. It was on the basis of this combination of experience and thorough analysis that he offered his constructive criticism.

Naylor discussed his views in a self-published pamphlet titled *The Teaching of D. S. Warner and His Associates.* With a frankness uncharacteristic of other Church of God writers of the era, Naylor candidly identified serious flaws in both Warner's theology as well as some of his actions. In Naylor's view Warner was wrong on a range of theological ideas and policies, methods of biblical exegesis and hermeneutics, from the return of Christ to strategies for the unity of all Christians. By extension, that the Church of God perpetuated such ideas and practices indicated that it, too, was flawed. Naylor's view of the church, however, included more than its theological warts. Those blemishes were not the whole story when it came to the movement's theology. Other voices had begun declaring a message that differed from Warner's in considerable measure, and in Naylor's mind they offered hope for the future. He also noted with some satisfaction the Church of God movement's rapid growth and the global reach of many of its programs and activities. In the middle of the twentieth century it was time to take stock theologically, discarding outmoded or mistaken ideas and incorporating new ones to frame the identity and mission of a church communion in which a considerable vitality not only remained but remained strong.

A little more than a half-century after Naylor offered his assessment of Warner and the Church of God, Gilbert W. Stafford published a small book that, like Naylor's pamphlet, assessed the Church of God in terms of theology and practice. Also like Naylor, Stafford was a veteran minister of the Church of God, having served churches in Massachusetts and Michigan before joining the faculty of the School of Theology at Anderson University. By the time Stafford had written this book,[1] he had taught systematic theology at Anderson for more than twenty years. Unlike Naylor, Stafford possessed the kind of academic credentials owned by none in Naylor's generation and by only a few of the people in church and academic leadership at the time Naylor wrote his pamphlet. In contrast, by Stafford's day academic credentials such as his were common among professors of theology and religious studies at Church of God colleges and its seminary.[2] That was but one index of the changes in the Church of God between the middle of the twentieth century and the beginning of the twenty-first. Another was Stafford's long history of interest and participation in ecumenical Christianity, one of the areas that Naylor had identified as a candidate for revision of earlier Church of God practice. In cèrtain respects Stafford embodied that revision.

As with Naylor, so also in the mind of Gilbert Stafford all was not well with the Church of God. His assessment of developments in the movement begins in recollections from his childhood and reaches to the turn of the twenty-first century, essentially the period between Naylor's pamphlet and his own book. Unlike his predecessor's study, Stafford stopped short of historical analysis, preferring instead to describe the Church of God in its present situation and the issues he saw at stake for its future. The church, said Stafford, was at a crossroads. Focusing on what he called the culture of the Church of God, Stafford noted a series of challenges, opportunities, and possibilities facing the people of the movement. The very first of the challenges that he addressed was the issue of self-understanding, asking, "What is the Church of God movement?" In the process he observed that very little by way of practices or theological commitments could any longer be assumed to connect all congregations. About the only assumptions that could be made for any church listed in the *Yearbook of the Church of God,* wrote Stafford, was that the congregation was duly approved for inclusion, assumed to hold regular public worship, and named Christ as Savior and Lord.[3] When one of the church's most distinguished and accomplished ministers makes such an assessment, eyebrows are sure to raise. A half-century earlier, Naylor had posed similar questions, although he did not state them as explicitly as

Stafford. Neither concluded that all was lost, but through the metaphor of a crossroads Stafford described the situation and issues confronting the Church of God under a note of warning: the time had come for the church to decide on the course of its future direction.

"I can only answer the question, 'What am I to do?,' " said moral philosopher Alasdair MacIntyre, "if I can answer the prior question, 'Of what stories do I find myself a part?' "[4] Humans are essentially story-telling creatures, said MacIntyre. Through our history we become "tellers of stories that aspire to truth."[5] In the process we learn who we are and what is expected of us. Storytelling communities also learn that they are not unencumbered selves but part of a people whose existence carries attachments and expectations. When such a people narrate their history they therefore engage in a political as well as a moral art.[6] Stated in its simplest and most direct form, Naylor's pamphlet and Stafford's book ask the same question, "What is the Church of God to be and do?" Neither leaves his readers without suggestions as to possible answers. However, before proceeding to answers prior work remains. In the following chapters a narrative unfolds that will inform and therefore should assist those who want to work on that question. If MacIntyre is correct, such a narrative is crucial to that task. Without a knowledge of the path that brought them to a crossroads, a people cannot have a clear sense of identity and therefore can have but little sense of the direction they are to take.

Before the story can begin, a few descriptions and explanations are in order. In the first place, what follows is not a full-fledged history of the Church of God (Anderson). Readers who open this book expecting to find a work similar to John W. V. Smith's *The Quest for Holiness and Unity* will be disappointed. There is a story here, but it is not a comprehensive narrative covering all aspects of the life of the Church of God movement. Little mention is made of important dimensions of that life such as the history of Church of God missions, or the development of specific institutions, important though each of those is in its own right. Neither does this story include every person important to the history of the Church of God or attempt to tell the story of the Church of God globally. Instead this book focuses on what might be called the Church of God movement's thought life or theology and practices that are so deeply intertwined with that life that it is at points impossible to separate them. However, even this narrower focus is limited. The story that unfolds in the following pages is not a complete history of theology in the Church of God. Aspects of various theological categories are considered as they bear on the discussion at hand, often at some length, but readers should not expect to find here an account of all the theological studies produced by ministers and writers of the Church of God.

Since the following chapters narrate neither a comprehensive history of the Church of God nor an overview of its theological history, readers are entitled to ask, "Then what is the subject of this book?" The short answer to that question could be stated thus, "This is an account that attempts to explain, from the movement's beginning, how it arrived at the crossroads described by Gilbert Stafford." What follows is a historical study of the ideas, personalities, events, and cultural currents that have combined to shape the identity of the Church of God movement. The Church of God was born as a protest movement concerned with the reform of the church. To consider the identity of this group is to study ideas and practices concerning its understanding of the church, a topic formally named by the theological category *ecclesiology.* The idea of the church—what it is, what God intends it to be, and how it is to order its life together and in the world—is the heart of the self-understanding of the Church of God. Scratch the surface of many a theological conversation in the movement's history, and its people will be found in actuality to be talking about the church. This book attempts to narrate that conversation through a consideration of those who contributed to it in print and in practice.

The second matter concerns the prominence that this study gives to certain practices of the Church of God. To talk about theology in the Church of God is to discuss what this book calls "doctrinal practices." People accustomed to reading theological studies may be surprised by the importance that a book claiming to be such gives to practices, as they usually have been connected to the culture of a religious body and not its theology. Others may be unfamiliar with the term as it has recently come to be used. On both accounts an explanation is in order. Religious practices and their importance to church groups and other religious bodies are a subject of keen interest in the work of a wide range of scholars and others with a professional interest in religion. Religious educators and theologians appreciate with a renewed conviction that active involvement in a religious community is more than simply sharing its belief system. In Christian terms, faith is shaped by practice as much if not more than by doctrine where doctrine is understood as a set of objectively and rationally stated propositions.[7] Historians of American religion now study religious practices in appreciation of the crucial influence they have in the formation of the identity of religious groups and their individual constituents.[8] Whether in current approaches to ministry in the church or in the scholarly study of religion, practices are taking a larger and larger role in framing the understanding of the identity and commitments of religious women and men.

Theologian James McClendon notes the unusual importance that practices have played theologically in the lives of certain church groups.

Taken together, he calls these groups "baptists." Note the small case *b,* for by it McClendon means to distinguish this large group of churches from specifically Baptist denominations. The baptists, says McClendon, share five distinctive characteristics: (1) "an awareness of the *biblical* story as our story, but also (2) of *mission* as responsibility for costly witness, (3) of *liberty* as the freedom to obey God without state help or hindrance, (4) of *discipleship* as life transformed into obedience to Jesus' lordship, and (5) of *community* as daily sharing in the vision."[9] Many church traditions share these characteristics, from churches of the sixteenth century Radical Reformation to some Methodist bodies to some churches of the American holiness revival. The Church of God (Anderson) is one such group.[10] In describing the baptist tradition McClendon notes that these churches have produced little theology in the sense of works with wide circulation in the broader Christian community. He offers several factors in explanation of this absence, but the one that is of telling influence here is his observation that in the baptist tradition practice has weighed heavier than systematic theology. Thus McClendon wrote a richly suggestive systematic theology in the context of the baptist tradition that, because of the tradition's emphasis on Christian practice, starts with a consideration of ethics. Theology in the baptist tradition begins not with a prolegomenon that explains the intellectual categories of the system about to unfold, but with ethics, because that is where McClendon's "baptists" begin in their practical understanding of the Christian faith. If one is to understand the theological life of the churches of his baptist tradition, it follows that such an account must intertwine the group's theology and practice. For a group such as the Church of God, which has been historically and militantly opposed to the use of creeds or doctrinal summaries as a test of fellowship, practices assume an even greater importance as the means by which people have learned what it means to be a Christian. This is not to say that doctrines have never been the subject of sermon or lecture in the Church of God. But it is a fundamental presupposition of this book that it is impossible to narrate the life of the Church of God theologically without attending to key practices so deeply and inextricably intertwined with the movement's theological vision that they may be referred to as "doctrinal practices." In the Church of God such practices have been, but are not limited to, forms of worship such as footwashing, holiness, divine healing, song writing, church membership, Christian unity, and the organization of the church's work.

How then shall *practices* be defined? The word is more familiar to social scientists, philosophers, and, more recently, theologians than it has been to historians and lay Christians. As employed in this study, the idea of practices is informed by the work of MacIntyre and McClendon. The former defines a practice as

> any coherent and complex form of socially established cooperative activity through which goods internal to that form of activity are realized in the course of trying to achieve those standards of excellence which are appropriate to, and partially definitive of, that form of activity, with the result that human powers to achieve excellence, and human conceptions of the ends and goods involved, are systematically extended.[11]

A definition that complex requires some explication. By way of example, following MacIntyre, we could say that putting a golf ball or executing a wedge shot accurately are not practices, but the game of golf is. It is important to note that practices are social or communal in nature; they are activities whose importance and conduct is shared by most group members. Secondly, as MacIntyre defines them, practices entail standards of excellence. Another name for such standards is virtues, qualities that enable an object or person to fulfill the purpose of its existence. The virtues necessary to a particular practice help to define that practice. Moreover, as the saying goes, "virtue is its own reward"; as internal goods these standards of excellence provide practitioners the satisfaction that comes with determined and skillful participation. A true golfer, even if a professional, plays for the sheer joy that comes with playing well–playing "virtuously" or achieving those standards of excellence, however infrequent and of temporary duration that may be–rather than for the external good of prize money or trophies. McClendon points out the importance of attitude to practice.[12] In his view, to participate in a practice involves not only certain virtues but a serious attitude as well. True golfers will play the ball where it lies and count every stroke. That is to say they will play by the rules that make the practice of golf what it is. By the same token, true golfers do not tee off with a shovel and a tennis ball; in this sense they "play" golf seriously.

Applied simply and directly to the church, practices are activities that "address fundamental human needs and conditions through concrete human acts" as they are "done together and over time."[13] "Enter a Christian community," write Craig Dykstra and Dorothy Bass, "and you will find that you are a part of a community that has been doing this thing for centuries–not doing it as well as it should, to be sure, but doing it steadily, in conscious continuity with the stories of the Bible and in frequent conversation about how to do it better. You join by jumping in where you are...."[14] Practices shape the life of the church. When a specific church tradition possesses no formally stated doctrinal consensus, no confession of faith to serve as the basis of fellowship, the practices of that group take on added importance. They become more than expressions or carriers of doctrine. At the very least, the practices of such groups embody their doctrine; in a very real sense they *are* the group's doctrine. Some Christian practices the Church of God shares with the wider fellowship of all Christians. However, and although they may not be hundreds of years old, other practices of the Church of God and the manner in which its constituents have followed them have defined the movement as they have also functioned as its doctrine. In the Church of God movement it has rarely been sufficient to agree to doctrinal propositions; doctrinal practice has been the proof of the pudding. It wasn't so much what people believed about holiness, the nature of the church, or the kingdom of God. Beliefs are important, but not finally the basis of fellowship. In the Church of God movement, what counted was doctrinal practice.

Since practices have played such a crucial role in the theological life of the Church of God, an important aspect of the history of the movement's theology turns on theology's location. For nearly five decades—almost half its life—the Church of God movement possessed no seminary or true college for the training of ministers. In those early years theology was a task open to any person with an idea and the will to express it in print, and doctrine was practiced by all who were committed to the movement and its vision of the church. To be sure, the editor of the Gospel Trumpet Company was the movement's key theological educator, but the home of doctrine was nonetheless the church at large. It was not the province of academic specialists, that is to say, those who taught theology in schools. In this open environment the church's doctrinal practices played a crucial role in educating the people of the Church of God movement. It was therefore a portentous moment in the movement's history when colleges and, later, a seminary were founded because in such institutions theology is not carried in practices as much as it is the subject of rational analysis and discussion. For example, it is very easy—one might say almost natural—for a seminary course on evangelism to consider theories and a theology of evangelism without providing student experiences in evangelistic techniques. It isn't that seminary professors are opposed to evangelism or the acquisition of skills in that area; it is just that skill development is not often thought to be on a par with the theoretical analysis that is the first consideration in most institutions of higher education. In this argument, when the academic institutions of the Church of God became the home of theology, the movement's doctrinal practices were bound to be affected by theology's new location. The institutionalization of theology is not the only factor to influence changes in the doctrinal practice of the Church of God, but it is a very important feature of the story.

Third and last, a word must be said about the audience, more properly audiences, for whom this book is intended. This book aims at informing two groups. On one hand it has been written for people of the Church of God movement who are engaged in the most fundamental discussions that any Christian community can pursue: Who are we and what is it we are called to be and do? Indeed such discussions, insofar as they attempt to understand the implications of their constitutive traditions for the present and future, perform a task so vital that engaging in this work may be said to create and sustain the community. People doing that critically important work, a work that incidentally is the province not only of church leaders but all who name this body as their home, must know the road that has brought them to their current standpoint. This book is written for people who want to engage in this task. On the other hand, this book also hopes to have an audience among those with a professional interest in the study of American religion. It narrates certain aspects of the development of one of the significant church groups to emerge from the American holiness revival of late nineteenth-century, part of the mosaic that is American religious history. To attempt to satisfy the expectations of multiple audiences is no small thing, and it becomes an even larger task when these audiences are church and academy, groups with often widely diverse standards and expectations. Nevertheless, that is the ambition of this book, and therefore it respectfully requests patience from both audiences. Theological terminology and the jargon of American religious history have been kept to a minimum, and where such terms do appear definitions or examples are supplied. Historians might consider these latter as unnecessary intrusions while church folk may be dismayed when they first encounter words or phrases of a technical meaning. But this book was written in the belief that historians, in this specific case religious historians, should consider writing for a reading public wider than their fellow historians and also in the belief that people of the church want to think seriously about the issues confronting them. The author therefore asks both professional and lay readers for a little forbearance in the hope that the exercise of this virtue will overcome whatever frustrations they may feel and thus allow this book to have the widest possible readership. Having made that request, the story can begin.

Notes

1. *Church of God at the Crossroads* (Anderson, Ind: Warner Press, 2000).
2. Stafford's degrees include baccalaureate and seminary degrees from Anderson College and a doctorate in theology from Boston University.
3. Ibid., 14.
4. *After Virtue,* 2nd edition (Notre Dame, Ind: University of Notre Dame Press, 1984), 216.
5. Ibid.
6. For a more detailed development of this idea see my essay, "History as a Moral and Political Art," in Merle D. Strege, *Tell Me the Tale: Historical Reflections on the Church of God* (Anderson, Ind: Warner Press, 1991), 137–157.
7. See, for example, the popular book edited by Dorothy C. Bass, *Practicing Our Faith: A Way of Life for a Searching People* (San Francisco: Jossey-Bass Publishers, 1997).
8. See, for example the collection of essays edited by David D. Hall, *Lived Religion in America: Toward a History of Practice* (Princeton: Princeton University Press, 1997).
9. James Wm. McClendon, Jr. Ethics: *Systematic Theology,* Vol. I (Nashville: Abingdon Press, 1986), 35. McClendon's emphases.
10. McClendon names the Church of God movement among churches of the baptist heritage. Ibid., 34.
11. MacIntyre, *After Virtue,* 187.
12. McClendon, *Ethics,* 162–166.
13. Bass, et al., *Practicing Our Faith,* 6–7.
14. Ibid., 7.

Daniel S. Warner, founding editor of the Gospel Trumpet. The first generation of the Church of God movement disavowed the idea that any individual or group of individuals should be referred to as "leaders" of the true church. Nevertheless, Warner was the inspirational visionary who voiced the message around which the movement coalesced.

Chapter 1
D. S. Warner and the Early Church of God

The central figure in the first decade and a half of the history of the Church of God (Anderson) was the religious reformer Daniel Sidney Warner.[1] He was born June 25, 1842 at Bristol, Wayne County, Ohio, the fifth of six children born to David and Leah Warner. In his later years Daniel looked back on his boyhood as a period of deep unhappiness. His father had kept a tavern for eight of those years and was given to heavy drinking. David Warner also tried his hand at working small farms in Crawford and Williams counties. Daniel remembered his father as a rough man, inconsiderate of his children and especially unsympathetic toward young Daniel, who was sickly from birth.[2]

Young Dan Warner demonstrated an aptitude for public speaking. He was naturally comfortable in front of an audience and also willing to entertain. His principle biographer describes him as a clownish and mischievous boy who sometimes endured schoolhouse whippings. Warner's schoolboy pranks may have merited an occasional whipping, but he was hardly incorrigible. Bright at school, young Warner was sociable, well-liked, and at ease on a soapbox making stump speeches for the Democrat party of which his father was a staunch member.

The Warners may have been Democrats, but they were also loyal Unionists during the Civil War. Daniel's older brother, Joseph, was drafted into the Union army, but because he was married and a father the draft law permitted him to find a substitute. Late in the winter of 1864–65 Daniel Warner accordingly volunteered for a one-year enlistment and was mustered into the 195th Ohio Regiment. Although the war lasted scarcely more than a month from the date of his enlistment, Warner nevertheless collected the one hundred dollar bounty then paid to volunteers. Though his time of service was very brief Warner contracted a serious lung condition during his regiment's lengthy forced march across West Virginia into the Shenandoah Valley. Ill health led to his early discharge, and he never fully recovered from this condition.

In his early twenties Warner took up teaching in the Williams County common school near his home. In February 1865, before volunteering for military duty, he attended a protracted revival not far from the family home in New Washington. Until this moment Christianity's role in his life was limited to his mother's influence. He had even flirted with what he later termed "infidelity," but a tender conscience undermined this brief dalliance. Upon returning home from a dance Warner was upbraided by his mother. She seized the opportunity to condemn her son's waywardness and religious indifference as manifested by his frivolous abandonment of a sister who lay seriously ill. Mother Warner's rebuke had its desired effect, and Daniel remained in a state of religious turmoil until his conversion later that month.

Following his discharge from the army in July 1865 Warner decided to attend college in hopes of improving his budding career as a teacher. That autumn he enrolled at Oberlin College. The first coeducational college in the United States, Oberlin had acquired a reputation for political, social, and ecclesiastical radicalism in the years preceding the war. Oberlin people were associated with the Liberty Party during the 1840s[3] and the college had been a way station on the underground railroad. Oberlin also was the home of a revivalist, perfectionist theology thanks to the influence of Asa Mahan, Professor of Theology, and President Charles Grandison Finney, also Professor of Theology. Finney was the more celebrated of the two men, although by the time Warner arrived on campus he was nearly past his prime. For more than thirty years he had held a reputation as one of the preeminent revival preachers in America. Neither Finney nor Mahan was Methodist or formally Wesleyan in theology, but both were associated with the holiness movement through their spouses' participation in Phoebe Palmer's Tuesday afternoon holiness meetings in New York City. Finney was also heir to the perfectionism that flowed from one stream of New England Congregationalism. These connections cast the light of holiness over Oberlin's religious atmosphere. Warner attended Oberlin twice but only briefly on both occasions. It is impossible to document its influence on him, or perhaps to believe that the college had any great influence on Warner at all. Nonetheless, it is interesting to note that later in life he adopted views on gender, race, and theology that closely resembled ideas in circulation at Oberlin during the middle of the nineteenth-century. Warner interrupted his first term at Oberlin to take a teaching position at Corunna, Indiana. Returning to college again the following autumn, he once again left in the middle of the term. This time he had felt a call to the ministry. Impatient at what seemed to him to be lengthy years of preparation, he returned to his father's home and spent the winter preparing himself for the ministry through prayer and Bible study. On Easter night 1867 Warner delivered his first sermon during a Methodist protracted meeting at Cogswell schoolhouse, not far from his family home.

First Glimpses of a Theology of the Church

Warner was licensed to preach in October 1867 by the West Ohio Eldership of the Church of God, a regional judicatory of the General Eldership of the Churches of God. John Winebrenner (1797–1860) had founded the group in 1830. Winebrenner was originally a minister of the German Reformed Church; however, he had fallen out of favor with church leadership and departed in 1825 over issues related to the revivalism that was increasingly popular among antebellum American Protestants. Revival preaching and "new measures" evangelism were controversial in churches that, like the German Reformed, were formed in centuries-old theological and liturgical traditions.[4]

Winebrenner and the comparatively independent congregations of the Churches of God can fairly be described as one of several primitivist strains in American Christianity.[5] "[W]hat Winebrenner and his followers conceived of as being the 'apostolic plan, as taught in the New Testament' [was] the concept of the local 'church of God.' "[6] The group professed no written or formalized creed, preferring to fellowship under the slogan "No creed but the Bible." They observed believer's baptism by immersion and footwashing, practices understood to be elements of the life of the church depicted in the New Testament. Winebrenner also envisioned a united church quite unlike nineteenth-century American Christianity's numerous denominations. His critics charged that he and his followers had succeeded only in creating one more church body. To this they replied that "the 'church of God' was merely the 'reemergence,' as it were, of the apostolic church. To be sure, there were Christians—'converted persons'—in groups other than the Churches of God, but only in the latter had Christians rediscovered and restored the apostolic plan of the church. Hence the Winebrenner group envisioned itself as a reform, and, to some extent, unity movement within the American church as a whole."[7] Another indication of Winebrenner's primitivism can be found in the great significance that he attached to the name "Church of God." He argued that the church is a biblical institution and therefore it should be called only according to a biblical name: "The sense or title, Church of God, is undeniably the true and proper appellation by which the New Testament church ought to be designated. This is her scriptural and appropriate name. This and no other title is given her by divine authority. This name or title, therefore, ought to be adopted and worn to the exclusion of all others."[8]

When D. S. Warner answered the call to ministry he affiliated with the Winebrenner group and enthusiastically espoused its ecclesiology and its underlying Christian primitivism. From the very outset he proved an energetic, able minister and quickly earned notice as a rising young pastor and evangelist. During the first six years of his ministry he served several circuits and conducted revivals in towns across northwest Ohio and northeast Indiana.[9] Warner threw himself unreservedly into his work, interrupting it only to send reports to the Church Advocate or write an occasional article for that paper. He sat on standing committees of the West Ohio Eldership, for a few years serving as its clerk, and willingly accepted special assignments from church leaders. In 1877 Benjamin Ober, a longtime friend of Winebrenner himself, offered this assessment: "D. S. Warner is a model young man, of deep piety and superior courage and means business in the work of the ministry, and if he continues he will make his mark in the church."[10]

Warner's ministerial future looked very promising. The single and very great blot on his personal happiness was his grief over Tamzen Ann Kerr, to whom Warner was married in September 1867. Tamzen gave birth to a son in December of the following year, but the child soon died. Little more than three years later Mrs. Warner delivered triplets, all three of which died almost immediately following birth. Tamzen herself died on May 26, 1872 of lingering complications sustained during the delivery. The grief-stricken Warner characteristically threw himself into his work. On the first anniversary of Tamzen's death he noted that date in his journal and then quickly proceeded to report in detail the outline of a sermon that he had delivered that same evening in Larue, Ohio. His topic had been "the church of God," and from this outline it is clear that Warner's ecclesiology was well developed and just as clear that it had been formed through his affiliation with the Winebrenner group.[11] Some years later Warner augmented this ecclesiology after rethinking the holiness movement's doctrine of entire sanctification, but he never abandoned the core convictions expressed in this 1873 sermon outline.

In June 1873 Warner traveled west to Nebraska under assignment as a home missionary for the Churches of God. He pursued this new work with the same industry and enthusiasm that marked his ministry in Ohio. He was also corresponding with Sarah Keller of Upper Sandusky, Ohio. Sarah's father was a well-to-do farmer and merchant and a devoted member of the Churches of God. Warner was thirty-one and Sarah eighteen, but she was said to possess an unusual maturity and their friendship blossomed into romance. They were married in June 1874, and Sarah accompanied her new husband back to Nebraska. After little more than a year on the prairie, the Warners and an infant daughter returned to Ohio.

The Holiness Movement

By 1875, the year of the Warners' return, the holiness movement was spreading rapidly across the United States.[12] Several decades before the Civil War, Methodists like Timothy Merritt and Phoebe Palmer had become burdened for the renewal of the doctrine of Christian perfection. Other individuals within and without the Methodist Episcopal church joined the growing movement proclaiming entire sanctification as a second definite work of grace subsequent to regeneration. Following the war, in 1867 at a camp meeting at Vineland, New Jersey, John S. Inskip and others formally organized the movement by creating the National Campmeeting Association for the Promotion of Christian Holiness. State, regional, and even ethnic holiness associations followed in train, including the Ohio Holiness Alliance. At their core many of these associations were a loose connection of minister-evangelists and their lay supporters who together sponsored and attended holiness camp meetings and assemblies.

An extant copy of an issue of the Ohio Alliance publication, the *Christian Harvester,* lists standing and special holiness meetings in towns across the state, including several in the region so familiar to Warner and his wife's family. By October 1882 holiness meetings were regularly convening at Bucyrus, Jerry City, Mansfield, and Upper Sandusky among other places. Upper Sandusky was of course the Keller family's hometown, but all of these locations became important centers of activity in the early days of the Church of God movement. Warner and other early evangelists fed off these centers of holiness movement activity. During the latter half of the 1870s holiness revivalists and General Eldership pastor evangelists were quite likely, if not inevitably, to encounter one another personally. They undoubtedly knew of the labors and messages of each other through the several publications that circulated throughout the region. These encounters were bound to produce some tension. The leadership of the Winebrenner group was lukewarm toward holiness preachers and their doctrine of the second blessing. On their side, radical holiness preachers could and often did employ harsh language to describe church groups that were perceived as less than enthusiastic for the cause of holiness.

After Warner returned from the Nebraska mission he met C. R. Dunbar, a Baptist holiness preacher. A. L. Byers reports that Warner "had been for some years honestly prejudiced against the doctrine [of entire sanctification]."[13] Warner himself described this prejudice as based in a technical theological distinction. Thus he explained: "I have always believed in a full salvation, and agree that it is usually obtained after the justified state. This was my experience as well as that of all believers in holiness; but I was inclined to attribute the deficiency of the justified state to infantile weakness, which through outward sinful influence, was not able to carry out the pure nature fully in practice. But he [Dunbar] and all sanctificationists attribute it to the remaining depravity of nature."[14] First Warner had to reconcile this theological difference, and secondly overcome his disapproval of the fanaticism of some holiness advocates, before he could join the holiness cause. A third factor must be included among his reservations. Warner believed that he already had been sanctified some ten years earlier. He recorded in his journal: "I enjoyed that blessing ten years ago, but I had all this time repudiated the second work and accounted for the wonderful change that God had wrought in me at that time to my yielding to the call to preach the blessed gospel of Jesus Christ, after being disobedient."[15] All three of these factors combined to make Warner reluctant to present himself at a revival altar seeking the experience of entire sanctification.

Several people were positioned to encourage Warner to overcome his reservations. Dunbar met with him and discussed at length Warner's theological concerns. Of greater personal significance was the example of Sarah Warner and her family, who had become very active participants in and supporters of the holiness cause at Upper Sandusky.[16] Sarah's parents, indeed the whole family, including most importantly Sarah Keller Warner herself,[17] had all experienced entire sanctification. Their influence drove Warner to a renewed study of the Bible in search of an answer to the question whether he had been in error. During the first week of July 1877 his inner debate finally was resolved. At a meeting on the evening of July 7, Warner walked to the altar to consecrate himself and receive the second blessing.[18]

Newly confirmed in his religious experience, Warner applied the same energy to campaigning for the cause of holiness that had sparked his career as an evangelist and home missionary. By the early autumn of 1877 he was in difficulty with the West Ohio Eldership of the Churches of God. On September 15 that judicatory brought him up on charges that centered on his advocacy of the doctrine of entire sanctification. Although the charges against him were sustained, the Eldership renewed Warner's license on condition that he refrain from bringing holiness workers to church meetings. Surprisingly, Warner consented to this limitation. At the same meeting he was appointed to the Stark circuit near Canton. He remained on this circuit scarcely more than two months before resigning to devote himself full time to the work of holiness evangelism. During the months of December 1877 and January 1878 Warner preached a lengthy revival in Findlay, where he once again was forced to defend his advocacy of the cause of holiness. On this occasion, however, the charges were more serious; if sustained Warner stood to be defrocked. The charges specified against him were: (1) transcending the restrictions of the Eldership, (2) violating rules of cooperation, and (3) participating in dividing the church.[19] On January 30 the West Ohio Eldership found him guilty on all charges and withdrew his ministerial license.

Warner responded to these developments with a renewed dedication to holiness evangelism. In the company of C. R. Dunbar and others Warner now added special services for divine healing. His defrocking also accelerated the development of Warner's ideas about the relationship of holiness to the church as organized into denominations. In a journal entry dated March 7, 1878 Warner wrote, "On the 31st of last January the Lord showed me that holiness could never prosper on sectarian soil encumbered by human creeds and party names; he gave me a new commission to join holiness and all truth together and build up the apostolic church of the living God. Praise be his name! I will obey him."[20] During that same spring and summer Warner widened the circle of his holiness movement relationships. In May he attended meetings at Yellow Lake, Indiana of the Northern Indiana Eldership of the Churches of God, a splinter off the General Eldership. The Indiana group had broken fellowship over two issues: (1) adoption of the doctrine of entire sanctification, and (2) opposition to the parent body's toleration of secret societies—namely membership in the lodges that were competing, often successfully, with Protestant denominations for male attention during the nineteenth-century. In September Warner returned to Ohio for the meeting of the Holiness Alliance.

Awareness of Warner's dispute with the Winebrenner group widened along with his increasing recognition in holiness circles. This news opened the doors of the Northern Indiana Eldership. They had a common enemy in the General Eldership, and that, along with the causes that they shared, was sufficient to earn Warner a prominent place in the tiny church body. While returning to Ohio after a second visit to Yellow Lake, he stopped at Auburn, Indiana to talk with I. W. Lowman, a man with religious convictions and ideas to match his own. Lowman was a strong holiness man with the money and desire to start a new journal dedicated to that cause. Warner's interest in writing and publishing had grown ever since his early submissions to the *Church Advocate.* By the time of this meeting he had already been working on a book-length manuscript.[21] Warner and Lowman also discovered that they saw eye to eye on the church, and that in fact both men "had been impressed with the idea of together printing a holiness and church paper."[22] The two men entered into a partnership, Lowman as publisher and editor of the church department and Warner associate editor responsible for the holiness page. Lowman owned the paper, but he and Warner were elected to their positions by the Northern Indiana Eldership. The paper made its first run in 1878 as the *Herald of Gospel Freedom.* From its very first issue the *Herald* was committed to wedding the idea of holiness to a "New Testament" view of the church. The paper's prospectus for 1879 said, "Viewed from a human standpoint the *Herald* may appear to possess two separate features: namely that of an organ of the Church of God and an advocate of holiness. But viewed from a pure Bible standpoint these distinct features naturally blend into one effort to restore and propagate the pure religion of the Bible. 'Church' signifies 'called out.' The divinely given title, Church of God, therefore denotes the called out of God or separated unto God. Holiness means the same thing; that is to be separated from all sin and wholly given up to God."[23]

Paradigmatic Events

Warner assumed his editorial duties in the fall of 1878. In November he and Sarah moved to Rome City, Indiana, only a short distance from Wolcottville where the *Herald* was published. The following March he paid Lowman two hundred fifty dollars for a half-interest in the paper. By the terms of this agreement the two men shared expenses evenly and income except for that earned by the job-work that Lowman did himself. They continued to share editorial duties until January 1880, when Warner assumed full editorial responsibility. In that year the Northern Indiana Eldership determined to merge the *Herald* with any other paper sharing its principles. Late in 1880 the Eldership's publication board accepted the offer of "G. Haines" to merge the *Herald of Gospel Freedom* with his Indianapolis based paper, the *Pilgrim.* This new holiness journal was christened the *Gospel Trumpet* and its first issue was published on January 1, 1881. After one more issue printed at Rome City the concern moved to Indianapolis.

As the winter of 1881 melted into spring Warner's stated views on the illegitimacy of what he termed "sectism," the division of Christianity into denominations that only partially represented the pure truth of the New Testament, simmered until they reached the boiling point. Approximately two years earlier he had concluded that no humanly devised rules of membership could properly constitute the church as mapped out in the New Testament. In April, after talking and praying with two fellow ministers at

Hardinsburg, Indiana, he declared, "The Spirit of the Lord showed me the inconsistency of repudiating sects and yet belonging to an association that is based on sect recognition. We promised God to withdraw from all such compacts."[24] Warner had in mind an article on membership in the bylaws of the Indiana State Holiness Association that required all members to hold membership in a recognized denomination. He had come to think of this article as the "sect endorsing clause," and was determined either to purge it from the bylaws or quit the association. Warner attended the May 20–21 meeting at Terre Haute armed with an amendment that he proposed to substitute for the sect endorsing clause. When association members voted down his proposal, he believed he had no choice but to withdraw.

Warner was one of a small but explosive group of holiness preachers who threatened the cohesiveness of the entire holiness movement.[25] The movement's leadership was drawn almost exclusively from the ranks of the Methodist church, and many of those leaders viewed the movement as the means of recovering the doctrine of entire sanctification for their denomination and thus its spiritual vitality. Methodists and members of Methodist-related denominations also provided the largest number of individuals to join the Church of God movement in its very early days.[26] Nevertheless, since the 1830s there stood alongside the traditional Wesleyans other holiness evangelists who possessed no loyalty whatsoever to Methodism. After his sanctification in 1877 Warner was to be found in this latter group. In his eyes John Wesley was a good man, an effective evangelist, and a great preacher of perfect love, but one who nonetheless did not possess all the light there was to be shed on the doctrine of the church. With no loyalty to either Wesley or the Methodist church to bind him to the holiness movement, Warner could walk away rather easily. In any case, he was not prepared to compromise his views on the church. He was the first preacher of consequence to leave the postwar holiness movement, and the Church of God movement that coalesced around him and the message of the *Gospel Trumpet* was the earliest of the holiness churches. For Warner and the early Church of God movement, however, the issue was never simply the cause of holiness. From its very beginning the Church of God was not a single-issue movement. Important as perfect love was in their eyes, from 1880 on it was always married to an equal if not greater commitment to a primitivist vision of Christian unity.

Later in 1881 Warner took a second and irrevocable step toward realizing his vision of the church. At an October meeting of the Northern Indiana Eldership at Beaver Dam, Indiana Warner again assumed the role of reformer, proposing to change certain articles of procedure for the little communion. The precise nature of those proposals is lost, but John W. V.

Smith infers, "It is likely Warner proposed that the Eldership abandon the practice of granting ministerial licenses and simply recognize all preachers who 'bore the fruits' of their call and also that former procedures for admitting church members be eliminated with each congregation opening its fellowship to all persons who had been truly regenerated and evidenced a sincere desire to do the will of God."[27] Warner had published these views at least a year previous to the Beaver Dam meeting, but whatever his specific proposals they were defeated by the Eldership. Warner then rose to his feet and renounced his association with the Eldership and all other church groups that participated in the sin of dividing the body of Christ. He then invited any like-minded persons in attendance to join him. Five people stood.[28]

Critical to the future of the tiny movement just inaugurated was the fact that when Warner and his five fellow believers walked out of the Beaver Dam church the *Gospel Trumpet* accompanied him. As early as the previous March the paper no longer identified itself as the publication of the Northern Indiana Eldership. The denomination had owned neither machinery nor supplies. All the *Trumpet* assets were held by the partnership of Warner and Haines, who Warner bought out for one hundred dollars before June of 1881. The arrangement between the *Gospel Trumpet* and the Northern Indiana Eldership followed a precedent established by the predecessor *Herald of Gospel Freedom.* The denomination had not owned either paper but employed each in turn as its official organ for announcements and doctrinal articles, granting a *de facto* blessing in the bargain. When Warner left the denomination he obviously forfeited the blessing, but took with him the paper and its assets, which were by then his personal property.[29]

Given Warner's theological convictions about the nature of the church and ministry, the *Trumpet* and later the Gospel Trumpet Company were more or less forced to play an indispensable role in the continuing existence of the fledgling group. He was unalterably opposed to church governance through boards or committees. As a consequence the Gospel Trumpet Publishing Company was the sole formal institution of the Church of God movement for more than thirty years. From the very beginning its pages carried doctrinal articles, testimonies, and announcements that were the standard fare in holiness journals of that era. By the end of the century the paper also advertised the company's books and products that went far in communicating a set of emerging practices that formed the life of Church of God people and the movement as a whole. The *Gospel Trumpet* itself tangibly and uniquely expressed the Church of God movement while it simultaneously conveyed a sense of identity through its sponsorship and legitimization of new religious practices. The paper also lent the air of printed authority to editorial pronouncements, thus conferring on its editor the role of primary theological educator of the new movement.

In the same month that Warner and the "Beaver Dam Five" departed the Northern Indiana Eldership, the name of J. C. Fisher appeared on the *Trumpet* masthead as editor and publisher. In 1878 Fisher and his wife Allie had joined the Michigan Eldership of the Churches of God. Like their sister splinter group in Indiana, the Michigan folk also had forsaken the General Eldership for the causes of holiness and the abolition of secret societies. During an 1880 visit to Indiana Fisher had heard Warner preach, and subsequently the Fishers invited Warner to Gratiot County, Michigan for a holiness revival. In October 1881 the Fishers started a holiness meeting in their home in Carson City. Immediately following his Beaver Dam stand Warner visited the Fishers and a meeting of the Northern Michigan Eldership; the events at Beaver Dam repeated themselves. Warner preached on the true church, elaborating on its divine government. When the Eldership resisted his ideas, the Fishers and approximately twenty others separated themselves to join the five reformist souls in Indiana. The group also drew up a set of resolutions stating its convictions on the nature and practices of the church and its ministry.[30] The first "come-outers" planned to hold camp meetings at Beaver Dam and Carson City, and the Church of God movement was born.

Notes

1. Currently there are three book-length treatments of Warner or his ministerial career. One of these is an older and celebratory biography, A. L. Byers, *Birth of a Reformation: The Life and Labors of D. S. Warner* (Anderson, Ind: Gospel Trumpet Company, 1921). There have also been two studies of his career, Barry L. Callen, *It's God's Church!* (Anderson, Ind: Warner Press, 1995) and Thomas L. Fudge, *Daniel Warner and the Paradox of Religious Democracy in Nineteenth-Century America* (Lewiston, NY: Edwin A. Mellen Press, 1998). John W. V. Smith wrote a chapter-length study of Warner published in *Heralds of a Brighter Day* (Anderson, Ind: Gospel Trumpet Company, 1955).

2. Later in life Warner composed a poem titled "Innocence" that summarized his unhappy childhood. The poem is printed in Byers, *Birth of a Reformation*, 35–36.

3. For a description of the relationship between Oberlin and the radical politics of the Liberty Party, see Douglas M. Strong, *Perfectionist Politics: Abolitionism and the Religious Tensions of American Democracy* (Syracuse: Syracuse University Press, 1999).

4. Although the printed version of this dispute was published after 1842, the nature of Winebrenner's problems with the German Reformed Church are illustrated in a prolonged debate between him and John Williamson Nevin, after 1840 a professor at the tiny German Reformed seminary at Mercersberg, Pennsylvania. Much of Nevin's criticism of Winebrenner is contained in a polemic titled *The Anxious Bench* (originally published 1843; reprint edition, New York: Garland Publishing, 1987).

5. One of the group's linguistic habits illustrates its primitivism. Habitually they referred to their church buildings as "Bethels," from the Old Testament Hebrew term for "house of God."

6. Richard Kern, *John Winebrenner: Nineteenth Century Reformer* (Harrisburg: Central Publishing House, 1974), 45.

7. Ibid., 46.

8. John Winebrenner, "History of the Church of God," quoted in Kern, Ibid., 46.

9. In a letter to the *Church Advocate* printed in its July 30, 1873 number, Warner summarized his activity: 1118 sermons, 501 conversions, 280 baptisms, 9 congregations organized. He accepted only free-will offerings for his support because he considered the salary system "antagonistic to the Word of God."

10. *Church Advocate*, January 10, 1877.

11. Speaking from Ephesians 1:10, Warner's sermon followed this outline: "1. Notice the purpose of God. 2. 'One' church. 3. Extent—heaven and earth. 4. Provisions for oneness: (a) one church typified, (b) one, bought, sanctified, made, built, (c) one faith, (d) one spirit to animate it, (e) one head, Christ, (f) one name, Church of God, (g) one law to govern it. 5. Standard of oneness—'As I and the Father are one.' 6. Time of this oneness. 7. To be visible, 'That the world may believe,' and so forth. 8. Object of oneness. 9. Apostasy and restoration of the church. 10. Illustrations: (a) paths, Jeremiah 6:16, (b) river, (c) house, (d) corner stone (sic)." Warner's sermon outline is printed in Byers, *Birth of a Reformation*, 72.

12. For histories of the holiness movement see Melvin E. Dieter, *The Holiness Revival of the Nineteenth Century* (Lanham, MD: Scarecrow Press, 1996); Charles E. Jones, *Perfectionist Persuasion: The Holiness Movement and American Methodism*, 1867–1936 (Metuchen, NJ: Scarecrow Press, 1974). See also Timothy L. Smith, *Called Unto Holiness: The Story of the Nazarenes*, Vol. 1 (Kansas City, Mo: Nazarene Publishing House, 1962).

13. Byers, *Birth of a Reformation*, 115.

14. Quoted in Byers, *Birth of a Reformation*, 119.

15. Quoted in Byers, *Birth of a Reformation*, 119.

16. The *Christian Harvester* reported favorably on the Kellers' organization of a holiness meeting in their hometown despite the refusal of local churches to allow them the use of their buildings. The Kellers could not be discouraged and moved the meeting to a building on one of their own properties, rededicating it to God in the process. Holiness services continued to be held in this "church." The West Ohio Eldership of the Church of God regarded these measures as highly irregular. Cf., "The Holiness Church," in *Advocate of Christian Holiness* (October, 1877), 239.

17. "Since seeing every day the change in my dear wife I thought was beyond doubt of this second work." Warner, quoted in Byers, *Birth of a Reformation*, 120.

18. Warner's journal records his experience: "Eve. met at a quarter to eight. Mighty power filled the house. The altar was filled from one side to the other. Several were seeking sanctification. Glory to God, this night he began to give me the evidence (besides my hitherto naked faith) that I had got out of the wilderness of Canaan. Jesus, my blessed Savior, just cut me off one bunch of the sweet grapes of this 'land.' Oh, glory to God, once more I was a little child! I felt the blood of Jesus flowing through my entire 'soul, body, and spirit.' Heaven on earth! Hallelujah, it is done." Quoted in Byers, *Birth of a Reformation*, 122.

19. Byers, *Birth of a Reformation*, 168.

20. Quoted in Byers, *Birth of a Reformation*, 173. It is worth noting that Warner received this vision and his commission from God only one day after losing a license conferred by mortals.

21. This manuscript was published in 1880 under the title *Bible Proofs of a Second Work of Grace*, although not by Lowman nor the publishing concern that he and Warner established.

22. Byers, *Birth of a Reformation*, 187.

23. Quoted in Byers, *Birth of a Reformation*, 194.

24. Warner reported this declaration in an editorial published in the *Gospel Trumpet* (hereafter *GT*) (June 1, 1881), 2.

25. Warner's equal in radical holiness was John Brooks, author of *The Divine Church*, and like Warner one of the firebrand radicals on the radical edge of the holiness movement.

26. Valorous B. Clear did some impressionistic research on the parent bodies of early "come-outers" to the Church of God movement. Cf. *Where the Saints Have Trod* (Chesterfield, Ind: Midwest Publications, 1977).

27. John W. V. Smith, *The Quest for Holiness and Unity* (Anderson, Ind: Warner Press, 1980), 44–45.

28. Mr. and Mrs. F. Krause, Mr. and Mrs. W. W. Ballenger, and David Leininger.

29. Cf. Smith, *Quest for Holiness and Unity*, 452, note 3.

30. The Carson City Resolutions are discussed in Chapter 2.

Chapter 2
The Theology of D. S. Warner

Charles E. Brown, fourth editor of the *Gospel Trumpet,* said that D. S. Warner was an original theological thinker, but that he and the early Church of God movement did not deviate from historic orthodox Christian teaching. Instead Warner's originality lay in the manner in which he combined a Wesleyan theology of salvation with the ecclesiology of the believers' church.[1] Ecclesiology and a theology of salvation were the twin foci of the ellipse that was Warner's theology. The two ideas were mutually interdependent. Wesleyans defined salvation as a "double cure" composed first of the justification that freed humans from the guilt of sin and secondly entire sanctification, which liberated them from sin's power and thus enabled the life of holiness. Even before 1880 Warner had reached the conclusion that the doctrine and practice of holiness could not prosper in a body of Christ hopelessly dismembered by denominational divisions. Similarly, without the teaching and experience of entire sanctification, there was no possibility of Christian unity and a church conformed to the teaching of the New Testament. In a very real sense, the early Church of God practice of the church was the corporate expression of its theology of Christian holiness. Later Church of God writers addressed additional aspects of Christian teaching, but in most cases and regardless the specific theological topic the movement's ecclesiology was often implicated and even a controlling factor.

Warner and the Theology of Entire Sanctification

Warner authored a lengthy pamphlet and one book-length discussion of his theology of salvation. Since the Gospel Trumpet Company possessed no equipment to publish books, he turned to the Evangelical United Mennonite Publishing Society to see his manuscript into print.[2] Warner's theology of salvation was consistent with views found in the nineteenth-century holiness

13

movement. A century and more earlier, John Wesley himself had described salvation as having both objective and subjective aspects. Justification, the objective, Wesley said was a "relative" change, meaning that the relationship between God and the believer was altered. Wesley went on to say that sanctification was the aspect of salvation that described a "real" change, by which he meant the new birth. Justification was what God does for human beings; sanctification is the divine work in them.[3] Together the two actions comprised salvation; to be saved was to experience both justification and sanctification.

In his pamphlet *Salvation: Present, Perfect, Now or Never,*[4] Warner defined salvation as deliverance. While he appreciated justification as the first work of salvation, Warner went to considerably greater lengths describing the many evils from which believers were delivered. Those who live in sin were trapped in a world where they were slaves to their own lustful desires and utterly incapable of self-control. In Warner's theology salvation offers an enabling power that delivers people from this bondage to an unruly self. That was the beginning point, for Warner added that salvation gave the believer victory "over all the elements of this world; over sin, fashion, and popular sentiments; and over the devil himself, who claims to be the ruler of earth, a master of the situation of life, with a peace that nothing disturbs."[5] Warner stressed the consequences of sin and the need for deliverance from them:

> Reader, Salvation means deliverance from all these elements of woe and misery. And should this picture fall short of the deep shades of your case, salvation yet means deliverance from the strongest chains of habit, the lowest depths of sin, the deepest hell of intemperance and debauchery. Deliverance from darkness into light, from the power of Satan unto God. From the woes of a guilty conscience into peace with God through our Lord Jesus Christ; from remorse into the joys of pardon; from the thralldom of sin into the glorious liberty of the sons of God.[6]

From deliverance Warner moved to a discussion of justification which he described as the first of two "accesses" through Christ, the second being sanctification. Justification is God's answer to the human predicament created by what Warner called "two-fold sin": the sin which all human beings inherit from Adam and the sins which they themselves commit. Of the first kind Warner said that it was a "moral element, or bent to evil, back of and distinct from all sinful actions that arise from it."[7] The two-fold nature of human sin required the remedy to which Warner referred in conventional holiness movement terminology as the "double cure" of justification followed by the second gracious action of God—sanctification.

Warner's theology of salvation followed standard holiness movement terminology and structures. However, the controlling idea by which he articulated this theology remained the idea of deliverance. In Warner's view, to be saved was to be delivered from the condemnation of sin and from the power of human sinfulness. Furthermore, to be saved was also to be delivered in the sense of being enabled to live a holy life. God's gracious empowerment of believers enabled them to "deny ungodliness and worldly lusts. Namely, it gives us power to fully abstain from all sin, and to say no to every presentation of evil."[8] Clearly a moral understanding of the human predicament controlled Warner's perception of sin. For him the human problem was not ontological; he did not think of this problem first in terms of the difference between and separation of humans from God. The problem, as Warner saw it, was that humans committed sins because they were in thrall to sinfulness. They needed God's gracious pardon, but even more than that they needed God's gracious empowerment.

The idea of salvation as deliverance was repeated in the writing of other early Church of God writers. H. C. Wickersham, a leading preacher and writer in the movement's first decades, defined salvation as "preservation from destruction, danger, or great calamity. [It is] the redemption of man from the bondage of sin and the liability of eternal death, and the conferring on him eternal happiness."[9] Like Warner, Wickersham divided salvation into the first work of grace, which he called regeneration, and the second work of sanctification. Instead of regeneration one would expect to find the word justification as the first work of grace. As Wickersham elaborated his theology, it appears that he collapsed the two ideas into one: "Regeneration is the first work of grace; includes the pardon of all past sins; the removal of all guilt and condemnation; adoption into the family of God; the witness of the Spirit, pardon and sonship; spiritual life and a new moral nature, including all of the Christian graces."[10] There is some overlap in Wickersham's view of the first and second works, for he says that sanctification "includes the destruction of all the works of the devil; the restoration of man to the state of holiness from which he fell, by creating him anew in Christ Jesus, and restoring to him all that image and likeness of God which he lost in the fall of Adam."[11]

The holiness movement, Warner included, understood sanctification to describe the event when believers were divinely empowered. Like other holiness movement figures steeped in the practices and conventions of revivalist preaching, Warner taught the theology of the "second blessing" as a work of divine grace instantaneously received. Since believers entered into the experience of sanctification by faith, no discipline or works were necessary to its reception. Warner emphatically asserted that sanctification was not the product of spiritual development. Just as much as justification, sanctification was not the result of growth or a gradual process. Believers laid hold of sanctification, which is another way of saying that they were "perfected in love," grasping it "as an instantaneous gift from God, purifying the heart by faith."[12] Added to the first grace of justification, the second grace enabled believers to live free of the power of sin as well as its condemnation. Taken together, they constituted salvation.

Warner taught a theology that viewed salvation as the means to a life of perfection. By the transforming and empowering grace of God believers were changed from sinfulness into a renewed and pristine image of God. Salvation makes believers perfect. Warner did not consider this transforming privilege to be an option available only to the especially zealous. On the contrary, he said that both the Old and New Testaments command perfection of all the people of God.[13] From the whole Bible Warner also adduced several texts to make the point that divine provision had been made to enable this perfection.[14] The text often employed as grounds for a doctrine of verbal inspiration Warner used to make a different point. Quoting 2 Timothy 3:16–17 Warner explained, "All scripture is given us of God for the purpose of making every real man of God perfect. Are you a man of God? If not, that accounts for the fact you cannot believe in and receive this state of Christian perfection."[15] To his claims that the Bible both commanded and promised perfection Warner added a third biblically based claim: perfection had been attained. He cited the Old Testament figures of King Asa, Job, and King Hezekiah as examples of perfection, and added numerous New Testament texts to underscore the point.[16]

The holiness movement's claim to the availability of full salvation in this life was not without controversy. Many Methodists challenged the holiness movement's theology of a second blessing as instantaneously appropriated; one of them, J. M. Boland, even regarded the doctrine as a problem for Methodism. If not all Methodists could accept the holiness movement position, then Presbyterians, Baptists, Congregationalists, Lutherans, and others were more likely to find it problematic. The "second blessing" was a controversial point of theology requiring argumentation and scriptural warrant. Warner took up that task in his *Bible Proofs of a Second Work of Grace.* Aware that other writers had taken up a similar challenge, Warner wrote his book with a different audience in view.

Bible Proofs of a Second Work of Grace is partly a collection of hundreds of proof-texts and in part an exposition of those texts elaborated as an apologetic for Warner's doctrine of sanctification. He aimed this discussion neither at those who already testified to the experience nor scoffers and avowed opponents of the doctrine. Although he wrote to defend his views, Warner also wrote to persuade the reader who was eager to love God more fervently and with a pure heart. In what is a glimpse of early Church of God evangelism, Warner targeted people who were already believers but who had honest questions about the doctrine of Christian perfection. Warner himself had once held similar reservations, and he intended his book for readers who might be persuaded to take a similar step and "launch away into the ocean of redeeming love."[17] More than a defense of sanctification as an instantaneous second work of grace, in this book Warner laid out an entire theology of sanctification.

Much of Warner's discussion presents a view of sanctification that is consistent with holiness movement teaching on the subject. Toward the book's conclusion, however, Warner considered the doctrine with special reference to the church. Before 1880 he had established a link between holiness and his understanding of the church.[18] He read Hebrews 12:25–29 and its reference to two "shakings" as an account of two divine actions toward the church. Rather than interpret the text as an eschatological warning of a day when heaven and earth will shake with God's judgment, Warner equated earth with the unconverted and heaven with the church as the body of believers.[19] The reason why the voice of Jesus shook the earth—sinners—only before his ascension and both the world and church afterward was clear to Warner. The text was a figure of the double cure of salvation: God's voice shook the world for the sake of its justification and that same divine voice shook the church for the sake of its need to press on to holiness.

> The voice that teaches the "first faith" only may move the world with conviction; but there sit unmoved, the members of the Church, steeped in tobacco, indwelt with pride, selfishness, covetousness, and other species of idolatry. Resting in a past experience and present profession, they smile complaisantly at, and give an occasional amen to the truth that hurts and agitates the poor sinner. But let one, who has tarried in the "upper room" holiness meeting, until filled with the old prophetic fire, grasp the two edged sword and definitely smite sin in the world and in the Church, how soon we see "shaken not only the earth but also heaven."[20]

In the context of his discussion of the second blessing Warner elaborated his idea of a corrupt and indifferent church. Old Testament prophets Ezekiel and Jeremiah were read as descriptions of a church and ministry contemporary with Warner. In his view this ministry lived sumptuously on fat salaries and was the real cause of spiritual famine in the churches. There is more than a hint here of the firebrand radicalism that put Warner on the fringe of the holiness movement and even a touch of social radicalism. He charged that ministers of his day made "a lucrative merchandise of [their] Christless sermons instead of administering the free Gospel of salvation."[21] Warner put the finishing touches on his baleful description of the church's condition with the following warning:

> It is an undeniable fact, that in most of our present day churches, a real convert can scarcely maintain spiritual life. The few that cannot be killed are usually driven or thrown out. O, ye shepherds, a crisis from the Almighty is coming upon you. As the Lord liveth the fires from heaven shall seep away your craft. "Howl, ye shepherds, and cry; and wallow yourselves in the ashes, ye principal of the flock; for the days of your *slaughter* and your *dispersions* are accomplished" (Jer 25:34). Their time of feasting upon, and dispersing the Lord's flock will come to an end.[22]

Warner found in passages scattered all through the Bible references to latter-day Christianity run amok. He took the judgment against Mount Seir in Jeremiah 35 as a reference to Catholicism. The Caucasus mountains mentioned in chapters 38 and 39 were references to sectism. Ezekiel's memorable vision of the valley of the dry bones Warner read not as a prophesy directed to the Exiles but as an account of a disintegrated church rendered powerless first through inbred sin that had been allowed to fester without entire sanctification and second by sectarian strife. Warner also mined Ezekiel for its vision of the climactic battle between Jehovah and Magog. Because the shepherds of the church had catered to their unholy lusts and truckled to the contamination of the church by the world, a terrible conflict would ensue whenever holiness preachers confront such sin. Thus, said Warner, the Holy Spirit speaking through the prophet "employs Gog and Magog to represent the acrid and intolerable Spirit of sectarianism, and its final overthrow."[23] In 1880 Warner was uncertain whether sectarianism would be overthrown by the "Wesleyan reformation" or the "present more general movement," but hosts of witnesses to the experience of entire sanctification were the holy army under divine commission to cleanse the church. Warner did not state clearly what he meant by the "Wesleyan reformation" or "more general movement." While tempting to read the latter as a reference to the holiness movement, that would make Wesley and Methodism the meaning of the former. Given Warner's anti-church rhetoric, not to mention the Church of God movement's tendency to use the Methodist Episcopal Church as a convenient whipping boy, it is unlikely that he would have thought it an agent of church renewal. Its membership, in his view, did not possess the right stuff.

Cleansing the church was no task for the timid or tactful. Warner caricatured "worldly preachers" as people who stood like beggars at the door of Satan's kingdom politely attempting to coax his subjects to the side of salvation and holiness. These preachers were "saying much about the duty and advantage of belonging to Church, and little about [people's] sin, and the duty of repentance; as though God were a dependent and the Devil a proprietor of the universe."[24] A church or ministry lacking the teeth of primitive, holy, gospel power would only prove pleasing to the Devil, but certainly brought no honor to God. A ministry truly fit for this work was bound to awaken persecution as it threshed out saintly wheat from the chaff of indifferent and worldly professors of faith. Warner expounded on several biblical references to threshing wheat as the proper metaphor for the work that holiness preachers were called to perform. Quite against the prevailing rage to enlarge churches, Warner contended that threshing them would reduce their numbers and that the consequent elimination of the weak and indifferent was precisely the medicine for a sick church; "there is too much of it such as it is: holiness beats it small."[25] "Threshing Babylon" became a favorite phrase to describe this work of separating saints from sinners and worldly professors in the church, reducing it to a cadre of tough and dedicated saints.

In 1880 Warner had concluded that the denominational system of American Protestant Christianity was not only problematic but wrong. According to Warner's interpretive lights "sectarianism" stood condemned in the pages of scripture. Logic also dictated such a conclusion. As historical bodies, no denomination could claim divine origin. "Christ is the source of all true union among his disciples, and all the divisions between them and the world; while the Devil is the instigation of all divisions in the Church, and all union between it and the world."[26] Warner was not alone in his perception that divisions between Christians poisoned the body of Christ. Many who attended holiness camp meetings testified to the love and unity that they experienced there among saints who were from many different denominations. Warner found evidence of the desire to transcend denominational barriers in the *Christian Harvester,* a journal associated with the

Ohio Holiness Alliance. Warner and other early Church of God people were acquainted with this journal; he described its editor as a "holy man of God." Warner and his wife, Sarah, continued to read the *Harvester* after they relocated in northern Indiana. Next to the *Gospel Trumpet* the *Harvester* seems to have been the holiness journal of choice among early Church of God people, particularly those with roots in Ohio holiness circles.

Warner cited one *Harvester* editorial in particular, commending its writer for correctly identifying "denominationalism" as a problem. Taken together, the editorial's points criticized denominational structures while allowing them to remain standing. (1) God has but one church on earth, singular and indivisible, and comprised of all who are born of the Spirit. (2) The scriptural and necessary polity of the church is the local congregation and it alone. (3) The Bible does not speak favorably of denominations in any sense as they are directly or indirectly the product of sin and therefore would be destroyed by the thorough and widespread experience of holiness. (4) The great mass of true Christians are to be found in evangelical denominations, and since the effort to abolish these would only add another to that number, the denominations must be regarded as a present necessity until holiness becomes more widespread. (5) The man or woman who has experienced entire sanctification and thus has been perfected in love regards all the sanctified—regardless of denominational affiliation—as brothers and sisters.[27] The editorial's position on denominationalism, critical as it was, nevertheless proved too moderate for Warner. To merely transcend some of the imperfections of a divided Christendom was too limited a view of the power of holiness. In his view the fire of perfect love could purge and remake the church. By 1880 Warner had abandoned the moderate position of holiness people whose views were represented by the *Harvester*. To him, denominational division was far more than problematic; it was a "monster evil; the fell destroyer of the purity and power and love of the Lord's [church]."[28] He could not accept the idea that denominations were a necessary evil to be endured until holiness became more widespread. Warner took the position that "sects" and holiness were mutually antagonistic. Anyone who thought that denominations should continue until holiness prevailed was an unwitting dupe of Satan.

"Sectarianism" could not be permitted to continue for two reasons. In the first place it was the great enemy of Christian love. How could Christians honestly speak of Jesus' commandment to love one another when they refused to act according to the dictates of the second commandment? Denominational barriers eventually became barriers to sympathy and a close feeling between Christians. Secondly, the division of Christians into denominations posed the single greatest impediment to the evangelization of the world. Citing Jesus' high priestly prayer in the Gospel of John, Warner intertwined holiness and evangelism in an interpretation that made John 17:13ff a favorite sermon text among Church of God preachers.

The purging fire of true holiness consumed all the fences that Christians had built up between themselves. In Warner's eyes that destruction was the real mission of the holiness movement. But this mission had been frustrated by the unwillingness of the sanctified to "[lift] up the sword of the Lord against sects, and attempt to abolish this evil."[29] Warner was under no illusions about the radicalism of his message. He clearly understood the course to which it committed those who agreed with him. He issued a call to arms. The denominational system had to be destroyed and scriptural holiness was the weapon.

> Can it be said of professors of holiness that they have "one heart" and "one mind," while some have a mind to be Presbyterian, others Baptist, others United Brethren, and others have a mind to adhere to one of the several sects of Methodism? Have they "one heart and one way," when they rise from the solemn altar, in the holiness meeting, and go, each in his own way, to the synagogue of *his own sect?*
>
> Now I must confess that I cannot see the necessity of this, unless it be to please the Devil, break the unity of the Spirit, and grieve away the heavenly Dove, bring to naught the divided house of the Lord and destroy the work of holiness as fast as it can be built up; to this end alone it is necessary.[30]

At this stage of his career Warner had emerged as a radical preacher moving toward the extreme edge of the holiness movement. He had concluded that the denominational system was Satan's tool for the weakening of the body of Christ and the destruction of human souls. Denominations were an "enormous sin" for which God would hold accountable their members and supporters, and the only cure for this plague was a thorough-going experience of sanctification that would melt believers into a spiritual and physical union. Warner was not an ecclesiastical anarchist. He did not envision a day when there would be no church. Rather, he looked to a future in which Christians returned to the fellowship described in the pages of the New Testament. Warner's message in 1880 was as yet insufficiently developed to label it a species of Christian primitivism. Nevertheless, he did envision "the one, holy Church of the Bible, not bound together by rigid articles of faith, but perfectly united in love, under the primitive glory of the Sanctifier, 'continuing steadfastly in the Apostle's doctrine and fellowship,' and taking the world captive for Christ."[31]

By the conclusion of the year following the publication of *Bible Proofs of a Second Work of Grace,* Warner had severed his ties with all institutional expressions of Christianity. He resigned his membership in the Indiana State Holiness Association, although he did continue to attend holiness meetings and read holiness journals, if nothing else than as a controversialist. By the autumn of 1881 Warner had also withdrawn from the Northern Indiana Eldership of the Churches of God. He had declared his views on the interrelationship between holiness and a unified church. Many ideas would have to be developed from that original premise. Many church practices would have to be either borrowed or invented if the little movement that coalesced around this premise were to survive. As those practices developed so did Warner and the early Church of God movement's more complete theology of the church.

Organization and Practices of the Church

By mid-October 1881 Warner and his new partner in the *Gospel Trumpet,* Joseph Fisher, had arranged for Warner to speak at meetings of the Michigan Eldership of the Churches of God. The two men seem to have worked out a plan that they hoped would produce results similar to those in Indiana a few months previous. One outcome of this plan was a set of resolutions adopted by the Carson City group. Given Warner's already developed animus toward any unity based on creeds or confessions of faith, it should be clear enough that the little band did not consider its resolutions as anything more than a stated declaration of intentions and convictions. As such, the Carson City resolutions offer a picture of the group's earliest ideas concerning the church.[32]

The resolutions begin with an apocalyptic preamble warning that in "these last days" the archangel Michael was championing the deliverance of the true saints while in the process building up the true church. In the midst of tumultuous times the saints at Carson City resolved, first of all, to live holy lives in anticipation of the return of Christ, "who we believe is nigh, even at the door."[33] This apocalyptic note, although not loudly stated in the very first days of the Church of God movement, certainly must be acknowledged; in time it crescendoed. Secondly, the saints resolved to abstain from any and all ecclesiastical organizations, save that body to which they referred as "the church of God, bought by the blood of Christ, organized by the Holy Spirit, and governed by the Bible."[34] The resolutions elaborated no further on the idea that the church is organized by the Holy Spirit, a concept that proved critical to the Church of God movement's later theology. However, two resolutions hinted at the meaning of that phrase by way of those practices that they either repudiated or asserted. One was the licensing of ministers, a practice for which the group could find no biblical precepts or examples. The rejection of conventional practices of ordination did not signify that the group wanted to abolish the distinction between clergy and laity. Rather, it wanted to alter the standards and practices by which ministers were recognized. According to the saints, the criteria of valid ministry were simply a godly life and a doctrine consistent with the Word of God.

It is interesting that two of the five Carson City resolutions pertain to the ministry, suggesting perhaps that ministers had a heavy hand in the preparation of the document. Only after dealing with the matter of a valid ministry did the resolutions turn to the composition of the flock that these holy and biblical ministers would oversee. Those who were truly regenerate and sincere and "who worship God in all the light they possess" the Carson City saints recognized as "members with them in the one body of Christ," and on that basis were offered fellowship. Such as would accept this invitation were also encouraged to "forsake the snares and yokes of human parties and stand alone in the 'one fold' of Christ upon the Bible and in the unity of the Spirit."[35]

The Carson City resolutions accomplished little by way of offering a platform or broad statement of convictions. Instead, they indicate what the very first of the saints believed could be stated and practiced in a manner that remained consistent with their interpretation of the Bible. The resolutions' emphasis on the ministry is quite consistent with Warner's hostility toward mainstream Protestant ministers. Warner was not, of course, advocating anticlericalism, but he was contending for a different standard for ordination. The idea of a church organized by the Holy Spirit was a key element of that standard and vital to his entire conception of the church. Better to describe the first saints as anti-institution, but even here their resolutions endorsed practices that confirm the ministry by the standards of holiness and sound doctrine. The test of ministers' validity was their talk and walk. This way of validating through practices could be applied to other aspects of theological and ethical life of the church as well. In fact, the development of a set of corroborating practices was critical to the survival of the fledgling Church of God movement.

Warner's ecclesiology was already well formed along some lines of the Carson City resolutions a decade before their adoption. In 1871 he had published a lengthy article spelling out his views on church membership. In addition to including baptism as a requirement for admission to the church,

Warner asserted that "salvation and entering into the church are insepara-ble."[36] Creeds, catechisms, and popular preaching might insist on baptism as the seal of salvation, but the only seal mentioned in the Bible is the Holy Spirit. Furthermore, church leaders were compelled to accept any person who claimed to be a child of God because Romans 15:7 commanded Christians to receive each other as Christ has received them. Additionally, in that same article Warner linked sanctification and church. "All the pure" he included within the church. In fact, wrote Warner, "the church only is sanc-tified and cleansed, by which we understand that persons being sanctified are thereby made part of the church."[37] In this article Warner focused on issues pertaining to church membership and not on the manner or extent to which a believer might be sanctified. That development awaited his associa-tion with the holiness movement. Insofar as his theology of the church was concerned, already in 1871 he was posing questions and answering them in a way that fitted easily into the framework of the Carson City resolutions a decade later.

The most complete expression of Warner's theology of the church is contained in an undated twenty-four page pamphlet titled *The Church of God: What the Church of God is and What it is Not.* Here Warner discussed a range of topics and questions, including membership, polity, ordination, Christian unity, and the problem of sectism. He concluded with a defense against the charge that in his appeal to Christians to leave their denomina-tions, Warner was merely creating one more. Warner preferred to translate *ekklesia* as congregation rather than church, but in either case the main interest was to see to it that no extra-biblical meaning intruded. That would be to pervert the Bible itself. So Warner employed New Testament texts such as Ephesians 1:22–23, and Colossians 1:24 as definitions of the word *church.* Put simply, he defined the church as the body of Christ. As such it must contain all of Christ's members, and therefore by Warner's logic no building or "organized division" can be the church because none contains all the members of the body. "No sect contains all of the body of Christ, therefore, no sect is the church of God. Then as honest men, who expect to be judged by the Word of God, let us never call anything the church but the body of Christ; i. e., all the saved, either universally, or in any given locality."[38]

Since the church is Christ's body, logically enough he is its head. Warner made this point by appeal to several explicit texts as well as by inference. He took quite literally such passages as Ephesians 4:15–16; 5:23–24; Colossians 2:18–19; Isaiah 33:22; and James 4:12. Warner insisted that head and lord of the church were more than titles; they also expressed a governmental function. As a consequence he denounced systems of denominational organization—"laws, creeds, disciplines, and systems of coop-eration"—because they denied Christ the active function of governing the church. The denominations' "law-making synods and general conferences ignore the Divine Lawgiver, usurp the place of Christ and sit in the stead of God, and are not Christ's church, which is subject to him."[39] Questions and practices associated with church membership touched the matter of Christ's Lordship of the church at a salient point. Jesus had said that he was the door and that if anyone enter in through him that person would be saved. Warner took this text from John 10 as well as Revelation 3:8 and Ephesians 2:18 to mean that Christ is the door of the church and that his gift of salvation is the only entrance. No human can control access to what is the gift of Christ. Warner asserted that all denominations construct their own door, some mechanism by which members are admitted, and that humans thus pretend to control access to the church. Such practices stand in direct contrast to the church that is governed by Christ, the door that "no man can open or shut." To this Warner added two corollaries: (1) since Christ is the door of the church he could not possibly be the door of a sect, and (2) since salvation did not constitute admission into any of the sects, no sect can be the church of God.[40]

Warner thought that the church is the visible people of God on earth. He did not accept the distinction between a visible and invisible church. If sal-vation was the door by which people were admitted into Christian fellowship, it followed that there could be no unsaved people in the church. Warner combined Ephesians 3:15 and 2:19 to say that the church was the household of God so that only those who are children of God, those who have been born of the Spirit, are the church. Moreover, since the one who commits sin is of the Devil and those who are born of God do not commit sin, there can be no sinners in the church. Warner reached this conclusion on the basis of 1 John 3:8–10. This was a juncture where his Wesleyan theology of salvation fitted nicely with his radical ecclesiology. Warner employed the doctrine of entire sanctification and the possibility of a holy life free from sin as the instrument to achieve the biblical description of a sinless church. Of course, in Warner's view the denomination's more or less complete rejection of the holiness movement only served to reinforce his conclusion that they could not be the true church: "There are no sinners in the church. But all the sects are more or less filled with sinners. Hence no sect is the church of God."[41]

That it may have been composed only of the saints did not mean that the visible church needed no organization. Warner knew that he was treading on difficult ground, for he noted that the Bible does not use the word *organize*. He avoided any hierarchical arrangement of church offices by appealing to the dictionary definition of organization: "to furnish with organs." From this Warner was able to describe the church's organization in a manner congruent with his favored description of the church as the body of Christ. In this view, then, organization must be organic. The organs of the church are its various functions and ministries as described by Paul in his list of spiritual gifts in 1 Corinthians 12:8–11. The Holy Spirit organized the church by providing some of its members with the gifts for ministry specified by this and other New Testament texts. Such a theology of church offices can appropriately be termed charismatic church government.

From Warner's functional understanding of the divine lordship it followed that God actively governed the church through the appointment of ministers to perform its several tasks. Warner read 1 Corinthians 12:27–28 both as a description of the life of the first century church and, therefore, the model for organization. God would provide the organs of the church through the charisms of the Holy Spirit and thus bestow on some the gift of preaching, on others the gift of teaching, on still others the gift of healing, and so forth.[42] Warner's view of charismatic government church precluded all human devices or measures that might guide church polity. Thus he anathematized the idea of apostolic succession as a superstitious delusion. He similarly condemned the practice of voting for church officers. That was nothing more than "Babylon formality, where God is not present to work 'all in all' by the selfsame Spirit, dividing to every man severally as he wills."[43]

Warner's theology recognized that some members of the church would be gifted for particular service or ministries. The New Testament clearly taught that some received gifts for ministry. The New Testament also referred to the practice of the "laying on of hands," but here Warner placed severe limits on the significance of this act. If God gifted a man or woman for ministry then it was the fact of that gift that fulfilled the fundamental requirement for ordination and not the act of undergoing the rite. However, since the laying on of hands was clearly a New Testament practice any true church must employ it, and so Warner assented. But he went on to say that the rite contains no power and confers no status. Warner repudiated his ordination by the General Conference of the Churches of God and underwent a simpler form of ordination that conformed to this understanding. The practice of ordination in the young Church of God movement was predicated on a theology of church and ministry that limited ordination to the necessary organization of the church; the rite of ordination had no part in organizing the body of Christ.

Warner's theology of the church necessarily led to a strong appeal for Christian unity. There was but one head, Christ, and therefore there could be but one body. All the members of Christ were to be united in one body, since that was the express intent of Jesus' prayer in John 17 as well as several other New Testament passages. Warner also invented some unusual arguments to make this point. He maintained, for instance, that the figure of Christ as the bridegroom of the church necessitated that all believers be united in one body. A multiplicity of brides would be tantamount to making Christ at least a bigamist, and such a monstrous moral contradiction only served to underscore the point that there was only one church and that all believers were to be one with it.[44] No human mechanism or polity could accomplish the union of all Christian believers. In Warner's view the only means by which Christian unity is accomplished was through the sanctifying work of the Holy Spirit. The bond of the true church's union was perfect love, the second blessing. Warner's idea that perfect love was the bond of Christian unity was an experience to which many holiness people testified. Often found in the letters printed in the holiness journals were testimonies to the unity and harmony of the campground and holiness meeting where the Holy Spirit had been present to meld Christian hearts together. It is common to read reports of these meetings that celebrate their harmony and the fact that people from many denominations could join together in the common experience of perfect love.[45] Warner attended holiness meetings and camp meetings and delivered sermons to their crowds. He had a first-hand opportunity to witness and experience the same unity that he asserted on the basis of Scripture and argument.

Warner often pled for Christian unity by appealing to John 17, adding several additional texts to this text so frequently cited by Church of God preachers.[46] Entire sanctification, the second work of what Warner called "Bible salvation," brought freedom from sin, and that freedom knitted people together in an all-sufficient love. No creeds or tests of fellowship were necessary for people who lived on the plane of Bible holiness. Warner believed that perfect love melded Christians together in a bond that transcended even theological error. The grace of God applied to the consecrated believer's heart instantaneously cleansed every sinful stain. Scrubbing away doctrinal error might take longer, "but the pure in heart have perfect fellowship, even though all previously educated errors have not yet disappeared."[47]

Warner clearly believed that entire sanctification produced a unity that he characterized as harmony. Those who had experienced Bible salvation would live harmoniously in worship and ethics. They would also achieve doctrinal harmony, but Warner also asserted that the one and true church must be prepared to extend the right hand of Christian fellowship to those with whom they theologically disagreed. This position led him to a delicate balancing act.

Fellowship is of the Spirit (Phil 2:1), and exists where heart purity exists. It is the conscious blending of hearts filled with the same Holy Spirit. One may have been led into all the [doctrinal] truth, the other not. This does not interrupt fellowship. Nevertheless, it is the duty of such as 'know the truth' in meekness to instruct others who do not. Ignorance of some truth does not destroy fellowship, but resisting the truth does; because it forfeits salvation. We must not sanction people's errors, but if saved, show our love and fellowship to them, so long as they do not get the evidence that their wrong doctrines have become willful, or they have in some way lost salvation. Then fellowship ends, but love and kindness still continue in faithful efforts for their salvation. *To ignore fellowship simply because of some doctrinal error is bigotry. To agree to disagree, or to put on equality truth and error, is babel confusion. To know the truth is our privilege; to teach the truth is our duty; but to have fellowship with the pure and upright of heart is an involuntary and spontaneous act.*[48]

Warner believed that the loving fellowship of those perfected in love trumped theological differences. He never minimized those differences, asserting the responsibility of those who had arrived at the truth to teach those who had not. Neither could there be any mincing of words nor an agreement to accept differences. But the fellowship produced by "Bible salvation" was involuntary, as automatic as a heartbeat. Warner's theological high wire act balanced a certain measure of toleration over against an abiding concern for the truth. Fellowship was the balance beam that kept him from falling off on either side. But for Warner, this was no act. It was to be the lived experience of the church. This vision of Christian unity would of necessity entail the development of some practices for which the previous church experiences of many early Church of God people had not prepared them. It also lent itself to differing interpretations with varying points of emphasis in the generation that assumed leadership in the two and a half decades following his death.

Warner could not complete any discussion of the church without lambasting denominations, for which his favorite term was "the sects." He took his lead from a small tract on sects written by B. T. Roberts, whom Warner identified as the founder of the "Free Methodist sect," doubtlessly enjoying what he would have regarded as the irony of a sect leader attacking sects. Warner's use of the term connoted nothing of the church-sect distinction employed by Ernst Troeltsch. A younger contemporary of Warner, the

German theologian distinguished sects as protest oriented, voluntary communities over against the established state churches of Europe. For Warner sects were sections, therefore only parts of the church, and they could never be the whole church. No person of ordinary intelligence could define sects as portions cut from the body of Christ and yet also agree that such sections were legitimate. "To justify and sanction such schisms from the general body is to sin against God, and utterly disregard His Word."[49] As such all sects were clearly heretical and utterly without merit.

No Christian needed to feel bound to a sect for any reason. Believers could freely gather for worship outside the province of the sects. Grace, said Warner, is freely available directly from God and no sect possessed custody of it or any so-called means of grace. It is no surprise therefore that Warner labeled as ordinances the services of baptism and the Lord's Supper. To these he added a third, footwashing. No Christian was required to join a sect as a condition of participation in acts of worship that the Lord himself had ordained for the "exclusive observance" of the members of the body of Christ. "Sectarians who do not discern the body of Christ are not even qualified for their observance."[50] In such a situation the only and the proper course of action for all Christians was to flee not merely the sects to which they belonged, but to quit the "sect system" altogether, to follow the plain counsel of the Bible and "come out from among them and be ye separate."[51]

A call to come out of denominational Babylon and enter into the one true church of God was liable to the charge that those who issued the call were merely the latest in a long line of sect creators. Warner answered that charge in a manner that satisfied him and others in the Church of God movement even if it did not quiet their critics. If sectism was a sin from which there was no escape then in vain God called people to holiness. That was an impossibility, and besides there was also the divine command to "come out," freely interpreted from several New Testament texts. Warner's theology of church membership provided the means of living up to this command. He reasoned that as soon as a sinner is converted that person has been made a member of the church of God. As yet the new convert has not joined any sect, but clearly is a member of the church. The Bible contains no command that new believers must join a sect, so the convert may live out his or her discipleship without ever disobeying scripture on this point. "He can obey all the Word and keep salvation, in the church, without ever joining a sect, and so can every saint on earth do the same."[52] Any current member of a sect has the same privilege. Later Warner would say that members of sects are obligated to leave them. But what prevents the new group from becoming another sect? Warner thought that creeds, confessions of faith, and other tests of fellowship were clear evidences of the process of sect formation. None of these could provide a suitable foundation for the Church of God. If believers were simply to acknowledge that they had been joined together by God's gracious salvation in the "bond of perfectness,"[53] then the true church was indeed present. "What foundation do all Christians actually and necessarily stand on? By abiding only in Christ, his body the church, we stand on the foundation that includes all Christians in heaven and earth; and not a member of any sect or cut-off faction."[54]

Notes

1. C. E. Brown, *When Souls Awaken* (Anderson, Ind: Gospel Trumpet Company, 1954), 54–68.

2. *Bible Proofs of a Second Work of Grace* (Goshen, Ind: Evangelical United Mennonite Publishing Society, 1880).

3. John Wesley, "The Great Privilege of Those that are Born of God," in *Sermons on Several Occasions* (London: Epworth Press, 1944), 174.

4. (Guthrie, Oklahoma: Faith Publishing House, reprint edition: n.d.)

5. Ibid., 6–7.

6. Ibid., 8.

7. Ibid., 17.

8. Ibid., 15.

9. *Holiness Bible Subjects* (Grand Junction, Mich: Gospel Trumpet Publishing Company, 1890), 54. In a brief set of opening remarks, Wickersham said that for his preparation of the subjects for this lengthy collection of proof-texts he had "selected richly" from the writings of A. J. Kilpatrick, S. L. Speck, W. G. Schell, and Warner.

10. Ibid., 63.

11. Ibid.

12. Ibid., 19.

13. Warner buttressed his assertion with several proof-texts: Gen 17:1; Deut 18:13; 1 Chron 28:9; Matt 5:48; Luke 6:40; 2 Cor 7:1; 2 Cor 13:9, 11; Heb 6:1

14. E.g., Ps 18:30, 32; Ps 25:9; Ps 85:13; Ps 91:11; Ps 119:3; Ps 138:8.

15. Warner, *Salvation*, 22.

16. 1 Cor 2:6; Col 2:10; Phil 3:15.

17. Warner, *Bible Proofs*, 11.

18. Warner said that God had given him a particular interpretation of the text of Heb 12:25–29 on August 30, 1879. Cf *Bible Proofs of a Second Work of Grace*, 367.

19. "The church may be denominated heaven, to indicate its source and the nature of its elements. Its Head and Founder, 'Is the Lord from Heaven.' " In what is surely a piece of questionable exegesis Warner proceeded to equate the church and the kingdom of God. *Bible Proofs*, 368.

20. Ibid., 371.

21. Ibid., 375.

22. Ibid., 375–376.

23. Ibid., 381–382.

24. Ibid., 408.

25. Ibid., 411.

26. Ibid., 419.

27. Warner summarized the points of the *Harvester* editorial in *Bible Proofs*, 119–120.

28. Ibid., 420.

29. Ibid., 421.

30. Ibid., 427.

31. Ibid., 429.

32. The full text of the Carson City Resolutions can be found in Barry L. Callen, Ed, *Following the Light* (Anderson, Ind: Warner Press, 2000), 71; they also are published in John W. V. Smith, *The Quest for Holiness and Unity* (Anderson, Ind: Warner Press, 1980), 46–47.

33. Ibid., Callen, 71; Smith, 46.

34. Ibid.

35. Ibid., Callen, 71; Smith, 47.

36. *Church Advocate* (June 21, 1871), 1.

37. Ibid.

38. *The Church of God: What the Church of God Is and What it is Not,* reprint edition (Guthrie, Okla: Faith Publishing House, n.d.), 1. Warner defined a sect from the Latin *secare,* meaning to cut. He used the term interchangeably with "denomination" to indicate any section, and therefore incomplete portion, of the church. "Sectism" thus denoted either the active belief in or acquiescence to an understanding of the church that accepted such division.

39. Ibid., 5.

40. On this last point Warner's logic runs in a very tight circle. Cf. *The Church of God,* 5–6.

41. Ibid., 7.

42. Ibid., 7–8.

43. Ibid., 8–9.

44. Ibid., 11.

45. E.g. *Advocate of Christian Holiness,* September 1877, 298; July 1878, 165; December 1879; September 1881;and October 1881, 309.

46. Heb 2:11; Eph 4:11–13; 1 Pet 1:18–19.

47. Ibid., 18.

48. Ibid., 19. Emphasis added.

49. Ibid., 20.

50. Ibid., 22.

51. 2 Cor 6:17; Rev 18:4; Isa 52:11, and Ezek 20:34, 41.

52. Ibid., 23.

53. A phrase from Colossians 3:14 and the title of a gospel song for which Warner wrote the lyrics. This song is one of the most succinct expressions of Warner's earliest theology of the church and the importance of the experience of entire sanctification to that theology. Cf. "The Bond of Perfectness," which was last published using Warner's exact language in *Hymnal of the Church of God* (Anderson, Ind: Warner Press, 1971), No. 456.

54. Ibid., 23–24.

Chapter 3
Challenges and Emergent Practices

The Carson City resolutions gestured toward the development of doctrinal practices of church and ministry. But this gesture was insufficient as either a theoretical or practical blueprint for such practices. Moreover, given D. S. Warner's antipathy for organizational ground rules, theoretical or otherwise, it was extremely unlikely that the fledgling Church of God movement would create a set of bylaws or a manual of discipline on which to found church practice. Nevertheless, shortly after its inception and for several decades afterward, doctrinal practices did in fact develop. However, this development occurred not first in a theory followed by practical application. On the contrary, practices that articulated the movement's vision of the church developed on the fly, as it were. Very early in its life, the Church of God was confronted by the first in a series of challenges that extended over a period of approximately thirty years. These challenges provided the crucible in which doctrinal practices concerned with identity and church discipline were forged. Two of these practices concerned the matter of church discipline *per se* and the practice of biblical interpretation. The latter was particularly crucial for a group that maintained no creed but the Bible, but in both cases doctrinal practices developed as the movement repeatedly faced challenges to order and identity during the last decades of the nineteenth-century and the first decade of the twentieth.

Personal Crises

D. S. Warner and the *Gospel Trumpet* lived almost constantly from one crisis to another during the paper's first six years. Finances were usually strained, often severely, and this forced the paper to abandon its location in downtown Indianapolis in favor of the Warners' kitchen. Warner hoped to build an office on the same lot, but that project also had to be laid aside for lack of funds. In the autumn of 1882 the Warners and their paper moved to Cardington, Ohio. Word had come of successful evangelistic meetings in that vicinity, and they hoped to find financial support for the *Trumpet* among the newly converted and sanctified. Finances worsened, however, so when a printing press broke down and local opposition intensified, the Warners relocated once again. The promise of land and materials for an office lured them to Bucyrus in nearby Crawford County. In June 1883 Warner moved the *Trumpet* to property that had been donated by a man named D. D. Johnson. Little is known of Johnson, except that in return for his generosity he was named the paper's publisher. The first three years of existence were dominated by financial problems so severe as to prompt Warner to relocate repeatedly wherever brighter prospects glimmered.

Better prospects in north central Ohio also returned the Warners to familiar personal surroundings and much closer proximity to Sarah's staunch holiness family. However, bright hopes quickly dimmed and eventually turned to near despair as D. S. Warner found himself embroiled in two crises, one of them personal, within a year of relocating from Cardington. The first crisis broke out when the fruits of Warner's radical ecclesiology ripened. The second grew out of the first and developed into a contest for ownership of the *Gospel Trumpet* that ended in the divorce of Daniel and Sarah Keller Warner.

On November 12, 1883, the first "general assembly" of the "saints," as Church of God people referred to themselves, convened at Conley Bethel near Bucyrus. Warner had announced the meeting in the paper, and since circulation was up to two thousand copies, most of them distributed in Ohio, Indiana, and Michigan, many readers lived close enough to attend. Warner envisioned a meeting that would be a foretaste of heaven, free of all church rules and regulations. He invited any and all who were dissatisfied with their church affiliation to join ranks with the new movement. Neither he nor the handful of souls associated with the Church of God had any idea, save the size of the *Gospel Trumpet* print runs, of the number or convictions of the people who may have been reading the paper or who numbered themselves among the "saints." On the first night of the meeting the Warners got a look at the movement's constituency, and a more dismaying sight they could not have anticipated. Those longing for a foretaste of heaven included a significant number of disaffected and highly vocal souls who may have been sympathetic to part of the *Trumpet* message but who also brought their own ideas concerning the theological and moral shape of the true church. Some strong holiness men from northwestern Ohio threw the meeting into confusion. They contended for the immorality of collars, collar pins, and

Sarah Keller Warner. A member of a staunch holiness family, Sarah Warner's part in an attempt to gain control of the Gospel Trumpet and her subsequent estrangement from her husband, D. S. Warner, were key elements in an early leadership crisis in the Church of God.

eyeglasses and insisted that all those in the crowd who were wearing such devilish devices remove them. To make their point further the men threw themselves on the meeting hall floor, moaning and groaning throughout the sermon.

What Warner had envisioned as an assembly of the saints he later described as a meeting where "Satan had also gathered his angels together where the sons of God came together to worship the God of the Bible."[1] Unfortunately for Warner and the saints, meetings on the second night of the general assembly degenerated into a confusion every bit the equal of the previous evening. Having adjourned to Annapolis, Ohio to escape the fanatics who had been so disruptive the night before, Warner and the saints found themselves greeted by L. H. Johnson, publisher of a Toledo paper called the *Stumbling Stone.* He had arrived early, and when the saints entered the hall Johnson was already in the pulpit preaching a doctrine that rejected the ordinances of baptism, communion, and footwashing as well as the doctrine of entire sanctification as a second work of grace. He had been attracted to the assembly by the anti-denominational side of the *Gospel Trumpet* and apparently hoped to sway the saints to his point of view. Heterodox on two of three theological issues, Johnson nevertheless remained in town to harangue the meetings for the next two days. Chaos threatened. Having had their fill of fanaticism and false teachers, Warner and those who followed the *Trumpet* straight down the line, now apparently greatly reduced in number, repaired to a private home where they attempted to continue the meeting. Even this second removal failed to discourage some of the fanatics who continued their pursuit of the saints. Only after yet another relocation were the saints able to separate themselves from these divisive elements and continue the little that remained of the "general assembly."[2]

The disastrous meeting of November 1883 illustrates two important aspects of the very early Church of God movement. First, Warner and his close associates had only a tenuous hold on the early Church of God movement. Not only had they no accurate idea of the movement's size, constituency, or theological opinions, but the movement's theology of church leadership also opened the door to rival claims based on the unmediated experience of divine illumination. Second, the saints were an amorphous movement composed of some true believers, but others who selectively embraced elements of Warner's message; these, nevertheless, could easily consider themselves members of a movement that possessed no rules or regulations except that members have experienced salvation. Warner's ecclesiology was too radical in its vision to survive without either modification or the development of practices that could sustain it.

The presence at the Annapolis meetings of so many people disaffected with American denominational life demonstrated that the Church of God movement was seriously crippled by the absence of institutional practices necessary to teach and reinforce its message. Despite the movement's positive doctrine of holiness such practices were essential if the saints—as well as potential saints—were to see the church in a positive light. Otherwise they would be left to define themselves largely according to the negative vision of what they found objectionable in the denominations. L. H. Johnson and the anti-eyeglass holiness people graphically demonstrated the possibility that people opposed the prevailing church system for many and varied opinions. To find commonality and cohesiveness on the basis of shared beliefs and practices was a very different matter. Warner never again made the mistake of inviting people to join the saints on the basis of dissatisfaction. Some might continue to join on such a weak reed. In a short time, however, doctrinal practices did develop whereby the saints were able to live out their vision of the church.

Practices did not emerge soon enough to allay the fears of some that Warner's ecclesiology was simply too radical. Among those was Sarah Keller Warner, and immediately on the heels of the Annapolis fiasco this fear led to a second crisis for the early Church of God movement. The new crisis was a dispute over control of the *Gospel Trumpet,* and it threatened to undo Warner personally even as it eventually undermined his marriage with Sarah.

One of the rising stars among D. S. Warner's associates was a young minister named R. S. Stockwell of Ada, Ohio. He had joined the Church of God movement a year before the Annapolis assembly, and his zeal earned Warner's public admiration and praise.[3] Alongside his prowess as a holiness evangelist Stockwell's theology also embraced the doctrine of "marital purity." Holiness movement radicals in and around Cincinnati interpreted the experience of entire sanctification in the extreme, restricting the sexual relationship of married couples. According to this view those who had been perfected in love were to live celibately—even if married. In 1883 Sarah accepted Stockwell's doctrine on this subject. Her husband did not and their marriage began to suffer.[4]

Warner had ample personal reason to resent Stockwell, but in the first months of 1884 the two men contested each other not for Sarah but for the *Trumpet.* Claiming authorization by divine revelation, Stockwell asserted that God had told him that Warner was to sell the paper to one of Stockwell's associates, a man known only as "Rice." Sarah concurred, and together the three of them persisted in encouraging Warner to agree to this divine leading. Their efforts proved persuasive and he eventually agreed, but only after originally declining their proposal. By the next morning, however, his resolve had returned and he informed the three of his change of mind. Reinforced by the friendship of John N. Slagle, Warner refused the trio's repeated overtures. When she saw that her husband was adamant in his refusal Sarah left him, taking their three-year-old son, Sidney, with her. Warner was devastated. Nearly four months passed without a single issue of the *Gospel Trumpet.*

After leaving her husband Sarah Warner publicly criticized her his teaching, pointedly repudiating "come-outism." She published her criticism in the pages of the holiness journals that were well known to the Warners and other holiness people, especially the *Christian Harvester.* This paper was the organ of the Ohio Holiness Alliance and its staff was well acquainted with the Warners as well as Sarah's own family. Her repudiation of Warner's theology is not extant but only reported. On the basis of her family's strong connection to Ohio holiness circles one can infer that Sarah's criticism of Warner may well have been connected to a return to a more conventional holiness ecclesiology. This inference leaves unanswered the matter of marital purity. Sarah may have set aside her belief in that doctrine, for within two years of leaving Warner she returned Sidney to the custody of his father and filed for a divorce which Warner did not contest. She later married B. P. Critchell. Sarah died at Carthage, Ohio, in the vicinity of Cincinnati, in 1893. Warner's associates in the Church of God movement cast her in the role of a fallen woman who had abandoned not only a faithful husband but her young child as well. The strict moral code of the holiness movement, not to mention the attitudes of late Victorian culture, inevitably combined to paint a highly unflattering portrait of Sarah Warner. But that portrait may not have accurately depicted the woman who sought control of the *Gospel Trumpet.*

Given the one-sidedness of the available source materials it is very difficult to fully reconstruct and assess the events involving the Warners and Messrs. Stockwell and Rice. Thomas Fudge argues convincingly that this was a contest for authority among the leaders of a group that had been democratically governed up until this moment. However, even at this early date, to control the *Trumpet* was in some sense to lead the Church of God movement. The paper's editor was the movement's principal theological teacher and voice. The move made by Sarah Warner, Stockwell, and Rice assaulted Warner's leadership. We cannot know the motives of the two men in this attempted coup, but Sarah Warner's are open at least to conjecture. It is quite conceivable that she sought control of the paper in order to steer the Church of God back toward the center of the holiness movement, especially where the doctrine of the church was concerned. Her family was very active in the Ohio holiness movement. Her father had organized an independent holiness church, for which initiative he earned the approbation of the *Advocate of Christian Holiness.*[5] Perhaps the outrageous fanaticism and confusion of the Annapolis meetings illustrated for Sarah the impractical dangers of a radical ecclesiology that strayed too far from traditional holiness teaching. In such a view, come-outism did not lead people out of the confusion of Babylon; in fact it only magnified confusion. The only alternative was to gain control of the paper and bring order to a movement threatening to degenerate into chaos. It may also have been the case that she was attracted to Stockwell, but his doctrine of marital purity would have made difficult any romantic entanglement. It is certainly plausible that theological issues were the motivating factors for Sarah in 1884.

Whatever the motivations of Stockwell, Rice, and Sarah Warner, the net effect of their action was an attack on Warner's leadership. Once he recovered his emotional and religious moorings he and his associates acted to consolidate his position and authority as leader of the Church of God movement. Stockwell was denounced and Sarah cast into an uncomplimentary role. Long after Warner's death his biographer, A. L. Byers, portrayed him as an innocent victim of Sarah's fallen ways. Byers' work tends to regard Warner in the uncritical light of hero worship, but it was scarcely necessary to protect his public image more than two decades after his death unless that view had been well established. Perhaps the single most important result of the crisis over control of the *Trumpet* was the emergence of D. S. Warner as the acknowledged leader of the Church of God movement.[6]

At the very least, it can be said that the Church of God emerged from the second crisis with an increased appreciation for the importance of leaders whose authority did not stem from democratic principles. In this sense the crisis and its resolution in favor of Warner reinforced views of the church and its organization that were implicit in the Carson City resolutions of 1881. Authority and leadership were not based in democracy but conferred through the charismatic work of the Holy Spirit, who appointed leaders by providing them with the spiritual gifts necessary to the performance of their duties. But the experiences of this critical period in the early history of the Church of God movement taught its leaders an important lesson. The movement would not survive without a polity, a way of being together. Church creeds and organizational forms might be convenient polemical targets, but their absence created a vacuum that any number of illuminati stood ready to fill. Over the next twelve years following the Annapolis meeting—up to Warner's death in 1895—a set of practices began to fill the vacuum created by Warner's anti-organizational bias. These and other practices that developed later were crucial to the formation of the polity of the Church of God movement even as they embodied much of its theology.

Emerging Practices in Controversy

In the aftermath of the Warners' separation members of the Church of God movement stepped in to end the four-month hiatus in publishing activity at the *Trumpet* office. In April 1884 Thomas L. Horton, a businessman from Williamston, Michigan, arranged for the shipment of *Trumpet* machinery and stock to that town. Joseph and Allie Fisher moved to Williamston and took a more active role in the paper's publication. The same year Joseph Fisher collaborated with Warner on the publication of the first book printed on *Trumpet* presses, a collection of gospel songs and hymns published under the title *Songs of Victory.* It was at Williamston that Warner and Fisher first invited saints to join in the publishing venture. Up until this invitation the *Gospel Trumpet* was almost exclusively the product of D. S. Warner's labor. But soon a handful of people answered the call.

By January 1885 joining the Fishers and Warner at Williamston were William and Jenny Smith, Jeremiah Cole, John Spaulding, Rhoda Keagy and Celia Kirkpatrick. The building that housed the print shop was large enough to offer living quarters for the entire group. They lived together in a communal society that soon became known as the "*Trumpet* Family" and offered a model that demonstrated how saints could live together under the leadership of the Holy Spirit without "man-made" rules. Within a decade "missionary homes" began forming in cities and towns across the United States and beyond. Taking the *Trumpet* family as their example, these homes played a key role in the transition from little or no local organization to settled congregations. In 1885 the missionary homes still lay beyond the horizon, but the emergence of the *Trumpet* family in that year indicated that brighter days were ahead.

In 1886 the Gospel Trumpet Company relocated once again, this time to a town in southwestern Michigan whose name belied its actual size—Grand Junction. Here the *Trumpet* and its family remained for twelve years. During the first six years of their existence the handful of people called the saints who had associated with the Church of God had endured hardship, crises, and hostility from critics. Hardly a dent had been made in the religious consciousness of denominational Christianity.[7] But the years in Grand Junction witnessed a dramatic spread in the movement's reach. The *Trumpet* family that departed in 1898 not only had grown markedly in size; it was sending literature around the world. At Grand Junction the leadership of the Church of God movement also began to set in place practices that shaped the movement's life together. It was not the case that any of these practices was the product of self-conscious activity aimed at creating them or a polity. On the contrary, they developed ad hoc, and occasionally as the answer to a challenge or even perhaps a crisis. The first of these involved Warner's part-ner and co-owner of the *Gospel Trumpet.*

Sometime early in 1887 Joseph Fisher's eye was drawn away from his wife, Allie, by a woman named Alice Davis. Not wanting to act without proper scriptural support, Fisher searched the Bible for warrants that would authorize the action he was contemplating. Finally he broached the subject of the biblical legitimacy of divorce to Warner, who suspected that Fisher's study of this particular topic was not disinterested.[8] This was for Warner a matter of sin taking root in the holiness camp. Fisher would have to repent or be disciplined. Either he would have to forsake this sinful doctrine and the relationship that spawned it or else relinquish ownership of the paper. Warner's ultimatum carried a considerable risk since Fisher held a large share in the financial interest in the Gospel Trumpet Company.[9] Given Warner's own personal past, the issue of divorce and remarriage was bound to be highly volatile as well. So the question at stake became a matter of church discipline. How would that discipline play out in a movement that shunned formal church procedures?

Warner was determined to follow his understanding of the Bible's teaching concerning divorce. It scarcely need be noted that he did not dis-tinguish between biblical teaching and his interpretation of that teaching; for Warner they were one and the same. His own divorce from Sarah had only recently been finalized, but Warner had determined that the Bible required divorced people to live celibately and not remarry. In his own case, Warner would eventually marry Frances "Frankie" Miller, but not until after his divorced wife's death. Since Warner regarded this interpretation to be the plain teaching of Scripture, he was adamant that it be operative not only in his personal life but for any church that claimed to be founded on the New Testament. However, his ultimatum did not cow Fisher, who divorced Allie and soon afterward married Alice Davis. Warner's only alternative was to require Fisher to give up his interest in the publishing company. Herein lay the test of Warner's determination to enforce discipline on a member and key leader of the Church of God movement. Fisher could not be expected to walk away from his financial interest, but Warner lacked the resources to buy out his one-time partner. Would he stand by and watch the dismantling of the Gospel Trumpet Company rather than be unequally yoked with an unrepentant sinner?

The timely appearance of Enoch E. Byrum of Randolph County, Indiana spared Warner the grief of sacrificing the publishing company to a point of church discipline. At the Grand Junction camp meeting of 1887 Byrum's uncle, H. C. Wickersham, introduced him to Warner, having been previously alerted by Wickersham to the fact that young Byrum had recently come into an inheritance. Warner then asked Byrum to consider buying Fisher's interest in the publishing company and Byrum agreed. The whole of his inheritance was consumed by this purchase, which made Byrum the publisher as well as part owner in the bargain. He had never seen the inside of a print shop. That Byrum's purchase freed Warner's hand to follow through on his ultimatum to Joseph Fisher should not be allowed to over-shadow Warner's determination to enforce church discipline. Nor was this lesson lost on Enoch Byrum, who was later called upon to discipline the church in three celebrated cases in the history of the Church of God.

In 1899 Byrum was confronted by the first major challenge to his author-ity. As in the case of Fisher, this challenge was at once personal and a matter of church discipline. Unlike that earlier affair, however, heresy was at the forefront of the confrontation. Since at least the 1870s the holiness move-ment had been troubled by the presence of a doctrine called "Zinzendorfism" after Graf Nicholas von Zinzendorf, the man generally reputed to be its originator. Zinzendorf was a key figure in the Moravian Church and John Wesley's associate from 1738 to 1742. Following Wesley, the leadership of the holiness movement described Zinzendorfism as a theory of entire sanctification wherein believers are said to be wholly sanctified in the same instant that they are justified and are neither more nor less holy from that moment until death.[10] Holiness leaders insisted that some degree of time elapsed between justification and entire sanctification; otherwise the change represented by the latter would signify the same relational change as the former. Wesley had asserted that justification was God's declaration of a changed relationship between himself and the believer; sanctification, however, signified a real change in the believer, a cleansed heart. Following this distinction holiness people asserted that Zinzendorfism either implicitly or explicitly asserted that holiness of heart was not real but imputed. From this conclusion some holiness advocates, E. E. Byrum included, dubbed the advocates of Zinzendorfism's advocates "Anti-cleansers."

Proponents of Zinzendorfism appeared in the Church of God movement after Warner's death in 1895. In November 1898 Byrum dismissed some members of the *Trumpet* family who had been teaching the doctrine. A significant number of the movement's preachers shared the views of the dismissed workers. Among these were some widely respected ministers, including W. A. Haynes, W. J. Henry, and E. G. Masters. Haynes frequently published articles in the *Gospel Trumpet* from 1894 to 1898. Henry had taken his stand for the Church of God in 1892, part of the holiness meeting at Jerry City, Ohio that contributed several individuals to the early Church of God movement. Such men were not to be regarded lightly. As the general camp meeting for 1899 approached both sides prepared for a fight. The "Anti-cleansers" went public with their teaching. For its part the paper, in Byrum's hands and therefore the trumpet of holiness orthodoxy, published several articles defending the doctrine of sanctification as a second definite work of grace that cleansed believers from all sin subsequent to the first work of justification.[11]

In the spring of 1899 A. L. Byers and W. G. Schell wrote articles for the *Trumpet* that took definitive positions on the issue that now percolated at full boil. Schell's piece ran in two installments under the title "Zinzendorfism Refuted." He was not afraid to label his opponents teachers of heresy as he laid out the standard holiness movement doctrine of sanctification. Schell reiterated the view that "inherited" or original sin remains in the heart of the believer following justification and that the second work—sanctification—eradicates this sinfulness at a moment that coincides with the baptism of the Holy Spirit. Sanctification was a cleansing that restored the believer to the state of Adam's soul prior to the sin in the Garden of Eden.[12] Schell might be said to have defended holiness orthodoxy on its merits alone. Byers, on the other hand, saw that Zinzendorfism undermined the Church of God movement's connection between heart holiness and authentic Christian unity: "To remove the doctrine of the second cleansing would simply be to quickly bring this reformation to naught, because it is just what the Church of God has needed to bring her out of spiritual Babylon into the glorious unity with Christ, and her members with one another."[13]

The pot boiled over in the camp meeting that convened at Moundsville, West Virginia[14] in June 1899. Byrum was determined to maintain strict control of the proceedings. As of that date, and as a matter of fact for the next eighteen years, the *Gospel Trumpet* was the sole institution by which any kind of order structured the informal ministers meetings that occurred during the general camp meeting. Since the editor ran the paper, he was also, *de facto,* the camp meeting organizer. Byrum closed off any opportunity for discussion or debate. After the camp meeting had adjourned he offered the following reasons for this move: (1) people were well aware of the issues surrounding the Zinzendorf doctrine that had been exposed and successfully criticized in print during the year just concluded; (2) proponents of the heresy had been privately advised at length that their doctrine rested on a false spirit; and (3) there was neither any wisdom nor any point in the public discussion of known heresy.[15] Whatever Byrum's reasons, his attempt at imposing a gag rule on the camp meeting did not intimidate the Zinzendorf faction. They met and published a written statement of their views. After two days of negotiating, they were permitted to read this statement. Evidently Byrum had put those two days to good use, because he reported afterward that the statement was "publicly refuted by the Word of God showing its falsity in doctrine and in spirit."[16]

It was one thing to refute heterodox teaching within the camp of the saints. Imposing a discipline to make that refutation stick was quite another, especially when the heterodox party numbered a very sizable minority in the movement's ministry.[17] Byrum proved up to the task. Risking the possibility of major defections he nevertheless imposed a strict doctrinal discipline. The Anti-cleansers walked out of the 1899 camp meeting and the Church of God movement. Byrum quickly followed up their departure with a notice in the *Gospel Trumpet* intended to enforce the majority's orthodox opinion. He published the names of the dissenters at Moundsville as well as those who shared their views but had not attended the meeting. Readers were strictly admonished: "To receive such persons or any one else teaching such who have faithfully been dealt with is to receive them and their doctrine at the peril of your souls. When they have seen the error of their ways and turned from it we shall be glad to inform our readers of the same."[18] Six months after the Anti-cleansing camp meeting, Byrum understandably remained worried about the effects of this schism.[19] The Zinzendorf theory had been propagated to some extent, and some of the saints were becoming confused, even "losing their experience." Byrum kept track of at least some of the Anti-cleansers. A few had repented and returned to the fold while others persisted in preaching false doctrine. Still others had left the ministry and had "gone to work with their hands," a step "which is much better," said Byrum, "than to go forth propagating something that would be detrimental to souls."[20] He remained adamant in refusing fellowship to the sizable number of ministers who remained outside the tiny fold. He encouraged the saints to pray for the restoration of the heretics, but he also took comfort in the fact that the Zinzendorfism episode "is only a fulfillment of the word of God." Invoking 2 Peter 2:1–2 as a forewarning of such episodes, Byrum made it clear that neither he nor the movement would turn back from this biblical standard.

To discipline the members of a church group is to follow a practice that at least aims at a modicum of consistency in thought and action. Without rules or formal procedures to follow, E. E. Byrum and the early Church of God nevertheless practiced church discipline in a manner that enforced theological uniformity on the movement. Otherwise events may have unfolded very differently. To be sure, Byrum and his supporters were immeasurably assisted by the Anti-cleansers' walk-out. That they did is testimony to the very tight control of the movement's one institution, the publishing house, by a very

small circle of men and women. In a very real sense their decisions constituted the disciplinary practice that they followed and that the Church of God
movement accepted. That practice needed to include elements for the
restoration of the penitent. Many of the Anti-cleansers left the Church of God
ministry and disappeared. Some few joined the Christian Church. Others
repented of their heresy and returned to the movement.

The doctrine of entire sanctification was a critical theological issue in the
Church of God movement at the turn of the nineteenth-century. Correlative
to that was a practical concern for the ethical consequences of that doctrine.
Once it had been firmly established that the experience of sanctification
entailed a cleansing from all inbred sin, it was perhaps inevitable that
attention quickly turned to the life of holiness that was the outcome of such
a cleansing. The saints became especially concerned about the marks of
sanctification in the daily lives of behavior. Pietists and their descendants
have often been susceptible to the charge of majoring in minors. This may
be the weakness of any group of Christians concerned that the roots of faith
must produce good fruits declarative of one's allegiance and faith. Whatever
the origins, just as repentant Anti-cleansers were returning some of the saints
became preoccupied with mild forms of asceticism as marks of holiness.

Like many groups with origins in the holiness movement and pietistic
Christianity, the Church of God movement kept a lengthy list of taboos
against "worldliness." The use of tobacco and alcoholic beverages was strictly
forbidden; so was the use of drugs—including caffeine. Many forms of
entertainment were also prohibited—dancing, the theater, and shows. In late
nineteenth and early twentieth century America these taboos reached far
beyond the confines of the holiness churches. The famed New School
Presbyterian revivalist Charles Finney had inveighed against the consumption of coffee and tea. Many Protestants joined forces in the crusade against
"demon rum." Catholic revivalists called Parish Missioners exhorted the
faithful to avoid the theater and the dangerous habit of novel reading even
as holiness advocate Phoebe Palmer had condemned *Uncle Tom's Cabin*
because it mixed fact and fiction. Concern for proper Christian conduct
extended across much of the religious landscape in late Victorian America.

John W. V. Smith and C. E. Brown agree that a spirit of competitiveness
pervaded the holiness churches on the matter of holy living.[21] They point to
exchanges between early Church of God figures and the leaders of other
holiness groups where one side challenged the other to live up to the
standard of holiness. Increasingly this standard was applied to articles
of clothing that were considered superfluous or prideful. Much of this
discussion applied to women's dress, particularly hats, jewelry, and even

undergarments such as corsets. Hats adorned with feathers were considered too fancy and necklaces and rings—even wedding rings—signs of worldly pride. Serious articles appeared in the *Gospel Trumpet* with titles like "The Evil Effects of Tight-Lacing"[22] to condemn corsets. Other articles doubted that holiness could long prosper in the heart of a woman who owned a large wardrobe, and another asserted that plain skirts were holier than those made with gores.[23] When it came to men, the article of clothing that attracted the most attention was the necktie. Ever since Warner's day the saints had considered the necktie to be superfluous and worldly adornment, but men were not barred from fellowship for wearing them.[24] After Warner's death attitudes hardened and the tie was increasingly regarded as a symbol of an unholy pride.

With the publication of Charles E. Orr's *Christian Conduct* in 1903, ascetics and watchdogs sniffing the wind for worldliness picked up the scent. Smith describes Orr as a very sensitive man of mystical and poetic bent. He possessed an extremely sensitive conscience as well, one that readily took up a heavy burden of guilt over even slight offenses. Orr also enjoyed a reputation for saintliness and extreme dedication to the message of the Church of God.[25] The saints knew him to be a man who lived up to the very high standard of holiness that he set for himself and for the movement as a whole. During the decade following the publication of *Christian Conduct*, Orr and like-minded individuals sought to further entrench their increasingly extreme asceticism. At the same time moderate voices urged that latitude be given to men whose businesses or occupations required them to wear neckties. That the two sides were becoming polarized is evident in an attempt at compromise through a resolution adopted by an ad hoc group of ministers at the 1911 camp meeting in Anderson, Indiana.[26]

> 1. That there is no good reason for a change in what for years has been the general attitude of the church in this country in regard to the matter, namely that the wearing of the tie is a thing to be discouraged as unnecessary and as tending to the spirit of the world.
> 2. That liberty be given to its being worn by those whose consciences do not forbid their doing so on occasions when their business or other extreme circumstances require it.[27]

Each side had won approval of its opinion, but such an outcome led Orr to view the resolution as tantamount to compromise. Two years later opponents of the necktie were back with another resolution, this one aimed at a stronger condemnation of the tie. Instead a group of leading ministers

Charles E. Orr. Of deeply sensitive temperament, the rigidly ascetic Orr refused to compromise on holiness standards and precipitated a divisive crisis in the early twentieth century Church of God.

adopted a substitute resolution that maintained the moral status quo. The group's failure to adopt a hard line on the necktie incensed Orr and others. Late in 1913 he began publication of a rival paper, the *Herald of Truth*. The *Herald's* appearance was not a signal of an imminent schism, but the growing polarization of viewpoints increased the likelihood of serious division. Orr used his paper as a platform from which to deliver his increasingly extreme view of personal holiness. For example, when he attacked those who sang worldly music, his broadax fell on tunes like "My Old Kentucky Home" as easily as Scott Joplin's rags.[28] The message of the *Herald* took on an ever more shrill voice.

E. E. Byrum and other leaders hoped that Orr would relent, but they also were losing patience under attacks in which he referred to them as compromisers. D. Otis Teasley, one of the early movement's more progressive thinkers, regarded Orr's actions and pronouncements as but the latest example of an impossibly high idealism. Teasley also expressed the hope that Orr would regain a more balanced view. However, Teasley, who in a few years would publish a book on hermeneutics that was quite advanced within Church of God circles, also criticized Orr's views because they rested on an unmediated inner illumination that appeared to supercede the Bible. Neither did he scruple to employ the word *heresy* in description of Orr's ideas. Speaking for the "great majority" of Church of God ministers, Teasley asserted as the movement's orthodox view that the Scriptures were the standard for instruction, the Holy Spirit guided readers to proper interpretation, and a conscience void of offense was the result of Christian obedience.[29]

Until February 1914 E. E. Byrum attempted to play a mediating role between extremists like Orr and moderates[30] like Teasley, H. M. Riggle, A. T. Rowe, and others. In the context of that day these men and their supporters were regarded as liberals for their view that neckties were morally unobjectionable. Given their convictions on most theological matters, it not only strains credulity to call them liberals, it is also historically inaccurate. In formal published opinion as well as in personal habit, Byrum had attempted to steer a middle course between extremism and compromise.[31] In late February, however, he took a step that followed the course he had taken in 1899. He published an editorial in the *Trumpet* warning readers that C. E. Orr had fallen under a spirit of heresy. He had established his own opinion as the norm of Christian conduct. To do so violated the principle of unity among the believers.[32] Apparently working in consort with Teasley, Byrum judged Orr to be not only a heretic but a schismatic as well.

Byrum's charges stung the deeply sensitive Orr. He continued to edit the *Herald of Truth* for another year, but in March 1915 he recanted some of his convictions in a letter to the *Gospel Trumpet.* However, by then a number of disaffected saints sufficient to keep the cause alive had emerged. Finally in 1923 a man named Fred Pruitt launched a successor to the *Herald of Truth.* Published at Guthrie, Oklahoma, the new paper was called *Faith and Victory.* Orr meanwhile lived theologically between the Church of God mainstream and his own recurrent extremism. The *Yearbook of the Church of God* listed him as a minister until 1926. He eventually started another paper, *The Path of Life,* which ultimately merged with *Faith and Victory.* Orr died in 1933, having become a page editor for that paper in December 1932.

The resolution of the necktie controversy provides a second example of the manner in which the early Church of God resolved theological disputes. The movement possessed no ecclesiastical machinery for dealing with theological mavericks like C. E. Orr. No leader stood forth to prefer charges to bring Orr to trial for heresy; no judicatory existed in which to conduct such a trial if charges had been preferred. What practice could E. E. Byrum employ to discipline his beloved, spiritually sensitive, but cantankerous brother? Byrum took what was still the only course open to him, the same steps that he had taken to deal with the Anti-cleansers in 1899. On his authority as editor and the movement's leading voice, Byrum labeled Orr a heretic and warned the saints against associating with him. Orr was left without recourse or due process. Byrum had a close grip on the *Gospel Trumpet,* the most authoritative and widely read source of information and doctrine in the Church of God movement. Using the medium of the paper, Byrum's familiar pattern of warnings and announcements constituted and reinforced the practice of church discipline.

By 1915 church discipline, authoritarian and without formal structures though it may have been, was becoming entrenched as an aspect of the doctrinal practice of the church. Warner and Byrum, particularly the latter, had theologically corrected some of the leading ministers of the Church of God. In Byrum's hands the practice had taken a definite turn in the direction of authoritarian control. Warner had said that only sin could break the bonds of Christian fellowship. But he had also asserted that obstinate refusal, when admonished by those who held the truth, eventually would constitute prideful disobedience. Byrum had thus judged C. E. Orr a schismatic as well as a heretic. The *Trumpet* editor could countenance diversity only so long before transforming obstinacy into sin against the loving fellowship of the church. Warner and Byrum, particularly the latter, had enforced doctrinal uniformity on some of the brightest lights in the Church of God ministry. However, none was brighter nor the struggle more protracted than in the case of W. G. Schell.

William Schell (1869–?) was still an adolescent when, mostly for curiosity's sake, one night in 1886 he attended a service during a holiness revival conducted by Church of God ministers A. J. Kilpatrick and J. N. Howard.[33] Schell had joined the Methodist Episcopal Church in the aftermath of his conversion in a revival meeting. But he decided that his experience compared unfavorably to the spirit manifested by Kilpatrick and Howard. Still seeking purity of heart, Schell returned for another service, but this time was introduced to the Church of God movement's vision of the New Testament church. That too attracted Schell, who after two sermons decided to leave the Methodists in favor of the Church of God. A few months later he answered a call to the ministry. Schell proved an able and effective preacher. He also wrote books and articles for the *Gospel Trumpet* and rapidly rose to prominence. When Warner died in December 1895 Schell was preaching in a revival at Castine, Ohio. His status in the eyes of the movement's leadership was such that *Trumpet* family members wired Schell the news of Warner's death along with a request to come to Grand Junction immediately and deliver the funeral sermon.

Warner's death raised the question of his successor as editor of the *Gospel Trumpet.* This was the first occasion when movement leaders faced the issue of leadership transition. It may have occurred to some that several individuals might be candidates to fill the vacancy. Several prominent ministers had contributed frequently to the paper and on that basis might be considered as potential successors to Warner. In some minds W. G. Schell was one of the strongest candidates for the position, but the problem of selecting a new editor was compounded by the absence of any formal institutions or procedures. Not only was there the matter of on whom Warner's editorial mantle was to rest; how to name that person was also at issue. Matters were further complicated by the special case of the Gospel Trumpet Publishing Company. It was still privately held in 1895 and would be for several years. Moreover, the other leading candidate for the editor's chair happened to be one of the principal owners.[34] E. E. Byrum's ownership and role in the company proved decisive. At Warner's request, Byrum had also assumed editorial responsibilities sufficient to place his name alongside Warner's as editor on the masthead the previous July.[35] That move answered the question concerning the identity of Warner's successor. Unfortunately, Byrum's assumption of the office did little to create procedures to fill vacancies even as it gave Schell the appearance of a mere pretender. Leadership transitions proved to be especially difficult for the Gospel Trumpet Publishing Company for the next thirty-five years.

Byrum's assumption of power hinted at what eventually emerged as a rivalry between him and Schell. The rivalry was one-sided, however, because Byrum's financial control of the publishing company was further consolidated only days after Warner's death. Frances ("Frankie") Miller Warner, newly widowed, asked that her late husband's interest in the company be liquidated and paid to her. Earlier Enoch Byrum's younger brother Noah had bought out Allie Fisher and Sebastian Michels. The Byrum brothers purchased Mrs. Warner's interest and thus became sole owners and proprietors of the Gospel Trumpet Publishing Company. If Schell ever was considered as Warner's successor, that candidacy appears to have been largely illusory. Nevertheless, he had already earned a reputation as an important preacher and writer. He continued a season in these capacities, writing books and contributing articles of critical importance during the showdown with the Anti-cleansers. It was only a matter of time, however, before serious friction developed between Schell and Byrum. The sequence of Schell's departure, return, and final departure from the movement illustrates once again the authoritarian way in which Byrum enforced theological discipline on the Church of God ministry.

As in the case of the Anti-cleansing disturbance the *Gospel Trumpet* played an important role in reporting heresy and lending authority to the church's judgment against individuals who deviated from church teaching. In the early 1900s Schell began expressing reservations about certain points of doctrine and was reported to be heterodox on three. He was alleged to have said that "he no longer considers the present reformation [the Church of God reformation movement, as it had begun referring to itself] to be of God."[36] Schell had set the Church of God in its historical and cultural context, attributing Warner's early insights to instruction he had received from the Winebrennarians. He concluded that had Warner and the other early leaders been affiliated with another denomination they would have borrowed elements of that group's doctrine, just as they had from the Winebrenner group. In 1903 Church of God preachers widely believed that the movement's doctrine derived from the Bible as it had been illumined by the Holy Spirit in the mind of the reader of Scripture. Schell's views clearly contradicted this belief. His other heterodox beliefs included a denial that the ordinance of foot-washing was authorized by the New Testament and a belief in triune immersion as the proper form of baptism. The latter two disputed points were serious, but the first struck at the movement's very roots. To say that any doctrine of the Church of God had origins in the world of denominational Christianity struck at the very roots of the movement's emerging sense of identity and invalidated its practices. It was the orthodox view of the movement that the teaching of the first generation must have emerged unmediated from its reading of the Bible alone. Any other source had to be part of the denominational system and therefore necessarily contaminated.

Schell had to be disciplined or defrocked. The Church of God congregation at Moundsville, West Virginia was reported as "suffering long and dealing with him in much leniency."[37] When he proved obstinate in his views, the church there expelled him. This was, however, no ordinary Church of God congregation. In 1898 the Byrums had moved the Gospel Trumpet Company to this Ohio River town, so the church in Moundsville quickly became one and the same with the *Trumpet* family. As a consequence many key movement leaders were members of the congregation or well known to it. In disputing with the Moundsville church leadership Schell was taking on the Byrums and other *Gospel Trumpet* writers and gospel workers. He suffered the same fate as the Anti-cleansers, the anti-necktie faction, and others who had opposed the movement's leadership.

Schell wandered in a far country theologically and economically for five years. Then in January 1908 the *Trumpet* published an open letter of confession in which he requested the prayers of Byrum and the saints. The letter was printed with an editorial introduction that described its writer as "one who once enjoyed the blessings of salvation and was a minister of the gospel." Readers were encouraged to offer the "united prayers of the children of God for his restoration."[38] The editors had withheld Schell's name intentionally, but when he sent word a week later that he had repented his sins and waywardness and found peace with God the *Trumpet* was quick to print his letter over Schell's signature.[39] On the basis of his public act of penitence he was restored to the Church of God movement and its ministry.[40]

Schell eventually left the Church of God movement again, this time for good. Subsequently he was led into the baptism of the Holy Spirit by a Pentecostal preacher and became a Pentecostal minister. Afterwards he published a book in which he repudiated the "modern holiness doctrine"; he also stated his intention to "sweep away, with an overflowing shower of Holy Scriptures, the false theories that are current in the minds of people concerning sanctification and holiness."[41] The book marks Schell's irreversible break with the holiness movement in general by attacking its mainstream elements as well as "Bro. Tomlinson's Church of God" and the extremism of the doctrine of "Social [marital] Purity."[42]

Church of God movement leaders, principally D. S. Warner and E. E. Byrum, developed elements of the practice of church discipline occasionally. They dealt with theological heterodoxy on a case-by-case basis, in the process building up that church practice. Throughout Warner's entire life in the Church of God and for most of Byrum's tenure as editor, the movement lacked formal structures by which orthodoxy could be enforced or easily defined. No creed or doctrinal statement existed—nor could one be written, if the movement were to keep faith with its original convictions—to serve as a doctrinal standard. The early Church of God movement insisted that its only creed was the Bible and the Bible alone. Despite the absence of the second-order language of creed or doctrinal statement, the movement and its leadership managed to practice a form of discipline that clearly defined group insiders from outsiders. The _Gospel Trumpet_ played a critical role in that practice as both the norm of teaching and the means of enforcement. But the _Trumpet_ could only include or exclude as determined by editorial decision. Ultimately it was the editor who shaped and defended theological orthodoxy in the Church of God. Neither Warner nor Byrum enforced orthodoxy on any basis other than their understanding of the requirements of Scripture. Byrum may have possessed a manager's mentality, but when it came to the ministerial functions of expelling sinners and restoring the penitent he followed what he took to be New Testament instruction. His practice resembled that of Mennonites and other Radical Reformation churches such as the United Brethren, the group out of which the Byrum clan had come. Warner appears to have been less inclined than Byrum to use the practice of banning. It is the case that Warner and other _Trumpet_ writers used the paper to portray Sarah Keller Warner as both theologically and ethically outside group norms.[43] However, on other issues Warner abjured heavy-handed authoritarianism in favor of a broadly democratic practice. This willingness clearly separates Warner and Byrum and sets the stage for a consideration of the practice of Bible reading and interpretation in the early Church of God movement.

Reading the Bible and Singing the Faith

Until the publication of Russell Byrum's _Christian Theology_ in 1925, the Church of God movement collapsed theology into biblical interpretation. Theology, which Church of God writers have until recently used interchangeably with the term _doctrine,_ assumed its importance in the closest possible connection with the Bible.[44] The movement's emphasis on biblical truth and practice inevitably stressed theology's importance where theology was understood to mean biblical interpretation that led to ethical living. To repudiate the use of creeds as doctrinal standards thus in no way weakened doctrine or signaled indifference to it. Rather, the absence of creeds combined with the equation of biblical interpretation and doctrine to create a very practical understanding of theology. Since the doctrine of the church, or ecclesiology, was at the very center of Church of God theological reflection, the *practices* of the church took on a crucial significance. The movement was to be what it claimed theologically, and right practice validated those claims. It is not too much to say that the practices embodied them. So, for example, beginning just after 1900 the saints began employing their own version of the classical theological idea of the "Notes" of the church. For early Church of God people the true church was the New Testament church, and the New Testament church was identified as that church where sinners were saved, believers were sanctified, and the sick were divinely healed. In other words, the validity of the movement's claim to be the New Testament church rested on the validity of its practices. Biblical interpretation, as with other practices, was of greater significance than doctrinal statements about inspiration and authority or manuals that published the findings of doctrinal study committees.[45] But to put the practice of hermeneutics at center stage placed a premium on such virtues as patience and flexibility. Late in Warner's editorial tenure there occurred a hermeneutical debate that illustrates what might be called the "ecclesial" practice of biblical interpretation.

The final two *Trumpet* issues for 1893 and the first issue of '94 carried a series of articles written by Warner that dealt with the interpretation of several Bible passages. However, Warner also situated his discussion of specific passages in the context of the movement's hermeneutical practice. He clearly regarded the former as particular instances of a larger issue. While he addressed the particular passages at hand Warner also spoke to the larger question. He adduced several texts to assert an ideal where the church's ministers "agree in faith and doctrine, being in the one 'faith of the gospel.' They are of the same mind, and that is not what they have compiled in a creed and subscribed to, but, that mind, faith, doctrine and practice is 'according to Christ Jesus.' This harmony of sentiment and teaching is attained, and can only be attained by having our former education and our wisdom destroyed and purged out; and be led by the Spirit of God into all truth, according to the promise of Christ" (John 16:13).[46] While such harmony was the ideal, Warner also recognized that not all of God's messengers possessed the same gifts and abilities. Nor had they attained the same measure of gospel truth. Nevertheless, "there is harmony in all that is taught, so long as each teacher is confined within that measure of truth received by the Holy Spirit."[47] How did this account of church and ministerial harmony actually play out?

Warner titled the first of his three essays, "Do the Ministers of God See Eye to Eye?" Within weeks he received answers to that question that prompted him to write a sequel titled, "The Ministers of God Must See Eye to Eye."

Evidently some readers, and some of them presumably ministers, disagreed over proposed interpretations of Jesus' saying that a camel could sooner pass through the eye of a needle than a rich man enter the kingdom. Warner offered a literal reading of the text and then encouraged his ministerial colleagues:

> And now beloved, if we are going to fulfil the prophecy of a
> holy ministry returned from Babylon confusion, to see eye to
> eye, and teach the same things, be sure that you take up and
> teach nothing that has the traditions of sectism to sustain it.
> Only teach what you know by the sure Word and Spirit of God,
> and there will be harmony.[48]

Despite clear differences of interpretation Warner did not use the authority of the editor's chair to enforce doctrinal uniformity. Instead he appealed to what he termed the "Word and Spirit of God" and implicitly trusted conversations between ministers and also between ministers and the *Trumpet* offices. Participants in these conversations together engaged in the practice of biblical interpretation, believing that the Word and Spirit of God would enter into their sincere efforts and guide them into "all truth." Warner's final article carried the title, "The Ministers of God See Eye to Eye,"[49] wherein he once again took up dissenting interpretations of biblical texts. As in the case of the second article he refused any claim to authority over his colleagues, nor did he claim greater light on the Scripture. Rather, Warner wrote in a tone that suggests that he engaged his ministerial colleagues in a conversation, preferring to leave guidance toward the truth in the hands of the Holy Spirit.

D. O. Teasley formalized the practice of biblical interpretation for the Church of God. Until 1919, his moderate theological voice held considerable influence among the movement's ministry. While superintendent of a missionary home in New York City, Teasley joined forces with George P. Tasker and A. D. Khan to write a correspondence course that directed home study for the ministry. Later he accepted an appointment to the staff of the Gospel Trumpet Company, eventually becoming managing editor. In 1918 he published the first book written in the Church of God solely devoted to hermeneutics, *The Bible and How to Interpret It.* There Teasley articulated the elements implicit in Warner's articles and, ideally, as they were to be practiced by sincere Christians, i.e., the Church of God movement at the very least.

Teasley began in his account with the two hermeneutical mainstays of the Church of God—Scripture and experience or, as those categories had previously been named, "Word and Spirit."

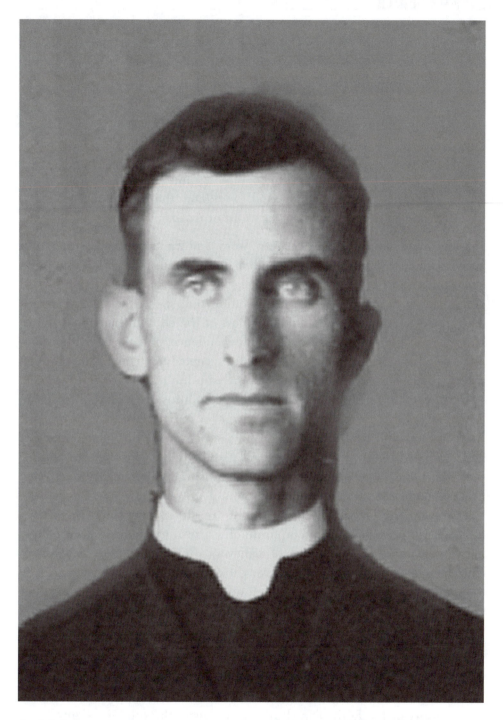

D. Otis Teasley. A voice for theological moderation during the Necktie Controversy, and a forward thinking leader during the first two decades of the twentieth century, Teasley authored several books on a range of theological topics from biblical interpretation to the organization of Sunday schools.

The interpretation of the Bible should be at the same time spiritual and literal. The two witnesses—the Word and the Spirit—should be allowed to testify to the truth of God. Interpretation should harmonize with both reason and experience; it should appeal to both the intellect and the heart. Without the aid of the Holy Spirit, a person cannot rightly interpret the Bible; yet he cannot depend on the Holy Spirit to do what he is expected to do for himself. We must search the Scriptures, give attendance to reading and study, and show ourselves approved unto God, workmen that need not be ashamed, rightly dividing the Word of truth.[50]

Teasley situated the balance between Word and Spirit within another balanced relationship, that of the individual and church. He insisted that both Protestants and Catholics tipped the balance too far in one direction or the other. The former "lost sight of the relation that should exist between the body of Christ and the individual members of the church. Individual rights have been exercised to the degree of independence, and the individual has interpreted the Scriptures contrary to the accepted doctrine of the church, and by propagating his interpretations without due respect for the accepted belief of the church has caused division and confusion."[51] Catholicism, on the other hand, "usurps the supreme right [of individuals] to interpret the Bible and to bind her interpretation on the consciences of men. Thus she destroys individuality and places a legislative body between the soul and its God. Jesus said, 'When he (not the church) [*sic*] the Spirit of Truth is come, he shall guide you into all truth.' "[52]

To avoid the errors of both extremes Teasley proposed the idea that biblical interpretation was a corporate enterprise, the mutual work of the individual and the community of believers. Both individual reader and church engaged in a conversation over the text of Scripture, taking care not to manifest any disrespect toward each other. As was inevitably the case for Church of God writers during the early formative period, Teasley also gave the Holy Spirit wide room in which to guide the search for biblical truth.

If the Holy Spirit shall guide us into all truth, we shall be guided aright and shall all finally reach the same conclusions and find ourselves, through the unity of the Spirit, led into the unity of the faith. The church is not given the supreme right to interpret the Bible for the individual, nor is the individual given the right regardless of unity and peace to interpret the Bible contrary to the general belief of the true church and force his interpretation upon others. The church should not interfere with the leading of the Holy Spirit in the individual, and the individual should not force upon the church what he conceives to be the leading of the Spirit faster than the body in general can comprehend and accept the truth.[53]

D. O. Teasley believed that his description of proper hermeneutical practice had been achieved in the Church of God movement. Because biblical interpretation equated with theology or doctrine in the early Church of God, it is fair to say that the movement achieved a practical understanding of doctrine. Teasley also followed Warner's implicit guidelines that insured mutual respect and a degree of flexibility among participants in the hermeneutical conversation. For Warner and, following him in the next generation, Teasley, the church's theological practices at least nodded in the direction of democratic participation to a degree considerably further than the more authoritarian Byrum.

Biblical interpretation and preaching was one of two practices that formed the worshiping community of the early Church of God. Alongside the Bible rested the hymnal, or, more properly until 1911, the songbook. The saints sang their faith, and the practice of singing carried an unusual weight in the early Church of God. Part of the extraordinary influence of singing rested in the remarkable productivity of poets and musicians during the first fifty years in the movement's existence. Singing the faith was a critical practice of the grassroots church, in part because the saints were singing and playing music written by other saints for use in Church of God meetings. Instructively, the first book of any kind to be published by the Gospel Trumpet Company was *Songs of Victory,* which appeared in 1885. Five more songbooks were published over approximately the next twenty years.[54] These early songbooks were almost exclusively dependent on Church of God writers for both texts and music. In 1911 the Gospel Trumpet Company published the first in a series of what might be termed major hymnals as opposed to songbooks. The first hymnal was titled *Select Hymns,* and aptly named, for its four editors had included favorite hymns and gospel songs from the previously published songbooks. The preponderance of Church of God writers is born out by the fact that 115 of the 633 songs in *Select Hymns* were written by D. S. Warner. However, his contribution was nearly tripled by the man who, more than any other, came to be identified with the Church of God practice of singing the faith.

Barney E. Warren (1867–1951), of Geneva Center, Michigan, was eighteen years old when D. S. Warner asked him to join his new evangelistic company. Warner had to persuade young Barney's father to grant his permission, and perhaps for good reason. The other members of the group included Warner and three women, none of whom was his wife. One of the women, Sarah Smith, had left her husband and family—with his permission—to take up the role of a "flying messenger" as they were called. Barney joined the group, which traveled the Midwest, South, and the Niagara Peninsula of southern Ontario for the next several years until it broke up in the early 1890s. He eventually married one of his fellow company members, Nanny Kigar, who died in the early twenties. He subsequently courted and won the hand of Lottie Charles, pastor of the First Church of God in Baltimore, Maryland. Warren contributed either words or music to more than three hundred of the songs collected in *Select Hymns,* but that was only a fraction of the more than seven thousand pieces that he composed over his lifetime.[55] Warren was the most prolific songwriter in the Church of God, but he was by no means alone in shaping this formative practice. Along with Warner, other songwriters included Clara M. Brooks, D. O. Teasley, A. L. Byers, and C. W. Naylor.

The practice of singing the faith was critically important because it was through song that the message reached furthest and deepest into the movement's heart. Church of God songwriters used a distinctive set of "symbol-terms" that "had a uniqueness about them that enabled all followers to relate with the doctrine or philosophy that was being identified."[56] Church of God songwriters employed these terms almost like code words to underscore or highlight core commitments of the movement. So, for example, the saints commitment to a life of holiness was symbolized in words or phrases like "holy life," "full salvation," and "cleansing/keeping." The gospel song, "I Will Trust Thee,"[57] used the phrase "safe within the vail" [*sic*] as a symbol of the typological interpretation employed by Warner and H. M. Riggle in *The Cleansing of the Sanctuary.*[58] Warner and the early saints wedded holiness to the ideal of Christian unity, and this unique marriage gave birth to equally unique musical children. Thus they sang:

How sweet this bond of perfectness,
The wondrous love of Jesus;
A pure foretaste of heaven's bliss,
Oh, fellowship so precious.

Oh praise the Lord for love divine
That binds us all together;
A thousand chords our hearts entwine,
Forever and forever.

"God over all and in us all"
And thro' each holy brother;
No pow'r of earth or hell, withal,
Can rend us from each other.

O mystery of heaven's peace!
O bond of heaven's' union!
Our souls in fellowship embrace,
And live in sweet communion.

Chorus: O brethren, how this perfect love
Unites us all in Jesus!
One heart, and soul, and mind, we prove
The union heaven gave us.[59]

As no theological writing from the world of denominational Babylon could contain the truth or articulate a faithful vision of the New Testament church, so none—or precious few—of the hymns and gospel songs of Babylon expressed the truth that the early saints had envisioned. So they produced the "truth in song." The practice of singing the faith was the most pervasive doctrinal practice in the early movement. Not all the saints read Warner's *The Church of God, Bible Proofs of a Second Work of Grace*, or W. G. Schell's *The Biblical Trace of the Church*. Doubtlessly, some could not read at all. But any saint could commit to memory and sing "The Bond of Perfectness," or the song that set to music the title of Schell's book. This practice formed the early Church of God into a community that clearly marked insiders as those who learned the songs and sang them in the full conviction that they indeed sang the faith that belonged to them and the movement.

It would be a fabrication, even a gross distortion, to say that the early saints worked out a theory of practice and self-consciously employed it to form the Church of God movement. Whether in the case of church discipline, biblical interpretation, or songwriting and singing, these formative practices developed on the fly, so to speak. Warner, Byrum, Teasley, and Warren did not have the benefit of preexisting rules and procedures by which to discipline wayward ministers, adjudicate hermeneutical differences, or develop a hymnody for a new religious movement. Neither was it possible for such rules to be formally adopted. None of those named, and few if any in the early movement, thought that governing procedures constituted any benefit at all. On the contrary, such procedures embodied the "man-rule" that crippled the church, preventing it from living up to the New Testament standard. Nevertheless, the Church of God achieved a measure of stability as the crucial doctrinal practices of church discipline, biblical interpretation, and songwriting and singing developed through crisis and challenge in the first thirty years of its life. In the process something like a consensus formed about these practices and a more cohesive movement emerged.

Notes

1. Quoted in Byers, *Birth of a Reformation*, 311.
2. One further episode is worth noting. A. L. Byers writes, "One sister ventured to stay in the room occupied by the false teachers. She was suddenly seized by the awful powers of darkness and she felt she was lost. To a sister who came to her she said, 'Oh, I feel so bad; take me to the altar!' She was led to the saints' apartment, where she bowed at the altar and soon began to manifest a frightful appearance. She jerked and cried, 'I have a devil; stay away from me!' Her face blackened and twitched with frightful contortions, her eyes glared, her tongue darted out like a serpent's, and when anyone approached her, she would spit and claw furiously. Hands were laid upon her and she was instantly delivered and clothed in her right mind." Ibid., 310.
3. "Brother R. S. Stockwell, of Ada, Ohio, expects to devote himself to the holiness evangelistic work. He is full of the Spirit, and the light of God's awful present truth. A mighty man of God. Send and get him to work for souls wherever the Lord wills." Quoted from the *Gospel Trumpet* in Thomas A. Fudge, *Daniel S. Warner and the Paradox of Religious Democracy in Nineteenth Century America* (Lewiston, NY: Edwin A. Mellen Press, 1998), 209–210. Fudge is unquestionably the authoritative study on this period of Warner's life.
4. In "Meditations" Warner wrote, "First there appeared mysteriously, withal, / Some leprous spots on our domestic wall. / The plague soon marred our holy fellowship, / Then ate like moth the threads of love that knit / Our hearts and souls in sweet connubial bliss, / And made us one in sympathetic flesh." Quoted in Byers, *Birth of a Reformation*, 313.
5. October 1877, 239. The organization of the church, which met on Sunday afternoons to avoid conflict with the established churches of Upper Sandusky, predates Warner's experience of sanctification. The Kellers were enthusiastic advocates of the holiness cause before their son-in-law applied Christian perfection to his peculiar, from their point of view, ecclesiology.
6. After Warner's death in 1895 the front page of the *Gospel Trumpet* announcing his passing carried a heavy black border. No other early Church of God figure was so honored. Furthermore, in his funeral sermon W. G. Schell speculated about the future of the movement now that it had lost its leader, a loss that Schell believed was God's judgment on the group for failing to live up to Warner's vision. *GT* (January 1896).
7. So reports H. C. Wickersham, one of the saints himself, an associate of Warner, and one of the influential leaders of this era, in *A History of the Church From the Birth of Christ to the Present Time* (Moundsville, WV: Gospel Trumpet Publishing Co, 1900), 290–291.
8. John W. V. Smith recounts this story on the basis of A. L. Byers' version. Cf. Smith, *The Quest for Holiness and Unity*, 67.
9. Along with Warner, Allie R. Fisher, in her own right, and Sebastian Michels held financial interests in the publishing company.
10. "What is Zinzendorfism?" *Advocate of Christian Holiness* (September 1878), 209.
11. Smith, *The Quest for Holiness and Unity*, 187.
12. *GT* (March 16, 1899).
13. "The Second Cleansing on Established Scriptural Doctrine," *GT* (May 4, 1899), 4.
14. The general camp meeting of the Church of God convened near the facilities of the Gospel Trumpet Publishing Company, which meant that when the company moved so did the camp meeting. In 1898 the company had relocated once again, this time from Grand Junction to Moundsville, on the banks of the Ohio River.

15. E. E. Byrum, "The Campmeeting," *GT* (June 22, 1899), 4.

16. Ibid.

17. Contemporary estimates of the number of Zinzendorf ministers ran as high as 50 percent of the total number of ministers in the Church of God. John W. V. Smith disputes the accuracy of those estimates, but still maintains that the Zinzendorf faction represented a "considerable" number. Many of the members of this faction were among the most able and popular preachers in the Church of God movement, meaning that the loss of quality probably outweighed the loss of quantity. Smith, *Quest for Holiness and Unity,* 189. In 1902 at the Moundsville camp meeting only ninety-one ministers attended, probably less than a fourth of all ministers in the Church of God. Cf. Ministers' Lists File, Archives of the Church of God. It seems reasonable to conclude that the Anti-cleansing heresy and its aftermath had dealt a heavy body blow to the young movement.

18. Byrum, "The Campmeeting," Ibid.

19. "Words of Greeting," *GT* (December 28, 1899), 1.

20. Ibid.

21. Cf. Smith, *The Quest for Holiness and Unity,* 194–195, and Charles E. Brown, *When Souls Awaken* (Anderson, Ind: Gospel Trumpet Publishing Co, 1954), 77.

22. *GT* (1898), n.p.

23. Pleated skirts were condemned outright as utterly worldly. *GT* (1908), n.p.

24. During this era many ministers favored wearing clerical collars.

25. *Quest for Holiness and Unity,* 199.

26. The general camp meeting began convening in Anderson after the Gospel Trumpet Company moved there in 1906. As of this writing "Anderson Campmeeting" as it is known colloquially, continues to meet annually, since June 2001 under the name "North American Convention of the Church of God."

27. Quoted in Smith, *Quest for Holiness and Unity,* 198.

28. "No one can sing 'Casey Jones' unto the Lord with grace in his heart.... We cannot sing or play rag-time music to the glory of God any more than we can smoke a cigar to his glory. "What Shall we Sing?" *Herald of Truth* (September 1, 1914), 1.

29. "The Inner Word Heresy," *GT* (February 12, 1914), 6.

30. Prominent preachers who shared their opinion on this matter included J. Grant Anderson, J. T. Wilson, C. W. Naylor, B. E. Warren, and E. A. Reardon. Cf. Smith, *Quest for Holiness and Unity,* 199.

31. John W. V. Smith recounts an anecdote that reports Byrum as shunning the necktie while fulfilling his ministerial duties in Anderson, but wearing neckties when out of town negotiating for the company in the larger world of business.

32. "A Warning to the Church," *GT* (February 19, 1914), 3.

33. An autobiographical sketch of Schell's spiritual pilgrimage, up to 1900, appears in Wickersham, *History of the Church,* 360–387.

34. In 1895 four people held financial interests in the Gospel Trumpet Publishing Company. On that basis the four individuals—D. S. Warner, Sebastian Michels, E. E. Byrum and his younger brother, Noah H. Byrum—referred to themselves as the company in "Articles of Agreement" drawn up on December 10, 1895, only two days before Warner's death. The articles laid the basis for the company's eventual reorganization as a not-for-profit corporation under the governance of the General Assembly of the Church of God. The Articles of Agreement can be found in Harold L. Phillips, *Miracle of Survival* (Anderson, Ind: Warner Press, 1979), 46.

35. Ibid., 52.

36. D. O. Teasley and H. M. Riggle, "Departed From the Faith," *GT* (June 18, 1903).

37. Ibid.

38. *GT* (January 30, 1908).

39. It didn't hurt E. E. Byrum's stature in the movement to print a letter from Schell that included the following confession: "I want to ask your forgiveness for every thought harbored against you. I have looked upon you as my enemy, but I must have been mistaken. I left you once, never to return; that was the decision of my mind. This I know was of the wicked one. Can you forgive me?" *GT* (February 6, 1908).

40. Two weeks later Schell published a lengthy article in the *Trumpet* detailing the woes he suffered during his apostasy. Cf. "Seven Years of Darkness, or, An Appeal to Backsliders," *GT* (February 20, 1908).

41. W. G. Schell, *Sanctification and Holiness: The False and the True* (Chicago, Ill: Herald Press, 1922), 15.

42. Schell uses exegetical arguments as well as logical moves to defeat the holiness crowd. E.g., If sanctification restores a couple to Adamic purity, then their children must be born without the stain of original sin. Or, he substituted "cleanse" for "separate" in translations of the word *hagiazo*, which led to a number of silly translations, e. g., John 17:19, where "set apart" meets the sense of the passage, but cleanse does not. Ibid., 67.

43. Thomas A. Fudge has rightfully noted the irony in the shift, from the democratic forms that made possible Warner's rise, to more authoritarian governance that he employed to consolidate power in the movement.

44. John W. V. Smith, *I Will Build My Church* (Anderson, Ind: Warner Press, 1985), 2.

45. On this issue John W. V. Smith put his historical conclusions prescriptively in his last book, "[As with all other theological writing in the Church of God], this is one person's voice. Some may differ at certain points. But that is part of the genius of the Church of God. In a group that takes a 'whole Bible' stance in regard to its creed, forgoing the practice of issuing official interpretations, there must be considerable room left for flexibility in both emphasis and exegesis. It is thus possible to hold different opinions and still maintain good fellowship as brothers and sisters in the Lord." *I Will Build My Church*, 4–5.

46. D. S. Warner, "Do the Ministers of God See Eye to Eye?" *GT* (December 14, 1893).

47. Ibid.

48. D. S. Warner, "The Ministers of God Must See Eye to Eye," *GT* (December 28, 1893).

49. *GT* (January 4, 1894).

50. D. O. Teasley, *The Bible and How to Interpret It* (Anderson, Ind: Gospel Trumpet Publishing Company, 1918), 110–111.

51. Ibid., 111.

52. Ibid.

53. Ibid., 113.

54. *Anthems from the Throne* (1888), *Echoes from Glory* (1893), *Songs of the Evening Light* (1897), *Salvation Echoes* (1900), *Truth in Song* (1907).

55. Cf. Axchie A. Bolitho, *To the Chief Singer: A Brief Story of the Life and Influence of Barney E. Warren* (Anderson, Ind: Gospel Trumpet Company, 1942).

56. Robert A. Adams, "The Hymnody of the Church of God (1885–1980) as a Reflection of that Church's Theological and Cultural Changes," (Unpublished Doctor of Musical Arts dissertation: Southwestern Baptist Theological Seminary, 1980), 38.

57. *Select Hymns* (Anderson, Ind: Gospel Trumpet Co., 1911), No. 167.

58. For a discussion of this interpretative method and the theology it underwrote see chapter 5.

59. *Select Hymns*, No. 472.

Chapter 4
Laying the Foundations of a Church

On Warner's death Enoch E. Byrum (1861–1942) succeeded to the editorship of the *Gospel Trumpet.* He did so for reasons as practical and down to earth as Byrum himself; he held a controlling financial interest in the company and for the previous six months his name had appeared alongside Warner's on the *Trumpet* masthead. By personality as well as position, Byrum had a profound influence on the history of the Church of God. It was observed of Byrum that when Warner died the movement lost a leader but gained a manager.[1] Even before Warner's death Byrum took advantage of his publisher's title to impose order on office procedures that tended to be neglected during Warner's lengthy evangelistic tours. While Warner sought platforms from which he might speak to thousands, Byrum was at home answering individual letters. His strong personality brooked no nonsense, an attitude formed early in life when his father's death thrust responsibility for the family farm upon the adolescent Enoch. He was extremely industrious and deeply respected authority; Byrum expected *Trumpet* family members to share those attitudes.[2] His personality suited him perfectly for the essentially conservative role of the second generation of a religious movement. If Warner and the first generation had sketched a dramatic vision of a truly reformed New Testament church, it was left to Byrum and others like him in the next generation to color in its details and consolidate the first generation's achievements.

Byrum grew up in a devout United Brethren family on their farm in Randolph County in east central Indiana. Eli and Lucinda Byrum reared their children in a religious atmosphere regulated by assigned times for prayer and Bible reading. Enoch attended Sunday school and early in life exhibited spiritual inclinations, reading the Bible from cover to cover. At fifteen he was converted in a revival meeting and soon after volunteered his services to the local church. He taught Sunday school and began to feel a call

Enoch E. Byrum. As second editor of the Gospel Trumpet and the de facto leader of the Church of God from 1895 to 1916, Byrum's strong personality steered the church through a series of theological crises and took steps that began to regularize its practices.

to the ministry. Enoch was not inclined toward preaching, so he started focusing on preparation for a missionary vocation. As long as he was responsible for the family farm, Enoch's plans for higher education had to be postponed. But when an older married brother was able to add the Byrum farm to his own, Enoch started attending classes at nearby Ridgeville College. Illness and family responsibilities continued to frustrate his plans. Finally Enoch was able to enroll at Valparaiso University where he completed a short course in speech. In 1886–87 he completed a year's study in Sunday school and Bible at Otterbein University. He had planned to enroll at Bonebrake Seminary in Dayton, Ohio, but after experiencing sanctification in a Church of God revival late in 1886 young Byrum's life took a dramatic new course. In the company of a friend he attended the Bangor, Michigan camp meeting the following summer. It was during this meeting that Warner approached him to purchase J. C. Fisher's interest in the Gospel Trumpet Company. Byrum agreed to the offer, remained in Grand Junction after the meeting, and when Warner departed on an evangelistic tour ten days later Enoch found himself in charge of the operation until Warner's return the following April.[3]

Byrum and his brother Noah decided to move the Gospel Trumpet Company from Grand Junction to Moundsville, West Virginia in 1898, and then again from Moundsville to Anderson, Indiana in 1906. Characteristically, practical business considerations governed both decisions. The company moved to Moundsville, on the edge of the West Virginia coalfields, to reduce operating expenses. The company's machinery ran on coal-fired steam, and coal could be purchased for seventy cents per ton in Moundsville, a savings of approximately 80 percent over costs in Grand Junction. The Byrums, driven by financial necessity to find bargains, purchased an abandoned shoe factory at a sheriff's sale to house the publishing work. Practical considerations also figured prominently in their decision to relocate later in Anderson. Moundsville city administrators were unwilling to run electrical lines to the publishing plant, and when inexpensive land became available in Anderson, a location more central to the movement's constituency, company officers determined to move once again.[4]

It is no accident that the years of Byrum's editorial tenure coincide with two decades of consolidation in the Church of God movement. What had begun as a movement took its first steps toward becoming a church during this period. He dealt firmly with the heretical Anti-cleansers and disciplined wayward opponents like W. G. Schell. Byrum also took a considered, moderate approach through the necktie controversy. He "wrote the editorials laying down the rules [and] shaped the communally organized missionary homes through which to promote both [Gospel Trumpet Company] literature and headquarters policy."[5] While Byrum laid down the rules, semi-official lists of Church of God ministers appeared for the first time. In the beginning these lists authorized railroad clergy bureaus to offer reduced rates to those ministers whose names appeared therein. The lists also served as the first step toward official determination of a Church of God clergy in a manner that resembled denominational practice. During that same period a group of ministers gathered at an annual "assembly" to create a missionary committee charged with the oversight of missionaries who were spreading in ever-widening circles around the globe. Missionary homes and preaching points also were transformed into local churches as the era of the "flying ministry" gave way to settled patterns of congregational life. During this same twenty-year period, doctrinal practices continued to develop and shape the movement's life.

Consolidating Practices

Divine Healing

For all of his managerial prowess, the name of Enoch Byrum was associated even more with the practice of divine healing. No person did more to shape that practice in the Church of God.

> During the last years of his life he was held in awe for his healing ministry. His office in the [Gospel Trumpet] Company held scores of relics—braces, crutches—gathered there in answer to prayer. He argued that healing was in the atonement—both cleansing the body and the soul, and that when man had met the scriptural conditions it was God who made good on his promises. He sent thousands of anointed handkerchiefs to those requesting prayer—which he and GT Company prayer groups had prayed over. He shaped the expectations for healing of the body throughout the church by his writing. His personal visits to pray for the sick ranged widely across the nation.[6]

Byrum emphasized the ministry of divine healing throughout his career. In addition to writing three books on the topic,[7] as editor he introduced a feature called "Divine Healing" to the *Gospel Trumpet*. For many years it filled the paper's back page with articles expounding the doctrine of divine healing along with countless testimonies from beneficiaries and witnesses. After Byrum left the editor's office in 1916 he devoted the balance of his ministry to the practice, traveling across the continent to answer requests for his presence and prayers.

Front page of the April 7, 1921 issue of the National Labor Tribune *featuring E. E. Byrum's ministry. After stepping down as editor, Byrum devoted the remainder of his life to the ministry of divine healing.*

Divine healing emerged as the dominant theme in a larger set of concerns related to health to which many early Church of God people were attentive. Some of these interests could be found on the fringe of late nineteenth-century American medicine. For example, D. S. Warner was interested in phrenology as it was taught in the work of Orson Squire Fowler.[8] His journal entries occasionally mention phrenological examinations of some of the people with whom he stayed while preaching revivals. Several saints, Byrum included, published books containing moral and lay medical advice to teenagers as well as parents. Thomas Nelson, a Danish immigrant who founded *Den Evangeliske Basun* Publishing Company, a Scandinavian parallel to the English language publishing work, authored a book in Dano-Norwegian titled *Hejm, Helbred, og Lykke* that proved so popular it was translated into English and published as *Home, Health, and Success.*[9] The book devoted a major segment to dietary concerns, recommending certain forms of food preparation as well as food groups. The *Gospel Trumpet* frequently ran articles that connected health to faithful Christian discipleship, even if those connections were sometimes strained. Thus W. J. Henry contributed an article titled "The Evil Effects of Tightlacing" condemning corsets not for moral reasons but because they squeezed a woman's internal organs to the detriment of her health. These and many other health-related issues concerned Church of God people because they took at face value the New Testament passage that described the body as the temple of the Holy Spirit. But all of these concerns paled in comparison to the practice of divine healing.

Shortly after Byrum joined the Gospel Trumpet Company and assumed managerial responsibility for it, the paper's emphasis on the doctrine began to increase. Warner and other early ministers had practiced divine healing, but not with Byrum's pointed interest or depth of personal conviction.[10] His ordination to the ministry in 1892 followed a growing reputation that associated Byrum with incidents of healing. At the Grand Junction camp meeting in 1895 an unusually high interest in the practice combined with a growing list of cases convinced him that he had received a special gift of healing faith from the Holy Spirit. He reported his belief to Warner, who gave his blessing to Byrum and his gift.[11] Byrum rapidly emerged as the movement's most prominent spokesperson for divine healing as a growing chorus of testimonies and ministers identified with the practice. Other important voices in the first two generations of Church of God leaders included Mary Cole and J. Grant Anderson.

Mary Cole (1854–1940) and her brothers George (1867–?) and Jeremiah (1841–1899) were raised in a devout, peripatetic Methodist family that moved from Ohio to Iowa to Illinois and, eventually, Missouri. Elder brother Jeremiah became a Methodist exhorter while George and Mary were still children. The Coles were radical holiness people whose formal association with the Methodist church was tenuous at best.[12] Jeremiah's enthusiasm for the cause of entire sanctification led him to the Western Union Holiness Association meeting in Jacksonville, Illinois in 1880. There he discovered that he shared a mutual interest in divine healing with another attendee, D. S. Warner. Jeremiah testified to a personal experience of healing, and his sister testified that he had been instrumental in her miraculous healing. Mary described herself as an invalid from birth, suffering seizures followed later by indigestion and dyspepsia.[13] Adolescence brought "female weakness" and spinal problems. As she described her physical condition, "altogether I was rendered useless for life."[14] She recounted the subsequent experience of her miraculous cure in a powerful testimony that lent increased validity to the doctrine as it served to enhance her stature in the ministry as a preacher and practitioner of divine healing. Younger brother George was about twelve years old when Jeremiah and Mary experienced these healings, and they reinforced in him a similar confidence in the doctrine. The Coles traveled as itinerant gospel workers and *colporteurs,* sellers of Bibles and religious literature, throughout much of the Midwest from Kansas and Nebraska to Ohio and Michigan. In 1898 Mary and George briefly joined Gorham Tufts at the Open Door Mission in Chicago. Later that year they opened a missionary home in the same city for evangelists and other gospel workers. From this location and in their role as home superintendents, as well as life-long evangelists, George and Mary Cole lent their influential support to the practice of divine healing and insured that subsequent generations of ministers would follow in their footsteps.

J. Grant Anderson (1873–1927) attended a revival meeting conducted by H. M. Riggle in Rootville, Pennsylvania in 1897. A student at the State Normal School of Edinboro, Anderson had walked four miles to hear Riggle preach on Christian unity.[15] The sermon convinced Anderson of the truth of the message of the Church of God and a friendship developed between the two men. A few years later Anderson, at that time teaching school, contracted tuberculosis and spent more than a year at Spencer Hospital at Meadville, Pennsylvania. After learning that his illness was terminal Anderson sent word for Riggle with a request that he come and anoint Anderson according to the instructions of James 5:14–15. An outbreak of smallpox at the hospital prevented Riggle and his wife from answering Anderson's request in person. However, as Riggle later testified, "My wife and I fell on our knees in our home and wrestled with God for [Anderson's] recovery. We stayed there until we received the assurance that the Lord had heard and answered. That was on February 8, 1903. On that very day Brother Anderson was instantly and permanently healed."[16] Following this experience Anderson gave his long-deferred consent to a call to the ministry. Highly regarded as a preacher and teacher especially in and around his home state, Anderson subsequently wrote a small, direct and plainly spoken book on the subject of divine healing. Like Thomas Nelson's earlier book, Anderson connected divine healing to larger issues of health and stewardship of the body.[17] In neither case, nor anywhere else, did the Church of God interest in divine healing reveal a larger fascination with the miraculous. On the contrary, beginning with Byrum and echoing in other writers there was the conviction that God intended that his children enjoy good health and that Christ's atonement had purchased it.

It is no accident that the title of E. E. Byrum's classic exposition of the doctrine linked the healing of soul and body. Byrum believed that Christ's atonement purchased the possibility of physical as well as spiritual wholeness. He grounded this belief in two ways. First, he employed a rough and ready syllogism to conclude that divine healing must have been purchased by Jesus' atonement. Along with separation from God, Byrum included sickness and death as elements of the human fallen condition for which Christ's sacrifice made restitution. To say that the blood of Christ did not cover the latter condition implicitly asserted that he was a less than perfect sacrifice. Byrum of course refused to accept such a view, and therefore concluded that Christ's perfect sacrificial death must have purchased God's healing for the body as well as the soul. Secondly, Byrum appealed to key biblical passages to anchor his belief. He frequently referred to such texts as Luke 4:16–21, Matthew 8:16–17, and 1 Peter 2:21–24 to portray Jesus as the fulfillment of Bible prophecies that include human sickness among the infirmities that Jesus took upon himself.[18]

Along with an expanded theology of the atonement and proof texts from scripture, Byrum and the early Church of God movement believed in and practiced divine healing for a third reason, although it was subordinated to the other two. Church of God practice also rested on the numerous testimonies of healing that appeared in the *Gospel Trumpet* and in the many books published on the topic. Personal narratives were crucial elements of early Church of God theological reflection and practice. Writers on the topic typically included such testimonies, often reprinted from the *Trumpet,* in their books. Fully half of *Divine Healing of Soul and Body* is taken up with testimonies of healing, and they comprise roughly 40 percent of J. Grant Anderson's *Divine Healing.* Byrum's *Miracles and Healing* devotes a third of its pages to "witnesses of today." Then there is A. L. Byers' compilation,

Two Hundred Instances of Divine Healing,[19] which recounts testimonies covering maladies as diverse as broken bones, consumption, rheumatism, nervous breakdowns, pneumonia, cancer, blindness, and the effects of swallowing rat poison. Letters and testimonies printed in the *Gospel Trumpet* were the primary source of information concerning instances of divine healing. To *Trumpet* readers these authors and their stories provided confirmatory evidence as they narrated the practice and its blessings.

The early movement's practice of healing turned on the conviction that no functional or material difference existed between the first Christian century and the twentieth. Byrum's *Miracles and Healing* clearly illustrates a hermeneutic that telescoped the centuries between Christ and the Church of God. The book's first part considers cases of divine healing in the Bible and then offers instruction in proper practice. Following these instructions is a third section that treats modern-day instances of healing in the same tone and acceptance as that employed where Byrum discussed biblical cases. James W. McClendon describes this collapsing tendency as a "this is that" way of reading the Bible and finds it to be characteristic of several Protestant groups associated with the Believer's Church tradition. He portrays this vision in a way that connects it with a specific approach to biblical interpretation: "So the vision can be expressed as a hermeneutical motto, which is shared awareness of the *present Christian community as the primitive community and the eschatological community.* In other words, the church now is the primitive church and the church on the day of judgment is the church now; the obedience and liberty of the followers of Jesus of Nazareth is *our* liberty, *our* obedience."[20] For the same reasons that some Church of God congregations could engrave the legend "Founded, AD 30" on the cornerstones of their church buildings, Byrum and others who wrote about divine healing admitted of no change, certainly no development in doctrinal practice between healing in the New Testament and their own day.

Church of God writers insisted that the day of healing miracles had not closed after Jesus' ascension. The movement sang its conviction as well in a gospel song written to underscore a polemical point against those in denominational Babylon who taught that the day of miracles was past. The refrain of Jacob Byers' 1897 gospel song "He Is Just the Same Today" asserted "Yes, he healed in Galilee, Set the suff'ring captives free, And he's just the same today."[21] By the late 1890s Byrum and others tied the practice closely to the movement's ecclesiology. That mainstream denominations insisted that the day of miracles had closed only served to prove further that such were part of a fallen and apostate church. If the New Testament provided the standard, then it stood to reason that any contemporary groups of Christians had to live by that standard in order to claim continuity with the church of the New Testament. Thus alongside the experiences of salvation and entire sanctification, early saints applied the practice of divine healing as the third mark of the truly restored church. Byrum therefore inferred that the denial of the doctrine of divine healing was one element in a general decline from the New Testament standard toward the confusion of "sectism."[22] By the same token, that the Church of God movement practiced divine healing served to validate its claim to be the New Testament church restored. Testimonies that narrated instances of healing proved more conclusive to the saints than theological polemics or any other form of argument that attempted to make similar claims.

Practice mattered more than theological discussion or exposition. Nearly all Church of God books on the topic contain a section that explains the procedures that were to be followed. Their writers were more interested in describing and teaching the practice than they were concerned to delineate an article of faith in which true Christians believed. The classic text for all practical guidance on divine healing was James 5:13–14. There readers found both a clear mandate for the practice as well as the instructions to guide it. The biblical text instructed the afflicted to call for the elders of the church, who gathered, anointed sufferers with oil and, with the laying on of hands, claimed God's promise for healing. On some points instruction manuals became very detailed, specifying, for example, the use of olive oil as the kind referenced in the Bible and therefore the only proper oil for use by New Testament Christians. Equally specific were Byrum's instructions to trust God utterly for healing and therefore forsake the use of medicine altogether.

In this connection Byrum may have been the movement's first doctrinal revisionist. Just prior to his death Warner wrote an editorial approving the use of "naturally occurring remedies"–herb teas, poultices, and other forms of folk medicine–on the precedent of Paul's advice to Timothy that he take a little wine for his stomach ailments. Warner was scarcely cold in his grave before his successor wrote, "During our absence an article was published in the _Trumpet_ in which the brother who wrote it lowered the standard below the Bible line while trying to expose certain lines of fanaticism, and since that time the Lord plainly showed him that he had lowered the standard and that fanaticism can be rebuked in the strongest terms and yet a radical stand taken upon the truth."[23] That was the end of the use of medicines–folk or prescription–in the Church of God movement. "The use of medicine is for two classes of persons; viz., those who are not acquainted with God and those of his children who are afraid to trust him."[24] In support of this position Byrum quoted an anonymous but "learned" physician as saying, "If all the medicines on earth were cast into the seas, humanity would be better off, but it would be worse for the fishes."[25] Byrum took a similar stand against consulting physicians, often citing their own acknowledgements of the limitations of medical practice as proof of the futility of their treatments. Byrum also objected to consultation with physicians on theological grounds; to do so manifested a clear want of the faith that was crucial to healing.

In a far-flung and widely dispersed movement like the early Church of God, it was sometimes the case that "isolated saints," as they were identified, had no nearby elders on whom to call. For their sake and because he found biblical warrants,[26] Byrum initiated the practice of anointing handkerchiefs and sending them to isolated saints who had requested prayer. He qualified the practice somewhat, saying that only those led by the Holy Spirit should send such a request. But for those who did, Byrum and a small group prayed over a small square of cotton muslin on which a drop of oil had been placed. This handkerchief was then mailed to the petitioner, who was instructed to place it on the afflicted site and agree with the prayer that had already been uttered over the cloth. In this manner no saint was truly isolated, and all were able to avail themselves of the plain teaching of the New Testament.

Not all prayers for healing were answered—not, at least, in the manner in which their petitioners desired. Although Byrum recognized that possibility, he also offered explanations to account for most instances where prayers for healing apparently went unanswered. He laid down the general principle that divine healing did not and would not occur until God willed it. Believers were expected to get an answer to the question whether God willed to heal them. Neither did Byrum insist that God would heal all who called upon him. Death was a fact for all humans, those who trusted in God as well as those who did not. Therefore believers had always to hold open the possibility that any illness could be their "sickness unto death," but if that were the case Byrum said that God would reveal that to the sufferer. Nevertheless, he was also convinced that people suffered physical maladies far more frequently than necessary. Some of these they brought upon themselves, and Byrum scoffed at those who prayed for healing but refused to abandon the habits that were the cause of illness. Dyspeptic men who chewed tobacco or women suffering from "dreadful problems" brought on by a cinched-down corset wasted their breath praying for God's cure if they were unwilling to forsake their sinful ways. In Byrum's eyes the root cause of their maladies was moral as well as physical. Thus he concluded, "When people get in line with God just where he desires them to be, they will either be healed, or God will receive glory through their sickness and enable them to rejoice through it all, with the comforting words, 'My grace is sufficient.' "[27] When God willed that a believer be healed, the individual was still responsible to appropriate it by laying claim to it in faith, "walking out on God's promise" to heal. Byrum did not reduce the mystery of divine healing to a calculus which, if rightly applied, would invariably produce the desired result. And yet on the basis of his writing it was also easy to conclude that those who were not healed lacked sufficient faith or harbored some secret, unconfessed sin.

After he left the editor's chair Byrum devoted his life to the ministry of healing. His views on certain aspects of this phenomenon appear to have softened to a degree. He cautioned his readers against fanaticism, urging them to follow common sense while awaiting God's healing touch. Thus he advised, "To take good care of yourself while well and be mean and neglect yourself when you are sick does not add to your faith or glorify God. Careful nursing when necessary, proper dressing of wounds and care of injuries, the use of disinfectants for sanitary purposes, and the observance of the proper laws of health are not unscriptural."[28] Although he suggested that vaccination against infectious diseases carried more imposition than benefit, Byrum also recommended that measure where smallpox was concerned because it was recommended by health officers and school boards. He advised people to report contagious diseases to the proper authorities as required by law. Broken bones and open wounds were to be treated by competent persons and the prayer of faith added to their efforts. As far as surgery was concerned, "the afflicted one or those responsible must decide whether or not there will be an operation. It should, however, be a matter of prayerful consideration, so as to not allow the enemy afterwards to accuse and harass the soul (Rom 14:22). God is, nevertheless, not only able to render the needed help in minor afflictions, but able to do what physicians and surgeons can do, and even do 'exceeding abundantly above all that we ask or think' (Eph 3:20). The only limit that Jesus placed on the things wrought by faith and on its development is our exercise of it (Mark 11:23, 24)."[29]

At the insistent examples of E. E. Byrum, Mary and Jeremiah Cole, J. Grant Anderson and others, the early Church of God movement took the practice of divine healing as one of its core doctrines. Church of God people claimed the experience of healing. They narrated these experiences in the *Gospel Trumpet.* They sang their conviction that God's healing power was as available in that day as it had been when Jesus walked the shores of Galilee. The doctrinal practice of divine healing was so crucial to early Church of God people that some were willing to be tried in court for their convictions.[30] The doctrinal practice of divine healing was a crucial element in the early movement's self-understanding, for healing miracles confirmed its claim to be the New Testament church restored.

"Face-to-Face" Polity

Just beneath the surface of many, if not most, theological conversations in the early Church of God movement ecclesiological issues lurked. The doctrinal practice of divine healing validated the movement's prior claim to be the true, New Testament church. Early twentieth-century opposition to premillennialism involved eschatology only indirectly; the more fundamental issue involved a reading of apocalyptic literature that focused on the history and future of the true church. Warner's emphasis on holiness was the lesser partner in the marriage he created between it and Christian unity. While it certainly is true that he believed holiness could not prosper on denominational ground, the fact that Warner made holiness the means to Christian unity could not but subordinate holiness to that great end. Questions pertaining to the church were almost always the driving force behind other theological issues.

Because matters of ecclesiology stood at the center of the Church of God movement's theology, *being* the church—i. e., engaging in the practices associated with that being—took on a role of critical importance. The presence of New Testament practices confirmed, at least in the eyes of the saints, if few others, that the Church of God was in fact what it claimed to be. In a movement that understood the Bible as the book to be lived more than simply believed, church practices could not but be emphasized. Moreover, since the Church of God movement insisted that it followed no creed but the Bible, on matters of ecclesiology church practice took center stage as the primary mode of theological reflection and education. Early come-outers frequently grounded their decision to leave denominational Babylon on the claim, "I saw the church." Seeing the church did not relate to subscribing to a set of propositions about the church or any other point of Christian teaching. Instead, as the saints understood it, seeing the church set a man or woman on a new path, a new way of life marked by a new set of practices. To live out those practices was to make a theological claim about the true church. That practices were lived made a saint's testimony the natural and primary vehicle of theological reflection. If practices are indeed lived experience, then a narrative gives the first-order account that most nearly approximates that experience. In this manner, practices pertaining to the church and the narration of them through testimony assumed a central role in explicating core convictions of the movement.

Church practices embodied and articulated several basic ecclesiological commitments.[31] The first of these commitments entailed a conviction among early leaders that they were indeed reformers of the church who had been privileged to receive from God a vision of the church as it had been divinely intended. Thus the first generations of Church of God people frequently testified to having seen the church. Secondly, early Church of God leadership utterly rejected all attempts to identify the true church with any group or denomination. All such churches were part of the "Babel of confusion" that the movement labeled "Babylon." The third commitment responded to the assessment entailed in the second, and that was an irrevocable and personal break with denominational Christianity entailed in the cry to "come out" of Babylon. A commitment to the church's holiness made up the fourth commitment. The church was holy because its members were holy. Church of God people were, fifthly, committed to the unity of all Christians. Here they followed Warner's original insight into the relationship between holiness and unity; the unity of the church was the product of the work of the sanctifying Spirit among its members. A sixth ecclesial commitment shaped the practices of governance. The early movement was determined to avoid "human ecclesiasticism," and "man-rule" and allow the Holy Spirit to govern the church through the charismatic gifting of men and women for the work that needed to be done. Finally, the early movement was committed to a qualified openness. "They believed that God, through the Holy Spirit, is continuing to reveal the knowledge of himself and the divine will to those followers who are faithful, diligent, and seeking. While all divine truth is contained in the Scriptures, human understanding of that truth can and should increase."[32]

The adoption of some ecclesial practices—worship, prayer, singing, and songwriting to name but a few—was uncontroversial. Such practices were intrinsic to the church's very nature. Others, however, especially those pertaining to organization and governance, were quite problematic because they raised ominous questions about the movement's central ecclesiological claims. The Church of God movement had come into being in protest of the excessive and sinful human organization of the church. "Man-rule" usurped the role of the Holy Spirit, who governed the church through the distribution of charismatic gifts. Any step toward organization was bound to be regarded as a potential descent into man-rule and, eventually, Babylon. Questions concerning church polity could not but raise theological eyebrows, and yet in the years after 1890 the movement's expansion forced the issue as it adopted new polity practices to meet the challenges brought on by growing numbers and new endeavors.

Early Church of God polity was characterized by what might be called "face-to-face" practice. Without an episcopal hierarchy or regional presbyteries, meetings of the saints became the dominant form of church polity. Whether in camp meetings, assembly meetings, or brush arbor meetings, early Church of God polity existed in a form where the saints gathered in face-to-face associations. This way of being together was, for them, the church. Evangelists and gospel workers were known as "Flying Messengers"; it was a period dominated by a rejection of the idea of settled pastors serving a single congregation or circuit. In its first decades a vision of the minister as evangelist controlled the movement's concept of church and ministry. By the end of the nineteenth-century much of American Protestantism was governed by a conception of the ministry that took its cue from nationally known evangelists like Charles Grandison Finney.[33] The revival evangelist pervasively shaped the saints' ideas of the ministry. Early Church of God writers attacked local pastors in the denominations as "hireling ministers" who had sold their divine call for a miserable mess of pottage called financial security. Warner discouraged local saints from attempting to persuade "Flying Messengers" to land and remain as a settled pastor. Even Sebastian Michels, an early minister and part owner of the Gospel Trumpet Company, was heavily criticized because the home that he founded to care for the children of Church of God evangelists during their gospel tours kept him at home and off the evangelistic trail.

Correlative to the "Flying Messenger" theology of the ministry was a practice of church polity as a gathered meeting of the saints. Such a polity functioned smoothly in the movement's early days, for one thing, because there were not many saints to be organized. Secondly, the Gospel Trumpet Company, as the only corporate entity in the movement, provided both a connection and a convenient reference when legal issues or organizational questions did begin to appear. Local gatherings of Saints were thereby freed of most questions concerning polity. It is no overstatement to say that the *Gospel Trumpet* was a key element in, if not in actuality, the movement's polity for several decades. It informed the saints about the travels and activities of the flying messengers as well as notified of future local, regional, and national meetings. Through testimonies and "News from the Field" the paper was the connective tissue of the Church of God movement. In addition to providing a real connection between readers the *Trumpet* served as a symbolic connection between far-flung members who eagerly anticipated its arrival and the larger movement. So long as the saints were provided with connections both real and symbolic, and so long as they were willing to wait patiently for the arrival of the next traveling evangelist, they practiced a polity sufficient for the movement's limited numbers and scope.

Missionary Homes and Leadership Development

Any polity that depended on face-to-face relationships of necessity placed a premium on meetings. Accordingly, state and regional camp meetings

The first generation of ministers in the Church of God movement described themselves as "flying messengers," and the evangelistic company was its standard form. Shown here are the members of the first such company, which served as the model for many others. L. to R.: Barney E. Warren, Daniel S. Warner, Nannie Kigar, "Mother" Sarah Smith, Frances "Frankie" Miller.

played an especially crucial role in the development of a polity. Even more important to the movement's life was the annual general camp meeting. Camp meetings had quickly become a feature of American Protestantism after they first appeared on the Kentucky and Tennessee frontier in the early nineteenth-century. The earliest meetings gathered frontier settlers regardless of denominational affiliation and often provided places for Baptist, Methodist, and Presbyterian preaching on the same grounds. These early meetings were boisterous affairs, and it was not uncommon for traffickers in vice to ply their trades just beyond the campground borders. Rather quickly, however, Methodists imposed a set of rules that simultaneously brought camp meetings under order while it transformed them into a largely Methodist institution.[34] A few decades later Methodists particularly concerned to renew the doctrine of Christian perfection noticed a diminished emphasis on that doctrine and a decline in Methodist camp meetings. Believing that the two phenomena were linked as cause and effect, proholiness Methodists attempted to reverse those trends by organizing the National Campmeeting Association for the Promotion of Christian Holiness in 1867. The camp meeting became the engine that pulled the holiness movement. Since many early Church of God preachers had connections to the holiness movement, it is understandable and natural that they continued the extensive use of camp meetings. Given the absence of formal organizational structure, camp meetings were bound to assume a critical role in the Church of God movement's polity.

The first general camp meetings in the Church of God began in the mid-1880s, and in 1886 the *Trumpet* designated the meeting that June at Bangor, Michigan to be a general camp meeting for all the saints. Twenty-four tents sheltered the saints, who could not have numbered more than five hundred souls. Soon the general camp meeting was located near the current location of the Gospel Trumpet Company, first Grand Junction, Michigan, followed by Moundsville and finally Anderson.[35] At these locations the saints gathered to sing, pray, seek God's healing touch, and fellowship with one another. They also gathered to informally assess the state of the movement and determine courses of action.

Writing twenty-five years after the first general camp meeting, H. M. Riggle, himself a preacher and camp meeting participant since 1893, described the general camp meeting in terms that leave no doubt as to its importance to the polity of the Church of God movement. Riggle's first point said that the general camp meeting brought together the only meeting of ministers in the Church of God. He also identified the following as special benefits of camp meeting attendance: (1) "It keeps us in touch with the general trend of the movement," (2) "promotes the spirit of unity," (3) "eliminates misunderstandings," (4) "dispels suspicions," (5) "heart-to-heart talks," (6) "consultation over local and national problems pertaining to our work," (7) "wholesome warnings against dangers," (8) "heading off wrong sentiment."[36] Clearly the general camp meeting was recognized to serve important functions of a polity as well as provide the occasion when the saints gathered for more overtly spiritual ends.

The meeting was also the dominant form in which the saints gathered locally and regionally. In fact, given the character of the flying ministry, periodic meetings provided one of the few occasions when early saints might gather under the ministry of an ordained member of the clergy. Beginning in the 1890s, however, the movement began a transition from meetings to settled congregations. This decade witnessed the emergence of the "missionary home," a key element in the transition from meeting to local church and a crucial location where ministerial candidates received practical training.

The *Trumpet* staff modeled local organized life for the Church of God while it published the literature of the movement. Members lived in a genuinely communal arrangement. None received a salary, but all were provided with room and board and a small travel allowance when it was necessary; later clothing was also provided. As the company grew, some family members were assigned to work that supported those who were directly involved in publications. Thus some family members could be found tending the dairy herd or the gardens while others worked as tailors, seamstresses, or laundresses. All family workers were housed in a large, multi-story residence that became known as the "*Trumpet* Home." In addition to providing rooms and dining facilities, the home also served as a center of evangelistic activity. *Trumpet* workers often spent some of their free time in street evangelism that featured singing and impromptu preaching. The *Trumpet* home served as a prototype in the founding of many other missionary homes across the United States and beyond.

While on an evangelistic tour of the western states in 1892, D. S. Warner became acutely aware of the problems of large cities and developed a strategy for answering those needs. Within a year Jacob W. and Jennie Byers founded a missionary home in San Diego. Saints eventually founded almost fifty homes in small towns as well as large cities in the United States and beyond. The homes were adapted to local needs. Some, like Gorham Tufts' Open Door Mission in Chicago, were primarily rescue missions. Others specialized in work among women or African Americans. However, support for evangelistic activity was a well-nigh universal characteristic of the missionary homes. Residents typically supported or themselves engaged in the work of colporteurs, and undertook evangelistic work in the neighborhood and surrounding region. The homes also served as hostels for traveling revivalists and missionaries. On the example of the *Trumpet* home, the missionary homes were also often organized as communes. None of the workers or residents was paid a salary, but they were supported through the free-will offerings of the saints and other supporters.

During the three decades of their existence, the missionary homes played a key role in the transition from loosely connected believers to a cohesive movement. They provided a catalyst in that transition in two ways. In the first place the missionary homes provided opportunities for inexperienced volunteers to validate and then develop their ministerial calling. The homes were magnets that drew young people, many of whom had "seen the church" as it was described in the "News From the Field" section of the *Gospel Trumpet*. For example, eighteen-year-old Otto Linn journeyed from Oklahoma to Anderson, where he joined the *Trumpet* family in 1905. Five years later he was in New York City working at the missionary home under the supervision of D. O. Teasley. Linn had left his home under a call to the ministry, and his work in the missionary homes gave him opportunities to exercise and improve his gifts. After two years of gospel work in New York, Linn returned to Kansas, serving churches there and in Oklahoma until he departed for a tour of duty as a missionary to Denmark and Norway in 1923. As in countless other cases, Linn benefited from an exposure to preaching and other ministerial labors through the on-the-job training that life in the missionary homes afforded. Scores of similar cases demonstrate that the missionary homes were important centers where the next generation of Church of God ministers received rudimentary training. During the decade 1910–1920 four homes—New York, Spokane, Kansas City, and the *Trumpet* home in Anderson—created more formal educational structures. Each founded a Bible institute focused on ministerial preparation. Cooperating with George Tasker and A. D. Khan, at the New York institute Teasley wrote a correspondence curriculum for ministers.

The second way in which the missionary homes accelerated the transition to a cohesive movement was through the opportunities they provided for what might be called advanced leadership training. The homes were managed by a superintendent and a "matron," often husband and wife. Superintendents acquired valuable experience working with people as well as managing a home's financial matters. When the Church of God movement further institutionalized after 1917 a host of practically trained men and women could step with some confidence into newly created agencies and departments of the church. The ministerial career of R. J. Smith

(1864–1925) serves as an example that was frequently repeated. Smith was one of many southern African Americans attracted to a Church of God vision of Christian unity that transcended social barriers such as race. He preached in both the South and North, and eventually took up the superintendency of the missionary home in Pittsburgh, Pennsylvania. In 1917 Smith was elected as the first chair of the General Ministerial Assembly of the National Association of the Church of God. The experience afforded by supervising a missionary home helped prepare Smith and dozens like him for leadership positions in new church agencies and departments. Many of the third generation of movement leaders acquired their skills as missionary home superintendents. Future *Trumpet* Managing Editor R. R. Byrum served a home in Boston. Influential pastor, missionary, and board member E. A. Reardon superintended the Chicago home. The Detroit missionary home was served for a time by the future fourth editor of the *Trumpet,* Charles E. Brown. Clarence and Nora Hunter supervised the home in Fort Wayne, Indiana years before she founded and presided over the National Woman's Home and Foreign Missionary Society of the Church of God.[37] Before the development of the missionary homes, ministerial or leadership training was largely nonexistent. Indeed, a bias against formal ministerial education existed among the movement's leaders in spite of the fact that many had undertaken postsecondary education. By providing training on several levels, the missionary homes hastened the Church of God through a transition from a loose association to a cohesive movement.

Governance and Ministerial Credentialing

Meetings provided the opportunity for ministers to gather in informal ministerial assemblies. No officers were elected, the very practice of voting being considered a Babylonish activity, and no agendas adopted. On a corner of the grounds ministers simply gathered to discuss the church and its current issues. "Leading" ministers, those who regularly published articles in the *Trumpet* or who enjoyed a reputation for strict, down-the-line preaching, had thereby earned an authority that gained them the ear of their ministerial brothers and sisters. Nevertheless, these assemblies were entirely ad hoc and without formal ecclesial standing, although they also were the locus of decision-making when warranted. One of the early examples of such action appears in the formation of the "Missionary Committee."

Cross-cultural missions began in the Church of God movement in 1892, when Benjamin Franklin Elliott took passage on a ship bound from San Diego to Ensenada, Mexico. Elliott, a former Methodist minister and professor of Greek at the University of Southern California, had joined the movement and started street-preaching targeted at Hispanics in Santa Barbara. In 1892 he decided to spread the message to the people of Mexico themselves. That same year J. H. and Hattie Rupert and W. J. Henry sailed to Liverpool, England to open a mission there. These individuals and their ministries were but the vanguard of missionary ventures that took men and women to several European countries, the Caribbean, and India by 1909. None of these early missionaries carried any authorization other than his or her personal sense of a divine calling. In these first decades the Church of God did not cooperate with any external sending agency and it lacked an internal agency to commission cross-cultural missionaries. Like those who remained in North America, early Church of God missionaries were flying messengers, except that they flew farther and returned home less frequently.

By 1909 the number and range of foreign flyers and their missions had begun creating problems. The Holy Spirit seemed to be leading some people into regions where they repeated or overlapped the work of other, earlier arrivals. Financial support also became an issue as missionaries requested contributions from local gatherings of saints as well as individuals. These requests were uncoordinated, arriving as they did individually from many quarters of the globe. Finally, at a gathering of ministers assembled at the 1909 camp meeting in Anderson, H. M. Riggle proposed the creation of a missionary committee. The matter was discussed and the question was resolved when the ministers voiced their approval with a collective "Amen." Seven ministers were appointed to the committee. In a correlative decision the assembled ministers also agreed to Riggle's second proposal, the founding of a new periodical focused on foreign missions.[38] In terms of doctrinal practice, the formation of the Missionary Committee took a momentous stride in a new direction.

The question begs to be asked, What had changed in the Church of God movement that its ministers were willing to step boldly toward "man-rule"? John W. V. Smith explains this willingness by reference to those who had departed the movement. The Church of God had lived through two major schisms, the Anti-cleansing heresy in 1899 and the necktie controversy between 1910 and 1914. Large numbers of ministers had left in the aftermath of these disputes. Smith contends that the departed ministers had held tightly to the movement's original commitments, including the ideal of a flying ministry. By the time Riggle made his proposals, in Smith's view, the likeliest source of their opposition was gone. Not that the Missionary Committee was readily accepted by all concerned. Voices were raised in objection to the creation of such an obviously Babylonish institution. But a question should be raised about Smith's easy identification of the

Anti-cleansers as conservatives; their doctrine of sanctification was, after all, a liberal departure from Holiness movement teaching. And the timing of the Anti-cleansers' departure does not quite fit Smith's analysis, because the Missionary Committee was created in 1909, before opponents of the necktie began leaving in earnest. Some ministers had left the movement, and others were soon to depart. However, those who had left would not necessarily have objected to a nascent organization, and some who might oppose it were still present.

So the question remains, What had changed to permit the creation of the Missionary Committee? It may very well be that little had changed in the movement, except for the attitudes of a small group of "leading ministers" who were privy to the growing administrative problems created by a flying ministry, foreign or domestic. H. M. Riggle stands out in this group. In 1908 he was president of the Gospel Trumpet Company. When the company had been reorganized in 1898[39] he had been named one of seven trustees, and Editor Byrum appointed Riggle a contributing editor in 1902. By 1924 Riggle had come to regret the era of the flying ministry for its inefficiency and repetitiveness. Ministerial labors were wasted when an evangelist started up a meeting of saints only to leave for a new appointment while the little band dwindled waiting for the next traveling preacher to hit town. Already in 1909 Riggle's various positions of responsibility predisposed him in favor of more efficient organizational structures. There is little doubt as well that Riggle's proposal for a missionary committee enjoyed the backing of E. E. Byrum. By then the two men had worked in close association for more than a decade. Byrum was one of the seven ministers recognized as the first committee. So was D. O. Teasley, who had gained administrative experience as a missionary home superintendent in New York and had served as managing editor at the Gospel Trumpet Company during Byrum's year-long absence on a worldwide missionary tour. These were people whose experience predisposed them to regard a missionary committee as the opportunity to eliminate overlapping appeals and missionary labors that stood to waste the movement's slender resources. In this view the missionary committee was the creation of a comparatively few ministers whose pragmatism inclined them to step away from the early bias against organization in the belief that the Holy Spirit could guide the hearts of committee members as readily as those of individuals.

Committee members had been selected on the basis of their capabilities of "advising, instructing, encouraging, and restraining."[40] Capabilities easily translate into responsibilities, but ironically the Missionary Committee received authorization in these four capacities from an ad hoc group without any formal authority to act. The assembled ministers would not have chosen the committee without a New Testament model. It was no accident that the same number of members composed the committee as there were deacons chosen by the Jerusalem church. Despite the apparent parallel, that the committee exercised a power by which to advise as well as restrain constituted a new element in the polity of the Church of God. Missionaries never again would be quite as free to follow the leading of the Holy Spirit on their own. After 1909 a committee existed that was ready to help them discern God's will. The creation of the Missionary Committee shifted the ground on which rested the movement's practice of church polity. It would not be too much to say that the committee was the first bureaucratic office in the Church of God movement. Formerly the movement was a loose confederation of preaching points, meeting places, and congregations glued together by the *Gospel Trumpet.* The creation of the Missionary Committee opened the door to a range of polity practices to which early Church of God writers and preachers had been militantly opposed. E. E. Byrum's personal predisposition to put matters on a sound managerial footing endorsed this development even as it meant that the theological issues opened in 1909 would be left for the next generation to resolve.

Byrum was only one of a group of nearly twenty ministers whose views on the need for improved cooperation and organization came to full expression after 1911.[41] Each of these individuals wrote essays for a ministerial newsletter inaugurated in 1912. Published by the Gospel Trumpet Company, *Our Ministerial Letter* attempted to change attitudes toward certain aspects of the church and its conception of the ministry. The very first issue aimed at shaping ministerial attitudes toward the new Missionary Committee and new forms of organization. At the request of the Missionary Committee J. W. Phelps prepared this first letter, which ranged over a variety of issues related to the question of organization. He appears to have taken this topic in an effort to calm fears that the Church of God movement had begun adopting the methods and structures of the very Babylonians that it was simultaneously thrashing.

Phelps assured his readers that there was nothing necessarily sectarian about organization.[42] He distinguished between biblical doctrine and the work of the church. Sects, i. e. denominations, err not in their attempt "to do the work of God in an orderly, systematic manner, but when they bind upon men as doctrines things not required by the letter or the spirit of the Word, or to release men from obligations which the letter or the spirit of the Word requires."[43] Phelps also made it plain that the Missionary Committee differed from the missionary boards of sectarian bodies in that the latter usurped the role of the Holy Spirit when they determined the qualifications of candidates for the mission field and sent them where they saw fit. In Phelps' view the Missionary Committee exercised "only that advisory power over the missionaries that the body of ministers exercise over the prospective candidates to the ministry."[44] Phelps further defended the Missionary Committee by saying that its actions had to that point been limited to raising support funds and disbursing them. Phelps' may have been guilty of splitting some fine theological hairs, but his work and that of his sixteen colleagues on *Our Ministerial Letter* indicated a marked dissatisfaction with the absence of institutional structures in the Church of God movement and a growing predisposition to develop some level of bureaucratic organization. The "Committee of Seventeen" also realized, however, that such moves required a careful restatement of the movement's theology and practice of the church.

E. E. Byrum and the Church of God movement adopted a second organizational practice during this period. Like the Missionary Committee, this new practice also laid the foundation of more "churchly" practices that followed a few years later. Also, like the creation of the Missionary Committee, pragmatic considerations played important roles in its development. This practice established patterns by which Church of God ministers were recognized and approved. As such it affected ordination practices and ministerial credentialing. In the nineteenth and on into the twentieth century American railroads offered reduced fares to ordained ministers. The railroads maintained clergy bureaus to oversee this program through a ministerial registration that distinguished the ordained from masquerading freeloaders. The clergy bureaus depended on denominational offices to supply them with the names of ministers recognized to be in good standing. Methodists and other denominations may not have regarded compliance with such a request as a theological problem, but the clergy bureaus' request for an official ministerial list had the potential to raise questions that impinged directly on the doctrinal practice of polity in the Church of God movement. Who determined ministerial "good standing" and by what criteria? Who would bear responsibility for securing names of Church of God ministers and for the maintenance of the ministerial list? About such questions there hung more than a whiff of Babylon and her corrupt practices.

There is little evidence that many Church of God preachers and writers picked up the scent during the editorial tenure of E. E. Byrum. The first ministerial lists to appear collected the names of ministers in attendance at the general camp meeting in Moundsville in the first years of the twentieth-century. Perhaps these sufficiently documented ministerial status to satisfy railroad conductors. However, from these early attendance lists it was a short but significant step to the creation of longer lists that aimed at including all members of the Church of God ministry.[45] The earliest extant such list was prepared by George Cole in 1905 for publication in 1906. To insure accuracy he distributed a proof along with a request for corrections and updates. Although compiled primarily for the railroad clergy bureaus, the fact that Cole asked for information that would drop "unworthy" ministers from the list indicates that it had other purposes. The 1906 list included only names and current state of residence. The names of unordained ministers were marked with an asterisk. The 1912 list added mailing addresses and one of four ministerial designations—pastor, assistant pastor, evangelist, or home missionary.[46] The 1914 list added a more ominous designation. That was the first year that a symbol marked the names of "colored" Church of God ministers.

Material Christianity

In 1896 Enoch and Noah Byrum decided to increase the number of products sold by the Gospel Trumpet Publishing Company. The previous year it had offered for sale a line of envelopes imprinted with scripture texts. Except for those envelopes the company had printed and published the *Gospel Trumpet,* books, tracts, and gospel songbooks, but in 1896 it entered the market of religious and inspirational products. A scripture-text calendar and Sunday school cards "with beautiful colored flowers, landscapes, figures, and so forth, with scriptural texts on them" were now available from the Gospel Trumpet Company. During the next decade the company expanded this product line to include post cards imprinted with Bible verses and wall mottoes—at first paper but in 1908 manufactured in art-velvet—also imprinted with a scripture text. Motto sales proved so strong as to prompt company officials to add a sales representative to demonstrate this "line of goods." By 1912, less than four years after their introduction, wall mottoes rivaled books as the number one seller among Gospel Trumpet Company products.[47] The company had opened these new product lines in part to supplement income derived from the sale of books and periodicals, but the sale of religious objects was never seen simply as a source of revenue. Mottoes, calendars, and post cards were regarded as evangelistic tools as well as the means for decorating the home with objects intended to encourage spiritual sensibilities. Through Gospel Trumpet Company products the Church of God movement drank deeply from the springs of nineteenth- and twentieth-century American Protestantism's "material Christianity."[48]

Historians and theologians of Christianity have generally regarded the ear as the critical organ of revelation for Protestants. Luther emphasized the

Word of God, especially as the act of preaching made the Word incarnate again. Zwingli's followers whitewashed the interiors of Zurich churches, obliterating the "graven images" portrayed in frescoes and paintings on their walls. The Lutheran and Reformed descendants of the sixteenth-century reformations may have retained the Reformers' emphasis on the spoken and written word, but other Protestants were receptive to a piety that included the eye as an organ of spiritual illumination. Nineteenth-century American Protestants purchased a wide range of religious objects, everything from drinking glasses etched with the Lord's Prayer or "Rock of Ages" to miniature Noah's arks and Bible puzzles.[49] Victorian attitudes in America encouraged a religion of domesticity that transformed the home into a shrine of family piety. Visual objects such as scripture mottoes and prints with religious scenes were hung on the walls of homes where parents wanted to influence the spiritual growth of their children.

The Gospel Trumpet Company was both the beneficiary and the agent of the parental desire to see their children saved and growing in faith. The company existed as a primary evangelistic arm of the Church of God movement; company literature and products advanced the movement's message. On the other hand, proceeds from the sales of religious objects also relieved some of the company's financial burden. However, it is also the case that by 1910 wall mottoes had forsaken sayings that were closely identified with the movement's doctrinal practices in favor of more generalized sentiments. The earliest mottoes had featured sayings such as "Be ye All of one Mind," "Is Any Afflicted? Let Him Pray," and "Without Holiness no man shall see the Lord." After 1909 these were replaced with such mottoes as "Prayer Changes Things," "Jesus Never Fails," and "Abide in Me."[50] The production and sale of religious objects was a point of convergence for three interests important to the company. First, religious objects increased revenue, no small matter for a company that was perpetually strapped for cash. Second, in their early years religious objects advanced the message of the Church of God movement and were thus regarded as a tool of evangelism. Third, religious objects were at the core of a doctrinal practice that might be called the formation of a Christian home.

The Church of God movement idealized the Christian home as the only safe alternative to that dangerous place called "the world." Sin lurked in the world and waited to devour any saint who was seduced by its temptations. The home was understood as a refuge, a harbor where the parents and children could rest, safe from worldly temptation. More than a resting place, the Christian home was also expected to fortify parents and children for necessary excursions into the world. Family devotions—prayer, Bible reading and parental commentary—staples of this fortifying process. But Church of God writers also encouraged the saints to make a sanctuary of their physical surroundings by decorating them with religious objects. A print of Heinrich Hoffmann's *Christ in the Temple* applied to an art-velvet motto did far more than decorate the home; it directed family members' attention toward matters of the soul and thus was thought to form spiritual character. A motto inscribed with the warning "Prepare to Meet thy God" reminded them that life was fleeting and therefore to be lived faithfully and in true holiness. Christian parents who loved their children would see to it that they were surrounded with reminders of their eternal destiny. Out of this concern developed the doctrinal practice of the Christian home. In the ensuing years the Gospel Trumpet Company became a leader in the sale of a wider and wider product line of religious objects that some later came to characterize as "holy hardware" or "Jesus junk." Whether "Sonshine Line" greeting cards, pencils inscribed with scripture verses, or electric lampshades imprinted with Warner Sallman's painting *Christ My Pilot,* the company's aim was never simply sales revenue. Such products also fed a visual piety that reinforced a doctrinal practice centered on the home as a refuge and place of religious formation.

Emergent Practices and Group Cohesion

The Church of God began as the loosest of movements, without formal organization of any kind and committed to the ideal of the charismatic governance of the church as the New Testament standard. By 1915 the movement had grown significantly, faced serious internal disputes, was forced to deal with external requirements, and extended its mission. In the process leaders like E. E. Byrum, H. M. Riggle, and others began employing practices that were quite pragmatic in origin. Railroad clergy bureaus needed a ministers' list. Local meetings of saints wearied of waiting for the next flying messenger to land. Foreign missionaries needed financial support while the saints needed relief from incessant requests for money. The saints were encouraged to develop their homes as Christian sanctuaries. In each of these areas of church life, a practice emerged to shape that concern. Because these practices governed the movement's life as the New Testament church they could not be regarded simply as pragmatic accommodations to the situation, even if they were. Rather, they came to be regarded as the means by which the church lived and worked together. In some cases, especially in divine healing, the movement employed a doctrinal practice that confirmed its claim to be the New Testament church.

The development of doctrinal practices was, from a sociological point of view, inevitable if the Church of God movement was to survive. Without institutions new religious movements ultimately fade out of existence. But when the new movement takes anti-institutionalism as one of its battle cries, the development of institutionalized practices becomes highly problematic. When the new movement also opposes the use of creeds or other similar instruments, practices—particularly doctrinal practices—assume crucial importance. Faced with a decision to develop rudimentary organizational practices or conventional creeds and institutions, Church of God leaders in the second decade of the twentieth century chose the former. It was scarcely a decision at all, but it was only the first step in what became a perennial issue in the Church of God movement.

Notes

1. Gale Hetrick and Company, *Laughter Among the Trumpets* (Lansing, Ill: The Church of God in Michigan, 1980), 105.

2. This sketch is indebted to Robert H. Reardon, "Movers and Shakers in the Church of God," unpublished ms., n.d.

3. John W. V. Smith, *Heralds of a Brighter Day* (Anderson, Ind: Gospel Trumpet Publishing Company, 1955), 54–58, *passim.*

4. Harold L. Phillips, *Miracle of Survival* (Anderson, Ind: Warner Press, 1979), 60–96, *passim.*

5. Robert H. Reardon, "Movers and Shakers in the Church of God," unpublished ms., n.p., n.d.

6. Reardon, "Movers and Shakers," n.d. Reardon adds a personal description of Byrum quite consistent with other descriptions of his personality and his managerial and leadership style: "There is abundant evidence that his ministry of healing inspired many miracles. His presence stimulated faith although he never led spectacular, highly emotionalized, present day type miracle healing crusades. He dealt primarily with individuals—those across the country who pled for him to come or those who traveled miles to Anderson for his prayer. I often heard him testify in P[ark] P[lace] Church [of God] and pray at the altar for the sick. It was in a quiet, matter of fact voice—no shouting appeals to the Almighty, no emotional outbursts."

7. *Divine Healing of Soul and Body* (Grand Junction: Gospel Trumpet Publishing Company, 1892); *The Great Physician and His Power to Heal* (Moundsville: Gospel Trumpet Publishing Company, 1899); and *Miracles and Healing* (Anderson, Ind: Gospel Trumpet Publishing Company, 1919).

8. Warner's library contains copies of four of Fowler's books, including *Physiology, Animal and Mental* (New York: S. R. Wells and Co., Publishers, 1875); and *Self-Culture and Perfection of Character* (New York: S. R. Wells and Co., Publishers, n.d.).

9. (Anderson, Ind: Gospel Trumpet Publishing Company, 1908). For example, Nelson was critical of white bread and offered instructions for baking good bread following the rule "the coarser the flour the better the bread." Nelson's general dietary rule could be summed up as "simple is better." He recommended only two beverages, milk and water, and advised readers that foods were healthier when consumed closest to a raw state—including eggs, 370.

10. Byrum himself reported an interest in divine healing that stemmed back to his boyhood. Cf., E. E. Byrum, *Life Experiences* (Anderson, Ind: Gospel Trumpet Company, 1928), 127–132.

11. Smith, *Heralds of a Brighter Day*, 70.

12. Mary gave "Babylon" no credit for her conversion and sanctification. Cf. H. C. Wickersham, *History of the Church; From the Birth of Christ to the Present Time* (Moundsville: Gospel Trumpet Company, 1900), 341; and *Mary Cole, Trials and Triumphs of Faith* (Anderson, Ind: Gospel Trumpet Company, 1914), 36–43.

13. Mary diagnosed the source of her many maladies to the fact that her mother had overheated during pregnancy. Ibid., 342.

14. Ibid.

15. One can only surmise the expository gymnastics of this sermon, based as it was on Matthew 24:28, "For wheresoever the carcass is, there will the eagles be gathered together." H. M. Riggle, "Introduction," in J. Grant Anderson, *Divine Healing* (Anderson, Ind: Gospel Trumpet Company, 1926), 5.

16. Ibid., 6.

17. The final chapter of Anderson's book is titled "Facts on Health" and discusses the health of the human body, "correct eating, drinking, breathing, and thinking," diet, etc. Ibid. Some of Anderson's advice anticipated later dietary advice: "Oranges, limes, and grapefruit are especially strong in vitamin and are excellent blood purifiers. Dr. Copeland (U. S. Senator) says, 'Mashed potatoes, fried eggs, fried bacon, boiled cabbage, and products made from refined (white) flour are not foods, and should not be eaten.' " 104–116. Anderson extended this interest to an area of married life rarely discussed openly in Church of God circles when he wrote *Sex Life and Home Problems* (Anderson, Ind: Gospel Trumpet Company, 1921).

18. Byrum, *The Great Physician*, 13.

19. (Anderson, Ind: Gospel Trumpet Company, 1911).

20. James W. McClendon, Jr., *Systematic Theology, Vol. I, Ethics* (Nashville: Abingdon Press, 1986), 31. Although writing a systematic theology, McClendon developed its structural themes from and for the specific historical tradition of the Believers' Church, as McClendon termed it the *baptist* tradition. The description quoted above is historically determined, not a category of systematic theology in the conventional sense of that term. McClendon goes on to say that the "this is that" vision of history and biblical interpretation is not meant as a denial of history. Perhaps not, but many Church of God writers in the first two generations either passed over much of Christian history between the subapostolic period and their own era or they repudiated those centuries as the history of an apostate church.

21. *Hymnal of the Church of God* (Anderson, Ind: Warner Press, 1971), No. 349.

22. *Divine Healing of Soul and Body*, 85.

23. Quoted in Smith, *Heralds of a Brighter Day*, 71.

24. *Divine Healing of Soul and Body*, 106.

25. Ibid.

26. Byrum found a precedent for this practice in Acts 19:12, where handkerchiefs attached to St Paul's clothing were given to the afflicted and effected miraculous cures.

27. *Divine Healing of Soul and Body*, 117–118.

28. Byrum, *Miracles and Healing*, 167.

29. Ibid, 165–166.

30. In 1898 a Grant County (Indiana) court indicted George and Mary Achor along with William Johnson on a charge of murder in connection with the death of his wife, Sarah. The three supported Mrs. Johnson's decision to halt the use of medicines prescribed for the treatment of complications following childbirth. When she died the Achors and William Johnson were arrested. The charge was later reduced to manslaughter, and their trial ended in a hung jury. As the case unfolded Editor Byrum made it a cause celebre in pages of the *Gospel Trumpet*.

31. John W. V. Smith describes these commitments as "facets" of "light on the church," a phrase widely employed by Church of God preachers and writers, as the third of four basic presuppositions that framed the early movement's self-understanding. The four presuppositions are: (1) the Bible is the sole foundation of the Christian faith, (2) the essence of Christian religion is experiential, (3) the Church of God movement was divinely called to proclaim and model the visible earthly expression of the one, holy, universal church, and (4) a belief among the movement people that "they were participants in the fulfillment of a segment of divine destiny for all humanity." Smith's discussion of these and related issues remains one of the most pregnant analyses of the early Church of God movement's self-understanding in the historiography of the Church of God. Cf., "A Developing Reformation Consciousness," chapter 5, in *toto, The Quest for Holiness and Unity*, 81–100.

32. Ibid, 88–94, passim.

33. On the dominance of this nineteenth-century view cf. Sidney E. Mead, "The Rise of the Evangelical Conception of the Ministry in America," in H. Richard Niebuhr and Daniel Day Williams, eds., *The Ministry in Historical Perspective* (New York: Harper and Row, 1956), 207–249.

34. For a study of early camp meetings and camp meeting religion, see Charles A. Johnson, *The Frontier Campmeeting: Religion's Harvest Time* (Dallas: Southern Methodist University Press, 1955).

35. For historical sketch of camp meetings in the Church of God, see Richard L. Willowby, *Family Reunion: A Century of Campmeetings* (Anderson, Ind: Warner Press, 1986).

36. *GT* (July 8, 1920), 11.

37. Cf. Smith, *Quest for Holiness and Unity,* 239–242.

38. Thus began the *Missionary Herald.* The paper had a short run, from 1910 to 1913, when it merged with the *Gospel Trumpet.* George Pease Tasker was named committee secretary. His minutes recording these events are quoted in Lester A. Crose, *Passport for a Reformation* (Anderson, Ind: Warner Press, 1981), 37.

39. In this reorganization the company became a stock-issuing corporation in an effort to raise capital. In essence stock purchasers agreed to loan the company money interest free for a specified term of fifty years. Neither would they receive any dividends. On the effective date of the reorganization Enoch and Noah Byrum received precisely the amounts by which they had earlier purchased the company, and by this transfer it became a corporation held in trust for the Church of God movement. In 1903 the company underwent a third reorganization, this time to incorporate as a not-for-profit religious corporation. Phillips, *Miracle of Survival,* 62–64, 91–92. That company officers led it through these maneuvers further illustrates their growing managerial expertise and a willingness to employ it in the service of a movement that they insisted was governed by the Holy Spirit.

40. Tasker, Ibid.

41. E. E. Byrum, D. Teasley, R. L. Berry, J. E. Forrest, E. A. Reardon, F. G. Smith, John A. D. Khan, G. Tasker, H. M. Riggle, George L. Cole, E. G. Masters, H. A. Brooks, J. W. Byers, George W. Olsen, Lena Shofner Matthesen, J. Grant Anderson, and C. E. Orr. With only a few exceptions, the list is a virtual "who's who" of second generation leadership among Church of God ministers.

42. The first page of this issue quoted from H. M. Riggle's address to ministers at Anderson during camp meeting the previous June: "Government and system need to be recognized in the church. Such recognition will not show that we are a sect; on the contrary, these things being God's order, our recognition of them will be one of the surest signs that we are the church of God." "Our Mission Work," *Our Ministerial Letter* (Anderson, Ind: n.p. 1912), 3.

43. Ibid., 8.

44. Ibid., 9.

45. The earliest extant attendance lists date from 1902. The earliest extant official Ministers List dates from 1906 and includes a total of 393 names. Archives of the Church of God. File "Ministers Lists."

46. That there was no designation for "missionary" suggests that the list was for American domestic use only. E. A. Reardon, Registrar, "The Church of God Ministerial List for 1912," cf. File, "Minister's Lists," Archives of the Church of God.

47. Harold L. Phillips, *Miracle of Survival,* 120–121.

48. The phrase is taken from Colleen McDannell's, *Material Christianity: Religion and Popular Culture in America* (New Haven: Yale University Press, 1995).

49. Ibid., 223.

50. Ibid., 234.

Chapter 5
Apocalyptic Identity

In 1897, a few months shy of his seventeenth birthday, Frederick G. Smith (1880–1947) went to work at the Gospel Trumpet Publishing Company. He had not been able to advance his education beyond grammar school, so the bright and adept young man trained himself in shorthand in the hope of eventually becoming a stenographer. This skill proved very useful in the company offices, and young Fred soon found himself in the position of private secretary to E. E. Byrum. Fred's parents, Joseph and Mary Smith, owned a farm near Lacota, Michigan, not far from Grand Junction. Never ordained, the Smiths nevertheless were something like lay ministers and opened their home to the preachers and gospel workers who constantly came and went from the *Trumpet* home. Their son grew up listening to conversations between evangelists and leading ministers of the movement who were refreshed at his parents' table. At age six Fred was converted in a children's meeting led by D. S. Warner.

Smith answered a call to the ministry in 1898. He was ordained two years later and left his secretarial position to enter full-time evangelistic work. About the same time a young woman named Birdie Mitchell arrived at the Gospel Trumpet Publishing Company and offered her services as a worker. Two years later Fred and Birdie were married. The young couple formed their own evangelistic company and for the next decade itinerated through the Midwest, particularly Michigan and Indiana, except for an evangelistic tour of the state of Washington the second half of 1906 and the first half of 1907. Prior to departing for the Pacific Northwest, Fred submitted a manuscript to Editor Byrum. The company's move to Anderson delayed publication of Smith's book, but in 1908 it appeared under the title *The Revelation Explained*. A detailed exposition of the Book of Revelation, Smith's book gathered up and extended lines of thought that had begun

Frederick G. Smith. Third editor of the Gospel Trumpet, his books articulated a method of biblical interpretation and a theology of the church that held sway in the Church of God movement for the first third of the twentieth century.

twenty years earlier in the minds of Warner, W. G. Schell, and other preachers who had sat in the Smiths' kitchen. Developed by Smith into a comprehensive interpretation of the apocalyptic books of the Bible—Daniel and the Revelation; that reading of the Bible served as the virtually unrivalled foundation of the Church of God movement's self-understanding from the early 1890s to 1935.

D. S. Warner and Uriah Smith

At some point between 1882 and 1884 D. S. Warner came across the ideas of an Adventist preacher named Uriah Smith, Professor of Biblical Exegesis at Battle Creek College. Smith had published several books, some of them dealing with typology and prophecy, but especially *Thoughts, Critical and Practical, on the Book of Daniel and the Revelation.*[1] Warner owned a copy of this book and read at least some of its sections with great care.[2] Uriah Smith interpreted the apocalyptic books, especially Daniel and the Revelation, church-historically.* According to this hermeneutical method apocalyptic symbols were understood as predictions of events in the life of the church read forward from the time of the biblical authors. Interest in biblical apocalyptic "prophecy" swelled in the last two decades of the nineteenth-century. The bulk of this interest centered in the interpretation that ultimately led to dispensational premillenialism and the Scofield Reference Bible. The church-historical interpretation differed from dispensationalist readings in the scope of its vision. The former read apocalyptic symbols as signs that revealed the future history of the church, the latter as signs predicting the sweep of world history at the end of time.

Smith's interpretation led him to the conclusion that 1844, a year of crucial significance in the Millerite Adventist movement, marked the beginning of "the final work for man's salvation"[3] at the end of the age. Warner agreed with Smith's schema, disputing only the dates that he used as anchors for the chronological application of apocalyptic numerology. At the

---

*A variety of methods have been employed to interpret the Book of Revelation. In addition to literary, allegorical, and dramatic approaches, the book has frequently been interpreted through what is generically referred to as a historical or historico-eschatological approach. This method treats biblical apocalyptic in the view that its authors predicted events under a chronological scheme. Some historical interpreters limit the sweep of Revelation to its own time; others interpret the book as a set of predictions focusing on events near the end of time. Still others interpret Revelation as a panoramic vision of world history. It is a variant of this latter approach that Uriah Smith adopted, and in which he was followed by Church of God interpreters in the tradition of W. G. Schell's *Biblical Trace of the Church.* The sweep of history is still the framework of this variation, but its subject matter is restricted to the history of the church, hence the use of the phrase "church-historical" to describe this interpretive method.

critical point in Smith's argument where he set the key date, Warner wrote "false premise" in the margin of the page.[4] He accepted the validity of Smith's hermeneutical method but rejected his starting point. Warner concluded that Daniel and the Revelation did in fact hold the key to unlocking the meaning of Christian history, but their symbols pointed not to William Miller and the Adventists. Rather, it was the Church of God movement that the Bible predicted as the restoration of the church at the end of the age.

Uriah Smith's work stimulated Warner's interest in the apocalyptic literature of the Bible, a literature that both men considered prophetic. His original views on the nature of the church were not tied to apocalyptic themes, but Warner began to publish articles employing Smith's church-historical hermeneutic as early as the spring of 1884. During the next few months he wrote articles that mined the text of the Revelation in either of two ways. At some points he interpreted apocalyptic verses in a manner that many nineteenth-century Protestant writers might have employed. But beginning in 1884 Warner also wrote articles that rested firmly on a church-historical foundation.[5] He became more strongly convinced of the truth revealed by this method, and the frequency of such articles increased up to the time of his death.

W. G. Schell, that theological wanderer, was the first Church of God writer to systematically develop in book length the ideas that Warner had adapted from Smith. In *The Biblical Trace of the Church,* Schell celebrated the arrival of the long-expected Evening Light and defended the interpretation on which that arrival was grounded. Schell wrote with a sense of urgency out of the conviction that the end of the age was imminent, that "the Lord will make a short work upon the earth."[6] Warner, Schell, and those they influenced were certain of the world's imminent end on the basis of their interpretation of Old and New Testament apocalyptic. Schell organized his book according to four great ages in the history of the church. The Morning Light Age extended from the New Testament to AD 270. He characterized it as an era when the true church declined and eventually was eclipsed by the rise of Babylon the Great, the Mother of Harlots, which he and Warner before him identified as the Roman Catholic Church. Catholicism's ascendancy began a Papal Age of spiritual darkness and the persecution of the true church that lasted for 1,260 years, or until AD 1530.[7] That year marked the beginning of the Protestant Age when the church began a long journey out of papal darkness into the half-light of a Protestantism that remained partially corrupted by deep divisions, man-rule, and remnants of Catholicism. The fourth and final period of Christian history had begun, said Schell, in 1880. This Evening Light Age marked the restoration of the true New Testament church in all of her original holiness and unity. The appearance of this church also signaled that the end of Christian history, and the world with it, rapidly approached.

Schell's schematization of Christian history rested on the church-historical hermeneutic applied to the books of Daniel, the Revelation, and the apocalyptic sections of Zechariah and other books of the Bible. Using these books and other New Testament texts, Schell created a picture of the Morning Light church, a golden age of Christianity which began a long declension as early as the subapostolic era. He criticized Ignatius of Antioch for his endorsement of a monarchical episcopacy, a deviation from the true apostolic church where leaders humbly regarded one another as equals. Schell also cited Ignatius' and Clement's references to schism as indicators of a lost original unity. The second-century church also demonstrated its apostasy, in Schell's view, by departing from apostolic example and teaching on baptism. He cited the Epistle of Barnabas for its doctrine of baptismal regeneration and criticized the church for admitting the use of sprinkling rather than immersion. Schell also noted declines in the number of miracles and the church's emphasis on holiness and the gifts of the Spirit.[8]

Schell relied heavily on Daniel and the Revelation to describe the second or Papal age. Deriving historical details from polemical Protestant histories such as Merle D'Aubigne's *History of the Reformation* and *Foxe's Book of Martyrs,* Schell interpreted Roman Catholicism as the successor to the Roman Empire and the persecutor of true Christianity. The Pope was the corrupt head of a degenerate church to which Schell and others referred apocalyptically named the "Beast" and the "Mother of Harlots."[9] Using symbolic numbers found in Daniel and the Revelation, Schell calculated the length of the Papal Age at 1,260 years and pinpointed its beginning in AD 270.

> The reign of popery, in Daniel's vision, was limited to "a time, and times, and the dividing of time." "A time" signifies one year; "times" two years; and "the dividing of time" a half year; in all, three and one-half years or forty-two months. Multiply forty-two by thirty, the number of days in a month, and we have twelve hundred and sixty days. Counting each day for a year (Num 14:34; Ezek 4:6), gives twelve hundred and sixty years for the papal reign. The real papacy was set up, not at the Nicean [sic] council, AD 325, as some affirm; but we find vivid traces of the very same beast authority as early as about AD 270.[10]

Schell regarded Catholicism as the product of a lowered standard of judgment in a clergy whose perceptions of truth had been corrupted and perverted. This debased clergy offered pagans admission to the church on the lowest of standards. After the Decian persecution subsided, "a pleasant opportunity was offered the heathen to exchange one profession for the other.... Many of the numerous converts received no change of heart, and were still pagans within. Thus, Heathen Rome, supposed by many to be overthrown, soon concealed herself under the garb of 'Christian Rome.' So Roman Catholicism is but the dregs of Paganism, blackened with fresh soot from the bottomless pit."[11]

In Schell's schematization of Christian history Protestantism defined the third great age of the church. Revelation 13:3, 14 stated that the beast received a deadly wound by the sword, which Schell read as a prophecy of the sixteenth century Protestant Reformation, "by means of which Romanism has been deprived of all temporal power and myriads of adherents."[12] Protestantism, however, in Schell's interpretation, turned out to be a very mixed blessing. The Reformation may have dealt a wound to the Mother of Harlots, but in this view Protestants were nothing more than wicked daughters. Relying once again on an inventive interpretation of the symbolic numbers of apocalyptic writing, Schell concluded that Protestants and the Pope alike shared title to the worst number of all—666.[13] Protestantism's two major parties, Lutheranism and the Reformed churches, made it the two-horned beast that emerged from the beast herself. They, too, were guilty of persecuting the true church, neglecting Bible teaching on holiness, and quenching the Spirit by insisting on formal liturgies. Thus, contrary to all claims, Word and Spirit lay as dead in Protestantism as in her mother. Revelation 11:7–10 makes reference to Word and Spirit laying dead for three and a half days, and "interpreted by the Holy Spirit," this signified three and a half centuries of Protestant hegemony.[14]

Schell calculated the Protestant Age to have begun in 1530 with the signing of the Augsburg Confession. Adding 350 years to that date yielded the year 1880 as the beginning of the fourth and final age of the church. "About that time," said Schell, "God, in fulfillment to that which had been written, began to send his messengers to and fro to gather together his elect, which had been scattered in the various Protestant sects."[15] Zechariah 14:7 prophesied this day of restoration: "It shall come to pass, that at evening time it shall be light." The two witnesses, Word and Spirit, that had lain dormant now returned to cleanse and restore the church with the fire of holiness. The collapse of the first Babylon in the Old Testament had set loose Israel to return to Jerusalem. Schell read these events typologically to conclude that once fallen, "sectism," i. e. Protestantism, the harlotrous daughter of the Mother of Harlots, would give up the true saints. They would answer God's call to flee this ecclesiastical Babylon and follow God to a new Mount Zion— "the church of the firstborn which are written in heaven. Sectism has now fallen, and the voice from heaven, saying, 'Come out of her my people,' is echoing in every clime."[16]

That the Evening Age of the church had begun also indicated that the history of the church, and with it the earth, was rapidly drawing to a close. Schell saw signs of Christ's return in world events and in the church situation of his day. These led him to conclude "that we are, therefore, to consider ourselves near the end of the last age of time."[17] He saw a further sign of the imminent return of Christ in the 1879 treaty struck between the Rothschilds of England and the Turkish government, permitting the return of Jewish people to their Palestinian homeland. Lastly, Schell regarded the emergence of the Church of God movement itself as a sign of the end of time. On the basis of Revelation 19:6–9 he wrote, "Here we have a likeness of the church dressed in her wedding adornments, anticipating the coming of the Bridegroom. She is now just in the act of placing these beautiful garments upon her person through the purification of all her members. This text is another proof that the evening light is a sign of the last days."[18]

Interest in Warner's and Schell's conclusions was not restricted to the small circle of Gospel Trumpet Publishing Company leaders and their friends in ministerial circles. Poets and songwriters set these ideas to music in gospel songs. Although he cites several poems and songs conveying the "Evening Light" message, Schell's own lyrics, "The Biblical Trace of the Church" set to music his historical schematization. When the Saints sang of the 1,260 years they called it "O, long dreary papal night," and the 350 years of the Protestant Reformation was the era when "Popery quaked with fear." Set to music, albeit not a particularly melodic tune, Schell and Warner's schematization became a key element in the Church of God movement's doctrinal practice of gospel singing. This practice played a powerful role in shaping the movement's self-understanding as the Evening Light, the last reformation, when God was gathering all the true saints into the Church of God reformation movement as the final moment in the history of the gospel. Already by 1880 Warner's views had hardened into an exclusivism that regarded all denominations and churches as pretenders to the name *church*. The Evening Light rhetoric gave a strident militancy to that exclusivism. Certainly by 1893 and perhaps even earlier, the saints were developing a perspective that left little room in the heavenly fold for sheep of any flock other than the Church of God movement. The doctrinal practice that taught and reinforced this perspective was a sectarianism that became ever more deeply entrenched in the ensuing decades. "Come-outism," paradoxically to movement outsiders, became the doctrinal practice of Christian unity in the Church of God.

By the end of his career Warner was an old hand at reading current events through an apocalyptic lens. When newspapers reported the problems created for Pope Leo XIII by Italian political ferment, Warner saw them as the fulfillment of the prophecy in Revelation 16:19: "But 'Great Babylon came unto remembrance before God, to give unto her the cup of the wine of the fierceness of his wrath.' "[19] A year after the World Parliament of Religions in 1893 Warner referred to that convention as a meeting of Gog and Magog. Furthermore, proposals to consolidate liberal religious bodies "will be one of the three wings of Gog and Magog, gathered by their unclean spirits that came out of the mouth of the dragon, out of the mouth of the beast, and out of the mouth of the false prophet."[20] When he learned that a group of Protestant ministers had met with Catholic priests in Bay City, Michigan, Warner interpreted the meeting in light of a church-historical reading of Revelation 13:12, saying, "The wound that Mother Rome received by the Reformation is being healed by Protestantism becoming corrupt enough to reassociate with this old mother against which they once protested. So Protestantism, in reality, has ceased to protest; and again she takes by the hand that wicked power that was made drunk with the blood of the saints. This is also Gog and Magog gathering together."[21] As he neared the end of his life Warner confidently interpreted events in light of the apocalyptic books of the Bible. He did not use these books to read the signs of the times on the stage of political history as in the manner of dispensational premillennialism. Rather, Warner believed that he had found the hermeneutical key that unlocked the meaning of historical events pertaining to Christianity and the church. The prophetic books of the Bible, as Warner read them, foretold events unfolding in his own day.

The Cleansing of the Sanctuary

In *The Biblical Trace of the Church* W. G. Schell had developed a second basis for his conclusion that the Church of God fulfilled the prophetic description of the Evening Light age. This ground he located in Daniel 8:13–14, which predicted the passing of 2,300 "days" before the Jerusalem temple would be cleansed of its defilement. Schell saw this as yet another prophecy of the Church of God movement. In the last years of his life Warner expanded considerably on Schell's ten-page discussion, developing a manuscript that would set a complete theology of the church in the context of the prophecies of Daniel and the Revelation. He did not live to finish the project; however a dynamic preacher and emerging authority in his own right took over the manuscript and brought it to completion. When published in 1903, *The Cleansing of the Sanctuary* bore H. M. Riggle's name as co-author alongside Warner.

The Cleansing of the Sanctuary is at least as much if not more the product of Riggle's mind as Warner's. Riggle wrote more than half of the completed book. Moreover, he also revised Warner's manuscript because, as Riggle declared in the book's preface, "Since Bro. Warner's death, the light of truth has kept rapidly increasing, and many things that seemed wrapped in mystery have since been made clear."[22] He did not elaborate, but Riggle published a sufficient number of *Trumpet* articles during the early 1900s to suggest that he was regarded as an expert on biblical typology relating to the Israelite tabernacle and temple.

The Warner-Riggle book is an ecclesiology in the form of an extended polemic against the Adventists. At issue was the chronology developed by Uriah Smith. It was, said Riggle, the product of a "disgusting theory that the cleansing of the sanctuary here referred to [Daniel 8:13–14] is a cleansing in heaven accomplished by Christ. The same was to begin in 1844. They endeavor to stretch out the 2,300 days to that time. Upon this calculation, U. Smith says the whole Advent [sic] movement is founded, and if not correct, 'It is a fraud.' We shall clearly prove it to be so by the Word of God."[23] Riggle labored mightily to make good on that promise by challenging the accuracy of Uriah Smith's dating and chronology. Ranging freely across the entire Old Testament, Riggle stitched together an exegetical quilt that read some texts as literal historical descriptions, others as prophecies of the future, and still others typologically. When completed the polemic laid Smith's chronology to rest. However, "were it not for the dark leaven of Adventism," wrote Warner, "a few plain scriptures were all that need be given to point out the sanctuary of the New Testament, for all spiritually minded readers are very naturally led to understand that God's church is the sanctuary."[24] Typological hermeneutics took over as Warner and then Riggle endeavored to demonstrate that the Church of God movement and its theology of salvation was prophesied in Daniel and Revelation.

Warner and Riggle interpreted the Israelite tabernacle as an Old Testament type for the New Testament anti-type or reality of the church and the salvation that gave entrance to her. In this view the tabernacle's two main sections, the holy place and the most holy place, corresponded to the two works of grace in the Wesleyan theology of salvation. In the view of Warner and Riggle, the former was the anti-type corresponding to the Holy Place and the latter corresponding to the Most Holy Place. Christ was the door through which sinners gained admission to justification, having made the sinner's offering typified by the brazen altar that stood in the courtyard of the tabernacle. Christ also was seen as the means of entrance into the most holy place, the golden altar on which believers consecrated themselves for entire sanctification. Thereby they gained admission into the Holy of Holies, entire sanctification or perfect love.[25] Warner and Riggle thus were able to establish that the Church of God movement's theology of the church and its theology of salvation not only formed a seamless robe; they were grounded, even predicted, in the prophetic passages of the Bible.

Having established the biblical legitimacy of the Church of God movement, a section of the book written by Warner turned to an extended discussion of ecclesiology. The subject was the primitive church, but Warner's church-historical interpretation, bolstered by his typological study, enabled him to speak of the Church of God as the restoration of the primitive church in all of its pristine beauty. In describing the characteristics of the primitive church of the New Testament, Warner thought that he also described the movement. What were those characteristics?

Warner detailed a list of ten attributes characteristic of the primitive church and any contemporary church that claimed to be faithful to the New Testament standard. That standard specified particular definitions under the following rubrics: (1) divinity, (2) organization, (3) visibility, (4) oneness, (5) unity, (6) universality, (7) exclusiveness, (8) holiness, (9) unchangeableness, and (10) indestructibility.[26] In one respect Warner repeated the claims and descriptions found in his writing of twenty years previous. What was new here was a sense of urgency and a confidence born in his application of the church-historical and typological hermeneutic. In 1880 Warner believed that much was amiss in the world of denominational Christianity. He believed that a divided church was a reproach to God and was convinced that holiness was the divinely appointed means by which the division of Christians was to be healed. He called upon all true believers to answer the biblical cry, "Come out from among them and be ye separate." Beginning in the mid- '80s he discovered the hermeneutical tools that enabled him to make strong claims about the biblical origin and divine purpose of the Church of God movement. These claims show themselves perhaps most strongly in Warner's description of the exclusiveness of the primitive church.

By exclusive Warner meant that "all who are not in the church that Jesus founded are excluded from salvation and the Christian's hope."[27] This sounds remarkably similar to the famous dictum of Cyprian of Carthage, "Outside the church there is no salvation." But Warner meant that salvation was the door into the primitive church. Warner worshiped an exclusive Christ, the only one under whose name people could be saved. "The faith that he gave us is an exclusive faith; no other saves the soul. The truth of God is exclusive in its nature; everything contrary to it is false.... The one church that Jesus founded and named, and which is his own body, is also exclusive, for there is only 'one body in Christ.' "[28] Those unwilling to comply with the conditions of this exclusive community searched in vain for another church "with a wider door"; in Warner's view there was no other. He was unwilling to compromise this point in the least and saw it as a bone of contention between the saints and "denominational Christians." He located objections to the sermons of "God's Messengers," i. e. the flying messengers of the Church of God, in the movement's refusal to "recognize their earth-born institutions as being also God's churches."[29] Buoyed by its interpretation of biblical prophecy, the Church of God movement steadfastly repudiated all gestures of coopera- tion and recognition. In the process Warner heaped apocalyptic scorn on all who refused to see the exclusive truth of the Evening Light.

> It is true there is in these last days a large sisterhood of Protestant bodies calling themselves churches, but the Lamb's wife owes no kin to them. They are of an entirely different family. There mother is 'Mystery, babylon, the mother of harlots.' As God is one, only one religion can emanate from him. As 'God is not the author of confusion,' his church cannot be a split up and confused lot of rival institutions. He recognizes no sisterhood of churches.... Men come to us and say just what the devil sought of Christ: 'Let us alone.' 'Go on and preach what you believe, but let everybody else alone.' This is great blindness. If the true God would reign, Dagon, and all other gods must fall down, and have their heads broken off. If Christ be lifted up, antichrist must be demol- ished. The kingdom of God and the kingdom of darkness can not jointly flourish, nor even co-exist in the same heart. No man can preach the truth without knocking down error, any more than the darkness can hold sway after the light has come. So likewise, the church of the living God, which is the pillar and ground of the truth, must utterly exclude and antag- onize every counterfeit church. Hence, in the present evening light, which reveals the true fold, 'every founder is confounded by the graven image, for his molten image is falsehood, and there is no breath in them. They are vanity and the work of

errors; in the time of their visitation they shall perish'
(Jer 10:14–15). That time has now come; for the preaching of
the 'pillar and ground of the truth' demolishes the 'work of
error.' "[30]

This kind of apocalyptic rhetoric, employed by many others in books and
in the *Gospel Trumpet,* underwrote a separatism that drove the Church of
God movement into the most sectarian phase of its life during the next thirty
years. The saints of the Evening Light claimed to be the restored church of
the New Testament, an exclusive church that admitted no sin, certainly
not the sin of dividing the body of Christ. During these three decades the
majority of saints refused to recognize the legitimacy of other Christian
bodies and therefore refused cooperation as well. Church of God ministers
were loath to join interdenominational ministerial fellowships. They warned
the saints to keep their children away from Sunday schools operated by the
"sects" and discouraged attendance at non-Church of God revivals; even holiness movement leaders were compared to Nehemiah's adversaries Tobias and
Sanballat. And the movement as a whole refused to participate—other than
by sending observers—in such nascent ecumenical ventures as the Universal
Conference on Life and Work in Stockholm in 1925.[31] Non-cooperation,
grounded in apocalyptic exclusivism, was the watchword of this era.

Riggle completed *The Cleansing of the Sanctuary* by rehearsing the lines
of the church-historical hermeneutic employed by Schell a decade earlier.
The book's final section is titled "Conquests and Victories of the Church of
God" and traces the primitive church's conquests and victories throughout
Christian history. By "primitive church" Warner and Riggle were not speaking only historically. That is, they did not restrict the meaning of primitive
church to the period of ancient Christianity. They also understood the
phrase qualitatively; the attributes listed and exposited in their book
described as well the characteristics of any body of Christians who practiced
the New Testament standards of church life. In this view the primitive
church could appear at any historical moment. Thus Warner and Riggle were
able to account for the presence of the true church during all epochs of
Christian history, and since in their view the Church of God lived by the New
Testament standard, it, too, was the primitive church. "Prophecy and
Revelation" portrayed the successes of the primitive church during the New
Testament era and beyond. Once again the Roman Catholic Church and the
papacy in particular served as an ever-present whipping boy, the source of
every evil and corruption of Christianity. Riggle supplied several diagrams to
eliminate any lingering reservations. There readers could see how Popery,
the first beast of Revelation 13:1–8, was followed by a second, Protestantism,

as prophesied in Revelation 13:11–18. Nevertheless, in the midst of corruption the true church endured. Through the long, dark age of "popery" she was the woman of the wilderness described in Revelation 12:6, 14. During "the 350 years of the" cloudy day of Protestant hegemony she was the church that survived the "sectism" prophesied in Ezekiel 34:12 only to emerge in the Evening Light of the gospel day, the fulfillment of Zechariah 14:6–7.

The Cleansing of the Sanctuary gave the clearest, most detailed, and most extensive expression to that date of a mindset that had been developing in the Church of God movement for twenty years. The book also validated that mindset by appealing to the apocalyptic writings of the Bible, principally Daniel and the Revelation, books that were understood to be prophetic and which, when properly interpreted, revealed the course of the true church, the primitive church, through the centuries. Warner and Riggle thereby gave the Church of God the means by which it could point to the pages of the Bible itself as the location of the movement's origins. Guided by Warner and Riggle, the movement discovered its identity as the restored church of the New Testament. The book's apocalyptic rhetoric encouraged readers to adopt exclusivist practices that refused to acknowledge any other Christian body as a legitimate church.

Solidifying an Apocalyptic Identity

F. G. and Birdie Smith traveled as itinerant evangelists until 1912, when they accepted a two-year assignment as missionaries to Beirut, Lebanon. Just prior to their departure he published *The Evolution of Christianity* and while overseas he completed a manuscript for a one-volume topical commentary on the entire Bible. Published immediately upon the Smiths' return as *What the Bible Teaches,* the book was destined to become one of the most successful in Gospel Trumpet Company history, selling well over one hundred thousand copies. Freshly returned to the United States the couple had only briefly resumed their itinerant ministry when he was invited to take a position with the Gospel Trumpet Company as an editorial assistant in 1915. The widespread success of his books made him the front-runner among candidates to succeed E. E. Byrum, and the following June, Smith assumed responsibilities as the third editor of the *Gospel Trumpet.*

In F. G. Smith the Church of God movement found a voice that confidently unlocked and declared the prophetic truths in the apocalyptic symbols of the Book of Revelation. He staunchly defended those truths, believing that to do any less would have compromised his integrity. Not blessed with a strong voice, Smith did not enjoy a great reputation as a preacher. However, a large majority of the movement's ministers placed unbounded confidence in him, and he was often invited to address ministers' meetings, especially on the topic of the church as revealed in "prophecy and history." He possessed a very orderly, perhaps brilliant mind, and like virtually all first and second generation Church of God leaders was self-taught in matters pertaining to the Bible and theology. Smith was also adept when it came to church politics. He "had the kind of mind that would have made him an awesome [chess] player. He would have been a thoughtful, brilliant strategist, aggressive, anticipating the opponent with uncanny skill and the ability to make dramatic moves."[32] Above his formidable political and intellectual personal assets, it was Smith's unshakable confidence in his prophetic understanding of the church that made him a force to be reckoned with for nearly forty years. "He was a strong defender of the theological house that he had built, guarded it jealously, and promoted it endlessly."[33]

By the time Smith assumed the editor's desk his books had already established him as the movement's authoritative voice on church history and prophecy. His expertise in these areas was grounded in the church-historical hermeneutic he had inherited from Warner, Schell and, to a lesser degree, Riggle. The key element of this hermeneutic was its belief that Daniel and the Revelation, along with apocalyptic sections of other books such as Zechariah, were prophetic rather than apocalyptic. As such they were thought to contain an encoded map of the future of the church from the close of the New Testament era to the present. Smith became the unchallenged master of this method. He lectured widely on the topic of the church in prophecy, augmenting the spoken word with several charts that covered the entire front wall of all but the largest of church sanctuaries. These vividly painted charts gave Smith's listeners a visual path through the prophetic and historical details specified in his lectures. The charts lent visual clarity and credibility to Smith's vision of a divine process that had unfolded throughout two thousand years of Christian history culminating in the Church of God reformation movement. The wide popularity of his books both established his reputation and further strengthened the movement's sense of identity. "Although other writers were published by the G[ospel] T[rumpet] Company these two books [*The Revelation Explained* and *What the Bible Teaches*] together with Smith's editorials were accepted generally as standard literature until the early thirties."[34]

In the minds of Church of God ministers and laypersons who read Gospel Trumpet Company literature, Warner and Riggle had demolished Adventist claims to be the church prophesied by scripture. Their book also successfully appropriated the church-historical hermeneutic for the Church of God movement. No writer of the movement put that hermeneutic to clearer or more extensive use than F. G. Smith. It was the backbone of his three books on prophecy and history,[35] and also informed his *The Evolution of Christianity*[36] and the extremely influential *What the Bible Teaches*.[37]

Smith's books combined the church-historical hermeneutic with the authority that was conferred on the editor of the *Gospel Trumpet.* From early on the paper's editors were the established teaching authorities for the Church of God movement. Warner was the visionary. By means of his decisiveness and strong managerial instincts E. E. Byrum had brought both the paper and the movement, if not to prosperity, at least to doctrinal and organizational stability. Other writers, principally Schell, Warner, and Riggle, had produced books that made use of the church-historical reading of biblical apocalyptic. By 1916, when Smith took office, the two streams converged and, when combined with Smith's considerable personal and intellectual abilities, gave his writing an almost unchallenged stature in the Church of God movement.

The Revelation Explained, as it subtitle states, is "an exposition, text by text, of the Apocalypse of St. John." Smith approached this exposition with a methodology that endeavored to find appropriate analogies for the symbols contained in the book. Thus a horn was said to symbolize strength, and an eye or scepter majesty. Smith also stipulated that analogies could not be arbitrarily applied but had to conform to nature. For example, "we violate nature when we attempt to make a ferocious tiger the symbol of an innocent child, or represent a blood-thirsty tyrant by the symbol of a lamb."[38] The only exception to this general rule gave a nod to typology; "certain things connected with God's chosen people under the old dispensation are considered proper symbols to represent similar things or events in the New Testament dispensation."[39] Thus, although inanimate, the vessels and furnishings of the Jerusalem temple could be analogically employed to signify matters pertaining to the life of the church. Smith was confident that "symbols are not words, but things, chosen [by the biblical writers] to represent other things; and by a careful study of the symbols themselves we can ascertain where to look for their fulfillment."[40] Smith did not base his interpretation of apocalyptic symbols on appeals to the work of other writers but on the nature of the symbols themselves.

Smith's interpretation of Revelation was based on the premise that the book's prophecies were arranged in six parallel series. Each series was thought to cover the same ground, sometimes with the same symbols, sometimes using new ones, but always capable of being understood by applying the method of natural analogies. Following the blueprint drawn by Schell, Warner, and Riggle, Smith constructed his exegetical edifice. Thus the numbers 1,260 and 350 figure prominently in his work, attached once again as they had been previously to the starting point of AD 270. Smith read the first series of prophecies, found in Revelation 6, to make the famous four horses conform to the church historical chronology. The white horse symbolized the pure age of the New Testament church and the red horse paganism's growing opposition to the truth. The black horse signified the church's apostasy and the pale horse the papacy down to 1530. The second series of prophecies, Revelation 7, recounted the future of the God's servants through the same period of history. The third series, Revelation 8–11, considered "Mohammedanism" as a subset of the general theme of the persecution of the true church by Catholics and Protestants. The fourth, fifth, and sixth series prophesied the coming of "Great Babylon," first as Catholicism, the "Mother of Harlots," and then secondly her daughter, Protestantism. Whether horses, dragons, horns, a woman and "man-child," or plagues, in Smith's eyes Revelation's symbols conveyed the same restorationist message. The church had fallen from a golden age of purity into 1,260 years of paganism thinly disguised as Catholicism. Protestantism represented a partial restoration of the truth but in the end was just as corrupt for having divided the body of Christ. Through the centuries a faithful remnant of true believers had endured fire and trial, often at the hands of the harlot and her daughter. At last, in 1880, the pure light of the gospel day had returned to shine on the final gathering of the saints before the end of time.

Smith asserted that the Church of God movement was the center of the final gathering of the saints. His exposition repeatedly claims that the movement is the fulfillment of Revelation's prophecies. One extended quotation will serve as an example.

> I call to witness every child of God who has been with the present reformation [i.e. the Church of God movement] from its beginning, if there were not three special phases of the development of the truth, as follows: 1. A wonderful revival of spirituality among a few of God's chosen ones, caused by the "everlasting gospel" being revealed to them as never before. 2. The knowledge of the truth and deep experience thus obtained prepared the way for the next step, which was the discovery that the "churches" were part of the great Babylon of Revelation and were in a fallen condition, "a hold of every foul spirit, and a cage of every unclean and hateful bird." Chap 18. 2, 3. Hence the cry went up, "Babylon is fallen, is fallen." 3. Then followed immediately the message to God's people to "flee out of the midst of babylon and deliver every man his

soul," warning them that no one could any longer bear the mark of the beast or worship his image without forfeiting eternal salvation and the fearful judgments of heaven that would soon descend upon every one who refused to obey the message and to walk in the light. The last two phrases, which apply to Babylon, are the same and in the same order as the description given in chapter 18:1–4. First an angel from heaven cries mightily with a strong voice, "Babylon the great is fallen, is fallen;" and then "another voice" from heaven says, "COME OUT OF HER, MY PEOPLE." The three successive phases of the message are now all combined in one, and God is gathering his holy remnant "out of all places where they have been scattered in the cloudy and dark day" (Ezek 34:12) into the one body of Jesus Christ. Hallelujah!"[41]

F. G. Smith's exposition of the Book of Revelation culminated more than a decade of growing interest in an interpretation of biblical apocalyptic that gave a fresh validation to the message of the Church of God movement. That this detailed exposition had come from the pen of the *Trumpet* editor only strengthened its appeal and credibility. Guided by Smith and others who wrote in this vein, Church of God people believed that their status in the Evening Light gave them a clarity of vision impossible to achieve for those who were still in Mystery Babylon's thrall. Since the Church of God stood clear of the apostasy, the saints alone saw the scriptural truth that Babylonian blindness obscured for all others. By 1910 a growing number of Church of God people believed that the movement was the culmination of the historical process by which God was bringing light out of darkness, holiness out of sin, and knowledge out of ignorance. To be a part of "this reformation," as they began to refer to the movement, was to be able to read scripture rightly. To do so meant the ability to read signs of the times that pointed to the movement's emergence in the Evening Light while they simultaneously warned of the imminent end of the age.

What the Bible Teaches—A Manual of Biblical Theology

Systematic theology is not a theological endeavor natural to the Church of God movement. This is not to say that the movement has lacked theology or methods for reflecting on it. However doctrine has expressed itself primarily as a set of practices, and the primary form for reflection and extending theological understanding has taken the form of narrative. In one sense the church-historical hermeneutic constituted an apocalyptically grounded narrative of the whole sweep of Christian history. But Church of God people were accustomed to narrative reflection on the much smaller and personal scale of their own lives. Whenever they stood in a prayer meeting or camp meeting service to testify to what God had done for them, whenever they wrote a letter of testimony to the *Gospel Trumpet,* Church of God people situated the story of their lives within the larger narrative of redemption. Such testimonies were the dominant form of theological reflection on the doctrinal practices that constituted them as a church. The enterprise generally understood by the phrase "systematic theology" did not appear in Church of God circles until 1925 with the publication of Russell R. Byrum's *Christian Theology.*

The most influential theological textbook for the two decades immediately prior to the publication of Russell Byrum's book was F. G. Smith's *What the Bible Teaches.* As with *The Revelation Explained,* in *What the Bible Teaches* Smith provided the Church of God movement with exactly the right kind of book at just the right moment. To begin with, Smith avoided the perjorative word *theology,* in favor of *Bible.* John W. V. Smith rightly pointed to the importance of the Bible in the early Church of God. There was a "Bible" way of salvation, "Bible" proofs of sanctification, "Bible" holiness, and when they gathered for worship Church of God people sang, "We will worship Thee in the Bible way as the evening light doth shine." It was important to believe only what the Bible taught and not worry about the integration of revelation with other forms of human knowledge. F. G. Smith's *What the Bible Teaches* aimed at systematically—meaning in an organized manner—presenting "the fundamental principles of truth contained in the Holy Scriptures."[42]

Smith thought of this book as a doctrinal presentation. One of its real virtues, in his eyes and in the eyes of his readers, was that it was written in "plain, easily understood language."[43] It is best described as a topically organized biblical theology. Although Smith arranged his discussion in a manner that resembled a classically organized systematics, that structure actually served only to organize Smith's exposition of the Bible. In the final analysis Smith's intention was to present "the true doctrinal standards of the Bible."[44] He employed a method that identified topics, e. g. God and his attributes, and then proceeded to exposit that topic by listing biblical passages that spoke to it. To explain God's self-existence, for example, Smith wrote, " 'The Father hath life in himself' (John 5:26). 'For with thee is the fountain of life' (Ps 36:9). He is underived and inexhaustible."[45] Whether in consideration of the doctrine of God, the conditions of salvation, Jesus' saving atonement or the call to holiness, Smith relentlessly piled text upon text to show the plain meaning of scripture. In the process the book also evidenced how completely he had mastered the Bible's contents.

It must be added that it seems never to have occurred to Smith that there might be a difference between what the Bible teaches and what he said it taught. It is not quite accurate to say that Smith thought that his interpretation of Scripture was correct. Rather, he thought that he simply was giving the plain meaning of the Bible; the idea of hermeneutics almost vanished. The singular exception was the apocalyptic or, once again, "prophetic" books, the symbolic nature of which required interpretation. But here *to interpret* meant to Smith only to disclose the plain meaning that was there in the texts themselves once decoded. Thus his exposition of the church is titled "The Church in Prophecy and History" and restates the position he elaborated in *The Revelation Explained.* In Smith's mind, the church-historical hermeneutic did not produce an interpretation of Revelation; it simply explained what the book in actuality taught.

Although one should not rely heavily on quantitative assessments in theology, it is noteworthy that the church assumed a disproportionately prominent place in Smith's discussion. It occupies two major sections of the entire book, and he devoted considerably more space to his discussion of the church than any other topic. For example, where Smith required just twelve pages to cover what the Bible teaches about God, eighty-two pages were required to discuss the church in prophecy and history. Smith's ideas about the church rested on his understanding of prophecy. This in turn meant that the idea of prophecy had assumed determinative importance for Smith. It had become much more than a key theological category. By 1914 he had concluded that Christianity stands or falls on "prophecy and its exact fulfillment," and that it was this that distinguished Christianity from all other religions of the world.[46] Prophecy had become a determinative idea for the man who less than two years after the publication of *What the Bible Teaches* became editor of the *Gospel Trumpet.*

In 1916 Smith assumed the most influential position in the Church of God movement. The editor was the movement's primary theological authority. From the very beginning, loose organization and an antipathy to anything hinting of "man-rule" made the editor the movement's *de facto* leader; somebody had to have a post office box. Time and the repeated public presence of the editor's name combined to reinforce his prominence. When, in 1914 the editor's office assumed responsibility for the ministers list, political muscle was added to a skeletal structure constructed by precedent and need. Smith did not create or manufacture this state of affairs; he inherited it from E. E. Byrum. In fact, Smith became the editor only after Byrum reluctantly resigned in response to mounting criticism that he wielded too much power, both within the company and in the Church of God movement.[47] Only one year later a momentous decade of institutionalization began, but two key buttresses supporting the editor's authority remained—his platform via the *Gospel Trumpet* and his supervision of the ministers list.[48] Other leaders were emerging, and their relationship to the editor would eventually have to be resolved. Nevertheless, at the beginning of his editorship Smith's theological voice was the loudest in the Church of God movement. The inherent authority of his office only amplified an enthusiasm for biblical prophecy that reached back to 1884 and bore the stamp of some of the movement's most highly regarded leaders. It should be no great surprise that Smith's books, especially *The Revelation Explained* and *What the Bible Teaches*, proved to be of such great influence for two decades and more.

The writings of F. G. Smith, as well as the earlier work of W. G. Schell, D. S. Warner, and H. M. Riggle, grounded the Church of God movement's identity in the apocalyptic books of the Bible. Church of God people sang, "There's a mighty reformation sweeping o'er the land," oblivious to contradictory statistics that made such singing appear little more than an overblown assertion. That they sang confidently despite all appearances to the contrary rested on their understanding of the church in prophecy and history. Unlike those two little horns of the apocalypse, the Lutheran and the Reformed churches, the movement could not point with pride to centuries of history and distinguished founders whose names all Protestants knew and revered. Instructed by Smith and the other apocalypticists, the movement trashed that history. Better than find themselves in the 350 years of the "cloudy day," the saints located themselves and the movement in the pages of the Bible itself. Why settle for a sixteenth-century historical location when a Church of God chart-lecturer could pinpoint the movement's origins in the words of St. John the Revelator? For little handfuls of saints who gathered in the face of the overwhelming Baptist presence in Alabama or the Lutheran hegemony in Minnesota, the awareness that the saints were part of a movement prophesied from of old gave them a heady confidence. The history of denominations was the story of a false church. Understood rightly, the Bible's prophecy corrected history and pointed to its fulfillment with the beginning of the Church of God movement. That was something to sing about, and sing lustily.

Notes

1. (Battle Creek, Mich: Review and Herald Publishing Association, 1882).

2. Warner's copy, complete with marginal notes and interleaved pages with notes for a planned book on topics similar to those Smith had discussed, is housed in the D. S. Warner Library, Archives of the Church of God.

3. Smith, *Thoughts on Daniel and Revelation*, 279.

4. Ibid., 267. This section is the only portion of the book where Warner underlined passages and made marginal notations.

5. John W. V. Smith, *The Quest for Holiness and Unity*, 98. For a detailed and complete early example of Warner's church-historical hermeneutic cf. "The Great Papal Beast," *GT* (August 1, 1886), 4.

6. W. G. Schell, *The Biblical Trace of the Church, from Her Birth to the End of Time: Showing the True Origin and Termination of Sectism and Proving that We are Near the End of the World* (Grand Junction: Gospel Trumpet Publishing Company, 1893).

7. Although he did not begin at AD 270 Uriah Smith identified the 1,260 years as the reign of papal darkness. Smith, *Thoughts on Daniel and the Revelation*, 351ff.

8. Ibid., 9–21.

9. Thus Schell, "Think of the victims of the papal bonfires in England under the reign of 'Bloody Mary'; the bloody fields of Scotland and the valleys of Piedmont; the gutters washed in the streets of Paris by the blood of the victims of St. Bartholomew's Day; and of the countless victims of the inquisition in Spain and other European states. Well has it been predicted of popery, he 'made war against the saints and prevailed against them.' " Ibid., 40.

10. Ibid., 40–41.

11. Ibid., 91–92.

12. Ibid., 93.

13. Schell employed the familiar device of adding the Roman numeral letters in *VICARIUS FILII DEI* to assign 666 as a reference to the Pope. In the case of Protestants Schell said that the number referred "approximately" to the number of Protestant denominations, a conclusion that he based on his own collection of Protestant denominations. Ibid., 110–111.

14. Ibid., 141–142.

15. Ibid., 143.

16. Ibid., 176.

17. Ibid., 209. Some of these conclusions were quite fanciful. Schell believed, for example, that as an eschatological sign the rumble of freight trains and the smoke and fire that belched from a steam locomotive fulfilled Nahum 2:3–5, "The chariots shall be with flaming torches in the day of his preparation and the fir trees shall be terribly shaken. The chariots shall rage in the streets, they shall jostle one against another in the broad ways; they shall seem like torches, they shall run like the lightnings."

18. Ibid., 212.

19. "Her Plagues Have Come," *GT* (Feb. 22, 1894), 1.

20. "Gog and Magog Gathering Together," *GT* (Mar. 1, 1894), 1.

21. "Healing of the Beast," *GT* (Feb. 21, 1895), 1.

22. D. S. Warner and H. M. Riggle, *The Cleansing of the Sanctuary* (Moundsville: Gospel Trumpet Publishing Company, 1903), 5.

23. Ibid., 38.

24. Ibid., 74.

25. Cf Riggle's diagram, *The Cleansing of the Sanctuary*, 98.

26. Cf, *The Cleansing of the Sanctuary*, 230–279. The last attribute was added by Riggle.

27. Ibid., 265.

28. Ibid.

29. Ibid.

30. Ibid., 266–267.

31. C. J. Blewitt sailed from New York to attend this meeting. He was accompanied by Carl Forsberg,

missionary to Sweden, who met Blewitt in Europe.

32. Robert H. Reardon, "Movers and Shakers in the Church of God," (unpublished ms: n.d.), 18. Other characterizations of F. G. Smith and his influence on the Church of God can be found in W. Dale Oldham, *Giants Along My Path* (Anderson, Ind: Warner Press, 1973), 251–2; John A. Morrison, *As the River Flows* (Anderson, Ind: Anderson College Press, n.d.), 19; and Robert H. Reardon, *The Early Morning Light* (Anderson, Ind: Warner Press, n.d.), 39–45.

33. Reardon, "Movers and Shakers," Ibid.

34. Ibid.

35. *The Revelation Explained* (Anderson, Ind: Gospel Trumpet Company, 1908); *The Last Reformation* (Anderson, Ind: Gospel Trumpet Company, 1919); and *Prophetic Lectures on Daniel and the Revelation* (Anderson, Ind: Gospel Trumpet Company, 1941).

36. (Anderson, Ind: Gospel Trumpet Company, 1911).

37. (Anderson, Ind: Gospel Trumpet Company, 1914).

38. Smith, *The Revelation Explained,* 23. To make sure that his readers got the point and the book's general direction Smith added one last example: "A disgusting, polluted harlot may be the proper symbol of an apostate church, but of the pure, holy church of God—*never*. A proper correspondence must be kept. We must follow nature strictly." Ibid.

39. Ibid., 24.

40. Ibid., 26.

41. Ibid., 274–5, Smith's emphases.

42. The phrase is the subtitle to Smith's book.

43. Smith, *What the Bible Teaches,* 7.

44. Ibid., 5.

45. Ibid., 42.

46. Ibid., 32.

47. John W. V. Smith, *The Quest for Holiness and Unity,* 213.

48. In 1917 the Ministers List was considerably expanded and became the *Yearbook of the Church of God.*

Chapter 6
Contended Practices

The early Church of God movement invited all Christians to take a stand for the truth with their brothers and sisters in true holiness and unity. During the movement's first three decades people from several denominations answered the summons. Methodist and Methodist-related bodies provided the largest source of "come-outers." Jeremiah, George, and Mary Cole were typical of many other Methodists who affiliated with the holiness movement. It was through that association that they came into contact with the Church of God, either with individuals or often simply through copies of the *Gospel Trumpet* left in a train coach, on a park bench, or likewise indiscriminately distributed. Jeremiah Cole met D. S. Warner for the first time at a meeting of the Western Union Holiness Association. Similarly, A. B. Palmer, licensed as a local preacher in the Methodist church at Oshtemo, Michigan, abandoned denominational Christianity after attending the Church of God camp meeting at Bangor, Michigan. The Jerry City, Ohio holiness association appears to have been a very important source of folk who, like Sarah Smith, "saw the church," came out of Babylon, and affiliated with the Church of God. Methodists were an important stream that fed the movement's widening current, but they were by no means the only denomination represented among the early come-outers.

Warner, of course, had belonged to the Churches of God. Other members of the Winebrenner group, notably Joseph and Allie Fisher, also affiliated with new movement. Another significant stream of come-outers flowed from churches of the Radical Reformation. The Byrum brothers, Enoch and Noah, who were such pivotal figures at the Gospel Trumpet Company, and their brother Robert, also heavily involved in the company's fortunes as a builder, were all raised in a United Brethren family as was their uncle, H. C. Wickersham. Another family that provided important leadership to the movement was Jacob W. and A. L. Byers, whose father, Andrew, had been a minister in a River Brethren Church near the family home at Albany, Illinois. The elder Byers came under heavy criticism for advocating the holiness cause, and after learning of the Church of God through the *Gospel Trumpet* he met Warner in 1888 and made his stand. The Byers and Byrum clans were but a small segment of a relatively sizable Radical Reformation element in the early Church of God movement. Between 1881 and 1886, 11 percent of those who corresponded with the *Gospel Trumpet* said that they were formerly of the Winebrennarian church. Come-outers from any of six different Methodist-related denominations accounted for roughly half of all correspondents. However, other than the Methodist church bodies, United Brethren and Mennonites comprised the largest group of come-outers, exceeding even the number of former Winebrennarians. Professor Val Clear contends that the determinative experience of the frontier prompted these refugees from other traditions to forget their European roots. "Nor were they concerned with religious matters from the east coast. They were as little aware of any social indebtedness they had to previous religious groups in the United States. As far as they were concerned the only wise men who came from the east were those in the New Testament. But of one thing they were firmly convinced: the religion they observed around them was false and despicable."[1] Roots may have been severed, but some inherited practices retained life. A former Mennonite, Mrs. C. E. Byers, whose husband pastored the saints in Springfield, Ohio and presided over congregations in the surrounding region, set very conservative standards of conduct for this heavily influential church.

The early come-outers were certain of their vision of a church that was made holy and one through the power of the Holy Spirit. They were equally certain that God had called them to embody that unity and they abandoned their former denominations to become members of the true body of Christ. However, they neither uniformly nor completely abandoned all the religious practices of their former associations. In fact, come-outers carried some practices into the Church of God movement where they became part of its doctrinal and practical life. Footwashing, for example, was practiced in the Winebrenner group as well as among several Radical Reformation denominations. That a significant number of saints had come out of these groups is good reason to think that footwashing was likely to become a permanent fixture of Church of God practice. However, not all practices were successfully transplanted. Two that were not, and which became quite contentious within the movement's doctrinal life, were pacifism and the practice of speaking in tongues.

Pacifism in the Early Church of God

The Church of God commitment to pacifism appears to have developed in the context of the Spanish-American War. Warner, himself a Civil War veteran, was gone, and the Byrums—Enoch and Noah—were owners of the *Gospel Trumpet* with Enoch the movement's leader. He espoused pacifism, understandable enough given his United Brethren upbringing, but by no means was Byrum alone in this commitment. Others in the movement who shared this conviction often grounded their views in the practice of holiness. As warclouds gathered, writers began voicing their convictions in the paper, which tutored its readers on the issues of war and peace.

In 1897 two *Trumpet* articles extended the practices of holiness and love of neighbor to include Christian pacifism. A writer named Ira Pendleton was not content to practice holiness only by refraining from certain forms of amusement or personal adornment. He insisted on enlarging the practice of holiness to include Christian behavior towards one's neighbors. Pendleton then defined the "neighbor" in the most inclusive terms possible, saying that those who live on distant continents are as much the Christian's neighbor as those who live next door. If people would keep the love commandment, which sanctified Christians were empowered to follow, then "wars and disputes would be at an end. No longer would we hear of army arrayed against army—taking the lives of their fellow human beings—but warfare would be considered a disgrace to humanity, and its instruments beaten into plowshares and pruning hooks; and the vast amount of wealth expended, be applied to a much better end."[2] Later in that same year another writer asserted that Christians not only were forbidden to injure their enemies, but also were forbidden even to delight in their afflictions. The natural human desire was to repay evil for evil, but such an attitude was as far from true Christianity as heaven from hell. Jesus set his followers the example of forgiveness, and only those who had been genuinely sanctified would enjoy his favor by following that example.[3]

Early in 1898 a reader sent the *Trumpet* this question for its "Questions Answered" feature: "If a man has enlisted in the service of the United States Army before he was saved, is it his duty to desert when he becomes a Christian?" For a pacifist, Editor Byrum offered rather strange counsel. Citing Romans 13 he declared that desertion would violate the command to be subject to the governing powers and advised the questioner to remain in uniform. Besides, Byrum was confident that "God can keep him saved where he is until he has served his time."[4] A few months later Byrum took a very different posture as he replied to a growing number of letters asking the

Trumpet's advice on the question whether a Christian should go to war. Byrum flatly stated,

> We answer no. Emphatically no. There is no place in the New Testament wherein Christ gave instruction to his followers to take the life of a fellow-man.
>
> In olden times it was an "eye for an eye and a tooth for a tooth." "Love your neighbor and hate your enemy."
>
> In this gospel dispensation it is quite different, Jesus says: "But I say unto you, do good to them that despitefully use you," and so forth—Matthew 4:44. Avenge not yourselves." "If thine enemy hunger, feed him; if he thirst, give him drink"—not shoot him.[5]

Byrum wrote in a tone suggesting that he expected his readers to follow the paper's position on this question. Furthermore, he advised men on how to establish status as conscientious objectors.

For nearly a decade following the Spanish-American War the *Trumpet* occasionally ran articles on the subject of pacifism. Readers would find the paper's position staked out in such sentences as: "As to going to war and fighting, there is one text that ought to settle this question for every spiritually minded person. It is Romans 13:10, 'Love worketh no ill to his neighbor: therefore love is the fulfilling of the law.' "[6] "I should refuse to go to war or obey an officer's command to shoot anyone. We are followers of the 'Prince of Peace' and 'the weapons of our warfare are not carnal.' "[7]

Byrum thought that Christians should not participate in warfare. As wholly sanctified believers they were empowered to follow Jesus' example regarding the law of love for the neighbor, even when that neighbor turned out to be an enemy. On the other hand, Byrum took seriously biblical texts such as Romans 13 that conferred on governments an authority not to be discounted. Just as in the necktie controversy, here Byrum also tried to steer something of a middle course. He thought that Christians should take the loving—not fighting—Savior as their moral exemplar on the matter of non-violence. But Byrum was also prepared to grant the state a moral legitimacy that eventually would undercut the church-wide practice of pacifism. He thought that pacifism was the right and proper practice for Christians while he simultaneously affirmed that those same Christians should always obey the governing authorities. In time these affirmations would pull in opposing directions, rendering pacifism untenable as a widespread practice in the Church of God.

World War I both disclosed and heightened the tension between the contradictory tendencies in Byrum's thought. In the years before the United States entered the fray, the *Gospel Trumpet* condemned war generally and encouraged Christians to refrain from participating. At the same time, the paper printed news from European battlefields, including some letters written by German soldiers. These men had been converted through the efforts of Church of God missionaries and evangelists who worked out of a mission established in 1907 at Essen. Once drafted into the German army, these men acted out the contradictory positions of Church of God leaders in the United States. Saints in the German army attempted to evangelize their comrades, but they also accepted their duty as soldiers. Some reported that they had been only slightly wounded, and they coveted the prayers of the saints that God would protect them from the sin that inevitably was part of military camp life.[8] The *Trumpet* passed these requests on to its readers while its editorials continued to condemn the war:

> Think of a man who has been taught all of his lifetime that it is a terrible crime to take the life of another, think of that man as he gazes upon his bayonet bloody from the charge!... Does he feel satisfied because he has risked his life in defense of his country? It would have been more natural to have risked his life in saving the life of others and he would have been deserving of much more honor."[9]

The early years of World War I presented conflicting images of Church of God pacifism. The *Gospel Trumpet* reported battlefield news from German soldiers without condemning them for fighting in battle. However, the paper also reported news from Denmark that two young men from Church of God missionary congregations there had been arrested and imprisoned for refusing to bear arms. While the *Trumpet* praised these Danish saints as Christian martyrs, it also printed this testimony from Robert Girke, a convert to the Church of God and a German soldier: "I am still saved and sanctified and my desire is to faithfully and firmly follow Jesus."[10]

The *Gospel Trumpet* continued its opposition to war after F. G. Smith succeeded Byrum as editor. In the last days of Byrum's tenure the paper's anti-war stance sharpened as it opposed the growing American sentiment for war preparedness and sharply criticized ministers who called for national mobilization.[11] Byrum also volunteered his advice to every Christian who refrained from going to war. However, some Church of God men did volunteer for military service, and to them Byrum promised that they would not be "un-Christianized" for going into battle.[12] He could make this promise because Byrum thought that "there is nothing wrong in being a soldier, but it is wrong to kill people."[13] Although he did not specify noncombatant service as an alternative, Byrum considered that an acceptable form of Christian military service despite his strong opposition to war.[14] Smith's pacifist commitments ran as deep as his predecessor's, if not even deeper. Along with Adam W. Miller and others, Smith was a cofounder of the Peace Fellowship of the Church of God. However, Smith was not reared in a historic peace church. His pacifism was an extension of the practice of holy living, and at least as early as 1911 he had asserted, "It is evident that the taking of human life is not in accordance with the spiritual precepts of the gospel."[15] As the United States hovered on the brink of war, Editor Smith spoke for the entire movement on the war issue. He said, "The general sentiment among us as the Church of God—a sentiment based on the teaching of the New Testament and enforced by our own religious convictions and conscientious scruples—is and has been adverse to our taking human life."[16] The *Trumpet* backed up this statement by repeatedly printing advice for male readers to follow when reporting to local draft boards.

In the face of the movement's clearly stated opposition to war it is somewhat surprising that the *Gospel Trumpet* also identified with patriotism and expressed its sincere appreciation for the United States flag.[17] However, in this and other ways the fundamental ambivalence inherent in Byrum's original view continued under Smith. Young men were never criticized and certainly not condemned for going into battle. Out of concern for the spiritual welfare of the troops the paper began a campaign to "Save Our Soldiers" through the distribution of religious literature. As the war progressed the advertisements for this campaign adopted an increasingly patriotic tone. Even as President Wilson had been unable to sustain a policy of neutrality, so also Smith and other leaders slid toward greater support for the war effort. Thus a 1918 *Trumpet* article ran out a logic that said any person who sells grain or buys postage stamps or pays taxes implicitly supports the war effort.[18] There could be no neutrality, and thus Christians had to come to terms, stated the article, with the fact that they held dual citizenship; they were citizens of the nation-state as well as the kingdom of God. Since the former claimed the duty to promote just relations between humans, and because "we owe a duty to the Government that has done so much for us," the saints were to prove themselves loyal citizens and buy Liberty Bonds.[19] The movement's ambivalence also appeared in the noteworthy absence of advice to its younger readers on the issue of pacifism. Throughout the period of the war the *Trumpet* made no statement on the practice in its regular feature, "Advice to Young People." Youthful readers were frequently warned of the evils of the dance hall, the theatre, movie houses, and immodest dress. But on the issue of war and killing, the issue on which it had spoken so candidly, the *Gospel Trumpet* offered nothing to young people between 1914 and 1918.

In matters of Christian truth the Church of God movement had taken an exclusivist position. The saints refused compromise with both the world and denominational Babylon. However, they did not see the struggle between allegiance to church and state in the same terms. In fact, the fundamental ambivalence of movement practices concerning war and peace appears to have largely eliminated a sense of conflict. Church of God writers distinguished between the spheres of civil and spiritual law. They affirmed the latter as the higher authority; Christians should obey God rather than human beings. And yet at the same time saints also affirmed the civil law as necessary to determine justice in a fallen world and consequently the state as the legitimate executive of that law. Believers were therefore to respect the civil law unless it conflicted with the spiritual, and the *Trumpet* extended this respect to the notion of a duty owed to the state "that has done so much for us."[20] Such an ambivalent position left the Church of God movement without a clear and consistent practice concerning Christian pacifism.

The Early Church of God and Glossolalia

Theologically speaking, the early Church of God depended heavily on the belief that the Holy Spirit actively engaged the church both corporately and individually. The Holy Spirit was said to govern the church through the spiritual gifts distributed to its members. The same Spirit worked the unity of all Christians by sanctifying them, perfecting them in the love that the saints insisted was the basis of Christian unity. The Spirit called people into ministry and flung them to distant missionary shores. Church of God writers frequently attributed their insights to the Holy Spirit, who had illumined their minds and hearts. It is not surprising then, that other Christian testimony to the Spirit's work attracted the attention of Church of God people. One such testimony involved the experience of glossolalia, "speaking in tongues," and the early Church of God movement manifested a wide range of responses to this experience and those who testified to receiving it.[21]

The phenomenon of speaking in tongues is widely associated with the emergence of the Pentecostal movement in American Christianity. That movement began in a revival that started in an abandoned African Methodist Episcopal church building at 312 Azusa Street in Los Angeles in 1906.[22] The Azusa Street revival and the Pentecostal movement that it spawned claimed far more than the ecstatic experience that many consider its trademark. The movement also claimed to have returned to the experience and practices of the first-century church formed on the day of Pentecost. This claim Pentecostals obviously shared with the early Church of God movement. The former referred in particular to the miraculous experience of the "baptism of the Holy Spirit," also following the Acts of the Apostles, marked by the experience of speaking in tongues. The Azusa Street revival is certainly neither the first nor the only incidence of glossolalia in the history of Christianity, but the movement that spawned has had the most wide-ranging impact.

The Church of God movement was directly connected to the Azusa Street revival through the preaching of William Joseph Seymour,[23] considered by some to be the founder of modern Pentecostalism. Seymour was born in Louisiana in 1870, where he taught himself to read and was formed by the African American Protestantism that was his cultural inheritance. At age twenty-five he traveled north to Indianapolis, where he joined a Black congregation of the Methodist Episcopal Church. Seymour's biographer believes that the decision to join a Black Methodist congregation rather than a congregation of the African Methodist Episcopal Church indicates that Seymour was particularly concerned to find racial reconciliation.[24] From Indianapolis he moved to Cincinnati in 1900, where he was influenced by the holiness preacher Martin Wells Knapp before affiliating with a group of people from the Church of God movement who were known simply as the Evening Light saints. Knapp and Seymour shared a fervent belief in the imminent return of Christ and the practice of divine healing. That the saints also shared these convictions and moreover practiced an understanding of Christian unity that transcended racial barriers made them especially attractive to Seymour. The early Church of God was one of the very few groups to ignore the color line drawn through much of American Protestantism. This feature drew African Americans to the Church of God movement.[25] In Cincinnati Seymour answered a call to the ministry and was ordained by the saints there. In 1903 he returned to the South and eventually made his home in Jackson, Mississippi.

In 1905, still in Jackson, Seymour learned from a Black holiness minister named Lucy Farrow how she had experienced the gift of speaking in tongues while serving as governess in the family of Charles Fox Parham. Parham was a one-time Methodist minister whose unorthodox theological views prompted him to leave that denomination in 1894. Once severed from these moorings, Parham sailed into many an ecclesiastical port, from the Bible and Missionary Training School of A. B. Simpson to Alexander Dowie's "Zion City." By January 1901 Parham, then leader of a small band of students at his "College of Bethel" in Topeka, Kansas, had become convinced that the experience of speaking in tongues was indisputable evidence of the baptism of the Holy Spirit. After a series of meetings in Kansas, Oklahoma, and Missouri, Parham moved to Houston, Texas in 1905 and opened an independent mission that quickly grew into a Bible institute. Upon hearing Lucy Farrow's testimony, William Seymour journeyed to Houston and enrolled in Parham's school.

From Houston Seymour moved to Los Angeles, where he began to preach the message that he had learned from Parham. Having been locked out of one holiness mission because of his radical teaching, Seymour started holding meetings in the home of a friend. Soon a revival began that swelled numbers to a point where a larger building had to be found. The group moved into an abandoned church building on Azusa Street, and the revival began to spread even further. Seymour preached a message that emphasized divine healing, the imminent return of Christ, sanctification, the experience of glossolalia as the sign of baptism by the Holy Spirit, and the unity of all believers who had been so baptized.[26]

The experience of speaking in tongues was discussed in the Church of God years before William Seymour's preaching ignited the Azusa Street revival. D. S. Warner and other early leaders saw the movement as the restoration of the New Testament church. This vision became more sharply defined after they learned to read biblical prophecy along church-historical lines. Committed as they were to the belief that the movement restored apostolic faith and practice, early Church of God leaders reflected on and believed in the manifestations of divine power recounted in the Acts of the Apostles. A group asserting that it bore the marks of the true New Testament church would have to come to terms with New Testament references to believers who spoke in unknown tongues. Early Church of God descriptions of their worship services placed such emphasis on the Holy Spirit's presence in and guidance of worship that other manifestations of the Spirit's presence, such as speaking in tongues, had to be seriously considered.[27] Those descriptions portray a style of worship that was "orderly," but also free, enthusiastic, and expressive.[28] It is important to note that the boundaries of the Church of God movement were quite permeable in the late nineteenth-century. The movement's affirmation that it had no creed but the Bible made room for people who had their own slant on one or another doctrinal practice. The broad interface between the early Church of God movement and other holiness radicals, as seen in the example of the Annapolis, Ohio assembly meeting, opened the door to advocates of radical holiness and, later, Pentecostal theology and practices. This blurred boundary between the saints and even more radical Christians existed within a broader interface between the holiness movement and emerging Pentecostalism.[29]

Already in the decade of the 1880s the saints described occasions where some worshipers spoke in tongues. Sarah Smith (1822–1908) was already a leader in the Jerry City, Ohio Holiness Association when she began reading the *Gospel Trumpet* in the 1880s.[30] Its teaching on Christian unity agreed with ideas that she had been forming, and Smith affiliated with the Church of God. In 1885 D. S. Warner invited her to join his "evangelistic company," a small band of five men and women that evangelized throughout the Midwest, South, and southern Ontario. In 1888 "Mother" Smith described meetings that were held not far from her Jerry City home in these words:

> Praise God this meeting will never be forgotten. It was a meeting of wonderful power, of joy and salvation. A few souls were gloriously saved and sanctified wholly, filled with the power of God, and were made to speak with new tongues. One sister came from Fayette, O. She was a member of the M[ethodist] E[piscopal] sect and thought we should not say so much against the sects. But she had an honest heart, and when she saw the pure light of the Gospel, she received the truth and the Lord saved and fully sanctified her by the Holy Spirit.[31]

Smith did not specify what she meant by "new tongues," but a year earlier Warner had left no doubt about his disapproval of disorderly or ecstatic outbursts in the midst of worship. At a meeting at St. James, Missouri, that soon acquired a degree of infamy, Warner confronted a band of people claiming a place among the saints but who were "dancing on one leg, some rolling their eyes in their head, others gibbering in tongues, or jerking, or falling stiff, and so forth."[32] Warner rebuked the spirit of these ecstatics, renouncing it as a work of Satan. Furthermore, Warner's description of the entire event heaped scorn on those engaged in such ecstatic practices as he had described. However, his description of the 1887 confrontation was not Warner's last word on the subject of speaking in tongues. Three years after this meeting, in the context of a *Gospel Trumpet* article endorsing a woman's right to preach and enter the ordained ministry, Warner referred to the practice of speaking in tongues, but this time in a more favorable light. Warner's exposition of Acts 2 did not dispute the fact that some in the crowd at Pentecost spoke in tongues; in fact, he took the narrative at face value. Furthermore, he described the manifestations at Pentecost, especially "prophesying in the Spirit," as continuing throughout the dispensation of the Holy Spirit. This prophesying was "to be one of the marked characteristics of this dispensation. For the 'last days' embrace the whole period of this last age," and in this context Warner stated, "The whole church may speak in tongues and prophesy."[33] Like Sarah Smith, he failed to elaborate on the meaning of the phrase "speak in tongues," now employed in a positive light.

J. W. Byers (1859–1944) was among the first Church of God leaders to qualify the meaning of the phrase "speaking in tongues." Writing several years before the Azusa Street revival, Byers limited glossolalia in two ways. First, he stated that even during the apostolic period not all members of the church received that particular gift. From this Byers concluded, "The gift of tongues is evidently a special endowment of the Spirit in the church to such as can make use of the same in God's appointed manner."[34] Secondly, Byers limited the practice of speaking in tongues to "intelligible speech." As he put it, "They may be the language of angels (1 Cor 13:1), but whether celestial or terrestrial, they are expressions of God's wonderful work of redemption in other languages from those commonly in use by the worshipers assembled at the time of such manifestations."[35] Byers thought that the practice of speaking in tongues was to be associated with the missionary outreach of the church, taking as his precedent the Acts narrative that describes the crowd at Pentecost as understanding in their native languages the words of the Galilean speakers. In addition to biblical precedent Byers also cited the testimonies of missionaries who suddenly and miraculously acquired the ability to preach in the native language of the people to whom they had been sent. Despite these warrants for interpreting the gift of tongues as the ability to speak a historical language, Byers' literal reading of the text also required him to leave the door open to other possibilities. While disputing the conclusion that the gift of tongues always accompanies the baptism of the Holy Spirit, Byers nevertheless also said that there was no reason why the manifestations of the Spirit as described in 1 Corinthians 12 and 14 "should not be brought into effect for the glory of God, in his own manner and time."[36] The fact that fanatics had distorted the practice gave no more warrant for its complete rejection than did fanatical practices of sanctification or divine healing.

Another person to write on the gift of tongues prior to the Azusa Street revival was Jennie Carpenter Rutty (1856–1942). Mrs. Rutty was a school-teacher and frequently contributed to the *Trumpet* around the turn of the century. She also did evangelistic work in the British Isles and started the Church of God congregation in Pomona, California. In addition to her letters and *Trumpet* articles, Rutty published advice books for young men and women.[37] The books covered a wide range of topics, from habits and

Jennie Carpenter Rutty. Minister and evangelist, Rutty wrote several advice books for young people as well as Gospel Trumpet articles on the practice of speaking in tongues at a moment when the Church of God was attempting to come to an understanding of the practice.

manners to domestic life and health to religion. Both of Rutty's advice books devoted a chapter length discussion to the topic of the baptism of the Holy Spirit. In each she defined this baptism in the conventional language of the holiness movement. The presence of the Holy Spirit in the human heart witnessed to the purity, sanctification, and perfection of the soul. "These three signify the same thing—purity—for the perfect man is one who has a perfect heart, made so by a cleansing from all imperfection—sin—and 'sanctified' means 'to be made holy, or free from sin; to be cleansed from moral corruption and pollution; to be made fit for the service of God, and the society and employments of heaven'; and 'purified' means to have been purged from moral defilement;... Sin being removed from the heart, the Holy Spirit comes in to be the controlling power in the heart and life.[38] This definition circumscribed Rutty's understanding of glossolalia.

Although she associated speaking in tongues with the manifestation of the Holy Spirit, Rutty emphasized *unknown* as the determinative qualifier regarding tongues speaking. She denied that the biblical phrase "unknown tongues" referred to ecstatic utterances and relegated the experience of Parham's Topeka, Kansas group to the status of counterfeit religion. Their "incomprehensible chatter" was part of a broader disobedience to the Bible and a spirit of disunity with God's true children.[39] Rutty's criticism of the Topeka group did not mean she altogether rejected the possibility of the experience. Indeed, she took Mark 16:17 and its reference to tongues as a sign that will follow Christian belief; Rutty wanted to know why more of the saints had not experienced the gift. However, by the gift of speaking in tongues she meant "that men naturally able to speak but one language should be anointed by the Holy Spirit as to speak in tongues before unknown to themselves."[40] Rutty thus laid down the following view: (1) speaking in tongues was a gift of the Holy Spirit but not the exclusive sign of Holy Spirit baptism, (2) ecstatic utterances were not accurate representations of the experience of the New Testament church, and (3) that "unknown" meant unknown to the one who uttered the language—not universally unknown.

The editorial staff of the *Gospel Trumpet* routinely observed events in the surrounding religious world and made them the subject of comment, often critical and occasionally condescending. As word of the Azusa Street revival spread in the years after 1906, the *Trumpet* was quick to criticize. G. T. Neal labeled the revival a heresy.[41] He had attended a meeting of an Azusa offshoot in Portland, Oregon and repeatedly used the word *hideous* to describe the ecstatic utterances of the worshipers and expressed his disgust at such outbursts.[42] E. E. Byrum implied that the tongues movement may have been the work of the devil, who was using it to engender revulsion in honest folk, an association also made by F. G. Smith.[43] J. W. Byers agreed with the sentiments of Byrum and Smith, calling the teaching of the Apostolic Faith movement a fallacy and naming the real bone of contention between that movement and the Church of God—the former's insistence that speaking in tongues was the sign of Holy Spirit baptism.[44] Not all Church of God people found these criticisms persuasive, however. Some, most notably the gifted but erratic W. G. Schell, abandoned the Church of God and affiliated with one of the new pentecostal denominations.[45] Others believed that the experience was a manifestation of the Holy Spirit, sought the experience, but remained within the Church of God movement, to the great consternation of people like Byers, Byrum, Smith, and H. M. Riggle.

The spread of what Church of God writers called "the tongues movement" elicited sharp but neither universal nor unison criticism from a majority of Church of God ministers who wrote on this subject. They agreed in their hostility to the Azusa Street movement without sharing a common definition of and attitude toward glossolalia. Riggle, J. W. Byers, D. O. Teasley, and J. E. Forrest all agreed that when the Bible referred to speaking in tongues it meant the use of a historical language even though speakers may not understand any part of their own utterance. Other Church of God people, notably Jennie Rutty and J. J. M. Nichols-Roy, held open the possibility that those who spoke in tongues might speak an unintelligible language without insisting that ecstatic utterances exhausted the meaning of glossolalia. This latter group took the position that while glossolalia normally signified a historical language, that definition did not fit all New Testament references. Since the Bible expressly affirmed speaking in tongues as a gift of the Holy Spirit, Christians should leave the future open to whatever the Spirit might choose. Nichols-Roy, one of several well-educated and bright Indian converts to Christianity and a leader in the Indian church, was especially concerned to leave the hermeneutical door ajar wide enough to admit the possibility of ecstatic languages. He read Acts 2 in the broadest possible sense, arguing the fact that the Pentecost listeners heard in their own language could not be taken as an indication that all the tongues spoken on that occasion were historical languages.[46] Other writers, notably Russell R. Byrum, distinguished between public and private glossolalia. A lack of understanding among those who heard the public expression of glossolalia was to Byrum a sign that the experience was not genuine. But he also said that no interpreter was necessary when a believer spoke in tongues privately.[47]

In 1914, but particularly again in 1919, F. G. Smith published articles on the practice of speaking in tongues.[48] He also addressed the General Ministerial Assembly on this issue and his comments subsequently were published in a small pamphlet.[49] Here Smith distinguished between the private and public practice of glossolalia. The private phase of the gift is a speech unintelligible to human beings. Smith viewed this speech as an expression of adoration or prayer through which the believer was strengthened. Hence, stated Smith, the practice "is prohibited in public unless interpreted ... [and] is not very profitable for public use even if interpreted."[50] The public practice of glossolalia was intended for the express purpose of building up the body of believers. As such it was uttered in "real languages of earth," constituted a helpful sign to unbelievers of the Spirit's presence, and need not be prohibited in the church.[51] But Smith adamantly opposed the claim of the "modern tongues movement" that glossolalia was the sign of the baptism of the Holy Spirit. In his view sanctification and holiness were the true signs of the Spirit's presence in the life of a believer. "Multitudes have, without the particular tongues manifestation, experienced the baptism of the Holy Ghost—purging and cleansing the heart from the nature of sin, filling with holy power and boldness, granting faith in abundance, the gifts of healing, and the working of miracles. All these are abundant in the church by the power of the Spirit of God."[52] Despite his argument, however, Smith allowed for the experience of glossolalia. He believed that the gift of speaking in tongues was being manifested in the church and that it arrived in a "joyful overflow of thanksgiving and praise to God at the time of [believers'] Spirit baptism."[53] However, it was also a dangerous gift that exposed a saint's soul to deceptive influence. Therefore, Smith warned, "Be sure that your heart is right with God, that you are walking in his word faithfully and walking in all the light that you have; that you are *free from all the deceptive influences of false doctrines and false teachers.*"[54]

By the early twenties the Church of God movement leadership had achieved something like a consensus on the question of speaking in tongues. It is also clear that some saints continued to practice glossolalia in the ensuing years. The consensus was that the phenomenon of "tongues speaking" that had erupted at Azusa Street and beyond was a heterodox movement. To make speaking in tongues the focal point of life in the Holy Spirit was a deceptive fanaticism, and the movements that it had spawned were generally regarded as doctrinally divided and spiritually confused. The consensus also tended to take the view that the New Testament's common references to glossolalia signified historical languages, although some individuals included the possibility of ecstatic language, particularly in the case of private religious devotions. Since the Bible clearly referred to speaking in tongues as a spiritual gift, the consensus maintained that the Spirit might similarly gift men and women at any moment. Therefore, sincere Christians needed to be open to the reception of that gift just as much as any other the Spirit might confer. However, F. G. Smith spoke for that consensus when he wrote to George Tasker, "Knowing what I do of this work [the Church of God movement] and contrasting it with the fruits of the modern tongues movement, I can say that I prefer the Holy Ghost which I know I have received, to the one that they say I have not received."[55]

Resolving Contentious Practices

Shortly after World War I leaders of the Church of God movement resolved their positions on both pacifism and glossolalia. Not all the saints agreed with these positions, and the difference of opinion disturbed local and regional ministers meetings and churches at various points during the following decades.[56] In the main the saints came to reject speaking in tongues as it was practiced in the various Pentecostal churches that formed in the twentieth century, although some did adopt the practice. It would not be as accurate to say that the saints rejected pacifism. Rather, the practice diminished in emphasis to a point where Church of God men entered the armed services during World War II at a rate comparable to the general population.[57] However, a small but determined minority kept this practice alive. Whereas the year 1920 marks a moment by which Pentecostal speaking in tongues had been rejected, it is also the date when the movement's leadership published a pamphlet that described pacifism and conscientious objection as the "teaching of the Church of God."[58] The passage of time, however, relegated this position to nearly the same status as the practice of glossolalia. In the fate of these two doctrinal practices different processes were at work by which the Church of God movement weighed both and found them wanting, even though one of them had enjoyed the early and determined endorsement of the movement's leadership.

Notes

1. Val Clear, *Where the Saints Have Trod* (Chesterfield, Ind: Midwest Publications, 1977), 74–75; 59.
2. Ira Pendleton, "Love Thy Neighbor," *GT* (May 20, 1897), 4. For chapter length studies of pacifism and the Church of God, cf. Merle D. Strege, "The Demise (?) of a Peace Church: The Church of God (Anderson), Pacifism and Civil Religion," *Mennonite Quarterly Review*, Vol. LXV No. 2 (April 1991), 128–140; and Merle D. Strege, "An Uncertain Voice for Peace: The Church of God (Anderson) and Pacifism," in Theron F. Schlabach and Richard T. Hughes, eds., *Proclaim Peace: Christian Pacifism from Unexpected Quarters* (Urbana, Ill: University of Illinois Press, 1997), 115–127.
3. W. D. Farnan, "Treatment of Enemies," *GT* (September 2, 1897), 4.
4. "Deserting the Army," *GT* (February 10, 1898), 4.
5. E. E. Byrum, "Should We Go to War?" *GT* (April 14, 1898), 4.
6. *GT* (May 30, 1907), 4.
7. *GT* (April 1, 1908), 4.

8. "Word from Germany," *GT* (November 26, 1914), 11–12.

9. "Inglorious History," *GT* (March 18, 1915), 1–2.

10. Cf. Nels Renbeck, "Young Men Refusing to Bear Arms," *GT* (August 26, 1915), 6; Girke's letter appears in *GT* (July 22, 1915), 6.

11. "Reaction Against Preparedness," *GT* (May 11, 1916), 16.

12. "Is it Wrong to be a Soldier?" *GT* (April 27, 1916), 3.

13. Ibid.

14. Byrum's position on war is summed up thus: "It is wrong to kill people.... War is cruel, and devastation, with foul murder, disease, destruction of property, breaking-up of homes, follows its track, leaving the land strewn with dead bodies of the best talent that the country can afford; and starving widows and fatherless children continue to partake of the miseries that follow in the wake of war. There are no humane bullets." Ibid.

15. *The Evolution of Christianity* (Anderson, Ind: Gospel Trumpet Company, 1911), 269.

16. "Our Attitude to War," *GT* (April 26, 1917), 12.

17. "Patriotism and Conscience," *GT* (May 17, 1917).

18. "Buying Liberty Bonds," *GT* (May 23, 1918), 12–13.

19. Ibid.

20. "Buying Liberty Bonds," *GT* (May 23, 1918), 12–13.

21. This discussion is indebted to the work of Kenneth R. Tippin, who gathered much of the primary source material on glossolalia in the early Church of God in *Powerful Words: Selected Radical Writings by Pioneers of the Church of God Reformation Movement* (unpublished ms., n.p.: n.d.). Tippin collects and reproduces early Church of God writing on the subject of glossolalia in an appendix to this manuscript.

22. For studies of the Pentecostal movement, especially in its connections with the holiness movement, cf. Vinson Synan, *The Holiness-Pentecostal Tradition*, 2nd edition (Grand Rapids, Mich: William B. Eerdmanns Publishing Co, 1997); Synan, ed, *Aspects of Pentecostal-Charismatic Origins* (Plainfield, NJ; Logos International, 1975); Donald W. Dayton, *Theological Roots of Pentecostalism* (Metuchen, NJ: Scarecrow Press, 1987); and Iain MacRobert, *The Black Roots and White Racism of Early Pentecostalism in the USA* (New York: St. Martin's Press, 1988).

23. Seymour is the subject of Douglas J. Nelson's *For Such a Time as This: the Story of Bishop William J. Seymour and the Azusa Street Revival*, unpublished dissertation, University of Birmingham, 1981).

24. Cited in MacRobert, *Black Roots and White Racism*, 49.

25. On the early history of African Americans and the Church of God cf. James E. Massey, *An Introduction to the Negro Churches in the Church of God Reformation Movement* (New York: Shining Light Survey Press, 1957) and Cheryl J. Sanders, *Saints in Exile: The Holiness-Pentecostal Experience in African American Religion and Culture* (New York: Oxford University Press, 1996). Cf. especially chapter 1.

26. For a lengthier discussion of this history see MacRobert, *Black Roots and White Racism*, 43–71.

27. Asked to describe the conduct of Church of God worship services, Warner answered, "We recognize Christ Jesus, and his representative—the Holy Spirit, as the only leader of the worship of God. Everybody is free to sing in the Spirit, to pray in the Spirit, to prophesy in the Spirit one by one, as the Spirit gives them utterance. And any one the Lord chooses to read the scriptures and teach the word is at liberty to do so." *GT* (November 1, 1883) quoted in Tippin, *Powerful Words*, 141.

28. Ibid., 141–142.

29. On the connections between Pentecostalism and the holiness movement see especially Dayton, Theological Roots of Pentecostalism, 63–84.

30. Cf. *Life Sketches of Mother Sarah Smith* (Moundsville: Gospel Trumpet Publishing Company, 1902).

31. Sarah Smith, "A Glorious Meeting," in "News From the Field," *GT* (June 15, 1888), quoted in Tippin, *Powerful Words*, 186.

32. A. L. Byers recorded Warner's narrative of this incident from the summer of 1887 in *Birth of a Reformation*. Sarah Smith and Mary Cole witnessed the event and described it, the former in a testimony printed in *Familiar Names and Faces* (Moundsville: Gospel Trumpet Publishing Company,

1902), 232–233, and Mary Cole in her autobiography, *Trials and Triumphs of Faith,* loc. cit, 144–148.

33. Warner, "Women's Freedom in Christ, To Pray and Prophesy in Public Worship," *GT* (April 1, 1890), reprinted in Tippin, *Powerful Words,* 135–136.

34. J. W. Byers, "The Gift of Tongues," *GT* (June 23, 1898), reprinted in Tippin, *Powerful Words,* 195–197.

35. Ibid.

36. Ibid.

37. *Letters of Love and Counsel for Our Girls* (Moundsville: Gospel Trumpet Publishing Co., 1898); *Mothers' Counsel to Their Sons* (Moundsville: Gospel Trumpet Publishing Co., 1899).

38. Rutty, *Mothers' Counsel to Their Sons,* 362–363.

39. Jennie C. Rutty, "The Gift of Tongues," *GT* (September 18, 1902), reprinted in Tippin, *Powerful Words,* 198.

40. Ibid.

41. "Unknown Tongues," *GT* (January 31, 1907), reprinted in Tippin, *Powerful Words,* 200.

42. Neal had already made up his mind about speaking in tongues before attending the service, as he said that he had wanted a better understanding in order to more intelligently warn people against the Apostolic Faith movement. Ibid.

43. Cf. E. E. Byrum, "Seeking Pentecost," *GT* (December 27, 1906); and F. G. Smith, "The Gift of Tongues," *GT* (December 12, 1907). Both men are quoted in Tippin, *Powerful Words,* 200. Smith spared no criticism of the " 'Apostolic Faith Movement,' with its false doctrines, false apostles, false spirit, upholding sectarianism, or millennialism, and other doctrines of devils; and with faces contorted, twitching, jerking, and unseemly actions they go about 'gibbering' in an unknown tongue, not knowing whether they are blessing God or cursing him." Ibid.

44. J. W. Byers, "The Tongues Spirit," *GT* (June 30, 1910), reprinted in Tippin, *Powerful Words,* 201.

45. By late 1915 Schell was publishing articles in the new Assemblies of God paper, *Weekly Evangel.*

46. J. J. M. Nichols-Roy, "The Gift of Tongues: What It Is," *GT* (January 14, 1915), quoted in Tippin, *Powerful Words,* 205.

47. R. R. Byrum, "Sources and Nature of Speaking in Tongues," *GT* (September 20, 1920), quoted in Tippin, *Powerful Words,* 206.

48. *GT* (November 12, 1914) and *GT* (December 11, 1919).

49. "The Gift of Tongues: What It Is and What It Is Not" (Anderson, Ind: Gospel Trumpet Company, 1929).

50. Ibid., 15.

51. Ibid., 18.

52. Ibid., 36.

53. Ibid., 53.

54. Ibid., 58, (Smith's emphasis).

55. F. G. Smith to G. Tasker, August 8, 1916, quoted in Tippin, *Powerful Words,* 206.

56. From time to time the practice of speaking in tongues has proved to be a serious and divisive problem in local congregations of the Church of God. In 1985 the General Assembly of the Church of God in Ohio presented a resolution to the General Assembly calling for a special study of glossolalia. Pursuant to this request, a committee composed of selected pastors, state coordinators, and professors of Bible, theology, and church history was commissioned to study the practice biblically, historically, and theologically. The committee presented its findings to the General Assembly the following June. The committee did not reach complete agreement, but its report was subsequently printed as a booklet for use by pastors and congregations. Along with recommendations for the life of the church, the booklet, while making the point that speaking in tongues was not part of the "doctrinal consensus" of the Church of God, also reported a range of three categories of response found in Church of God literature. The three categories are: (1) "Avoid: It (glossolalia) causes division"; (2) "Permit: But do so only with considerable caution"; (3) "Welcome: All gifts are needed. Those who have held this view have been reluctant to discourage the presence and practice of any New Testament gift, including 'tongues,' ... if that gift is disciplined appropriately and is not demanded of all believers." *Biblical Guidelines for the Local Church* (Anderson, Ind: Executive Council of the Church of God, 1986), n.

An abridged version of this statement is published in Barry L. Callen, ed., *Following the Light* (Anderson, Ind: Warner Press, 2000), 300–303.

57. This is not to discount the Church of God men who registered as conscientious objectors, or in one or two instances, left the United States. But in the main, those who elected to register as conscientious objectors were either clergy or studying for the ministry. Conscientious objection does not appear to have been an option considered by many laypersons in the Church of God during WW II. Moreover, during and after the war some Church of God pulpits were denied to those who were known to have taken C. O. status. Taken together, this is hardly the experience or witness of a historic peace church however much some continued to describe the Church of God during the Korean and Vietnamese wars.

58. The pamphlet was published by the Executive Committee of the Missionary Board of the Church of God over the signatures of F. G. Smith (President), E. E. Byrum (Vice-President), and J. W. Phelps (Secretary-Treasurer). The pamphlet concluded with the following declaration: "As a minister of the church of God, I, in agreement with my fellow ministers, hereby declare: That I believe in being a loyal citizen of the Government under which I live in so far as its requirements do not conflict with my duty to God as enforced by the law of my conscience. That ... it is contrary to my religious convictions as a follower of Christ for me to take human life. My religion and my conscience forbid my taking up arms for the slaughter of my fellowmen." Note that the language of the declaration implicitly distinguishes between clergy, to whom it applies, and laypersons, who are not mentioned.

Chapter 7
Institutional Revolution

F. G. Smith served the Gospel Trumpet Company as editor from 1916 to 1930. His predecessor had been coerced out of the editor's chair and it is perhaps no mere coincidence that Smith was even more rudely dismissed. By the time of their departures both men were widely perceived as wielding too much power. Before E. E. Byrum left office, leading ministers had taken the first steps toward the development of new organizational forms. Smith departed Anderson in 1930, and he left behind a Church of God movement that had undergone revolutionary structural changes. When he took office the Gospel Trumpet Company was the sole corporate entity in the movement and the face it presented to legal, business, and political communities at home and abroad. More than its business manager or president, the editor called the tune for the company and, through its books and periodicals, for the movement as a whole. By 1930 an entire family of church "agencies," as they were known to Church of God people, had been created, and over them the General Ministerial Assembly indirectly presided. In the process the Gospel Trumpet Company was reduced from the movement's sole legal entity to one agency among several. The new structure redistributed power and influence more evenly, but even more was at stake in the organizational revolution of these years.

The changes that occurred in the Church of God between 1916 and 1930 must be understood as more than the development of a polity, as if one were making alterations on a vehicle while leaving its contents undisturbed. Because so much of the movement's identity was carried by its theology of the church, to create a new polity of any kind, let alone a managerial bureaucracy, inevitably worked to alter the movement's self-perception. At the beginning of this period, movement leaders expressed their concern that something ominous was about to happen; at the period's conclusion they worried that it had. As institutionalization began, F. G. Smith brooded over what such changes might portend. As the period closed, his successor, Charles E. Brown, soothed the movement's theological conscience with a rationale assuring them that alterations in polity had not organized the church at all. That both men felt it necessary to state their respective fears or confidence signifies their belief that the change then unfolding carried an unusually large potential. Moreover, the idea of leadership itself became an issue in the movement, shifting from a "leader mentality" when Smith took office to the early stages of Brown's theory of "spiritual democracy" in the 1930s. The matter of leadership was anything but an academic dispute. It was resolved only through the most prolonged and deeply divisive struggle in the movement's history and in a manner that left other issues unresolved. On several fronts then, the period from 1917 to 1942 marks a tumultuous period in the theological history of the Church of God.

A New Assembly and New Agencies—1917

At least by the turn of the century and likely before, whenever ministers of the Church of God gathered at a camp meeting or grove meeting, a "general assembly" occurred.[1] These assemblies were informal discussions of matters that ministers found important to their labors. The regularly recurring business item in these early assemblies related to the perennial need to secure reduced clergy rates as railroad passengers. Otherwise it was homiletics—as in actual sermons as opposed to theoretical discussions—and not economics or business that held ministerial interest in the assemblies. Senior and influential ministers exhorted their brothers and sisters of the cloth on important doctrinal themes. On those occasions when a theological issue came under discussion, any difference of opinion was allegedly resolved when one of the influential ministers rose to the platform to explain to his or her colleagues the movement's position on the question.[2] Informality characterized the tone of these early assemblies, which in point of fact were little more than ministerial discussion groups.

The creation of the General Ministerial Assembly closed the era of informal assemblies. It was the Gospel Trumpet Company that put forward the action that prompted the creation of a formal ministerial organization. To the assembly that met in association with the general camp meeting—from 1906 forward in Anderson—the company proposed a slate of nominees for membership in the Gospel Trumpet Company, i. e., the name by which its governing board was known. Prior to this proposal the twenty-four company members had functioned as a self-perpetuating board. The motives prompting this organizational change are shrouded in some obscurity.[3] The proposal to select company members by assembly election was tantamount to giving up the autonomy enjoyed by the publishing house from the very first days of its existence. It is difficult to discern the motives behind a proposal by company officials that would so dramatically change its relationship with the church, other than the prospect of securing financial support for the cash-starved publishing work. On the other hand, many of the movement's ministers also favored a more formal relationship in order to have a voice in the company's direction.[4] In this latter sense the move to create a General Assembly can be regarded as the culmination of a restiveness among ministers within and without the Gospel Trumpet Company. Fermenting among the ministers was a desire to broaden participation in decision making, and it led to changes accomplished through a year that began with the resignation of E. E. Byrum and concluded with the creation of the General Ministerial Assembly.

The change proposed by the Gospel Trumpet Company altered its relationship with the church, but the same proposal transformed the movement's self-conception and assemblies even as it changed their function. Acting as a corporate body was new to the Church of God ministry. Moreover, to elect a slate of nominees for the Gospel Trumpet Company created moral and potentially legal responsibilities for a general assembly when it came to potential relationships with boards or agencies not yet in existence. More than precedent setting was on the minds of some ministers in attendance. At an assembly on June 14 they voted into place a few modest procedural rules and authorized the appointment of a committee of five to draft a constitution and permanent set of bylaws.[5] The gathered ministers next moved to elect Eugene A. Reardon, pastor at Chicago, chair *pro tem.* The committee warmed to its task, and on June 21 read its report to the assembled ministers. They approved it and thus brought into being the General Ministerial Assembly.

The newly organized Assembly appears to have been the brainchild of a group of progressive ministers many of whom had been instrumental in the organization of the Missionary Committee a decade earlier. They appreciated the likelihood that formal ministerial organization would not be welcomed by all, so they took steps to ensure that the new Assembly would be presented in the most favorable light. The June 28, 1917 issue of the *Gospel Trumpet* carried an article positively inclined toward the change adopted only seven days earlier, justifying it on the basis of two needs: (1) more attention to the movement's "business interests," and (2) the means to take advantage of "unparalleled" evangelistic opportunities that only a formal organization could afford.[6] The article, which reported the motivating causes of the recent actions only in the passive voice, further stated the desirability of a more direct and legal relationship between the Gospel Trumpet Company and the movement.[7] A generation had arisen that knew not the antipathy toward organization that had breathed sulfur and brimstone at denominational Babylon. The new generation had been schooled at organizing and maintaining good financial and organizational practices in the places of responsibility that multiplied as the movement grew after 1890—principally the missionary homes and the increasingly complex Gospel Trumpet Company. It was also the case that business and political life in the United States was becoming more complex, especially after 1920. The bureaucratic organization of the Church of God movement has been justified as an innocent response to the rapidly changing social and political culture surrounding it. And yet, when the church and its ministers desired, they could and did resist mightily other aspects of cultural change. Movie theaters, flappers, and many another feature of the changing culture remained taboos long after the ministers decided that its new organizational structures could be adopted without compromising the essential nature of the church.

Ministers in the state of Michigan quickly followed the precedent established by the creation of the General Ministerial Assembly. At the urging of C. E. Brown, a young pastor in Detroit, in late 1920 ministers created the Michigan State Assembly. Their principal motive was a desire to create an organization by which to discipline the ministry. In addition to a bylaws provision that authorized lay representation from each congregation, the other noteworthy feature was the new state assembly's self-imposed restriction on its responsibilities; the assembly limited its power to disciplining wayward ministers.[8] The news that Michigan ministers had organized a state assembly did not set well with prominent, nationally recognized movement leaders. At Anderson Campmeeting the following June, Michigan leaders were taken to task for their actions. Even supporters of organization wanted to keep it under a tight rein.

The era witnessing the organization of assemblies on national and state levels also saw refined organizational principles extend into the grassroots church. Issues and techniques of local church government were directly addressed in Russell Byrum's *Problems of the Local Church*.[9] Another of the movement's progressive ministers, Byrum offered his book as a manual to guide the functions of local congregations. He accepted the movement's fundamental ecclesiology and directed his discussion toward other matters of practical concern. In this Byrum reinforced the movement's growing ecclesiological distinction between the church's functions—an appropriate human concern—and organization, which was understood to be the special province of the Holy Spirit. Concerning the church's functions, Byrum acknowledged his debt to "the experience of Christians of the generations past" and their works of church law, handbooks, and manuals.[10] He stipulated that he would take from those sources only such ideas as were consistent with the theology of a divinely organized and governed church. Earlier Church of God writers had acknowledged the contributions of a Luther or Wesley as the work of people "living up to the light that they had" but simultaneously insisted that those authorities did not shed all the light there was on the church. Byrum's use of external sources on a matter of such importance as the practical life of the church extended the admission that the denominational world was not entirely in the dark. Russell Byrum believed that local congregations were in serious need of assistance, and so they were. Churches were making an organizational transition that had begun in brush arbor meetings, camp meetings, and periodic local revivals. A few locations were fortunate to be the site of a missionary home. But the vast majority of Church of God congregations had begun as preaching points of one kind or another. They were sorely in need of assistance when it came to adopting an organization without violating one of the movement's cardinal theological tenets.

Byrum's manual offered advice on a wide range of local church policies and functions. He covered the relationship between pastor and congregation, including a list of pastoral duties and an explanation of the congregation's obligations to its minister. Byrum outlined the procedures for conducting a church trial, distinguishing between trials for laypersons and clergy. He also discussed procedures for organizing a congregation's business functions and explained the rules of order that guided the conduct of a local church business meeting. In the midst of this discussion Byrum provided the bylaws model that was widely adopted by Church of God congregations in the United States and beyond.[11]

Problems of the Local Church addressed practical matters of congregational life. Concerning the specific function of religious education, it was anticipated by more than a decade by D. Otis Teasley's *How to Conduct a Sunday School.*[12] Teasley (1876–1942) was in the vanguard of the progressive ministers of the Church of God movement. Converted and called to the ministry in his early youth, he had begun preaching as an adolescent in Missouri when he heard the preaching of A. B. Stanberry and stood with the Church of God in 1896. A correspondence course in music was the limit of Teasley's formal education, and he put it to use when the Gospel Trumpet Company issued a call for helpers to produce a new hymnal. After the project's completion Teasley returned to the life of a flying messenger until 1904, when he and his wife, the former Ora Howard, and their two children moved to New York City where Teasley superintended the missionary home. In 1910 he and his family followed the Gospel Trumpet Company to Anderson, where he took the assignment of general manager of the new missions paper, the *Missionary Herald*. Three years later the paper was incorporated into the *Gospel Trumpet*. No longer with an assignment Teasley moved to Bessemer, Alabama, where he again assumed responsibility for superintending a missionary home. In 1917 he and his family returned to Anderson because he had been elected to chair the Gospel Trumpet Company directors' board. In effect he became the company's general manager, and it was Teasley who guided the company through a transition from religious commune to a corporation.

D. O. Teasley was an exceptionally bright man—some of his younger contemporaries called him a genius—with an attractive personality that drew people to him and elicited their respect. He authored or edited seventeen books and several hymnals,[13] and himself composed numerous gospel songs and lyrics. Teasley thought and wrote about subjects considered by few Church of God ministers of his era. He conceded little if anything to the anti-necktie faction, championing a more moderate interpretation of personal holiness. He advocated causes and took stands on issues that put him on the cutting edge of the Church of God ministry. Among his many books was one that addressed hermeneutics, a topic unknown to many of his contemporaries. His book on the organization of Sunday schools espoused a cause that had only recently begun to win the movement's grudging acceptance. But Teasley made his case for Sunday schools with an argument that suggested some Church of God leaders peered over the wall into denominational Babylon only to find ideas and methods worthy of adoption. Cracks were developing in a wall that had hermetically sealed the Church of God movement from the denominations. The organization question was among the first of those cracks.

Early attitudes toward Sunday schools were anything but favorable. Church of God people suspected them to be little other than incipient breeding grounds of lukewarm religion that substituted rote memorization of the catechism for soul-stirring religious experience. Still worse, worldly professors were thought to use Sunday schools as places to show off their wealth and status by dressing their children in fine clothing. Bad enough to use one's children as expressions of adult pride, but even worse to train them in prideful ways as a consequence. Although this attitude softened before Warner's death, the appearance of Teasley's book was still something of a watershed. It accelerated the acceptance and development of Sunday schools in the Church of God movement. Scarcely more than a decade later the national Board of Religious Education and Sunday Schools was created.

Teasley refused to honor the movement's past attitude towards Christian education. He recognized Sunday schools for their "marvelous achievement" and the "inestimable value" of a properly conducted Sunday school. The era of the flying messengers and its emphasis on evangelism still bulked large in Teasley's conception of just exactly what constituted proper conduct. "First, last, and always," soul-winning was the purpose of the Sunday school: "Every lesson, from the infant class to the highest grade, should point to Christ as the central theme and as the Savior of the world."[14] Appropriate to the movement's need to find biblical warrants for any new development, Teasley found in the Scriptures ample illustrations, if not Sunday schools *per se*, of the propriety of the people of God as teachers. He wrote approvingly of Robert Raikes' efforts in religious education, especially among the poor, and went so far as to assert that it was no great objection to Sunday schools if children therein received instruction in the peculiar doctrines of the sects. Teasley even approvingly described the work of the International Sunday School Union and its system of lessons, citing favorably its adoption by every major denomination except the Episcopalians. His approval and that of others had led the publishing house to adopt the use of the outlines in 1910. Clearly Teasley, like Russell Byrum, represented a new and more discriminating theological attitude.[15] They were two of a growing number of ministers who refused to condemn out of hand all the ideas and practices of the denominations.

Other church bodies may not have regarded as controversial the adoption of new methods of church government and institutions like Sunday schools. However, for two decades and more the Church of God had roundly condemned all such practices and institutions as human creations of denominational Babel. During those years its theology of the church committed the movement to the attempt to be the church without any formal structures and procedures—all the way down to rejecting ballots and voting. That the movement began to adopt formal structures must be seen as more than a concession to the need to organize. On the contrary, the development of new procedures and practices implied that substantive ecclesiological changes were also underway if not yet readily perceived or appreciated. The rationalization that they were organizing only the functions or work of the church served to obscure or perhaps even hide the theological change implied in new organizational practices.

Some ministers worried that these new developments might lead the movement over the cliff into Babylon. Chief among those was none other than F. G. Smith. Who but the editor was likely to chair the meetings that led to such sweeping change? At least one writer attributes the new organization to Smith's astute legal mind.[16] However, Smith also saw a darkening cloud in the growing number of organizations that came into being in the wake of the new General Ministerial Assembly. He weighed ideas and judged developments according to theological rather than sociological or organizational categories. From such a vantage many human problems—individual and corporate—could be neither solved nor even ameliorated by improved communication or organization. Like the founding generation, Smith looked at problems in the church or between people and identified sin as their most likely cause, and he warned the movement against placing too much confidence or authority in the new structures.

In a 1919 *Gospel Trumpet* editorial Smith vented his theological misgivings. He thought that a crisis borne of growing numbers and success was brewing. Mining the Christian past once again with his own interpretive pick-ax, Smith held up to the movement a nugget of wisdom that combined numerical growth and a consequent desire for organization with a slide into apostasy. Subtly Satan was using the new boards and corporations to impose a "sectish" understanding of the church on the movement, especially where the new agencies had been ascribed with "ecclesiastical authority and rule over the church."[17] In Smith's view the only means of preventing apostasy was to clearly distinguish between the divine government of the church and a "mere business arrangement for caring for certain phases of the church's work."[18] They were, after all, "humanly created positions," and whenever ecclesiastical authority, i.e. the authority by which the church is governed and directed, is thought to exist in such positions, said Smith, there is found the assumption that is "the very thing that the Papacy was made of."[19] No form of governance but a theocracy appropriately described the divine government of the church. "Christ rules by a moral and spiritual dominion, and his ministers and workers share in this oversight and rule *in whatever proportion they are able to put forth the same moral and spiritual influence.*"[20] Smith made as clear as possible the doctrinal position that church leadership was spiritual rather than structural:

> There is *divine authority* in the church. It is bestowed upon individuals by the Spirit of God. There can be no higher authority than this. Boards and committees may be formed to look after business matters, but the entire authority belonging to positions in such corporations is human; and such bodies must be made to realize that they are utterly subservient to the spiritual authority of the church, instead of being masters or administrative directors of ecclesiastical affairs. It matters not what the humanly created positions may be—whether

president of a missionary home, or of a camp meeting association, of an evangelistic board, or the president of the Gospel Trumpet Company—such positions are altogether human. *The authority of God in the individual soul, a divine commission direct from heaven, is greater than all of these.* To vest ecclesiastical authority in such positions is to head directly toward ecclesiasticism and apostasy. If men who are in such official positions possess spiritual gifts and qualifications which give them moral and spiritual influence in the church, they are expected to use such influence for the glory of God. But we must remember that that sort of rule is altogether different in character and in results from that assumed authority proceeding from a humanly created position.[21]

Smith saw signs of creeping ecclesiasticism in the positive attitude that some of his ministerial brothers and sisters took towards the new organizational structure. He was determined to root out the weed and keep the garden clear of any further infestation. New organizational practices had sprouted, and Smith wanted to separate and deny them any influence on the doctrinal practice of the church. That practice remained grounded in and articulated the idea of the divine organization of the church. Leadership in a truly theocratic church was spiritually and morally based. Smith's argument drew a clear distinction between theocracy and "man-rule." In theory the Church of God movement accepted this difference. The larger question was whether later practice would conform to the theory or would changes in practice and new ideas about leadership combine to overturn Smith's theoretical distinction.

Rapid change in many other areas of the corporate life of the Church of God came about in 1917. The *Trumpet* family disbanded that year and family members moved out of their quarters in the *Trumpet* home. For nearly forty years the men and women who worked for the Gospel Trumpet Company had been organized as a communal society. As long as the number of family members remained small, the commune functioned smoothly. With size came problems, and by the time the company moved to Anderson the *Trumpet* family had already outgrown its newly constructed quarters. Sheer numbers increased the complexity of company operations even as they created a housing shortage. The company attempted to meet all the family members' needs, which required the operation of a small farm—including a dairy herd as well as other livestock, poultry flocks, gardens and orchards, laundry, cobbler's shop, seamstress and tailor shop, food services, commissary, home for the aged, and cemetery, not to mention plumbers, carpenters, electricians and other skilled workers. Even when family members married and lived outside of the home, the company attempted to underwrite their living expenses just as if they remained residents. During the decade from 1907–1917 company directors meetings were taken up with the need to make more and more policy decisions concerning the *Trumpet* family's living arrangements.[22] Faced with mounting operational debt in 1917 the Gospel Trumpet Company finally liquidated all the home's ancillary operations, disbanded the *Trumpet* family and adopted a system of wages based on a measurement of each employee's work and skill level.

Inside the Gospel Trumpet Company and in the movement at large the elimination of the *Trumpet* family's living arrangements was greeted with equanimity and little sense that something important had been lost. From its very first days the *Trumpet* family was a pragmatic living arrangement rather than the product of an idealistic religious vision. As long as it was able to function reasonably well, the "family arrangement" was retained—probably due more to the weight of custom than a determined commitment to the ideal of a religious commune. Once company directors decided to disband the family, they acted quickly to resolve the company's financial liabilities according to what company President J. T. Wilson[23] called "the introduction of up-to-date business methods" and "careful economy."[24] Instrumental reason and rational calculation replaced a system of operations that many had come to believe was outmoded. Shortly after disbanding the *Trumpet* family an "Efficiency Committee" was appointed, and workers were subsequently retained on the basis of their skills and potential contribution. During 1917–1918 the Gospel Trumpet Company cut its work force by one-third while simultaneously improving productivity. Company managers may not have seen the connection, but in adopting the dominant culture's procedures and criteria of bureaucratic management they opened the door to systems of planning and management current among leaders of major Protestant denominations and interdenominational campaigns.[25]

"Need" was the oft-stated justification for the creation of boards, agencies, and committees during the period from 1917 to 1930. An individual or group of ministers identified a problem or lack of resources in the life of the movement, and a new agency was brought into being to address the problem. The manner in which the Missionary Committee, later the Missionary Board, developed was a model often followed in the decade that followed the founding of the General Ministerial Assembly. So, for example, after a small group of concerned individuals began noticing the near absence of Christian education programs and activities in the movement, the Board of Religious Education and Sunday Schools was created in 1923 to assist congregations in

organizing and promoting Sunday schools and other programs. The first
Board of Church Extension and Home Missions was ratified in 1920 to
foster new church development and support the missionary evangelism of
Native Americans and Hispanics in particular. In no case did an agency
possess an organizational authority that might be employed to require
individual congregations to follow its advice. Agency heads possessed broad
powers within the area of their "portfolio," so to speak, but were trumped by
the loose congregational polity of the Church of God. As one new agency
leader after another eventually discovered, no agency executive in Anderson
possessed the organizational muscle to bring local churches and pastors
into line.

An absence of muscle did not automatically hamstring movement leaders
committed to up-to-date systems of management and church finance. The
leadership's ability to change church perceptions and practice during this
period can be illustrated by changes that occurred in attitudes towards
tithing. At the turn of the century people in the Church of God opposed the
practice of systematically giving one-tenth of personal income to the church.
This is not to say that the saints did not give to the Lord's work; they simply
did not believe in tithing. J. C. Blaney, a pioneer evangelist in Canada, suggested that individual churches follow Jesus' practice of keeping a treasure
box to collect gifts "for the needs of the work and for the poor."[26] People in
the New Testament church of 1903, said Blaney, should be afforded the same
opportunity to give under the same circumstances as Jesus' followers in the
ancient church. Even the imposing figure of E. E. Byrum waded into the
discussion as an opponent of tithing. In his words, "Tithing was a doctrine
and practice [sic] of the Old Testament, and is not of the New. Nowhere is it
commanded or even recognized as practice for New Testament saints."[27]
Byrum's radical interpretation of the New Testament took him to the
conclusion that saints will consider all their possessions, not a mere tenth,
under God's ownership.

R. L. Berry (1874–1952) echoed Byrum's sentiments in the middle of the
following decade. New Testament giving, said Berry, rested on the principal
of love rather than law. Like Enoch Byrum, Berry thought that the saints
should give regularly to the work. But he offered a new criticism of tithing
when he said that to give one-tenth of one's income worked a hardship on
some while it let others off the hook. The "perfect equality" of the "New
Testament financial system lays financial responsibility on each according to
his ability.... The poor get all they need and the rich have nothing to waste."[28]
Byrum and Berry were both members of the group that sponsored *Our
Ministerial Letter,* so it is not surprising that the generally pro-organization

newsletter sidestepped the practice of tithing. Although the Old Testament endorsed the figure of 10 percent, said J. W. Phelps, no percentage was stipulated in the New. About all that he could say was that the New Testament endorsed "systematic giving."[29]

In less than a decade Berry reversed his position. As early as 1923 he proposed a unified budget for the five new agencies created since 1917. In 1925 Berry asserted that tithing rested on the principle that everything belonged to God and the tithe was the portion to be set aside in recognition of God's sovereignty. If not precisely New Testament in origin, tithing had certainly become biblical in the most approving sense of the term. It is no accident that Berry's financial conversion coincided with the organizational change going on in Anderson. The new agencies, and the Gospel Trumpet Company as well, operated according to budgets and systems of rational planning that required reasonable estimates of income and expenses. The practice of tithing in local congregations laid a fiscal foundation on which the agencies eventually could build. The arguments of leaders like R. L. Berry proved convincing to the saints. Per capita giving rates in the Church of God, as with the growth of the constituency, led or were very near the top of the charts in comparison with mainline Protestant groups during the decade of the 1930s and 1940s.

A Backward Step from the Practice of Unity

In the first decades of the Church of God, the practice of Christian unity overcame the racial divisions that scarred American society. During the years of organizational expansion, however, strains developed between Whites and Blacks in the movement. While changes in structure forced revisions in the practice of the church, growing distance between African Americans and Anglos first undermined and then altered the movement's practice of Christian unity. In the same year that witnessed the organization of the General Ministerial Assembly, Black saints also took steps to create an African American fellowship inside the Church of God movement. It was not a move they made willingly.

The history of African American connections to the Church of God movement runs back to the years before the turn of the twentieth century. In 1886, some three years before the arrival of White Church of God evangelists in South Carolina, a Black woman by the name of Jane Williams gathered a small congregation at Charleston. This church was something of the mother church for work among and by African American preachers in the South.[30] In these early decades White and Black Church of God evangelists cooperated extensively across the region. It was not uncommon

Jane Williams. Credited as the person whose ministry opened up the message of the Church of God to African Americans, she served as pastor of a congregation in Charleston, South Carolina.

for members of both ethnic groups to attend the same tent meetings and revivals, on occasion drawing the ire of local residents for transgressing such racial taboos as mixed seating.[31] In some instances Whites served as ministers to biracial gatherings; in other cases Black ministers took the lead. The pattern of racial unity in the movement's early decades was driven by a literal reading of Galatians 3:28 as the normative status of the true New Testament church: "In Christ there is neither Jew nor Greek; there is neither bond nor free, there is neither male nor female: for ye are all one in Christ Jesus."

The New Testament ideal proved difficult to sustain against the racism of early twentieth American society, whether northern or southern. Before 1910 a *Gospel Trumpet* reader asked Editor E. E. Byrum to explain the paper's request that camp meeting announcements include the word colored if the meeting was intended for African Americans. Another reader asked whether members of the two races should extend each other the "holy kiss" that was the saints' customary greeting.[32] In 1910 C. W. Naylor wrote a *Trumpet* article that outlined the emerging racially separatist attitude of the White Church of God leadership. He contended that while race mattered not with regard to salvation, "there are social differences that we cannot ignore without serious consequences. These social differences in no way affect the spiritual unity or fellowship. Both white and colored are better off as a result of social separation than they would be mixed together in these relations."[33] Within two years the paper took the position that racial separation advanced evangelistic efforts better than integrated congregations, which the paper believed inhibited evangelism among Whites.

The *Trumpet* attitude translated into camp meeting policy during the same period. In 1913 the "Camp Meeting Committee," a committee of persons who worked at the Gospel Trumpet Company, considered E. E. Byrum's suggestion that the "colored brethren" meet separately for worship in the German tent following the German language worship service. The committee agreed and directed Byrum to consult D. F. Oden, a leading African American minister to determine whether Blacks were agreeable to the proposal; they were cool enough to the idea that no such service apparently was held. However, the camp meeting committee attempted the same move the following summer. Byrum and Floyd W. Heinly were asked to once again broach the subject with the Black ministers and again they demurred. African Americans feared that once the practice of racially separate services began it would escalate into the feeling that Blacks were generally unwelcome at Anderson Campmeeting. Over these reservations, however, the committee proceeded with plans for a separate meeting as an experiment.[34]

A strong oral tradition among African American people of the Church of God says that White camp meeting organizers encouraged Blacks to organize a separate camp meeting.[35] Without documentation this tradition has been passed down through a series of historical essays. It may be the case that the repeated requests of the camp meeting committee in 1913 and 1914 are the origin of this tradition, in which case it would not be quite accurate to say that Whites asked Blacks to form a separate camp meeting. This much is certain: White camp meeting organizers were intent on trying to separate the races at least temporarily. It is even more certain that after 1900 White saints were willing to question the movement's practice of Christian unity insofar as race was concerned. What once had been a nearly unique practice of Christian unity that overcame racial separation began to erode.

In 1917 Elijah and Priscilla Wimbish led the organization of a meeting in West Middlesex, Pennsylvania. Since 1904 Elijah Wimbish had nurtured the vision of a camp meeting in the region. Realized in 1917, the West Middlesex meeting began in a determination to practice open, interracial fellowship, for White and Black ministers had partnered in the work of the Church of God in western Pennsylvania.[36] Nevertheless in that same year, at the West Middlesex meeting, African Americans organized the National Association of the Church of God and a General Ministerial Assembly as well, with R. J. Smith elected its first chair. The National Association did not exist as a separate Black denomination as, for example, the African Methodist Episcopal Church was distinct from the Methodist Episcopal Church. The National Association did not grant ministerial credentials independently, but it did maintain its own administrative offices and institutions. At the same time, African Americans continued to attend the general camp meeting in Anderson, and several Black ministers were elected to trustee boards of agencies of the Church of God. The presence of Black board members in essentially White institutions somewhat obscured the fact that after 1917 Blacks and Whites in the Church of God movement tended to operate in increasingly separate spheres.

A New School and A New Teaching Authority

After *Trumpet* family members moved out of the *Trumpet* home in 1917, another new agency, Anderson Bible Training School, occupied the vacant building that later generations of students came to call "Old Main." The Bible Training School remained a department of the Gospel Trumpet Company until 1925, when the school was reorganized and chartered as Anderson Bible School and Seminary. Four years later the school again renamed itself, this time Anderson College and Theological Seminary.[37]

R. J. Smith, superintendent of the Pittsburgh, Pennsylvania missionary home and first chairman of the General Ministerial Assembly of the National Association of the Church of God.

John A. Morrison, first president of Anderson College. Morrison's belief in the need for higher education in the church and his theological disagreements with F. G. Smith put the two men on a collision course in the early 1930s.

A Bible training school in Anderson was an idea hatched in the mind of J. T. Wilson, newly elected president of the Gospel Trumpet Company. By the time Wilson thought of the idea, other saints already had founded Bible institutes at the missionary homes in Spokane, Kansas City, and New York. The New York and Kansas City schools soon closed their doors in favor of Anderson's location near the geographical center of the Church of God constituency. The school at Spokane struggled for life until eventually reborn as Pacific Bible College.[38] Anderson Bible Training School took center stage as the educational work in the movement. For the first eight years of its existence the Bible training school was little more than the education department of the Gospel Trumpet Company. Wilson served as principal of the school while he presided over the publishing house. Most of the first students were Gospel Trumpet Company employees, as were many of the first faculty members. But substantial changes were in store, particularly after the school was rechartered in 1925 and became an independent agency of the church under the leadership of John A. Morrison and G. Russell Olt.

John Morrison (1893–1965) was born in Phelps County, Missouri and spent his childhood wandering with his family from one house to another in the Ozark highlands. Almost constant relocation and the need to do his part with the chores of farming prevented young John from completing so much as a single full year of school. Despite his near complete absence of formal learning, Morrison deeply valued education and was determined to become a teacher. After twice failing the Missouri teacher's examination he enrolled at Steeleville Normal School. At the end of the term he successfully completed requirements for a license and began teaching at Wesco, Missouri. Later called to the ministry, Morrison and his wife, Eunice, had moved to Delta, Colorado when Wilson invited him to come to the Bible training school as a teacher and assistant principal in 1919. Ministers who possessed an educator's credentials were not unheard of in the Church of God, but neither were they superabundant. Very few possessed Morrison's sharp, ready, wit and his effectiveness as a speaker. His sense of drama combined with homespun humor and the native charm of a born storyteller to give him command of any speaker's rostrum or pulpit. Beyond his many personal gifts John Morrison was committed to the cause of higher education in and for the Church of God. When Wilson left the school in 1923 Morrison succeeded him and remained its chief executive officer until retirement in 1958.

Morrison had the good sense to recognize his severely limited educational experience in and trust the better-trained Russell Olt (1895–1958) to guide the curricular development of the young school. Olt was born and raised in Dayton, Ohio, where John Taylor, the part-time pastor of a local

G. Russell Olt. First dean of Anderson College, Olt was the architect of Anderson College's expanded, liberal arts curriculum and both advocate and activist in numerous social and political causes.

congregation of the Church of God modeled the ministry for the young man. After simultaneous careers as a student and teacher at Wilmington College in southwest Ohio, Olt earned a master's degree at the University of Cincinnati. By 1925 he had become dean of the college at Wilmington and then was also installed as pastor of Walnut Hills Church of God in Cincinnati. In that year Morrison persuaded Olt to come to Anderson but he continued to serve the Walnut Hills church, returning on weekends for twenty-four years to fulfill his pastoral duties. In some respects Morrison and Olt could not have been more dissimilar. The former loved to return to a cabin near the Meramec River in his native Ozarks whenever possible while the cosmopolitan Olt headed for the cultural opportunities of major metropolitan centers. Morrison's formal education was limited to, as he put it, "parts of" nine years, averaging not more than half a year when he did attend.[39] Olt's graduate degree was the highest held by any minister in the Church of God until the 1930s.

Olt was a many-sided individual. His social and economic views distanced him from the generally Republican Church of God ministry and Park Place neighborhood of Anderson where the campus was located. He was a deeply committed pacifist and internationalist whose understanding of Christian ethics extended into the realm of social justice. When blue-collar workers at the General Motors plants in Anderson demonstrated for union organization, Dean Russell Olt marched with them. He appointed several distinguished women to the Anderson College faculty during an era when males dominated American college faculties and helped to organize the local chapter of the Urban League.[40] Olt also gained an unfortunate notoriety among Church of God ministers for arranging an experiment in which his secretary, Mary Husted, underwent a dental operation while under hypnosis; many of Olt's ministerial colleagues believed hypnosis to be dabbling in magical arts. A professor of psychology, Olt put his learning to administrative use in some odd if clever ways. For example, he constructed an intimidating reputation for inflexibility by sawing an inch off the front legs of the visitor's chairs in his office, thereby forcing occupants into the posture of a supplicant. By all accounts he and Morrison formed an admirable partnership for the thirty-three years of their joint service, not that they did not occasionally disagree. On one occasion the two men differed on a key faculty appointment in Bible. When Morrison did not offer a faculty position to the candidate of Olt's choice, the dean avoided the president for a week.

By 1928 the new dean had set about the transformation of a curriculum that had featured such courses as "Evangelistic Piano Playing" into a liberal arts college. From the very outset the Bible training school had operated with

a utilitarian conception of education. Wilson and others believed that learning was to be put to useful purpose rather than pursued as an end in itself.
In the school's first years that purpose intended that its graduates use their
training in the service of the church in the form of a better-prepared
ministry, albeit that the church at large was not very interested in a formally
trained clergy. Olt's plan for curricular reorganization built on that utilitarian concept rather than discarding it. Nevertheless, the expansion of the
curriculum on a liberal arts model represented a significant change in
the school's self-understanding. Faculty recruitment was one of the first
aspects of the college's life to reflect these changes. A godly life and broad
ministerial experience no longer would suffice as credentials for a faculty
appointment. Beginning with the appointments of Amy Lopez, a student at
the University of Wisconsin from the Church of God in Jamaica, and B. F.
Timmons, Olt hired people with solid academic credentials as well as a faith
unfeigned and a saintly reputation.[41] Morrison completely supported Olt's
planned expansion, and when it was proposed to the college's trustees in
1928 they voted the addition of a liberal arts curriculum. As a further step
the revised curriculum then was presented to the General Ministerial
Assembly for its approval. Over the reservations of some that the church had
no business offering secular courses in its college, the curriculum once again
passed. However, that action combined several highly volatile elements in
both the college and the still relatively new organizational structures of the
church. These elements exploded in 1929 and continued to burn until 1933.
By the time the fire had burned out, both college and church structures
emerged with a new sense of themselves and their relationship to the Church
of God movement.

One of the key members of the young Anderson College faculty was
theology professor Russell R. Byrum (1889–1980), nephew of Enoch Byrum.
Russell had taught courses at Anderson from the earliest days of the Bible
training school when he was a full time member of the editorial staff, eventually managing editor, at the Gospel Trumpet Company. During his
boyhood and early adolescence Russell lived in Moundsville with his parents.
There he fell completely under the spell of George Tasker's example of
serious, scholarly study of the Bible. Russell and a friend asked Tasker to
teach a Bible study class for young men, and when Tasker left for the mission
field Byrum assumed leadership. As a teenager Russell moved to Anderson
with his father, Robert, as a member of the advance party that constructed
the several buildings needed to house the company's operations and workers.

Robert Byrum had built the *Trumpet* home in Moundsville, where
his son was converted and called to the ministry. Russell learned the

Russell R. Byrum left a post on the editorial staff of the Gospel Trumpet to take an appointment as professor of theology at Anderson College. His differences with the theology of F. G. Smith led to charges of heresy in 1929. Acquitted on all counts, Byrum nevertheless resigned his position, never to teach again.

construction trade and used his spare time to start congregations in nearby
towns. Later he took a pastorate in Boston. Others recognized in him a talent for writing, and in 1916 he accepted assignments writing for the *Trumpet*
as well as Sunday school lessons. His own voracious reading habit and thirst
for scholarship also turned him toward writing for the church and ministry.
In the same year he married the former Bessie Hittle, a one-time missionary
to Syria, who shared Russell's concern that education take a larger place in
the church's life. One of Bessie's co-workers in Syria had been Minnie
Criswell, George Tasker's first wife. The Taskers and Byrums formed a close
friendship as kindred spirits who shared similar commitments and ideas concerning the church.[42] Bessie's primary commitment lay in the area of
Christian education. She was a member of the first Board of Religious
Education and Sunday Schools, an innovator in Sunday school curriculum
development, and for decades a leader in Christian education at Park Place
Church of God. At the same time that they were married, Russell accepted a
position at the Gospel Trumpet Company and shortly afterward became the
paper's managing editor.

Like many people of his generation Byrum was without advanced formal
education and thus largely self-taught. He published several books on a range
of subjects, but he read further and more broadly in the area of theology and
in 1925 published *Christian Theology,* a one volume systematic theology.
Byrum's work prompted F. G. Smith to realize teaching authority on theological matters was shifting away from the editor's office at the Gospel
Trumpet Company. Part of the story of the revolutionary institutional
changes of the 1920s involves Smith's determined but failure effort to reverse
the direction of this shift. That effort brought Smith and Byrum into direct
conflict after 1925 and culminating in 1929.

Beginning in the 1920s the ground of teaching authority in matters
theological began shifting in two ways. The first was connected to the nature
of language and the second to the changing fortunes of two institutions,
Anderson College and the Gospel Trumpet Company and its editorship.
Russell Byrum resigned from the company in 1927 in order to join the college faculty full-time, a decision that demonstrated the changing lines of theological authority. Two years earlier he had published *Christian Theology,* a
book that reflected changes in theological discourse underway in a vanguard
of the ministry. Byrum structured his work according to the categories of
conventional systematic theology, especially as it had been written by
Baptist theologians such as A. T. Robertson. One of the clear indications of
this debt shows in Byrum's position on Christian unity, which differed sub-
stantially from the apocalyptically based come-outism of Smith and others.

That *Christian Theology* bears marks of Byrum's indebtedness to a Baptist theologian is but one illustration that his work departed from the pattern set by F. G. Smith. Beyond matters of structure, however, Byrum's theological vocabulary also turned away from Smith's, and nowhere is this more clearly demonstrated than in a comparison of the terminology the two men employed in their discussions of the church. Byrum exchanged Smith's apocalyptic vocabulary for a discourse more at home in New Testament exegesis and conventional theological discussion. Although the former was fluent in the movement's use of typology, he discarded that language for terms appearing in the theological literature with which he had become familiar.[43] Byrum applied the restorationist scheme of Christian history as it had been worked out by Schell and Smith, but he also employed the definition of the New Testament Greek word *ekklesia* as his normative referent for the church. His favorite figurative representations for the church were terms like *body, house, flock, city,* and *family.* Notably diminished was the presence of Smith's apocalyptic references, positive and negative—"woman in the wilderness," "Babylon," "Mother of Harlots," "Dragon Power," and so forth.

Despite their terminological differences Smith wrote a commendatory introduction to the first edition of Russell Byrum's *Christian Theology.* After explaining that the nature of systematic theology requires restatement from one age to the next, Smith described his younger associate's work in a way that suggests the editor thought it would have an audience larger than the Church of God movement. Part of the book's appeal, in Smith's view, lay in the fact that Byrum's theology was among the first to answer the challenges to "historic Christianity" laid down by the higher critics and "modern religious liberalism."[44] He read the book as concentrating on theism, apologetics, and the doctrines of God and human nature because these topics comprised the foundations on which the entire structure of Christian doctrine rested. Other systematics had not been written with an eye on the "general drift ... toward religious liberalism," so Smith commended Byrum's theology to theological students and "all truth-loving people everywhere."[45]

Byrum developed *Christian Theology* from his lectures at Anderson College. He anchored his study on the Scriptures alone, rejecting tradition, mysticism, and rationalism as proper sources of theology. While appreciating the importance of religious experience, he nevertheless also denied that such experience could provide the revelation upon which theology could be built. Byrum did not deny revelatory experience, but he thought that such experience was not crucial to the work of systematic theologians. They needed to rely on the Bible, which contained "supernatural and direct" revelation as opposed to the indirect revelation of nature. He singled out for criticism those "theologians who assume that revelation was originally given only through experience, and not in words; that the truths contained in the Scriptures were originally the result of inner experience only, and that consequently truth may be learned from Christian experience today as a source of theology."[46] Smith accurately read Byrum's opposition to those theologians who traced their lineage back to Schleiermacher, but his theology was not primarily an antiliberal polemic. It was in fact a textbook that introduced its readers, primarily his students but Church of God ministers as well,[47] to the subject of systematic theology. Byrum knew that such an audience had to start at the beginning, and so he defined terms that for many in this audience were strange and new—exegetical theology and exegesis, historical theology versus practical theology, and the different uses for the word *theology* itself. In this sense Byrum had written an extensive primer in theology and employed conventional theological terminology to introduce the subject to his readers.

While F. G. Smith commended Bryum's theology he also regarded it of secondary importance for the doctrinal instruction of the Church of God movement. The book's shortcomings, in Smith's eyes, were to be found in its departure from the apocalyptic language employed in his books and others. In Smith's view, authoritative discussions of the church, be they theological or of any other variety, rested on the understanding of the "church in prophecy and history" that had been forged in his work as well the writing of Schell, Warner and Riggle. Discussions that proceeded along other lines might be useful, but in Smith's mind they did not carry the same authoritative weight. However Byrum's lectures took other positions that upset Smith, even further disqualifying the younger man's work from the status of "standard literature." For example, Byrum was telling his students that the interpretive formula on which rested the church's apocalyptic self-understanding—that a prophetic day equaled a chronological year—could not be proven true.[48] After Byrum left the Gospel Trumpet Company, Smith took steps to formally relegate *Christian Theology* to secondary status as theological literature for the Church of God movement.

The General Ministerial Assembly had a decade of experience under its belt when Smith brought a resolution on "standard literature" to the floor. This was the weightiest theological issue yet confronted by the still maturing assembly. Smith's resolution called for adoption of a date to demarcate so-called "standard" literature. Books published prior to this date would carry the full weight of teaching authority for the Church of God, while later books would be considered useful but of secondary importance. Smith proposed the year 1924 as the doctrinal watershed; Byrum's *Christian Theology* was published in 1925. In the so-called "standard literature resolution" Smith, for all intents and purposes, contradicted the position he had taken in his 1919 editorial on creeping ecclesiasticism. An assembly that could demarcate standard from secondary doctrinal literature would have an authority considerably greater than that of an advisory body. Such an action was tantamount to the Assembly arrogating to itself the ecclesiastical authority to write a creed for the church. To identify a standard literature may not have produced a simple creed for memorization, but it would have elevated the status of the apocalyptic self-understanding in the Church of God movement to a level comparable to Ellen G. White's writings among Adventists.

The General Ministerial Assembly voted down Smith's standard literature resolution. Deprived of a formal, if oblique, downgrading of Byrum's work, Smith determined to move directly against the young theology professor. In the spring of 1929 Byrum gave Smith the opportunity he had been seeking. Speaking to the Indiana Ministers Assembly, Byrum outlined his theology of Christian unity. He derived that theology from the gospels and letters of the New Testament and, perhaps of greater significance to Smith, did not refer to the Book of Revelation. Byrum noted that calls for Christian unity were increasing among Christians outside the Church of God movement, some of whom, he feared, took "the real unity of all Christians more earnestly than some of our own good brethren."[49] Byrum also cautioned his ministerial colleagues against degenerating into "mere Church of God sectarians."[50] He contended that Christian unity was not to be found in uniformity of doctrine or practice. Instead Byrum described Christian unity as a loving fellowship that is achieved as humans obey the two great commandments, i.e. love God and neighbor. Such fellowship "was the purpose of God in creating us; it is the source of the highest human happiness and it is the end of our existence."[51]

Byrum could have stopped there and still have said enough to raise ministerial eyebrows, but he proceeded to attack the doctrinal practice that had been associated with the apocalyptic understanding of the church for nearly three decades. He argued that come-outism was an outmoded belief. Said Byrum, "Our contact with other Christians has led us to see that many more are saved than was supposed, and as a consequence of this and for other reasons the hope of all coming to us grows weaker."[52] Byrum was nothing if not candid. His bluntly stated argument threw the gauntlet down at the feet of those ministers who saw the church in an apocalyptic light:

> Few thinkers among us at present expect all true Christians to
> come to us, or to come into an operative unity with us as we
> as a group are with one another. Some still try to hold that

position or shrink from recognizing that they no longer hold
that narrow theory, because it would be unorthodox, and
seems to them to be a surrender of the Bible doctrine of unity.
Such brethren need to find a truer ground for unity.[53]

A more solid ground of unity anticipated Christian cooperation that was
not the forced product of human conferences, denominational compromises,
or concessions to each other. Neither would arguments or polemics unite
Christians. Instead Christian unity was coming about through a "spiritual
gravitation"; Byrum thought that God was drawing believers together, that
as they fellowshipped with one another in love they would in their consciousness realize that God had been at work among them. The task, then,
for the Church of God as he saw it was to continue to witness to Christian
unity but also to refrain from all sectarianism and especially from the
imposition of an unwritten creed.[54]

Byrum seriously overestimated the number of ministers ready to concede
the wisdom of his argument. His paper could not but have created controversy, and it did. Ministers formally complained that Byrum's views were out
of harmony with the movement's generally accepted teaching, the ecclesiology
connected to come-outism. They urged that the true practice of Christian
unity required a repudiation of Christianity's denominational structure. A
sufficient storm was brewing to warrant John Morrison's decision to distrib-
ute Byrum's paper to all Church of God ministers along with an invitation to
send him their comments in reply. Opinion varied widely; some thought that
Bryum's views were quite contrary to Church of God belief and practice.
Others thought it was time that the movement give up come-outism and the
apocalyptic self-understanding on which it rested; they welcomed Byrum's
work as a fresh alternative. Still others were uneasy with his ideas and
expressed the desire that he return to the traditional doctrinal fold.

Anderson Campmeeting annually brought together more ministers than
any other meeting on the Church of God calendar. As such it offered the best
forum to consider the hornet's nest that now buzzed around Russell Byrum.
Accordingly, at the camp meeting that gathered in June 1929, he was
required to answer a bill of particulars charged against him. Ostensibly a
hearing, the inquiry's atmosphere and structure more nearly resembled a
full-fledged heresy trial. Witnesses were called for both the defense and prosecution. A jury of eighteen—three college trustees and fifteen ministers—was
impaneled to render a verdict. In a move that could not fail to increase the
uneasiness of just about anybody in Byrum's shoes, college trustee R. L.
Berry took the role of prosecutor. Berry had succeeded Byrum as managing
editor at the Gospel Trumpet Company and was deeply sympathetic with

Smith's theology. That such a person was appointed prosecutor seems more than a little coincidental and strongly suggests that Berry was acting as Smith's agent throughout the proceedings.

The prosecution brought several charges against Byrum. They were not focused on one or two issues. On the contrary their scattershot nature suggests that Byrum's accusers were looking for anything that might warrant a conviction. Thus he was charged with (1) depreciating the guidance of the Holy Spirit in achieving Christian unity in favor of a sociological approach; (2) failing to emphasize the supernatural aspect of the kingdom of God; (3) undermining the faith of students and, therefore; (4) causing much confusion.[55] After hearing testimony from Byrum and witnesses for both the prosecution and defense (including one prosecution witness who changed his mind after hearing the accused testify), the panel of jurors acquitted Byrum of all charges. However, the flame of suspicion against Byrum spread to the college faculty in general, fanned by alarm over the recently adopted liberal arts, i. e. "secular," curriculum. To quell suspicion in the ministry, as well as among some members of the trustee board, college trustees developed a statement of belief that they intended all faculty members to sign. Byrum regarded such a measure as unfairly limiting the teaching approaches of professors, whose task it was to train young minds to think broadly. Rather than see it adopted Byrum resigned his faculty appointment. Later he said that he was surprised when Morrison accepted it. Scarcely forty years of age, Byrum was about to reach the height of what might have been a distinguished academic career. Instead he left the ministry when his career at Anderson prematurely ended. Although his departure also meant the end of nearly every personal working relationship that Byrum prized, he bore neither Morrison nor the college any ill will.[56]

John Morrison's decision to accept Russell Byrum's resignation yielded several different kinds of fruit. It accomplished the goal that F. G. Smith had twice sought but had been unable to achieve—the diminishing of Byrum's theological influence. However, Smith had taken aim at the wrong target, as he soon realized. Events were to play out in such a way as to make it clear that a theological teaching authority to rival the editor and paper was not to be located personally in Russell Byrum but institutionally in the young college growing on the opposite side of the street from the Gospel Trumpet Company. Another fruit to ripen in the wake of the Byrum affair was a settled conviction in John Morrison's mind that Smith had grown too powerful. This certainty combined with Morrison's strong theological reservations about Smith's apocalyptic come-outism, to convinced Morrison that the editor should be denied another term.

It took years, perhaps decades, to recognize that Morrison's decision bore fruit in another way. Byrum's departure may have eliminated a principle source of the church's suspicion toward Anderson College, but it also forestalled a badly needed conversation on issues such as the nature of education and learning at a church-related college as well as its relationship to its sponsoring church. These conversations did not occur and an opportunity was lost to achieve broad mutual understanding, perhaps a consensus, on such matters. Instead, Russell Byrum's heresy trial and the subsequent departure of the movement's most promising theologian became the opening gambit in the larger question of F. G. Smith's role as theological authority and leader of the Church of God movement as well as the specific theology associated with his name.

Notes

1. For a history of the General Assembly cf. Marvin J. Hartman, "The Origin and Development of the General Ministerial Assembly of the Church of God, 1917–1950," unpublished B. D. thesis, School of Religion, Butler University, 1958. Cf. Barry L. Callen, ed., *Following the Light* (Anderson, Ind: Warner Press, 2000), 157–309. Charles E. Brown described the proceedings of a 1902 assembly that he, not yet twenty years of age, attended at Yellow Lake Campmeeting in northern Indiana: "The ministers present assembled in the men's dormitory and sat around on the beds and talked. The only touch of a formal organization in this meeting was the appointment by this informal gathering of one man to represent the group in talking to the railroads concerning the availability of clergy rates." Quoted in Callen, Ibid., 160.

2. This is Hartman's description as summarized by Callen in *Following the Light,* 160–161.

3. In 1916 the company members, i. e. the twenty-four member board, appointed a committee composed of Vice-President A. L. Byers, D. O. Teasley, a rising star in company management, and F. G. Smith, who was to become editor within a month, to construct a proposal to create closer ties between the company and the church.

4. Phillips, *Miracle of Survival,* 142.

5. The committee members appointed were J. W. Phelps, A. B. Frost, H. A. Sherwood, O. E. Line, and R. R. Byrum. Phelps and Byrum both worked at the Gospel Trumpet Company.

6. The article is quoted in Callen, *Following the Light,* 162–163.

7. e.g. "It has been felt for some time that there should be....." Ibid., 162.

8. Gale Hetrick and Company, *Laughter Among the Trumpets,* 118–120.

9. (Anderson, Ind: Gospel Trumpet Company, 1927).

10. Ibid., v.

11. Many congregations simply lifted the bylaws section directly from Byrum's text. So, for example, the familiar article on voting membership that bases congregational voter eligibility on three conditions: (1) sixteen years of age, (2) six months previous attendance, during which period (3) prospective voters must have lived "in harmony with the doctrines and practices of the Church of God." The membership article also stated that the above conditions could be waived if the prospective voter was approved by a two-thirds majority of the congregation. Cf. Byrum, *Problems of the Local Church,* 204–209.

12. (Anderson, Ind: Gospel Trumpet Company, 1911).

13. His books covered a wide range of topics beyond the works on hermeneutics and the Sunday school: biblical geography, manners, counseling books for men and woman, sex and reproduction, the doctrine of salvation, and the Holy Spirit.

14. Ibid., 9–10.

15. In 1919 Teasley resigned from the Gospel Trumpet Company under heavy suspicion of adultery. A young woman had followed him from Anderson to Bessemer and rumors of impropriety abounded.

The matter was further compounded by an unhappy marriage and home life that appeared to lend some credence to the rumors. Rather than see Teasley accompany F. G. Smith on an announced world missionary tour, people from Bessemer stepped forward to accuse Teasley of adultery. He resigned his positions at the Gospel Trumpet Company, referring to himself as "your unworthy brother," and left the Church of God movement.

16. Reardon, "Movers and Shakers in the Church of God," 18.

17. *GT* (June 5, 1919), 1.

18. Ibid.

19. Ibid.

20. Ibid. Smith's emphasis.

21. Ibid., 1–2. Smith's emphasis.

22. In addition to familiar religious and moral issues, e.g. "How often may persons of the opposite sex hold private conversations with one another?" directors found themselves dealing with the following: How long did a family member have to remain in the Home before being considered for "outside" living? If a carpenter in the Trumpet family helped another family member build a house for a few weeks, does the latter owe the company at least for the carpenter's board? Should the company pay for the installation of a telephone in the home of a family member? For a complete discussion of the Gospel Trumpet Company's transition from commune to wage paying employer, cf. Harold L. Phillips, *Miracle of Survival* (Anderson, Ind: Warner Press, 1979), 147–155.

23. Wilson was elected president in 1917. He succeeded E. E. Byrum, who had continued in that office for one year after his resignation as editor in 1916.

24. Ibid., 155.

25. For a study of the application of business methods in a post-WW I Protestant inter-denominational crusade, cf. Eldon Ernst, *Moment of Truth for Protestant America: Interchurch Campaigns Following World War One* (Missoula, Mont: American Academy of Religion and Scholars' Press, 1974).

26. "The Treasury Box," *GT* (July 23, 1903), 6.

27. "Tithing," *GT* (March 24, 1904), 4.

28. "The Tithing System Compared with the New Testament System," *GT* (September 16, 1915), 8.

29. *Our Ministerial Letter,* "Our Mission Work," (n.p: n.d.), 13. At the very end of that issue of the newsletter, James R. Tallen added a short essay titled "Financial Possibilities." Without appeal to any biblical text Tallen used the figure of 10 percent as he illustrated how such an amount could be divided in support of various aspects of the church's work. Ibid., 28–29.

30. James Earl Massey, *An Introduction to the Negro Churches in the Church of God Reformation Movement* (New York: Shining Light Survey Press, 1957), 19.

31. One such incident occurred at an 1897 camp meeting in northern Alabama. Cf. "Haunted by the Past," in Merle D. Strege, *Tell Me the Tale: Historical Reflections on the Church of God* (Anderson, Ind: Warner Press, 1991), 6–8.

32. A fine study of the change in racial attitudes in the early Church of God is Greggory R. Giles, "Black-White Relations in the Church of God, 1880–1918," unpublished course paper, Anderson School of Theology, 1986, revised 1993). Archives of the Church of God.

33. *GT* (March 11, 1910), 10.

34. The minutes of the Campmeeting Committee from 1910 to 1916 are collected in a volume housed in the Archives of the Church of God.

35. The oral tradition took written form in Katie R. Davis' account of the African American camp meeting, *Zion's Hill at West Middlesex* (Corpus Christi, Tex: Christian Triumph Press, 1951). Subsequent printed references to the event all cite Mrs. Davis' account. John W. V. Smith cited it in *The Quest for Holiness and Unity,* as did Samuel Hines and Cheryl Sanders in subsequent works. Mrs. Davis relied on the recollections of Joseph Crosswhite, manager of the West Middlesex campground, who recalled hearing Samuel and Laura Moore's account of a request from Whites that African Americans "get a meeting of your own" because they were attending the Anderson meeting in growing numbers. It is this tradition that has been passed down without documentation in the African American church. However, the recently uncovered minutes of the camp meeting committee document the request, cited in the above narrative. Camp meeting organizers did request Blacks to hold a separate service one afternoon during the Anderson meeting. The camp meeting committee micromanaged

the meeting's every detail, down to the straw ordered to stuff into mattress ticks. Given this tendency, and coupled with the detailed accounts in its minutes, it seems the better part of historiographical wisdom to err on the side of caution and rely on information that can be documented.

36. On this matter and much else about African Americans and the Church of God see Cheryl J. Sanders, *Saints in Exile: The Holiness-Pentecostal Experience in African American Religion and Culture* (New York: Oxford University Press, 1996), especially pages 22–27.

37. The "Theological Seminary" portion of the title was a bit grandiose. A seminary would be founded on the Anderson College campus, but not until 1950. For histories of Anderson College, nee University, cf. John A. Morrison, *As the River Flows* (Anderson, Ind: Anderson College Press, 1962); Robert H. Reardon, *The Early Morning Light* (Anderson, Ind: Warner Press, 1979); and particularly Barry L. Callen, *Guide of Soul and Mind* (Anderson, Ind: Warner Press, 1992).

38. Pacific Bible College, under the leadership of its founder A. F. Gray, later moved from Spokane to Portland, Oregon where it eventually grew into Warner Pacific College.

39. Morrison, *As the River Flows,* 75.

40. According to Robert Reardon, in addition to the Urban League, Olt aided in the organization of the United Way in Anderson, the Peace Fellowship of the Church of God, the International Youth Convention of the Church of God, and the first World Conference of the Church of God. "Movers and Shakers in the Church of God." Olt also led a group that arranged for the relocation of displaced persons after World War II.

41. Lopez joined the faculty in 1927, interrupting a formal education that later included an M. A. from Columbia University and graduate study at Oxford. She taught English at Anderson College until her retirement in 1950. Timmons began teaching at Anderson in 1928, soon afterwards received a Ph. D. from Ohio State, and taught ethics and sociology.

42. Years later Byrum wrote a reminiscence of his old friend Tasker. Mrs. Earl Martin appended a comment wherein she noted that Byrum could not read "Tasker's sad story" without weeping. In his reminiscence Byrum attributed to George and Minnie Tasker considerable influence on his and his wife's intellectual and spiritual development. The typescript and Mrs. Martin's handwritten appendix is housed in the Archives of the Church of God.

43. The movement's apocalyptic ecclesiology and the hermeneutics behind it were widely read and taught by rising leaders in the decade 1910–1920. Byrum published a book on typology, *Shadows of Good Things* (Anderson, Ind: Gospel Trumpet Company, 1923), and future New Testament professor Otto F. Linn lectured on the church and prophecy. Both men later set aside this exegesis in favor of methods and constructs more at home in the world of scholarly exegesis and theology.

44. Russell R. Byrum, *Christian Theology* (Anderson, Ind: Gospel Trumpet Company, 1925), 8–9.

45. Ibid., 10.

46. Ibid., 34.

47. Byrum's *Christian Theology* has been in print continuously since 1925 and despite several newer works remains on the list of books suggested for candidates for ordination to the Church of God ministry. But this recommendation belies the fact that early on the book's sales gave no promise of such longevity. Cf. Harold L. Phillips, *Miracle of Survival,* 177.

48. R. R. Byrum, "The Byrum Family," unpublished ms., Archives of the Church of God.

49. R. R. Byrum, "Christian Unity," mimeographed paper, Archives of the Church of God, 1.

50. Ibid., 1.

51. Ibid., 3.

52. Ibid.

53. Ibid.

54. Ibid., 4.

55. Robert H. Reardon, *The Early Morning Light* (Anderson, Ind: Warner Press, 1979), 57–58.

56. R. R. Byrum, "The Byrum Family," unpublished memoir, Archives of the Church of God, 19. Russell Byrum returned to the construction trade he had learned from his father. Bessie Byrum taught at Anderson College for another two years and continued her work in behalf of Christian education while her husband became a prosperous contractor who made significant financial contributions to Anderson College.

Chapter 8
A Spiritual Kingdom

Until their deaths in the 1940s and 1950s, key members of the first generations of the Church of God were known for their expertise on certain of the movement's distinctive doctrines. Thus E. E. Byrum was a noted authority on the subject of divine healing and F. G. Smith was identified with the doctrine of the church, especially as it had been revealed in prophecy and history. The movement also had a distinctive perspective on the doctrine of the kingdom of God, and the person who wrote and spoke extensively on that topic was H. M. Riggle.

Herbert McClellan Riggle (1872–1952) was raised in an Evangelical Lutheran family against a community backdrop shaped by the deep holiness piety of the Free Methodist Church, the Welseyan Methodist Church, and the Mennonite Brethren in Christ.[1] He was converted in 1891 and experienced entire sanctification in 1893 in revival meetings conducted by G. T. Clayton after approximately four years of attentive listening to preachers such as W. G. Schell and A. J. Kilpatrick. That same year Riggle married Minnie Shelhamer, the daughter of the first come-outer at Cochran's Mills, Pennsylvania and a cousin of Free Methodist evangelist E. E. Shelhamer. Minnie was also a preacher, and after a brief sojourn in the Puget Sound area the young couple returned to their home in western Pennsylvania to form the Riggle Evangelistic Company. The Riggles held pastorates in several states, sometimes Herbert serving one congregation and Minnie another, but their real skills were in itinerant evangelism. Together they started numerous congregations in Pennsylvania, Ohio, Indiana, and elsewhere.

By the time that *The Cleansing of the Sanctuary* was published, H. M. Riggle was already an accomplished writer. He had published a sufficiently large number of articles that E. E. Byrum named him a contributing editor to the *Gospel Trumpet*. Riggle also had published numerous books, including the first of several on the subject with which his name came to be

H. M. Riggle, The "Boy Preacher of the Reformation," Riggle authored several books on the topic of the kingdom of God. He staunchly and aggressively defended the movement's theology of the kingdom as a present reality against premillennialists.

associated, *The Kingdom of God and the One Thousand Years' Reign*.[2] Riggle was also a leading controversialist for the Church of God, defending its ideas and practices in the schoolhouse debates common to nineteenth- and early twentieth-century American religion.[3] His youthful appearance, oratorical skill, and expertise on topics crucial to the movement's identity earned Riggle the sobriquet, the "Boy Preacher of the Reformation." Later the Canadian H. C. Heffren also published smaller works on eschatology, as did Gulf-Coast Bible College founder Max Gaulke along with professor E. I. Carver and others. But Riggle's work was the earliest and most extensive on the topic.

The rise of the Church of God movement coincided with the waning influence of postmillennial eschatology among American Protestants and the emergence of premillennialism.[4] Puritans were by and large premillennialists although not dispensationalist, but it was postmillenialism that enjoyed a brief season of popularity between Jonathan Edwards and the Civil War. In the early national period, numerous Evangelical reform and missionary societies busily set about building the kingdom of God in America. The career of the Liberty Party in the 1840s and '50s illustrates the manner in which perfectionist, revivalist-oriented Protestants were deeply invested in the political process in the belief that through such involvement Christians would cooperate with the Holy Spirit to build the Kingdom on earth.

In the wake of the Civil War's terrible slaughter it became increasingly difficult to sustain the optimistic belief that Americans were cooperating with God in the construction of the Kingdom. At the same time, a new form of premillennialism called dispensationalism began rising in popularity. A popular teacher among the Plymouth Brethren, John Nelson Darby, developed the doctrine in England in the years before the American Civil War. Its later growth in the United States was fueled by the publication of the Scofield Reference Bible in 1909 as well as dispensationalists' growing participation in the Niagara Bible Conferences and a series of conferences on biblical prophecy that they sponsored in major American cities after 1878. Later leading premillennialist spokespersons such as Reuben A. Torrey and William Bell Riley thought dispensationalism to be an indispensable weapon in the fight against theological liberalism, and this made dispensationalists allies of scholarly Fundamentalists such as A. A. Hodge and J. Gresham Machen. But it would be a serious mistake to conclude that all Fundamentalists advocated a dispensationalist eschatology.[5] Nearly all dispensational premillennialists may have been Fundamentalists, but not all Fundamentalists, particularly those affiliated with Princeton Theological Seminary, espoused dispensationalism.

After it adopted Uriah Smith's church-historical hermeneutic for its own, the Church of God movement rejected both post- and premillennialist eschatologies. Its preachers and controversialists strenuously maintained the view that Christ would never again return for the purpose of establishing an earthly Kingdom—before or after Judgment Day. Instead they insisted that his rule had already begun; the kingdom of God was a spiritual reign situated in the hearts and minds of human beings. Church of God preachers expected the return of Christ, and many believed that return to be imminent. But they asserted that the Lord's return would simultaneously ring down the curtain on world history; there would be no literal divine rule on the earth.

Over a two-week period in March 1901, H. M. Riggle and Elder F. J. Ebeling of the Reorganized Church of Jesus Christ of Latter Day Saints met at Blystone, Pennsylvania to debate four separate theological issues. Riggle took the negative side of the first proposition: "*Resolved,* That the kingdom of God will be a literal kingdom, and its complete establishment is yet future." Riggle had already published the first of his three books on the Kingdom as related to eschatology. He also had in hand and was soon to complete D. S. Warner's unfinished manuscript as *The Cleansing of the Sanctuary.* Guided by these works, W. G. Schell's *Biblical Trace of the Church,* and works by other Church of God writers, Riggle closely intertwined doctrines of the Kingdom, the church in prophecy and history, and eschatology.

Riggle opened the debate by defining the nature of a Kingdom. He stipulated that any kingdom has five characteristics: (1) a ruler, (2) a throne from which the ruler governs, (3) a territory over which the ruler has jurisdiction, (4) subjects in that territory who are governed by the ruler, and (5) laws by which the subjects are governed.[6] Against the view that the kingdom of God was to be fulfilled in the future Riggle contended that Jesus had satisfied all five criteria during his earthly ministry. If that were so, premillenialists who looked toward the future establishment of the Kingdom were in error. Of course Riggle did not pin his argument on a debater's ploy. He adduced numerous biblical texts to support his claim that Jesus had already satisfied all the conditions of kingly rule. Riggle read John 18:36–37 and John 1:49 to make the point that Jesus claimed kingship and that others confessed him so. Hebrews 1:7–8, Hebrews 4:16, and Psalms 47:8 established Jesus as ruling from a throne of grace and holiness. Third, Christ himself claimed the whole of heaven and earth as his dominion in Matthew 28:18. Fourth, said Riggle, 1 Peter 3:22 described the angels and principalities as subject to Christ, and Ephesians 5:21 made it clear that the church also submitted to him. In the "gospel dispensation," in Riggle's favored phrase, Christ has subjects both in heaven and earth. Fifth, "the laws which govern the subjects of Christ's kingdom in this dispensation are, First, the law of truth. Psalm 119:142–'Thy righteousness is an everlasting righteousness and thy law is the truth.' Second, the law of holiness. Third, the law of love."[7] Having thus made his case, Riggle pressed the view that the kingdom of Christ was therefore a present reality.

Riggle's conclusion was a bedrock theological commitment of the first generations of Church of God leadership. From far-off India John A. D. Khan echoed Riggle's position. Since the beginning of time, said Khan, the righteous accept God as their sovereign Lord who rules over them and controls their lives and actions.[8] In Khan's view it was "according to Scripture,... nothing but a Utopian dream to look for the establishment of the Messianic kingdom at the second coming of our Lord; and such expectations are certain to end in a great disappointment."[9] Khan and Riggle also shared similar views of millennialism's origins. Both men found its source in what they termed ancient Judaism's false hope for a literal kingdom of God. In this Riggle self-consciously followed the judgments of noted church historians such as Augustus Neander and Phillip Schaff.[10] Khan developed his ideas from other sources that located the origin of such "gross materialistic ideas" in Judaism's abandonment of a purely spiritual conception of the Messianic reign under the influence of pagan sources such as Zoroastrianism.[11] Regardless of their explanations of millennialism's ultimate source, both men agreed that its great fallacy began in Jewish hopes for a future, earthly messianic reign. Khan developed his views in India, but wherever English language hymnals of the Church of God were used, D. O. Teasley taught singers the same conclusion in the lines of a polemical gospel song titled "We'll Crown Him Lord of All": "While others dream of an age to come, He's reigning in our hearts today."[12]

No biblical text was of any greater importance to the theology of the present Kingdom than Luke 17:20–22: "And when he was demanded of the Pharisees when the kingdom of God should come, he answered them and said, 'The kingdom of God cometh not with observation: neither shall they say, Lo here! or Lo there! for, behold, the kingdom of God is within you.' " Riggle and the early Church of God movement took this text to mean that Jesus located the Kingdom within the hearts of believers. It was not a literal, earthly kingdom but a spiritual reign over the minds of those loyal to Christ.[13] The version of the Bible quoted by Riggle was the King James, which Riggle favored but did not use exclusively. That version's translation of the Greek *entos* as "within" seems to confuse the sense of the encounter the passage describes. Riggle knew of other translations that preferred "among" over "within," but thought the change to be of no great consequence. He thought that "within" was the proper rendering, interpreting it thus: "By using the words 'within you' Jesus did not mean to teach that the kingdom was in those wicked Pharisees, but simply wished to convey the truth to them that his kingdom, throne, and reign was not temporal, but spiritual in the hearts of his people."[14] As Riggle stated, "This is positive and clear, and should stop the mouth of every latter-day advocate of a literal reign upon the earth yet future."[15]

That the Kingdom was spiritual rather than temporal was the most important of the reasons that Riggle and the Church of God opposed all forms of millennialism. In their eyes, opponents who looked for a future literal reign of Christ on earth had fundamentally misunderstood the nature of the Kingdom. To be mistaken about the Kingdom also indicated that they had not seen the church. A spiritual Kingdom required a spiritual mode of entrance, and salvation was the name of that door. Jesus had told his disciples that they must be converted, and as little children at that, or else they would never enter the Kingdom. Thus Riggle concluded:

> Entering the kingdom and getting saved is the same thing. Here again we see the spiritual nature of Christ's kingdom. Since it is through the new birth that men enter the kingdom, there are none in the real kingdom of God but those who are saved. The work of placing men and women in the kingdom belongs to God, "who hath delivered us from the power of darkness, and hath translated us into the kingdom of his dear Son" (Col 1:13). Since the new birth is a spiritual birth, and the door into the kingdom is a spiritual door, it is further proved that the kingdom of God is a spiritual kingdom; for how could a man enter a literal kingdom through a spiritual door?[16]

Riggle's description of the believer's relation to the Kingdom was reminiscent of the language that Church of God writers employed when discussing the church. In point of fact Riggle equated church and Kingdom: "When a soul fully complies with all the Bible conditions, then by the work of conversion—the new birth—it enters through Christ the door into the church, or kingdom, of God."[17] A mistaken theology of the Kingdom therefore equated to an erroneous vision of the church. If the movement's exegesis of Daniel and the Revelation was correct then premillennialists had to be wrong. Riggle opposed millennialists of all descriptions exactly on the grounds that they practiced a faulty and inconsistent exegesis. Indeed, he loved to employ the rhetorical device of piling up the apparent inconsistencies of millennialism.[18] But the crucial aspect of his rejection of millennialist eschatologies centered in the movement's conviction that the Kingdom was a present spiritual reign. Premillennialists believed in the temporal reign of Christ. Against this view, Riggle and other Church of God writers insisted that the Kingdom was located within the hearts and minds of believers.

The Kingdom and Holiness

Given the Church of God movement's tendency to equate church and Kingdom, and coupled with the insistence that the latter is a present spiritual reality, it is not too much to say that the practices of holiness embodied the practical aspect of the movement's doctrine of the Kingdom. Even before Riggle began debating millennialists and publishing his books on the Kingdom, songwriter Barney E. Warren had penned the words to a gospel song that closely connected holiness and the present spiritual reign of Christ: "'Tis a kingdom of peace, it is reigning within, it shall ever increase in my soul; We possess it right here when he saves from all sin, And 'twill last while the ages shall roll."[19] The affirmation that Jesus had saved from all sin was familiar to singers affiliated with the holiness movement. To be saved from all sin entailed both freedom from the power of sin as well as its condemnation. Hearts obedient to the spiritual reign of Christ walked in the way of holiness.

As articulated in the work of H. M. Riggle, the Church of God stated that conversion was the doorway into the Kingdom. But the saints also understood conversion under the familiar holiness description of the "double cure"; it was the first of two steps necessary to complete the work of salvation. The second, of course, was the experience of entire sanctification. The connection that Riggle made between sanctification and the Kingdom is clearly seen in the following extended quotation.

> But even after conversion there yet remains in the heart of the believer a sinful nature, the carnal mind. This causes an inward warfare between the flesh and the spirit. Before Christ can reign supreme, this inward foe must be destroyed, the throne of iniquity must be obliterated. This is accomplished in the glorious work of entire sanctification. So the fullness of God in the baptism of the Holy Ghost and the complete establishment of his throne of holiness in our hearts is something for which the believer must seek, therefore he prays, "Thy kingdom come" (Matt 6:10). There is a sense in which God's

people can pray this prayer in any meeting where they desire the salvation of the lost. Their cry is that the kingdom of God may come into the hearts of the people by the salvation of their souls. The promise is, "Fear not, little flock; for it is your Father's good pleasure to give you the kingdom." "The very God of peace sanctify you wholly."

When the believer presents himself as a living sacrifice upon Christ the altar, when the last condition is fully met in a complete death to sin and self, then the Holy Ghost, with the blood of Christ, destroys the body of sin and moves in, in all his fullness as a personal comforter, to abide with the soul forever. "God sitteth upon the throne of his holiness." "The reign of God is within you." This is the sense in which the "saints of the most high" "take the kingdom and possess the kingdom forever, even forever and ever. The kingdom is "righteousness, and peace, and joy in the Holy Ghost."[20]

Riggle refused to concede the term *dispensation* to premillennialists. He maintained that history had been divided into three dispensations of God's presence: the era of the biblical patriarchs, followed by the Mosaic dispensation of the law, followed in turn by the final, Christian dispensation that began with Christ's advent and ministry. This last dispensation Riggle subdivided into the four periods that he and others had worked out in their apocalyptic ecclesiology: (1) the morning light of the gospel day, (2) the long years of apostasy that were followed by (3) the partial light of Protestantism culminating in (4) the evening light of the restoration of the true church. The widely held view among the saints of "this present reformation," as they liked to refer to the Church of God movement, was that they were living in the last era of the last dispensation. Many expected the Lord to return soon, but without a period of tribulation and prolonged opportunity for repentance. Riggle insisted, "Now is the day of salvation" for the Kingdom was at hand. Possessing it and enjoying the glorious reign of Christ in the soul were not to be found in some future age, but at the front of a camp meeting tent or revival meetinghouse at an altar of prayer. Those who lived in sin were slaves to their own lusts and unable to control themselves: "... but salvation makes us 'kings' in rule over our own selves; over our passions, appetites, and desires."[21]

The present spiritual rule of God in the soul brought the believer victory over sin. Indeed, said Riggle, the redemption of humanity was the special aim behind Christ's establishment of the Kingdom during his earthly ministry.

The powers of darkness were broken when the redemptive reign of Christ began and Jesus gave his disciples power over Satan's tottering kingdom. Among the broken powers was sin's hold on the human heart. Through Christ's death and resurrection God had clothed him with all power in heaven and earth: "power to fully save, sanctify, and redeem mankind from the last effects of the fall."[22] Those who were sanctified had been freed not only from sin's condemnation but sin's power as well. Life in the Kingdom equated to the life of holiness.

That holy living was equated with the present reign of Christ in the soul only added to the significance of the practices of holiness embedded in the life of the Church of God. Under the doctrinal rubric of the Kingdom, the reign of God and holiness mutually reinforced each other. The shibboleths and taboos familiar to the holiness movement—plain dress, refraining from beverages containing alcohol or caffeine,[23] shunning the theater and movie house, novel reading, the dance hall, and others—were the manner in which the saints gave evidence of and practiced the present rule of Christ. To engage in prohibited forms of entertainment or wear jewelry or, for some, a necktie, were signs of "worldliness," proof that one's allegiance was not to Christ but to the principalities and powers that ruled the earth. The saints may not have separated themselves from the surrounding culture as completely as the Amish, for example, but where they did distance themselves it was with a determination and an understanding similar to H. Richard Niebuhr's classic expression, "Christ against culture."[24] "The world" stood over against the present Kingdom. Men and women had to choose one or the other. To accept God's offer of salvation's double cure set one under Christ's rule and on a new way of life that shunned worldliness. To live according to the holiness taboos was, in the Church of God movement, to practice Kingdom living.

The Kingdom and the Church in Prophecy and History

H. M. Riggle noticed an important difference between the Church of God movement and millenialists when it came to biblical sources. The former generally developed its understanding of the Kingdom from the Gospels and the letters of the New Testament. On the other hand, said Riggle, "Modern Millennium-teachers dwell very little in the plain Gospels and Epistles to prove their doctrines, but speculate in prophecy and [R]evelation."[25] Riggle could not resist associating such teachers with the "ungodly heretic Cerinthus," an ancient millennial teacher who rejected the Gospel of Matthew and many of the Pauline letters as non-canonical.[26] "Modern millennium-teachers" may not have excluded the Gospels and letters from the canon, but in Riggle's mind they neglected the primary sources of biblical teaching on the Kingdom. The difference in sources notwithstanding, Church of God opponents of millennialism were nevertheless compelled to dispute premillennialist readings of biblical apocalyptic, but for reasons that ran far beyond variant views of the kingdom of God.

An important ground for Church of God opposition to the idea of a future literal kingdom took the form of a hermeneutical battle over the apocalyptic sections of the Bible. Premillennialist eschatology and the apocalyptic ecclesiology of the Church of God both were grounded in that literature, but they reached mutually exclusive interpretations. If the premillennialists had their eschatology right, then the church-historical reading of biblical apocalyptic was in error. By the same token, if Schell, Warner/Riggle, and Smith were right, then the premillennialists had to be wrong. But this dispute was more than a disagreement over eschatology. The doctrine of the church that had developed after 1885 depended on the church-historical hermeneutic. The debate over eschatology and the nature of the Kingdom thus entailed what was in Church of God doctrinal practice the correlative topic of ecclesiology. If the premillennialists were right about eschatology, then the Church of God reading of biblical apocalyptic had to be incorrect, and if so the foundation of the movement's self-understanding and sense of mission of necessity had to collapse. The movement would then be left without a place in the Bible or history and therefore be devoid of a reason for being. Although this conclusion was rarely if ever stated, it nevertheless was an important aspect that drove Church of God polemics against all forms of millennialism.

Church of God writers and dispensationalists shared a common appreciation of the dialectic of prophecy and fulfillment, but there were also important distinctions. One difference came at the point of assigning a historical location to the idea of fulfillment. Whereas dispensationalists looked to the future, near or otherwise, when it came to the fulfillment of prophecies concerning the Kingdom the Church of God insisted that they had already been fulfilled. In terms of the Kingdom, movement writers said that the Old Testament prophets had foretold a coming king and kingdom and that Jesus was the fulfillment of that prophecy; ergo, the Kingdom began in Jesus' lifetime and continued down to the present.[27] Another hermeneutical difference that separated the Church of God from premillennialists involved the way each read apocalyptic. Dispensationalists tended to read this literature as predictions concerning world history, whereas the apocalyptic ecclesiology of the Church of God limited the scope of Daniel and the Revelation to prophecies concerning the church. But here again the movement argued that those prophecies had been fulfilled. They saw themselves as living in the "evening light" of the gospel day, the final era of the last dispensation of history. All that had been prophesied in Daniel and the Revelation concerning the church had been fulfilled, and there remained only Christ's return before time would be rolled up like a scroll.

The significant differences between the Church of God and millennialists—dispensationalist and otherwise—demanded attention. H. M. Riggle warmed to this polemical task. He told his "dear readers," for example, that Nebuchadnezzar's vision of the great statue in Daniel 2 prophesied the four kingdoms that would rise and pass away as precursors to the establishment of the Kingdom. In Riggle's view "history had proven this to be true": the Babylonian, Medo-Persian, Greek, and Roman empires had succeeded each other in turn and the advent of Christ during the last had fulfilled Daniel's prophecy. Therefore no future kingdom was possible; it had already come in Christ.[28] But according to Riggle and the church-historical hermeneutic, Daniel prophesied events beyond the fall of Rome. It also foretold a time when "the saints of the Most High shall take the kingdom and possess the kingdom forever, even forever and ever" (Dan 7:18). Riggle identified these saints as the children of the woman described in Revelation 4:1–2. In his view as with other Church of God writers, the woman was symbolic of "the true church of God—the bride of Christ—in her primitive unity and purity."[29] Her children, all the saints, were to rule in fulfillment of Daniel's prophecy concerning the church, the afore-quoted Daniel 7:18. From this foundation Riggle reiterated W. G. Schell's interpretation and periodization of the epochs of Christian history, an interpretation soon to be restated in *The Cleansing of the Sanctuary* and preeminently in the books of F. G. Smith. As Riggle read the prophecies of Revelation and described them for his readers, their only possible reference was to the history of the church marked by successive eras of purity, papal apostasy, partial restoration, and complete return to the holiness and unity of the primitive church.[30] Those who could not see the truth that these prophecies were now in their final stage of fulfillment had eyes that were simply too blind to see what God had plainly revealed.

In Riggle's antimillennialist polemic this positive interpretation of Daniel and the Revelation was accompanied by a sharply negative examination of millenialist hermeneutics. In some cases he employed a debater's maneuvers, often pointing to what he considered inconsistencies or contradictions. More often he disputed the interpretations of key biblical passages or conclusions. A case in point involved the question whether Christ presently sat upon the throne of David or would he wait until the establishment of a future kingdom to claim that exalted position. Riggle took it as axiomatic of

Max R. Gaulke, founding president of Gulf Coast Bible College and a mid-twentieth century apologist for the movement's theology of the kingdom of God.

the "millennium heresy" that it claimed that Christ did not sit on David's throne at present. If the Bible contained sufficient warrants to believe that Christ currently held the throne, "then why look for another [dispensation] in which to accomplish that which is being fulfilled in this present one?"[31] Riggle mined texts from both the Old and New Testaments to argue his case. The famous Messianic passage from Isaiah 9 was a prophecy of Christ's enthronement fulfilled at the beginning of his reign "in the days of his incarnation."[32] Riggle similarly interpreted the angel's word to Mary in Luke, rhetorically asking and then answering, "Do we have presented before us in this prophecy two dispensations? Not by any means. The birth of Christ, his name, his origin, his throne and reign, are all connected and must be in one dispensation—that is the present one."[33] In other texts Riggle interpreted Christ as a "title name" for David in order to appropriate for Jesus the present possession of David's throne.[34] Riggle drove home his conclusion with a patented rhetorical flourish:

> We that are now translated into the kingdom of his dear Son (Col 1:13) know that his kingdom is righteousness, and peace, and joy in the Holy Ghost (Rom 14:17), and a scepter of righteousness is the scepter of his kingdom (Heb 1:8). He reigns over us in mount Zion and in Jerusalem (Isa 24:23; Heb 12:22). And he must reign (continue) till he hath put all his enemies under his feet. The last enemy that shall be destroyed is death (1 Cor 15:25–26). This is accomplished at his second coming. Then the end, when he shall have delivered up the kingdom to God, even the Father (1 Cor 15:22–24). The time when the Millenarians expect him to begin his reign is the exact time that these texts declare that he ceases to reign, having delivered the kingdom to the Father. Hence if Christ does not reign over us in this dispensation, he never will. May the deceived ones learn this before the coming of the Lord. Amen.[35]

The early Church of God movement took Jesus at his word when he said that his Kingdom was not of this world. They interpreted this to mean not that he had no kingdom or that its fulfillment was postponed to some prophesied future, but that he reigned presently as the ruler of a spiritual Kingdom that included all those who had experienced salvation.

After Riggle

Riggle's body of work, a substantial portion of it derived if not lifted directly from his first book on the topic, remained normative for the movement in the years up to his death in 1952. Other voices added their interpretations, but they were largely consistent with Riggle's writing. In 1959 Max R. Gaulke, founder and president of Gulf Coast Bible College in Houston, Texas, published a small book that recapitulated some of Riggle's main themes. However, Gaulke laid even greater stress on the significance of the doctrine of the Kingdom. For him, "all the doctrines in the Bible converge upon this one—the kingdom of God. Christ came to establish this kingdom. The Bible is the divine document that presents the history of God's redemptive plan as he endeavored to make his kingship acceptable to the world. Everything else the Bible says can be incorporated into this briefly stated—but major—thesis of the Word of God."[36]

Dispensationalism's growing popularity particularly troubled Gaulke, and he made that eschatology the special target of his polemics. He was equally concerned that "those who teach the true 'faith once delivered to the saints' remain patiently quiet.' "[37] Popular preaching was not Gaulke's only concern, however. Even more than Riggle he took aim at dispensationalism, which, for Gaulke, muddied the theological waters of eschatology even more than earlier forms of premillennialism. He described dispensationalism as a "strange admixture of speculation and 'private interpretation' " and an unquestioning literalism that naively shifted to figurative or symbolic interpretation when the purpose suited.[38] Gaulke regarded all of this as highly questionable, and additionally he was irritated by dispensationalists' tendency to scorn as unbelievers and modernists all who did not agree with them. He wrote to champion an interpretive approach to the Bible and, specifically, the Kingdom that Gaulke called "pragmatic conservatism." Such interpreters, said Gaulke, "seek what is the practical, workable, revealed truth of the Bible. They hold that the Bible brings to us the divinely inspired message of God to man for all time and that within the limits marked by divine revelation there is always room for increasing light, even though its main elements are clearly discernible so 'that he may run that readeth it' " (Hab 2:2).[39]

Many of the theological lines that Riggle had developed Gaulke followed. Like Riggle, for example, Gaulke maintained that the Kingdom is spiritual rather than temporal. He also developed his theology of the Kingdom almost exclusively from the Gospels and the letters of the New Testament rather than the Revelation. Also, like Riggle, Gaulke argued that Jesus had inaugurated the Kingdom in his own lifetime as the fulfillment of Old Testament prophecy. However, Gaulke departed from the earlier teacher when it came to the relationship between the Kingdom and the church. Riggle had equated them, but Gaulke followed such scholars as Herman Ridderbos to another conclusion. Thus Gaulke said that the church was the divinely appointed agent whose task it was to proclaim the Kingdom. "The church is both within the kingdom of God and an agency [sic] thereof. However it controls neither the means of grace nor the door into the kingdom. The kingdom of God is the supreme value (Matt 6:33). The church's purpose is to promote the eternal, spiritual kingdom of God by exalting Christ, its Savior, Lord, and King. The Kingdom, in this way, is actually given to the church."[40] A close relationship existed between the church and the Kingdom, but on Gaulke's view they were not identical.

Gaulke differed from Riggle in another respect, and this difference he shared with other Church of God writers of the era. Neither Gaulke nor such authors as H. C. Heffren or George P. Tasker followed Riggle down the trail of church-historical exegesis. They apparently did not see dispensationalism as a threat to their ecclesiologies, anchored as they were to biblical grounds other than the apocalyptic literature. The writers of the 1950s did not repudiate or otherwise dispute the church-historical work of Warner, Riggle, Smith, and others. Rather their work passed by it in silence. They were more concerned with defending what they considered a biblical doctrine of the kingdom of God than defending an exegesis that many in the movement eventually came to consider problematic.

Other Church of God writers occasionally entered the theological lists on the subject of the Kingdom in the same decade as Gaulke. H. C. Heffren published books and tracts on the Kingdom, and the Canadian-American retired missionary George Tasker also wrote on the topic. His small booklet on the Kingdom was self-published whereas Heffren's works were published by the Gospel Trumpet Company and the Gospel Contact Press, the publishing arm of the Church of God in Canada.[41] These works repeated the familiar main lines of the movement's theology of the Kingdom. Like Riggle's work and Gaulke's, these books and pamphlets taught the view that the Kingdom of God was a present, spiritual reign in the hearts of believers. The promised fulfillment of God's rule had come in Jesus' lifetime; there was no need to look to the future for such a realization. The Kingdom was already here in all of its fullness. All that remained was for the Lord to return and claim his own.

Notes

1. Biographical information on Riggle can be found in John W. V. Smith, *Heralds of a Brighter Day* (Anderson, Ind: Gospel Trumpet Company, 1955), 76–99; H. M. Riggle, *Pioneer Evangelism* (Anderson, Ind: Gospel Trumpet Company, 1924); and s. v. "Riggle, H. M.," *Historical Dictionary of the Holiness Movement*, ed. by William C. Kostlevy (Lanham, Md: Scarecrow Press, 2001).

2. (Moundsville: Gospel Trumpet Company, 1899). Riggle's books include, among others: *The Christian Church: Its Rise and Progress* (Moundsville: Gospel Trumpet Company, 1911); *Christ's Kingdom and Reign* (Anderson, Ind: Gospel Trumpet Company, 1918); and *Jesus Is Coming Again* (Anderson, Ind: Gospel Trumpet Company, 1942).

3. The proceedings of two of his debates were published. *The Ebeling-Riggle Discussion* (n. 1901) is the transcript of a debate on a range of theological issues, including the idea of a literal millennial reign of Christ, between Riggle and Elder F. J. Ebeling of the Reorganized Church of Jesus Christ of Latter Day Saints. *The Riggle-Kesler Debate* (n. 1915) recounts a debate focused on the doctrine of the church between Riggle and Elder B. E. Kesler of the Church of the Brethren.

4. For a fine study of American premillennialism cf. Timothy Weber, *Living in the Shadow of the Second Coming: American Premillennialism, 1875–1982,* enlarged edition (Grand Rapids, Mich: Academie Books, 1983).

5. Ibid., 28–29.

6. *The Ebeling-Riggle Discussion,* 14. Riggle consistently made these five criteria of a kingdom the lynchpin of his opposition to the idea of a future kingdom. Cf. *The Kingdom of God and the One Thousand Years Reign,* 69–70; *Christ's Kingdom and Reign,* 9; and *Jesus is Coming Again,* 62–63.

7. *The Ebeling-Riggle Discussion,* 31. While Riggle cited no texts here in support of the laws of holiness or love, he had no difficulty in finding such to apply in his other works. The first and second commandments underscored the law of love, and Colossians 1:13 described the law of holiness when it said that Christ had delivered believers from the power of darkness, i. e. sin. Cf. *Christ's Kingdom and Reign,* 24–25.

8. *God's Kingdom and the Millennium* (Anderson, Ind: Gospel Trumpet Publishing Company, 1923), 23. This posthumously published pamphlet (Khan died in 1922) began with the publishers' extraordinary stated premise that since the Bible was largely an "oriental book" much of its meaning has been lost to occidentals who fail to comprehend that fact. They added, "An Oriental can shed light on Scriptural truth that we never dreamed of." That "the publishers," key leaders of the Church of God movement, did not consistently so regard Khan's conclusions adds more than a touch of irony to their use here of the fact that he was born and reared by Muslim parents in Bengal.

9. Ibid., 34.

10. *The Kingdom of God and the One Thousand Years Reign,* 24–31; *Christ's Kingdom and Reign,* 43–51.

11. Khan, *God's Kingdom and the Millenium,* 5–22.

12. *Select Hymns* (Anderson, Ind: Gospel Trumpet Company, 1911), No. 54.

13. *The Ebeling-Riggle Discussion,* 21.

14. Riggle, *The Kingdom of God and the One Thousand Years Reign,* 21.

15. Ibid., 18.

16. Riggle, *Christ's Kingdom and Reign,* 31.

17. Ibid., 42.

18. Cf. *The Kingdom of God and the One Thousand Years Reign,* 69–70, 99; and *Christ's Kingdom and Reign,* 103–104.

19. "The Kingdom of Peace," *Hymns and Spiritual Songs* (Anderson, Ind: Gospel Trumpet Company, 1934(?), No. 220.

20. *Christ's Kingdom and Reign,* 41–43. The passage quoted is a slightly revised version of the same statement Riggle had written in *The Kingdom of God and the One Thousand Years Reign,* 22–23.

21. Riggle, *The Kingdom of God and the One Thousand Years Reign,* 19.

22. Riggle, *Christ's Kingdom and Reign,* 125.

23. Some preachers received dispensations where caffeine was concerned. Riggle was a notorious coffee drinker and F. G. Smith drank a six-pack of Coca-Cola every day in his study at McKinley Avenue Church of God in Akron, Ohio.

24. The phrase comes, of course, from Niebuhr's classic, *Christ and Culture* (New York: Harper and Row, 1951). Riggle gave Jesus' parable of the wheat and tares precisely this two-kingdom reading. Cf. *Christ's Kingdom and Reign,* 34–36.

25. *The Kingdom of God and the One Thousand Years Reign,* 28.

26. Ibid.

27. Riggle, *Christ's Kingdom and Reign,* 100–101.

28. *The Kingdom of God and the One Thousand Years Reign,* 32–38. Riggle also supplied a diagram or chart, complete with timeline, to visually reinforce his interpretation.

29. Ibid., 150.

30. Ibid., 151–171.

31. Ibid., 62.

32. Ibid., 63.

33. Ibid., 64–65.

34. Cf. Jer 30:9; Ezek 34:23, 24; 37:24–28; Hos 3:5; and Heb 4:7. Riggle, *The Kingdom of God and the One Thousand Years Reign,* 67.

35. Ibid., 70.

36. Max R. Gaulke, *May Thy Kingdom Come—Now!* (Anderson, Ind: Warner Press, 1959), 11.

37. Ibid., 19. Gaulke was especially annoyed by dispensationalists' use of radio to broad and damaging effect. "Recently a popular radio preacher proclaimed over his network: 'When Christ comes to reign you farmers in Texas will be raising watermelons so large it will take a pickup truck to haul one of them. Your cantaloupes will be as large as bushel baskets.' Such nonsense makes sensible Bible scholars blush." Ibid.

38. Ibid., 15–17.

39. Ibid., 17.

40. Ibid., 72.

41. G. Tasker, *The King is Coming!: A Study for the Times* (Penticton, B. C., Canada: n.p.), 1953; H. C. Heffren, *The Signs of His Coming,* 1950.

Chapter 9
Challenging the Apocalyptic Identity

Russell Byrum's heresy trial brought into sharp relief growing differences of theological opinion in the Church of God. However, his differences with F. G. Smith were not the beginning of theological dissent. Opposition to Smith's views began simmering more than a decade before Byrum's disagreements earned him a heresy trial. Some of the best and brightest among the saints had begun raising questions about the apocalyptic hermeneutic that anchored the movement's widely received ecclesiology and, consequently, its self-understanding. Because the freight of Smith's articles, editorials, books, and sermons carried this identity it was only natural that he was closely identified with it. Indeed, to challenge the apocalyptic identity was tantamount to challenging Smith and vice versa. His failed effort to establish a normative body of theological literature coupled with the Byrum trial steeled the resolve of a small group of ministers determined to remove Smith from the editor's chair. These individuals acted out of different motives, not all of them shared by each member of the group. A few had grown to regret their earlier endorsement of the doctrinal practice of come-outism. Some disagreed with Smith on theological grounds. Others believed that too much power was concentrated in his hands. Still others thought that as long as Smith sat in the editor's chair he threatened the development of Anderson College. From any one or more of these motives, opposition to F. G. Smith and his theology increased between 1920 and 1930. That rising challenge and its aftermath tell a crucial tale in the theological life of the Church of God movement.

H. M. Riggle had been closely identified with the movement's apocalyptic self-understanding. Not only was his name alongside Warner's on the title page of *The Cleansing of the Sanctuary,* but Riggle himself had authored several books on the topic of the kingdom of God, and the earliest of these shared Smith's interpretive method. On his own testimony, Riggle later came to regret the apocalyptically grounded come-outism that his early books espoused. As early as 1920 he stopped teaching the church-historical interpretation of the Book of Revelation.[1] Although he may have stated them *sotto voce*, Riggle was by no means the only Church of God minister with reservations about the apocalyptic self-understanding. John Morrison, for one, had told Smith openly that he did not agree with the argument made in *The Last Reformation*.[2] Morrison may have disputed Smith's conclusions publicly, but even louder theological demurrers came from other quarters, one from an influential American pastor and another from one of the movement's brightest intellectual lights on a mission field halfway around the world.

India, 1915–1925, and George Tasker v. F. G. Smith and the Missionary Board

When he and his wife Minnie took passage for India in 1912 few stars shone brighter in the Church of God firmament than George P. Tasker.[3] Born in Nevada and orphaned in infancy, Tasker (1872–1958) was reared in the home of a maternal aunt in Montreal. His aunt and uncle were people of strong religious commitments as articulated by the Scottish Presbyterian Church of which they were members and Mr. Tasker an elder. They saw to George's religious upbringing and education, and upon graduation from high school he enrolled at McGill University in Montreal. After a year he left school to be apprenticed to a diamond setter. Before reaching his twenty-first birthday he returned to the United States, living first in Philadelphia and then Chicago. These were also years of religious turmoil and questing for the young man. He had experienced conversion and was devoting considerable time to his own ideas about the church in 1897 when he met Gorham Tufts and George Cole at an evangelical mission in Chicago where Tasker was working. The two visitors were connected with the Church of God mission there, and Tufts was recently returned from India, where he had taken funds intended for the relief of a massive famine. The three men found themselves kindred spirits and Tasker was won to the Church of God movement.

Although he spent but one year in college, Tasker's native intelligence and other abilities quickly propelled him to leadership positions. By 1900 he was in Moundsville as part of the Gospel Trumpet Publishing Company staff. His Bible study courses in the *Trumpet* home attracted a large following, including the teenaged Russell Byrum, who later said that it was Tasker who had fired his interest in serious, disciplined Bible study. In addition to his own writing Tasker also evaluated book manuscripts and likely sat in for Editor Byrum while he was away on speaking tours. He also served as assistant superintendent of the New York City missionary home and collaborated

George P. Tasker, whose theological and administrative disputes with F. G. Smith and the Missionary Board provided the opening challenge to Smith's leadership.

with D. O. Teasley and A. D. Khan in the development of a ministerial home study course. When the movement's ministers decided to form the Missionary Committee in 1910, Tasker was named its recording secretary. During his years of spiritual seeking Tasker had heard an Indian convert preach in Chicago. Tasker's early associate Gorham Tufts also was deeply committed to the Christian mission in India, so when the call came inviting missionaries to join the growing Church of God work in Bengal, George and Minnie Tasker did not refuse.

The Taskers arrived in India to join four Church of God missionaries who preceded them on site. As many as seventeen North Americans had already served missions in India, invited by Indian church leaders to join them as co-laborers. The mission had begun nearly two decades before the Taskers' arrival when a young convert from Islam, John A. D. Khan (1878–1922), requested samples of Gospel Trumpet Company publications. E. E. Byrum obliged him with two tons of literature and a hand operated printing press. A small circle of well-educated and deeply devoted converts— J. J. M Roy (later, after marrying missionary Evalyn Nichols, he became Nichols-Roy), Mosir Moses, R. N. Mundul, and P. J. Philip—provided visionary leadership for the Church of God in India well before the first missionaries arrived. In their minds the North Americans were fellow laborers, whereas the Missionary Committee seems to have sent Tasker to India with the idea that he was to be an unnamed field secretary with the assignment of regularizing an Indian church that the Americans believed lacked order. For his part Tasker was not at all heavy-handed as an administrator and in fact held the Indian leadership in very high regard, especially Roy and Khan, the latter with whom Tasker formed a very close friendship. Unlike many Anglo-American missionaries of that era, Tasker did not insist on speaking English and in fact learned Urdu and Hindi. He could also understand Bengali. His decidedly anticolonial attitudes and his affectionate regard for the Indian church leaders made Tasker's administration—if it may be so labeled—of the Indian church very low key. The situation in India remained largely as it had been prior to the Taskers' arrival.

During the years between 1912 and 1920, when the Taskers' took their first furlough, George Tasker's practice of Christian unity embarked on a path that clearly diverged from the apocalyptic ecclesiology widely practiced back home. Tasker's practice was to accept preaching or teaching invitations from virtually any Christian group in the belief that they had been extended by fellow members of the body of Christ. Thus, for example, he gave Bible lectures in the YMCA in Lahore. While North American saints were denouncing all denominations as a Babel of confusion, Tasker became friends with an Indian convert and pastor of a Presbyterian church just outside of Lahore who offered Tasker the regular opportunity to occupy his pulpit. Word of Tasker's actions reached the Missionary Board, whose secretary-treasurer, J. W. Phelps, reproved him for not insisting that Indian converts forsake their denominations by the same logic that underwrote American preaching and practice. Tasker disagreed and answered Phelps with a statement that clearly differentiated the missionary's doctrinal practice from that which held sway in the United States:

> We would be wasting money as well as serving ill the cause of Christ here by preaching "comeoutism" around the country through men who would have to be supported by us even as they were by other missions. When the time is ripe for such a message, the fruit will be ripe too. As things are at present we must let in a little more <u>sunshine</u> and bring down some more <u>refreshing rain</u> before we can apply our sickle with hope of satisfaction or success. We must <u>work with God</u>. If we don't know his voice and can not see his hand, but know only our own doctrines and are able to see God only in our own works, we have no business here but had better go home. The country and God's cause will get along better without us in such a case until we had learned wisdom.[4]

Tasker also expressed his reservations about the growing tendency toward becoming a denomination he saw in the movement's organizational developments after 1917. Missionary Board forms that requested statistics and used the name "Church of God" in a way that made it the movement's name raised Tasker's hackles. To him such usages perpetuated rather than protested denominationalism, and he complained, "My whole soul protests, Brother Phelps. 'Church of God' is the status not the name of any one community of Christian people. If we must legalize by use this name exclusively we must *qualify* it by some other definition."[5] Members of the Missionary Board read Tasker's position to mean that he considered the Church of God movement a "sect among sects." From Tasker's own writing, said Board Secretary-Treasurer J. W. Phelps, "We would have thought that the Church of God, this reformation, or whatever you choose to call it, is but a church among sects and on a par with the Methodists, Baptists, and so forth."[6] Phelps also rebutted Tasker's criticism of F. G. Smith's work on Revelation and the doctrinal practice of come-outism.[7] A rift had opened between the movement's leadership in the United States and one of its most talented and scholarly-inclined minister-missionaries.

To its credit the movement's leadership made repeated overtures attempting to close the breach between themselves and Tasker. Phelps conducted a lengthy and detailed discussion of theological issues in his numerous letters to Tasker. Smith and E. A. Reardon visited the Indian mission and its leaders during their round-the-world missionary inspection tour of 1919–1920. When the Taskers returned to the United States on furlough during 1920, Missionary Board members held out some hope for clearer understanding and reconciliation through face-to-face conversations. None of this availed very much, and the issues were still largely unresolved when the Taskers returned to India. However, while they were en route to Anderson the Missionary Board took an action that exacerbated the situation when it appointed Floyd W. Heinly field secretary for India. The position had been created with an eye towards the Indian church; no other mission had a field secretary in 1920. Although inexperienced as a missionary, Heinly was an able administrator and, more importantly, theologically in line with Smith. He was dispatched to India for the dual purpose of bringing order to its financial and theological house. Heinly's appointment demoralized Indian church leaders; A. D. Khan was so dispirited that he died of pneumonia in 1922 without a struggle. Having lost his closest friend and in many respects his alter ego, Tasker ran out of patience and reasons to cooperate with the Missionary Board, which voted to dismiss him on June 11, 1924. Later that year Tasker delivered a manifesto aimed at Smith's apocalyptic ecclesiology and the exclusivist practices of come-outism that derived from it. Tasker's broadside was entitled *An Appeal to the Free and Autonomous Churches of Christ in the Fellowship of the Evening Light.*[8]

George and Minnie Tasker had no intention of returning to the United States after their dismissal. Instead they remained in India as independent missionaries underwritten by the financial contributions of friends and churches that remained supportive of their work. The *Appeal* was intended to encourage that support by setting the record straight with regard to the issues that had arisen between George Tasker and movement leaders. To accomplish this end the pamphlet reprinted selected correspondence bearing on the issues between Tasker and the Board. That correspondence shows Tasker to be deeply troubled by two developments, one of a more recent vintage and the other a longstanding problem. The more recent concern was his perception of a growing tendency toward denominationalism in the Church of God. This point summarized the misgivings that Tasker had expressed to Phelps five years earlier. He regarded policy changes at the Missionary Board as a salient example of this development. Only a few years had passed since the Board functioned as a loosely structured committee. However, Tasker regarded changes since its reorganization as a declension. Once it had been reorganized in 1917, in Tasker's view the Missionary Board had begun to govern in a manner not unlike the missionary boards of denominational churches.[9] Thus he wrote, "We did not use [sic] to have a regular Missionary Board, as you know, and certainly not an 'official' agent of such Board on the field. Rightly or wrongly we had somehow been led to believe that such things were inimical to the truth and so we came out of and held aloof from all organization potentially restrictive of 'the free expression of the Spirit of God in the hearts and work of the ministers.' "[10] The institutionalization that had begun in the Church of God movement so aggressively in 1917 troubled George Tasker, for whom these developments raised crucial questions regarding the movement's theology of the church.

Ecclesiology was also implicated in the second dispute between Tasker and the Missionary Board. In this case the specific issue concerned the doctrinal practice of Christian unity. Tasker routinely preached in churches and missions affiliated with Protestant denominations. This practice he thought to be in keeping with the movement's commitment to the ideal of the unity of all Christians. In this regard his missionary experience, like that of many other Protestant missionaries, had broadened the grounds on which he fellowshipped believers from other denominations. While his ministerial colleagues back home routinely "thrashed Babylon" Tasker categorically rejected all attempts to portray Christians in the denominations as unbelievers in any serious sense of the term.[11] But it was not only experience that led him to dispute such attempts. He also dismissed them as examples of poor biblical exegesis; as employed by Phelps and others such Bible references were nothing other than proof texts. On these two points Tasker widened the breach that had opened between him and Smith's understanding of the Church of God. In case there was any doubt that Tasker and Smith differed on these important issues, the former also decried the apocalyptic ecclesiology's insistence that Christian unity was achieved as believers in the denominations forsook them to affiliate with the Church of God movement. Tasker labeled what he called "our 'doctrine' of comeoutism" to be "a positive incubus on this work as a fundamentally *spiritual* reform."[12] He also subjected the practice of come-outism to a christological critique, saying that it was ultimately not the church but Christ to whom each believer was drawn; Christ and not the church needed be held up as "the one center and point of gathering."[13] Come-outism forgot or neglected that all-important point; moreover, any church that wandered down that path had also forgotten Warner's original insight.[14] In this connection, and as with a growing number of Church of God ministers in the 1920s, so also Tasker looked beyond the movement's boundaries and saw the positive results of evangelism and a yearning for closer fellowship among the Protestant denominations. This perception prompted Tasker to view the movement's early history in terms that Smith and others had to regard as revisionist:

> Seeing the spiritual darkness and deadness in the existing situation we went at it from *without* and taking our cue from the Book of Revelation we cried valiantly, "COME OUT." *Some* "heard" us and come [sic]. More heard us and smiled, but they did not ignore all we had said. Many waked up, saw light in much we taught of real Christian experience and privilege, and all though they did not see that they could better things any by coming to us, our *spiritual* testimony has had its effect. But *they did not come out,* and I scarcely think any reasonable mind will question the truth of the statement that today, with all the truth and light that God by the Holy Spirit has been causing to break forth from his Word all over the world through many agencies, organized and otherwise, and the room being given to that truth and light, there are a far greater number of real children of God *within* the denominational system today, and far more liberty is being accorded them therein, than was the case when D. S. Warner first stepped out of the Church of God (Winebrennarian).[15]

After their dismissal George Tasker decided on a course of action that permitted him to remain on mission in his beloved India. His actions and statements had opened a large rift between himself and the Missionary Board. In 1924 the president of that board was none other than F. G. Smith. It was Tasker's views, bearing such a departure from Smith's on matters of ecclesiology and church practice so crucial to the self-understanding then prevailing in the movement, that had opened the rift. For its part the Missionary Board refused to close that gap from its side. Its members took the view that they championed orthodox practice in the Church of God and those who deviated from that practice had to be in the wrong. As in nearly all other areas of the movement's national life and thought, Smith was in a position to deal with those who disputed or otherwise disagreed with that self-understanding. That a talented and highly regarded minister such as George Tasker could be a casualty in one such difference of opinion illustrates, however, not only the power of the editor to enforce orthodoxy. It also indicates that after 1920 some ministers in the movement were beginning to see the Church of God and its cardinal practice of Christian unity in a new and different light.

E. A. Reardon. A leading minister since his work on Our Ministerial Letter, *Reardon's Anderson Campmeeting sermon criticized the sectarian attitude prevalent throughout the Church of God and set the stage for the dispute between colleagues of F. G. Smith and Anderson College alumni and supporters.*

Anderson, 1929, and E. A. Reardon

The dismissal of George Tasker illustrated the lengths to which Smith and those who shared his ecclesiology were prepared to go in defense of their position. That Tasker's voice spoke halfway around the world from Anderson may have made his theological dissent appear inconsequential. He remained in India, financially supported by a handful of Church of God congregations and individuals personally loyal to him.[16] While the loss of so widely respected an individual created no general hue and cry in the movement, the reasons behind it were an early expression of a theological perspective that grew throughout the decade. More and more ministers challenged the apocalyptic ecclesiology and its insistence that Christian unity would be achieved as true believers came out of denominations and into the Church of God. By the time of the Taskers' dismissal Russell Byrum was within a year of publishing *Christian Theology* and was himself discounting Smith's hermeneutics in courses at Anderson College. Popular preacher H. M. Riggle was in the process of abandoning some of his earlier apocalypticism. In 1929 Russell Byrum repudiated the apocalyptically grounded approach to Christian unity publicly at the Indiana State Ministers Meeting. But the most dramatic restatement of Christian unity occurred only a few weeks later on the movement's center stage.

When E. A. Reardon (1874–1946) took the pulpit at Anderson Campmeeting in June 1929, he had earned the broad and deep respect of the Church of God and its ministry. Born to Roman Catholic parents in West Liberty, Ohio, Reardon graduated high school and taught school in that vicinity until 1898. In that year he experienced conversion during a three-week revival meeting in his hometown. Through the influence of Barney E. Warren, Reardon took his stand with the Church of God and soon departed for Chicago where he joined the gospel workers at the Chicago Missionary Home. Ordained in 1902, Reardon took a wide range of assignments that marked him as a rising minister in the movement: Superintendent of the Chicago home, missionary tour in Egypt, service on the original Missionary Committee, and election as the first chair of the General Ministerial Assembly. He was also a member of the "Committee of Seventeen" responsible for the creation of *Our Ministerial Letter.* From 1920 to 1926 he served Park Place Church of God in Anderson as its pastor and was the confidant of many agency leaders. In 1929 Reardon was in the middle of what would be a seven-year pastorate at North Denver Church of God.

Tall and lean, E. A. Reardon brought an air of gravity to any pulpit he occupied. The topic and approach that he took in June of 1929 could only have added to his stature. He delivered a sermon on the subject of Christian unity defining his topic in a way that challenged the movement's generally received understanding and much of its practice with regard to Christians beyond the Church of God fold.[17] Reardon followed Russell Byrum's optimistic assessment of unity movements arising among other Christians. New spiritual winds were blowing, said Reardon, who concluded that the desire for unity carried by such winds required the saints to reexamine some of their attitudes and practices. He attacked the idea prevalent among some ministers that the Church of God was the "hub of Christendom," insisting that the first allegiance of Christians was to Christ rather than the church. As Reardon put it:

> I am convinced that the gathering that God is most interested in is our gathering unto Christ, and [that] there never will be one centralized and centrally-governed movement that will take in all the children of God on earth. There is no one place on earth from which God is directing all the affairs of his Kingdom and salvation work. There is no one body of people on earth who can claim an exclusive right to Christ and to all his light and truth. If Christ were here in person, he would certainly put to confusion those bodies of his professed followers who make themselves his exclusive people.... I cannot conceive of him as confining his operations exclusively to this movement, and I am quite sure that the representative minds and spiritual hearts of our people do not hold such a view.[18]

Reardon appealed for a broader understanding of fellowship and greater spirit of cooperation toward Christians in other church bodies. Some of those people, he contended, possessed a reach and influence broader than the Church of God, an influence that would only be constricted were they to join the movement's narrow confines. Reardon stopped well short of advocating federation, but he pointedly questioned the practice of withholding cooperation from other Christians unless assured of virtually complete doctrinal agreement.[19] The absence of cooperative efforts Reardon laid squarely at the feet of those in the movement who built barriers and fostered an unholy "spirit of exclusiveness to the extent that they are seriously prejudiced against even that which is good in others, simply because it does not have our stamp on it. They have shut themselves up in the reformation and bolted the door."[20]

Reardon closed his sermon with a warning against a sectarian spirit that he saw creeping through much of the Church of God. If this tendency were allowed to continue the movement would soon die. The challenge, he said, was to speak with a clear and distinctive voice without allowing distinctiveness to become a preoccupation. As Reardon colorfully put the matter, "I believe in a clean, separate, and distinct work for God, but I also believe that we should keep the sectarian stink out of the distinction."[21] He cautioned the saints to be on the watch for a spirit that would appear disguised as loyalty to the Church of God movement. As he said, "There is such a thing as stressing the reformation to such an extent as to cause our people to be reformation centered, reformation sectarians."[22] To make certain that his hearers got the point, Reardon concluded with a sentence that could not but inflame those in the crowd who were the target of his sermon: "If we yield to any influence that will sectarianize [the movement], we will soon fossilize and be in the Babylonian Museum ourselves."[23]

The immediate effect of Reardon's sermon was not long in being felt. Apparently those "representative minds and spiritual hearts" to which he had referred were not to be found among the majority of members of the General Ministerial Assembly. When the results of elections for agency trustee boards were posted, they reported that Assembly members had voted Reardon off the boards for which he stood for re-election. When camp meeting concluded he returned to Denver, but Reardon was not a man to console himself by licking old wounds.

E. A. Reardon, F. G. Smith, and John A. Morrison

As 1929 drew to a close, the events of that year impressed on the minds of E. A. Reardon, John Morrison, and influential company member A. T. Rowe the idea that F. G. Smith was a roadblock to the broader, more open future they envisioned for the Church of God. Morrison's concerns centered in the development of Anderson College. R. R. Byrum's heresy trial illustrated Smith's determination to restrict the college and its curriculum. Morrison, Reardon, and Smith had been acquainted with each other and were friends for many years.[24] The issues that separated them in late 1929 and 1930 were not personal conflicts but rested instead on variant conceptions of the church. Reardon shared Morrison's concern for the future of education in the church, but to this he added reservations that had first dawned a decade earlier. During his 1919–1920 missionary tour with Smith, Reardon noted with uneasiness the editor's tendency to present himself as the leader of the Church of God movement. While on the trip he confronted Smith over this matter. Reardon and Smith viewed the practice of church leadership in different lights. The former was part of that rising generation of ministers given opportunities for leadership in the missionary homes and other newer places of service. Although six years younger than Reardon,

A. T. Rowe opposed a monopoly on theological ideas in the Church of God. His belief that the Gospel Trumpet Company needed to publish authors of different views combined with his influential role in the company to make him one of the leaders in the effort to remove F. G. Smith from office.

Smith remained the staunch defender of the older view of leadership that regarded it as charismatically endowed. Although he agreed that the Holy Spirit gifted men and women for their place of service in the church, Reardon worried that Smith had arrogated too much of the idea of "leader" to himself.[25]

The issue came to a head in 1930, when Smith's term as editor was due to expire. That meant he would first have to stand for reelection by Gospel Trumpet Company members, in effect the trustee board for the publishing house. Following reelection, Smith would still need to be ratified by a simple majority in the General Ministerial Assembly. His influence and the popularity of his books rendered the latter decision pro forma. But Reardon was a member of the Gospel Trumpet Company and in the spring of 1930, he led a coup against Smith, along with Morrison and Rowe, chair of the company's board of directors,[26] persuading a majority of members to vote against Smith's reelection. This action was highly controversial. Many ministers did not take kindly to the rude dismissal of so widely a respected leader. Smith had been deprived of the office to which he believed he had been divinely appointed by his charismatic gifts. A sizeable segment of the Assembly sympathized with him, and when the camp meeting convened they were in a fighting mood. The Gospel Trumpet Company elected H. M. Riggle to succeed Smith, but the Assembly refused to ratify him.[27] The company then turned to Charles E. Brown, who accepted election on the condition that Smith would endorse his ratification on the Assembly floor. Ever the loyal churchman, Smith consented, and Brown was ratified as the fourth editor of the Gospel Trumpet Company.

F. G. Smith left Anderson to take the pastorate of the McKinley Avenue Church of God in Akron, Ohio. He had lost his platform, but neither he nor his ecclesiology and views concerning the movement's best future went quietly into the night. His many friends and admirers were ready to seize control of the movement, and a key element in their plan was a restriction in the development of Anderson College. Accordingly they embarked on a course aimed at denying President John Morrison another term. If Morrison had helped engineer Smith's removal, the latter's allies among ministers in Ohio would return the favor by defeating Morrison's bid for ratification in 1934.

During the years from 1929 to 1934 F. G. Smith and John Morrison represented divergent conceptions of the Church of God movement's ecclesiology and its correlative practices. Each man stood for reelection or ratification as a symbol of those often opposing viewpoints. It would be patently unfair to Smith and his position to portray him and his ecclesiology as anti-intellectual and backward looking. He was not opposed to higher education or to new forms of ministry. However, he did insist that any such ideas be held up to a doctrinal standard that rested on those truths he believed were revealed in the apocalyptic books of the Bible. Neither was Smith a sore loser ready to take his ecclesiastical ball and go home when he saw the game going against him. Although it is unfair to ascribe the practices of his followers to Smith, one must also admit that his ecclesiology encouraged a mindset that practiced the church as a closed, exclusive, narrowly focused community. For his part, Morrison was at least Smith's equal when it came to playing political hardball after prayer meeting had dismissed. Morrison looked toward a church that was open to new ideas, and he believed that education was the key to that future. He was also more pragmatic than Smith when it came to the steps necessary to secure that future for both college and church. The election disputes involving Smith and Morrison were never fights between two individuals; at stake rather was a key element of Church of God ecclesial practice and thought.

Morrison stood for ratification in 1934, and Smith's followers, located primarily in Ohio, were determined to deny the college president another term. They tied his defeat to a plan that would return the college's curriculum to that of the Bible institute it once had been. First and foremost the Ohio Ministerial Association desired that Anderson College be financially and administratively separated from the General Ministerial Assembly of the Church of God. The Ohio ministers had come to regret chartering the college and now characterized that action as hasty. But they were politically savvy enough to recognize that they would not likely achieve their objective, so they insisted that at the very minimum the college administration be replaced by people willing to alter the curriculum.[28] Moreover, the content of this revised and restricted curriculum was to conform to the "doctrinal teaching as has, and still does, characterize the great body of our ministers; including such truths as the present-day call of God to his people to come out of all sectarianism, Papal and Protestant, the modern Babylon."[29] In December 1933 the Ohio Ministerial Assembly had adopted a resolution calling for, among other objectives, the college to "be placed in the hands of, and directed and managed by, men who are wholly committed to the TRUTH; men who can and will pass it on, both in theological instruction and in burning reformational [sic] emphasis, to the body of students."[30]

The controversy that raged through the Church of God movement during 1933 and the first half of 1934 brought to head two different theological and ecclesiological sores that had been festering for nearly six years. First of all there were those in the movement who continued to worry that the expansion of bureaucratic organization was a step in which the movement had lost its first love and gone a whoring after the style and patterns of denominational Christianity (see Exod 34:15–16). In their eyes a church-sponsored college was but the latest example of this growing tendency, especially after that college had succeeded in getting the General Ministerial Assembly to endorse its plan for a liberal arts curriculum. Opponents of this move had nothing against "cultural colleges," as they termed them, but such institutions followed an agenda that had nothing in common with the church of the New Testament. The real problem was a threat to gospel freedom in what appeared to be an ever-expanding ecclesiastical bureaucracy consolidating power to itself. To separate or at least curtail the development of Anderson College would set the necessary limits to this expansion.[31]

Second, the Ohio resolutions expressed deep concern over the content of theological instruction at Anderson College. The focal point of this concern centered in the belief that the college no longer taught Church of God doctrine. Given the fact that there existed no judicatory or official body empowered to determine doctrinal standards, establishing orthodox Church of God doctrine was a dicey proposition. Ministers in Ohio, a fertile garden for the apocalyptic ecclesiology of its most famous minister, demanded that the college administration declare itself "as being out and out for ALL the fundamental doctrines taught, AND AS TAUGHT, in this reformation and published in our standard literature."[32] That a resolution calling for a "standard literature" had failed several years earlier apparently did not inhibit people from using the phrase as if such a body of authoritative teaching existed. In the minds of many it did. Supporters of the Ohio resolutions wanted a doctrinal standard to be recognized and enforced, but without a central authority—that would have infringed on congregational autonomy—to enforce them. That college administrators and faculty members were at best cool toward the theology of this so-called "standard literature" made Morrison the focal point of this concern.

One further element appears to have contributed to the Anderson College controversy of 1933–34. As already noted, there is reason to believe that some ministers sought Morrison's ouster in reciprocity for the action taken against Smith in 1930. Professor Otto F. Linn argued to the college's critics that if the content of theological instruction was the issue then their complaint was with the theological faculty, of which he was a member, and not the administration. But he was assured that no criticisms were associated with his teaching and that the fault lay with the administration.[33] Critics of the college may have labored under the assumption that its president and dean controlled classroom instruction. Academic freedom certainly did not exist at Anderson to the degree that it did at Indiana University. Nevertheless, Morrison's open antipathy to Smith's views coupled with his role in Smith's ouster and Smith's reluctance to criticize Linn and other members of the theology faculty point to reprisal as a possible motive in the drive to eliminate Morrison.

Both sides lobbied the entire movement through the spring of 1934. Ministers' meetings were full of talk about "Morrison and his boys," i. e. the freshly trained candidates for ministry graduating from the college. The college newsletter, *The Broadcaster,* devoted its pages to the advocacy of a college free to grow and develop. Finally June and camp meeting arrived and with it the annual meeting of the General Ministerial Assembly. By the narrow margin of thirteen votes out of more than seven hundred ballots cast, Morrison was ratified for another term. The college's intellectual future, and in some measure the theological future of the Church of God, would not be tied to a narrowly framed ecclesiology that a growing number of people considered outmoded. And yet the vote tally also indicated a deep theological rift in the Church of God movement. After months of intense lobbying, only the slenderest of majorities had ratified Morrison, signifying that the Church of God was virtually equally divided when it came to the college president and the views of the church symbolized by him and his opponents.

Years later John Morrison described the efforts at reconciliation made by the winning side in the factious debate of 1933–34.[34] From a distance of nearly three decades he saw those efforts as largely successful. To be sure, not all of his opponents were satisfied by the outcome, and they would not willingly support the college. But most of the opposition, thought Morrison, had been reconciled to the fact that he would remain in office and that the college would continue to develop. Generosity often comes easier to the victor than the vanquished, and time also tends to rub the edge off what had once been sharp differences. Morrison's recollections may have been accurate, but if in 1934 he thought that matters between the college and its opponents were finally resolved, he was mistaken. The fight over ratification was only the first round of a longer contest pitting the apocalyptic ecclesiology against new theological ideas and methods. A challenge was indeed mounting against the come-outism that was still entrenched as the movement's practice of Christian unity. In the wake of the ouster of F. G. Smith and the ratification of John Morrison, new faces entered the picture to complete that challenge.

Notes

1. Riggle told this to Russell Byrum who reported it in his family memoir, "The Byrum Family," unpublished memoir, Archives of the Church of God, 17.

2. John W. V. Smith, *The Quest for Holiness and Unity*, 249.

3. For Tasker's biography cf. Douglas E. Welch, *Ahead of His Times: A Life of George Tasker* (Anderson, Ind: Anderson University Press, 2001).

4. Tasker to J. W. Phelps, February 25, 1919, (Tasker's emphases), File "Missionary Board Correspondence," Archives of the Church of God. Two weeks earlier Tasker had written Phelps in the same vein: "I do not believe that we have any call to require others to separate from their Christian missions in which they have been converted, educated, and employed when by so doing they become just as dependent on us (who have no suitable institutions for them or fixed employment under oversight) as they were upon their former mission. Tasker to Phelps, February 8, 1919, File "Missionary Board Correspondence," Archives of the Church of God.

5. Tasker to J. W. Phelps, February 18, 1919, (Tasker's emphases), File "Missionary Board Correspondence," Archives of the Church of God.

6. Phelps to G. Tasker, September 25, 1919, File "Missionary Board Correspondence," Archives of the Church of God.

7. Ibid.

8. Calcutta, India, 1924.

9. Tasker may have been somewhat naïve on this point, failing to appreciate the possibility that even loosely organized committees and boards nevertheless manifest a tendency toward institutionalization and expansion of their responsibilities. That which takes its first breath as an advisory body is not by that definition exempted from expanding its assignment and power.

10. Tasker, *An Appeal to the Free and Autonomous Churches*, 14–15.

11. "A man who has worked any length of time among the heathen, for example, and has arrived at what might be called a Missionary definition of Christianity, would never be guilty of applying 2 Corinthians 6:14, 'Be not unequally yoked together with unbelievers.' To PROFESSING CHRISTIANS! as Brother Phelps does on page 3 of your letter. They are NOT unbelievers in the Scripture sense of the word at all." Tasker, *An Appeal to the Free and Autonomous Churches*, 17.

12. Tasker's use of scare quotes to surround the word doctrine implies that he did not consider it doctrine per se, but something less. Tasker continued, "We have been altogether too revolutional [sic] and impatient in this respect, reaping a few ripe ears of grain and leaving bushels behind with the gates of the field shut and barred against us for the future or until we had learned wisdom. You all know this is true. Can't we learn a bit from our experience the necessity of revising our doctrine a bit?" Tasker, *An Appeal to the Free and Autonomous Churches*, 29–30.

13. Ibid., 27. Tasker wondered whether "ego" had not become unwholesomely entangled with the Church of God movement's insistence that believers must come out of the denominational world.

14. "No oriental Bride ever dreams that she is the center of the doings. It is the Bridegroom. Brother Warner, I think, caught that vision. They say he was full of Christ. I could almost think so from many of his hymns. They breathe Christ-consciousness." Ibid., 27.

15. Ibid., 32, (Tasker's emphases).

16. One of Tasker's key supporters was Fred Bruffet, who gathered about himself a significant number of ministers disenchanted with Smith and the general direction of the movement. Bruffet served as the pastor of an independent church in Lincoln, Nebraska and as vice-president of the American Conference of Undenominational Churches. Among the ministers attracted to Bruffet's group was George Cole, whose name disappeared from the *Church of God Yearbook* in 1918. Cf. Douglas E. Welch, *Ahead of His Times*, 110–113.

17. E. A. Reardon, "Problems of Christian Unity," reprinted in part in Barry L. Callen, ed., *The First Century*, Vol. 2 (Anderson, Ind: Warner Press, 1979), 635–638; also reprinted in Callen, ed., *Following the Light*, 134–136. The complete manuscript of Reardon's sermon, along with earlier drafts, is housed in the Archives of the Church of God.

18. Ibid., 143–145.

19. Thus Reardon rhetorically asked, "Is it not a fact that, while some of them have what we would say is 75% of the truth, yet we are not able to cooperate with them to the extent of 5%?"

20. Ibid., 135–136. During the first fifty years of the Church of God movement's existence but especially after the rise of the apocalyptic theology, preachers commonly referred to the movement as "this reformation," or "the reformation."

21. Ibid., 136.

22. Ibid.

23. Ibid.

24. The Reardon and Smith families were neighbors in the Park Place neighborhood on the east side of Anderson. When E. A. Reardon died in 1946, F. G. Smith was among his pallbearers.

25. Reardon's travel diaries are held in the Archives of the Church of God. His views concerning Smith are summarized in Robert H. Reardon, *The Early Morning Light*, 49–50.

26. Rowe served the company from 1931 to 1949 as General Manager. By 1925 he had already emerged as a key member of the company.

27. As of this writing Riggle remains the only person ever to have failed at ratification by the General Assembly of the Church of God.

28. Cf. "To the Concerned Ministers of the Church of God Concerning the Much-Discussed 'Toledo Resolution.' " The Ohio ministers sent this open letter to all Church of God ministers clarifying the issues that were raised by the "Toledo Resolution." A copy of this letter is shelved in the Archives of the Church of God.

29. "Resolution Passed Unanimously by the Ordained Ministers Assembled at the Regular Mid-Winter Session of the Ohio State Ministerial Association," (December 28, 1933), Archives of the Church of God. To insure that their grievances were not ignored the Ohio ministers mailed a copy of the resolution to every minister registered in the *Yearbook of the Church of God.* F. G. Smith thought that the college administration had ignored earlier expressions of similar concern. He quoted a letter from A. F. Gray, then chair of the Anderson College Board of Trustees, in which Gray said that he had only learned of an earlier version of the Toledo Resolution (adopted at Springfield, Ohio in August 1933) when he read it in the college newsletter. The Springfield Resolutions had been addressed to the college trustee board. Cf. F. G. Smith, letter to Otto F. Linn, February 7, 1934, photocopy in the Archives of the Church of God.

30. Ibid. Emphases original in the sources.

31. "To the Concerned Ministers of the Church of God...." The open letter also pointed out that denominational colleges tightly controlled by governing hierarchies such as the Lutherans and Catholics remained true to their doctrinal traditions. The problem for "freedom loving" churches (the letter does not specify which groups) is that loose control of their colleges was the doorway through which liberalism entered first the colleges and then the ministry trained there. The Ohio ministry appeared to be caught in a double bind: either endorse the recent development of the college and therefore expanding ecclesiasticism or separate the college from the movement and invite creeping secularism.

32. Ibid. Emphasis original in the sources.

33. Cf. Linn's letter to F. G. Smith, Mrs. [Rachel] Lord, and C. E. Byers, dated February 2, 1934 and Smith's reply dated February 7, 1934. Photocopies of this correspondence are housed in the Archives of the Church of God.

34. *As The River Flows* (Anderson, Ind: Anderson College Press, 1962), 182.

Chapter 10
The Triumph of History

The departures of Russell Byrum and F. G. Smith left two very large holes in the theological leadership of the Church of God movement. The latter had magnificently played the role of theological teacher to much of the church. The former had quietly but firmly played the antagonist in the drama in which the two were intertwined. Without question, the church was far more concerned about Editor Smith's successor than it was for the appointment of a professor to fill the vacancy created by Byrum's resignation. The importance of college professors, even those who taught Bible or theology, grew only as the decade of the '30s wore on and gave way to the '40s. In 1930 the person who held the office of editor still flexed the political muscle that shaped the theological life of the Church of God. If college professors did not yet possess the ability to immediately affect the movement, they certainly were in a position to shape its theological future through the influence of their ideas on generation after generation of students. The loss of Byrum and Smith left both the movement's present and its future uncertain.

The vacancies at the college and publishing house were filled by two men whose careers played a key role in advancing theological change in the Church of God.[1] Like nearly every previous movement leader, one of these men was largely self-taught. The other, however, established a new precedent for the academic study of Bible and theology. Despite substantial differences in educational background, the two were linked by their regard for history. In the case of Charles Ewing Brown, who became the fourth Editor of the Gospel Trumpet Company in 1930, the study of church history cast the Church of God movement in a new light that required a serious reconsideration of earlier theological claims. For Otto F. Linn, who joined the Anderson College faculty in 1930, it was not only history's subject matter but the historical-critical method of biblical study that prompted him to challenge

Otto F. Linn, scholar-teacher, Bible commentator, college administrator, and the first Church of God minister to hold an academic doctorate.

an entrenched hermeneutic in a manner that led to sweeping changes in the movement's theological self-understanding. Taken together, Brown and Linn produced a body of scholarship that insisted on historical understanding and the application of historical method. To the extent that the church found their work persuasive, the decades after 1930 witnessed what might be termed the triumph of history.

Otto F. Linn and the Historical-Critical Method

Otto Fernand Linn (1887–1965) was born in the tiny Swedish-American settlement of Falun, Kansas. Raised against a backdrop of Swedish pietism, Linn experienced conversion in 1905. He had been a member of the Swedish Evangelical Church, but under the influence of itinerant Church of God preachers he testified to undergoing entire sanctification and shortly thereafter left Oklahoma to join the Gospel Trumpet Company. Having received a call to the ministry, he began preaching during the two and more years that he stayed in Anderson. While there Linn almost assuredly read F. G. Smith's *The Revelation Explained,* newly published in 1908 and the summary statement of the movement's apocalyptically grounded ecclesiology. In 1910 he left for New York to work in the missionary home. At that time D. Otis Teasley served as home superintendent and spoke with a voice of theological moderation. To have moved from Smith to Teasley meant that Linn had seen firsthand just about the entire theological spectrum of the Church of God in his first five years among the saints.

Linn returned to Kansas in 1912 to take up work as a pastor and evangelist, serving churches at Anthony and Caldwell. In 1923 he began a two-year missionary tour in Denmark, where he spent some of his time delivering chart lectures based on Smith's work. Linn returned to the New York missionary home in 1925, but soon departed for his native Kansas. In 1926 he took the pastorate at Enid, Oklahoma and enrolled at Phillips University. Linn's quick mind enabled him to complete baccalaureate and master's degrees at Phillips within four years. He then accepted an invitation to join the Anderson College faculty as an instructor in Greek and dean of men for the 1930–31 academic year.

Linn had little to say concerning the dispute that had created the vacancy he filled. He thought that Russell Byrum was clearly out of harmony with the mainstream of the movement's theology, but Linn also thought that Byrum was not necessarily wrong. Linn was revising his own assessment of Smith's work. Revision turned to radical departure during the course of Linn's doctoral study at the University of Chicago from 1933 to 1936, at the conclusion of which he became the first minister of the Church of God to hold an academic doctorate. That he earned this degree studying with Edgar J. Goodspeed, Shailer Mathews, and Shirley Jackson Case profoundly shaped Linn's exegetical methods in ways that could not fail to bring him into conflict with Smith's views and the ecclesiology that they underwrote. During his brief tenure at Anderson College he introduced the historical-critical method of biblical study* to a generation of students, not to mention colleagues, who were thus equipped with the tools to refute the church-historical hermeneutic.[2]

Linn taught at Anderson only until 1936, when he resigned over a curricular dispute with Dean Russell Olt. Linn wanted the college to develop into a graduate school of theology whereas Olt was laying groundwork for an undergraduate liberal arts college. Each was impatient to see his goal achieved first, and when that proved impossible Linn departed—not the last person on the losing end of a dispute with the iron-willed Olt. A consummate teacher, the modest but unbending Linn preferred to leave rather than become embroiled in an open dispute with the college dean, not that opportunities for self-promotion were unavailable. During the campaign to oust John Morrison, F. G. Smith had intimated to Linn that he was a likely candidate for the college presidency once Morrison was eliminated. Linn turned a cool shoulder toward such overtures.[3] From 1936 to 1942 he served the Church of God in Dundalk, Maryland, just outside of Baltimore. While at Dundalk Linn decided to write a commentary on the New Testament that would rest on the historical-critical approach. Volume I was released in 1941, but Linn's exposition first appeared as a serial in the *Gospel Trumpet* beginning in December 1939.[4]

Editor C. E. Brown announced the editorial plan that would publish Linn's work eleven months out of each year until the entire New Testament was covered. In making this announcement Brown also noted Linn's

---

*By Linn's day it had become customary to refer to the critical study of the Bible as "lower" or "higher." The former was another term for textual criticism, the comparative study of the ancient manuscripts used to establish the Hebrew and Greek texts which are then translated into vernacular languages—English, for example. "Higher" criticism is an umbrella term that names several methodologies, including historical and literary criticism. These were the two methods commonly employed by Linn and his students and successors. Historical criticism is interested in such questions as What historical factors can be discerned from work behind and within the Bible? What were the special aims of the writers and the particular interests of their audiences? What social and cultural factors helped to shape the text as we now have it? Literary criticism developed especially during the nineteenth-century and was particularly focused on sources believed to lie behind the biblical writings. Perhaps the most famous example of this particular method is Wellhausen's "Documentary Hypothesis," the theory that several literary streams contributed to the composition of the first five books of the Old Testament. Linn and others employed both methods; and by the term "historical critical method," I mean both historical and literary criticism.

Charles E. Brown. Fourth editor of the Gospel Trumpet, *Brown used his prolific pen to ground the Church of God movement's identity in historical understanding.*

exceptional qualifications for this assignment, taking pains to mention his doctorate from Chicago.[5] The methodology that he had learned there appeared in the very first installment, when Linn discussed basic matters such as the manufacture of papyrus, extant manuscripts, and the fact that the original manuscripts had long since vanished.[6] The serial continued until the November 30, 1940 issue, when it abruptly concluded with Linn's exposition of Jude. No explanation was given for the absence of any comment on Revelation. He had submitted his material, as often was the case, perilously close to deadline. When his manuscript arrived, the editorial staff immediately realized that Linn's radical departure from Smith's work and the so-called "standard literature" would create serious problems were it to be published.[7] Editor Brown, rarely a fighter and always one to keep peace in the church, killed the serial.

Brown's decision only postponed the inevitable. Plans were already underway to publish Linn's serialized exposition as a three-volume commentary. Volumes I and II appeared as scheduled, but because the final volume contained the controversial commentary on Revelation the publication committee had to be convened. In 1941 that committee was composed of Brown, Book Editor Harold L. Phillips, Earl L. Martin, A. F. Gray, and F. G. Smith. By a margin of three to two the committee approved publication, but by company rule a split vote required the decision to be referred to the full publication board. Linn's advocates within the company, principally A. T. Rowe, knew they would lose that decision, so they pressed the issue no further.[8] Instead they resorted to an alternate route to the publication of *Studies in the New Testament*, Volume III.

General Manager A. T. Rowe (1874–1967) was the driving force behind the publication of the third volume of Linn's commentary. Neither a theologian nor exegete, Rowe was nevertheless a published author ready to show his tough side when circumstances warranted; rumor had it that, because he was the target of violent threats, Rowe once carried a pistol during labor disputes at the Gospel Trumpet Company. He supported Linn's work out of the same conviction that had made him a key player in Smith's ouster in 1930. Rowe strongly opposed the idea of a "standard literature" by which the views of a small group or even an individual could dominate movement thought. Through the influence inherent in the editor's office, Smith's views had achieved something very near an intellectual, if not doctrinal, monopoly. Rowe consistently opposed such tendencies, and thus his sponsorship of Linn's work must be understood as an effort to give space to alternative theological viewpoints. Rowe saw to the publication of Volume III by using Commercial Services Company of Anderson as the printer. Commercial

Services was the wholly owned subsidiary of the Gospel Trumpet Company by which it made use of its presses for contract print jobs. Rowe ordered Commercial Services to print one thousand copies of the book. Two hundred copies went to Linn in payment for his manuscript. The remaining eight hundred became the property of the Gospel Trumpet Company when Rowe signed a purchase order that authorized Sales Manager Charles F. Wilson to buy them. The entire run quickly sold out and thus it was that Linn's third volume saw the light of day. Despite the board of directors' favorable decision, the book did not appear in the company's wholesale catalogue. But its shape, size, and cover exactly replicated the format of its two predecessors; the only difference was to be found on the imprint page of Volume III. Careless readers might easily overlook that variation.[9]

Linn's work differed from that of earlier Church of God writers in several respects. Almost without exception the movement's previous expositors worked from the King James Version whereas Linn preferred a translation that remained closer to the original Greek and Hebrew—the American Standard Version—for his English language text.[10] Earlier writers premised their cases on, and typically stated that they were prompted by, the motive of "shedding new light." They often prefaced their books with appeals to the illumination of the Holy Spirit. Linn sounded the notes of conventional academic writing. Buoyed by the conviction that the "open, unprejudiced and energetic mind has ever been the medium through which revelation has come," he encouraged his readers to make up their own minds after carefully deliberating his argument and the facts on which it rested. That Linn was the first Church of God writer to employ advanced methods of criticism in biblical study also distinguished him from all who had gone before. However, although Linn had applied the historical-critical method consistently throughout his exposition of the New Testament, his use of that method remained uncontroversial until he reached the Book of Revelation. It was not the method that had created problems for the editorial staff. Linn's work only became problematic when he applied the historical-critical method to the biblical book that had been famously exposited by Smith, thereby contradicting the exegetical conclusions that underwrote much of the movement's ecclesiology.

The fundamental difference between Linn and the "standard literature," preeminently Smith's work, was that the former's method presumed a different understanding of time and prophecy. Linn interpreted Revelation as a prophetic sermon addressed primarily to an ancient church undergoing persecution. Since he regarded prophecy largely as a preaching function he saw no need of schematizing apocalyptic symbols in an effort to unpack any predicted future for either the church or world history in general. This essentially preterist hermeneutic differentiated Linn from church-historical interpreters and dispensationalists alike. He was fully aware of the controversial nature of his exposition within Church of God circles. Nevertheless he stood his ground and asked only for a fair and unbiased reading while he proceeded with a full-scale assault on Smith's work. Linn conceded that time had "tended to make sacred" that earlier exposition, and obliquely criticized ministers who let others do their thinking for them. "Such intellectual indifference," said Linn, "contributes to the tyranny of an opinion that may have established itself."[11] Then he turned one of the movement's longstanding convictions against any present or future critic by claiming that anti-creedalism rested in a dread of intellectual tyranny. As he put it, "Dangerous as independent thinking may be, it is less dangerous than the crushing of individual initiative which inevitably leads to stagnation."[12] Having thus challenged his readers, Linn turned to his exposition.

Linn approached the Book of Revelation in the conviction that the interpreter's first obligation was to attempt to understand the book as its original readers would. In essence he read Revelation in a preterist light. According to Linn the book had been written after the beginning of Roman persecution and its message was addressed to a suffering church that needed encouragement to believe that the final verdict of history was assured. It might be the case that Christians in other times and places had also found encouragement from apocalyptic. For Linn that signified the potential timelessness of the Book of Revelation. That the apocalyptic message was timeless meant that it was not addressed only to ancient Christians. He did not think Revelation to be a dead letter. Rather, its lessons could be applied in any repetition of the circumstances that threatened the first-century church.[13] Relentlessly situating the Book of Revelation in a context of Roman persecution, Linn insisted that "the great issue of the book is the struggle between Christ and his church against the antichrist emperor and his worshipers."[14]

F. G. Smith interpreted Revelation as an apocalyptic map by which accurately guided readers could understand the history and prophetic future of the church. He schematized apocalyptic imagery in a way that both harmonized and validated that history. The lynchpin of the system was his interpretation of symbolic numbers such as 42, $3 1/2$, and 1,260. In this reading Smith largely concurred with D. S. Warner, W. G. Schell, H. M. Riggle, and others who had written in this vein. That these authorities spoke as it were with one voice lent further veracity to the literature they produced. Nevertheless, Linn challenged this entrenched interpretive tradition head-on, asserting that approaches that literalized symbolic numbers resulted in "endless confusion." Careful study of the context, a hallmark of Linn's exegesis, revealed that the number 1,260 could not be associated with the Roman Catholic papacy. Neither St. John the Divine nor St. Paul had in mind the papacy when they spoke of the great apostasy and the antichrist.[15] Linn also heaped criticism on those interpreters who calculated history by applying symbolic numbers in a chronology that began with a peg driven according to their "personal theological bias."[16] He scorned by example such calculations. Referring without name to Smith's chronology Linn exposed its fallacies in a passage that deserves extended quotation:

> A position held by some who explain the 1,260 days as 1,260 years is that the beast of chapter thirteen is the papacy which was the successor to paganism, the dragon.... According to this position the beginning of the 1,260 years would be at the triumph of Christianity over paganism. Galarius placed Christianity on a plane of equality with paganism in AD 311 and in 313 Constantine made Christianity the official religion of the Empire....What date could be more significant than this for the driving of our peg? By following this method we would add 1,260 to 313, which would give us the year 1573 as the end of the era in question. But this is not a significant date, or at least does not contribute to the theology of those who would so use the number. They pass mutely over this supposed transfer of authority and select some particularly important date that fits into their trend of thought and then count backwards regardless of what happened at the time at which they arrive. If we, as some, were to choose the very important date of 1530 we would count backward to 270, which certainly was not an important date in early history. We might find some significant events during that year as we could during many subsequent years, but that proves nothing. Such a literal reckoning is what led the Adventists to announce a date for the Second Coming, as also it has in other instances. It is a confusing and erroneous method which ignores the symbolic force of the number.[17]

D. S. Warner and H. M. Riggle had argued that the Adventists were incorrect primarily in the application of their hermeneutical method and not the system itself. In this they were followed by F. G. Smith and others. Nearly forty years after the publication of *The Cleansing of the Sanctuary* Otto Linn argued that the method itself as well as its application was fallacious. He based his argument in a critical methodology that nearly all of his readers found unremarkable except for Linn's exposition of the Book of Revelation. Even at that a growing number of his readers agreed with his conclusions. Working independently of his former professor, Adam Miller, who succeeded Linn as a professor of Bible at Anderson, reached very similar conclusions in a thesis written for the M. A. degree at Butler University in 1942.[18] Several of the sources in his bibliography were works written by the men who had been Linn's professors at Chicago. First through Linn and subsequently through Miller's work, a crack had been opened in the formidable façade of the movement's church-historical hermeneutic. The tool employed by both men, professor and student, was the historical-critical method.

A. F. Gray, president of Pacific Bible College and one of the members of the publication committee who had voted to publish Linn's work, invited the Dundalk pastor to accept an appointment as dean of the tiny school in Portland, Oregon. In 1942 Linn left Maryland to take up this assignment. He remained at PBC as dean and professor of New Testament until Parkinson's Disease forced him into early retirement. Until then he remained an extremely popular teacher and respected scholar. Some of his students remember running to class sessions rather than miss any part of his lectures. At the same time he served on a subcommittee working on the translation of the Revised Standard Version New Testament. As dean of Pacific Bible College Linn may have thought that finally the opportunity had come to realize his old dream of a graduate theological institution for the Church of God. At least he set about the task of recruiting a faculty worthy of such a project and by the early 1950s had assembled the best-trained collection of Bible and theology scholars to be found in the movement.[19] As at Anderson so also at PBC, Linn's dream evaporated in the hot sun of a liberal arts curriculum plan that hoped to generate larger enrollments. But his scholarly approach to biblical exegesis by then had sunk deep roots in generations of students at both institutions.

Charles E. Brown and "Genetic" Church History

In December 1894 a flying messenger named Willis D. Bunch stepped off a train in southern Illinois. He had spent his last dollar to pay a fare that took him as far as his faith told him God wanted him to go. Eventually Bunch arrived in the small town of Mt. Zion and began a revival wherein Willis M. Brown was converted. Brown had been a hard-drinking infidel who loved gambling and a good time and who wandered Mississippi River towns in search of fast entertainment. Brown thoroughly repented his ways and invited Bunch to stay at his home, which the latter used to start another meeting. It was there that Brown's son, Charles, age eleven, was converted in January 1895. Father and son both received a call to preach, first Willis and then Charles, in September of that same year. Thus began the ministerial career of one of the most influential and prolific writers in the history of the Church of God movement.

Charles Ewing Brown (1883–1971)[20] prized education and learning. The boy preacher began his schooling in the common schools of Hardin County, Illinois. When he was fifteen he was in a revival meeting with a group of ministers whose sermons he later characterized as ignorant. The younger Brown realized that if he remained in their company he would suffer a similar fate. Conversations with a Methodist minister in Kentucky prompted him to apply for admission to the preparatory school at Asbury College; his inadequate common school education required Brown to take this step before enrolling in the college. The minister promised to underwrite Charles' expenses, so he asked permission of his father to enroll. Willis Brown objected to his son's attendance at a "sect school," but against his father's wishes young Charles enrolled anyway. When the generosity of the Methodist minister failed to materialize, Charles was left with an unpaid tuition bill and forced to drop out of school. Willis Brown took this as a heavenly sign that his son was wasting his time on education. Although it took years to repay, Charles eventually squared his account at the preparatory school. Later, after the family moved to Hickman, Kentucky, Charles completed three months of study at the local high school. His thirst for learning remained insatiable throughout his entire life. He took correspondence courses in a variety of subjects including Greek and Latin. He arranged to be tutored in Hebrew by a rabbi who had converted to Christianity. Brown also studied German in night school. Eight years after Brown became editor John Morrison wrote, "He insisted on going to school when opportunity afforded, and when opportunity was not afforded, he insisted on the privilege of constant and diligent study."[21] Near the end of his editorial tenure Brown could still be found after hours in his Gospel Trumpet Company office reading and reflecting on theology and church history.

Willis Brown worried that his promising boy preacher would be ruined by education, especially if it was acquired under the auspices of Methodists. His worst fears were realized when Charles announced that he had joined the Methodist Episcopal Church. Wherever Willis preached he requested prayer for a son who had wandered into the far country of "sectism." Invariably the saints prayed fervently for the prodigal's return. At last, at Claypool camp meeting in northern Indiana, Willis later wrote, "God answered my long continued prayer, and flashed the light on my son Charley's heart and mind. He is with me now and says he is done with sectism and this [the Church of God movement] is the only way. Glory to God."²² One year later Charles was ordained to the ministry on the same campground.

After his marriage to Carrie Becker in 1907 Brown slipped back and forth between the roles of itinerant evangelist and pastor. He had been trained as an evangelist by years of travel with his father, but the demands of a growing family pressed him into the more settled life of a pastor. After brief pastorates in Ohio and Indiana he stayed for two years in Philadelphia. After one last attempt at evangelistic work he assumed a pastorate in Detroit in 1915. There Brown remained for the next eleven years. It was during this period that Brown's reputed "liberalism" developed. Older, more seasoned ministers considered him far too progressive and "too much of a thinker."²³ He opposed C. E. Orr and the anti-necktie people, including his father, who edited the *Herald of Truth.* Shortly after his arrival in Detroit the congregation began the practice of collecting offerings as an element of worship, one of the first in Michigan to do so. Brown was also one of the key figures in the organization of the Michigan State Ministerial Assembly, a bold step that earned him and his associates the ire of leaders in Anderson.

Brown's liberal reputation did not tarnish his stature so much as to prevent the ministry from electing or appointing him to important leadership positions. He served as recording secretary during the meetings that led to the organization of the General Ministerial Assembly in 1917, the same year in which he was named a regular contributor to the *Gospel Trumpet.* In 1921 he was elected to the board of directors of the Gospel Trumpet Company and to the Missionary Board, on which he sat for thirty-seven years. Brown was also elected to serve his first term as chair of the General Ministerial Assembly in 1925, and in 1927 he was appointed secretary-treasurer of the Missionary Board. In 1926 he had resigned the pulpit in Detroit to take a pastorate in Huntington, Indiana which he continued to serve after accepting the Missionary Board assignment. Then in 1929 he resigned both positions in order to accept the pastorate at Belden Avenue Church of God in Chicago.

Brown's stay in Chicago lasted but a year. In the summer of 1930 he was elected to succeed F. G. Smith as editor of the Gospel Trumpet Company. Brown assumed this key post at a moment when the Church of God movement was tossing and turning on a sea of theological disputation, reaction, and political maneuvering. In a sense, Brown was a beneficiary of this upheaval; he owed his editorship to growing theological dissent. However, Brown's candidacy would have ended in defeat had it not been for Smith's charity and commitment to a cause larger than his own personal career. H. M. Riggle, a man much more widely known and approved than Brown, had failed in his attempt to be ratified as Smith's successor. Brown realized that he would suffer the same fate, so he asked Smith for his endorsement. His agreement secured Brown's ratification. Within a month he explained to Trumpet readers that he had not sought the office and was not particularly elated to hold it; an enormous burden of responsibility outweighed his feelings of gratitude at being chosen for an office of such historic significance in the Church of God movement.[24]

Brown soon began to make use of the weighty influence of his new office, but with a characteristic caution that avoided polarization. This appeared to him as the strategic policy needed to hold together a movement that was already divided at the time of his election and which quickly became even more deeply so. In the realm of church politics he took a neutral or perhaps mediating posture, deciding issues and casting votes on the basis of their prospects to avoid controversy and maintain peace in the church. Brown was also a master of indirect discourse. He frequently employed parables and sometimes spoke rather cleverly in double entendres to avoid confrontation, at times masking his own views behind words that might convey alternate meanings.[25] At the same time, soon after becoming editor, Brown began writing a long string of books that separated him from the so-called standard literature of the apocalyptic ecclesiology.

Brown had already produced several works before he was elected editor in 1930, but shortly after assuming that responsibility he wrote a book that signaled a conception of the church and Christian unity that clearly separated him from the practice of come-outism.[26] He titled this work *A New Approach to Christian Unity.*[27] Brown's approach to the topic was new both with respect to the denominational community he had in mind as well as Church of God readers who could be forgiven for wondering why Brown's argument sounded like nothing they had previously read in Gospel Trumpet Company literature. This book differed in tone, perspective, and content from all earlier Church of God writing on the subject of Christian unity. The triumphalist voice of come-outism was completely absent, replaced by a tone that remained confident while it asked readers to evaluate the book's argument reasonably. Brown's genuinely historical perspective replaced the idea of "the church in prophecy and history," and this led to subtle but crucial shifts in the idea of the church and the relationship of individual Christians to it.

Brown had read deeply in the history of Christianity and the product of this exposure was a generous appreciation for the achievements and accomplishments of Christians past and present. *A New Approach to Christian*

Unity argued that Christians should not settle for the "spiritual unity" of the church but must press on to what Brown called "organic unity." He cited many Christians of the opinion that a spiritual unity was the best to which they could aspire. Brown disagreed without demonizing, and in so doing gratefully acknowledged the contributions that earlier Christians had made to the general progress of the faith. To be sure, he extended the criticism first made by D. S. Warner, namely that creeds have had a divisive affect on the church. Brown employed his historical knowledge to make the same point more effectively, and he sometimes did so in a manner that displayed a Pietist's preference for lived experience over rationalist theological distinctions. So, for example, to illustrate the divisiveness of creeds he wrote, "Personally, I have known godly persons very much used of the Holy Spirit ... who never in their lives once heard of the 'filioque' controversy; and who would not be able to give an opinion as to whether the Holy Spirit 'proceeds' from the Father 'and the son' or only from the Father; or even whether he 'proceeds' from either in the metaphysical sense signified by the ancient creeds. Upon such a far-fetched and trifling quibble does the major division in Christendom depend!"[28] Catholic and Orthodox theologians would not share Brown's estimate of the significance of the *filioque* dispute, but that is beside the point. Neither are some of his historical judgments when measured against a more academic and scholarly foundation. The point is not so much Brown's historical conclusions, but that he possessed some and was the first editor to think out of a historical understanding. Brown may have mistakenly assessed the significance of the *filioque* controversy, but he could also heap praise on a Reformed tradition that contributed "great scholars and great saints" to the cause of Christ and acknowledge that "the world would be immeasurably poorer if bereft of the great saints of the Lutheran communion."[29]

Brown's historical understanding also prompted him to what might appear to be surprisingly charitable judgments of Christian movements that were part of his contemporary world. He was acquainted with the Social Gospel movement and generally sympathetic with its goals. If Brown avoided the use of a phrase such as Walter Rauschenbusch's "Christianize the social order," it was not because he disagreed with the importance of that objective. Rather, Brown thought the phrase excited unnecessary and misguided passions; instead he substituted "exert the proper Christian influence upon the social order."[30] For Brown the more pressing concern was that the divided nature of Christendom inhibited the exertion of such influence, and that this division stood in the way of a growing desire for unity among Christians of many persuasions.[31] Brown thought that the renewal of American society, and not just that of the church, depended on the recovery of unity among Christians. This breadth of vision as to disunity's consequences further separated him from many of his predecessors in the Church of God. Although only implicit in *A New Approach to Christian Unity*, given the absence of the phrase "come-out" from its pages, Brown's idea that a Christian did not have to leave a denomination in order to be part of God's church was certainly in gestation.

Brown published books nonstop from the 1930s through the '40s and into the early '50s. The three that most clearly illustrate the historical perspective that shaped his work are *The Church Beyond Division* (1939), *The Apostolic Church* (1947), and *When Souls Awaken* (1954).[32] He taught church history at Anderson College for several years and used the titles "Lecturer in Church History" and "Lecturer in Christian Doctrine" on the title pages of several of his books. Clearly he relished the role of scholar-professor. Although he served full-time as editor from 1930 to 1951 Brown dedicated *The Apostolic Church* to his undergraduate students with an academic's feeling and rhetoric. The earliest of this trio of books is a full-fledged ecclesiology dependent on his earlier *A New Approach to Christian Unity*, but intended by Brown to be read first in sequence. *The Apostolic Church* Brown subtitled "a study in historical theology," but it is more properly described as historical ecclesiology. Here Brown examined the church, its purpose and ministry, from the New Testament era to modern times. *When Souls Awaken* originally was a set of four special lectures delivered at the invitation of Anderson College's School of Theology. These lectures explore what had become Brown's favorite theme—the church historically considered. But in this case the church under examination he described as "radical Christianity." He wanted to explore the church's historical roots and connect them to later branches of the church, especially that branch called the Church of God movement.

Brown lamented the absence of historical perspective among many Christians. Those who lacked this perspective he labeled "thoughtless." Without a historically informed viewpoint they could not stand against fads and "sensational religious doctrine."[33] Accordingly, he wrote to inform, but his several books in this vein were never simply narrative church history. Brown rested his ecclesiology on a foundation of historical understanding. To write ecclesiology out of that understanding would lead readers to a point where they would have to make up their minds about basic convictions concerning the church. Well read in church history and the history of dogma, Brown was conversant with some of the traditional heavyweights of church historiography—Neander, Harnack, and Latourette—and handled the definitions of critical and dogmatic history with facility. For that reason he also knew and accepted the limitations of his preparation and therefore his writing. He made no pretense of writing scholarly books, but called himself a popularizer and justified the usefulness of such writing even though he could not resist exploring an occasional criticism of academic historians. However, the focus of Brown's work never blurred. He aimed at lifting the Church of God out of a sea of historical ignorance. Until its feet rested on the solid ground of historical understanding, he feared that the movement floated on uninformed prejudice, erroneous descriptions, and therefore was subject to the winds of any new idea or enthusiasm.

Brown approached the study of church history as a Christian primitivist. He thought that the Apostolic age set the standard for the church in all subsequent eras, whether in doctrine, spiritual life, fellowship, evangelism, as well as the "overwhelming experience of the Spirit's complete control of our lives."[34] He denied that Christianity developed in any positive sense after the close of the Apostolic era. In fact he thought that any dissenter from the Orthodox or Catholic churches had to deny that they were the continuous development of Christianity from the New Testament era. If their claims of doctrinal development were true, an apostasy from Apostolic Christianity never occurred. In that case, said Brown, all Protestant dissenters would necessarily deserve the labels "heretic" or "apostate." "Dissenters from the ancient [Orthodox and Catholic] communions are therefore bound to take the positions that the apostolic church is the true norm of Christianity and that the ancient communions have apostatized by deserting that standard."[35] The Apostolic church expressed "radical Christianity," a phrase that Brown used to signify the root, from the Latin *radix,* commitments of believers, whether in the first century or the twentieth. Thus he mined Christian history for examples of Christians whose lives and beliefs exemplified radical Christianity. He shared this conception with earlier figures such as D. S. Warner and with his own contemporary, F. G. Smith. But Brown differed in his refusal to dip into apocalyptic waters and likewise in his far more positive assessment of the contributions made by radical Christians of times and places other than the Church of God of 1881 and after. If Brown failed to endorse a conventional church historian's standard assumption concerning development, he nevertheless introduced a measure of historical understanding to the Church of God by insisting that it open its eyes and mind to the presence of many groups of radical Christians throughout the history of the church. Brown's view required of Church of God people the confession that the movement was not the goal of the divinely directed historical process but instead the latest example of a radical Christianity that had been present all along the road from the Apostles forward.

Brown put historical understanding to the service of the movement's doctrinal practice of the church. At the core of his conception of the Apostolic church stood the idea of "spiritual democracy." By this term he meant the spiritual equality and universal priesthood of believers coupled with the unity of the church.[36] In his view, this principle of church life and organization appeared in the New Testament church and was valid for the church in all times and places. He did not think that twentieth-century Christians were required to reproduce first-century administrative techniques, which Brown distinguished from the timeless principle of spiritual democracy. In fact, he saw different stages of the development of this principle among the various churches of the New Testament. That some of those churches may have been led by bishops did not validate episcopal government. In Brown's eyes it indicated a less developed stage of spiritual democracy. A church that aspired to be the gathering of radical Christians needed to be ordered by that practice.

Brown applied his notion of spiritual democracy to the growing network of bureaucratic agency offices in the Church of God. He thought that opposition to all forms of organization was one of the most serious errors made by the early pioneers of the Church of God.[37] Failure to organize led to an atomized, individualistic church without hope of cooperation, and as Brown put it, "There can be very little cooperation among people who regard all organization as sin."[38] He did see a positive side to the movement's animus toward organization in what he called the "leader principle." Brown regarded D. S. Warner as the "universal leader" of the early Church of God movement, a position in which he was followed by E. E. Byrum. But Brown also considered the "leader principle" to be in tension with the idea of spiritual democracy, and the transition from the former to the latter he regarded as the most significant change in the history of the Church of God. Brown was himself a catalyst to that process in two ways. In the first place he introduced the concept of spiritual democracy, and in the second he implemented organizational changes in accordance with that idea. Shortly after his election and ratification as editor, Brown disbursed responsibility and practices concerning ministerial ordination to state and regional assemblies. The authority to determine valid ministerial credentials had rested with the editor since the first ministerial lists were compiled. But in Brown's view that practice was a holdover from the days of the "leader principle." By 1930 there no longer was a mere handful of leading ministers. Moreover, the church controlled leadership through a democratic process. Broader based leadership forced the issue of spiritual democracy and required the power of ministerial credentialing to be distributed throughout the church, and the new editor acted accordingly.[39]

The concept of spiritual democracy served as the criterion by which Brown assessed the Protestant Reformation. While it was true that reformers such as Luther and Calvin had recovered the New Testament's gospel of redemption, Brown regarded the radical reformers, or as he called them the Anabaptists, as the highest expression of sixteenth-century Christian reform. It was their practice of spiritual democracy that gave them this stature and made them the true torchbearers of Christianity in the sixteenth century. As Brown interpreted Christian history it was Warner's combination of Anabaptist spiritual democracy with Wesley's essentially pietist soteriology and the goal of Christian unity that ignited "one blazing ideal of New Testament Christianity."[40] Brown did not claim that Warner was an original thinker in the realm of Christian theology. The latter was in Brown's view orthodox in every respect. But he regarded Warner as original in terms of his combination of these three streams of the Christian impulse to reform. It may not have created a huge blaze of new truth, but as Brown said, a fire is a fire, and even a spark may eventually set a whole forest aflame.[41]

C. E. Brown changed the language by which the Church of God communicated its understanding of the church. In the simplest terms, he gave the movement a historical reference point. In changing the language of description he fundamentally contributed to the alteration of basic doctrinal practices, and especially in one case this was critical to any future self-understanding. In the first place Brown replaced apocalyptic language with historical reference. This replacement did not occur overnight; the movement was too accustomed to thinking in the terminology of Schell and Smith. But over time people became increasingly aware that Brown's vocabulary and his vision of the church differed markedly from F. G. Smith, and they began to adopt that language.[42] Brown's historical vocabulary situated the Church of God movement in history rather than at the end of history. As Church of God people came to the view that the history of Christianity was a story they shared in common with all Christians, reference to that history as a tale of apostasy declined. Correlatively, the fervor generated by Smith's apocalyptic vision began to wane, especially as the movement settled into the American middle class.

The second alteration caused by Brown's historical perspective followed directly from the first. His body of work encouraged the Church of God movement to abandon the language and associated practice of come-outism. Brown's positive assessment of past and present Christian achievement in the denominations rendered increasingly untenable the position that regarded them as daughters of Mystery Babylon. Even more telling was Brown's conviction that faithful followers of Jesus were already members of the church of God, regardless of their denominational home.[43] Implicitly this view did more than tolerate denominations; it gave them a measure of legitimacy. As the Church of God movement granted legitimacy to the denominations, it moved from being a sectarian protest group to one of the members of the system—even though many in the movement stubbornly refused to use the label denomination as a self-description. Gradually shorn of come-outism's insistence that true believers must quit denominations and denominationalism, the Church of God movement was forced to find a new identity. Brown guided that search through his many books as well as editorials written over more than twenty years, and in a limited respect he succeeded. The Church of God first became tolerant of believers in denominational Christianity and then embraced them even as many in the constituency stopped thrashing Babylon. These revisions owed a great deal to Brown's historical understanding, one that made increasingly common sense in the growing religious toleration of post-World War II American culture.

Brown developed his idea of spiritual democracy historically, and in this, too, church practice was altered to the extent that the movement adopted his view. He thought that spiritual democracy characterized the New Testament era and appeared in the subsequent history of the church wherever Christians were faithful to that standard. Mennonites and Pietists were two of his favorite examples in this regard. That he saw such historical examples at all set him over against the older and still majority viewpoint that affirmed the Church of God movement as unique and unprecedented in Christian history. Brown held the movement's practices up to the standard of spiritual democracy. Where they failed that test he set changes into motion. The first of these changes were those he implemented concerning ordination and ministerial recognition. Others followed in train, most notably broadened ministerial participation in corporate decision-making.

During the teens, twenties, and thirties it was no exaggeration to say that the Church of God movement was governed by a small circle of "leading ministers." One person has termed these individuals the "national elders" of the Church of God. The original members of this select circle were most of the membership of the "Committee of Seventeen" responsible for the creation of *Our Ministerial Letter.* Many were members of the Gospel Trumpet Company. After bureaucratic organization began in 1917, these same individuals were elected to memberships on several boards and agencies. Although the number of agency boards gave the appearance of broadening participation, in actuality the circle of agency membership remained disproportionately small. For example, the odds were quite high that A. F. Gray would be named to any and every special committee during the 1930s. These assignments were in addition to his memberships on several agency boards and service as chair of the General Ministerial Assembly. A. T. and Ida Byrd Rowe offer another illustration in the extreme. During a portion of the 1930s the Rowes could discuss any aspect of the movement's business at their kitchen breakfast table. Between them this couple sat on every Church of God agency board. Brown's ideal of spiritual democracy contributed to the elimination of this prevailing practice of "interlocking directorates," resulting in reforms that ultimately prohibited multiple agency board memberships. Perhaps no other alteration in practice deflated the oft-heard criticism that "the big boys" were running the church. In this respect Brown's principle of "spiritual democracy" broadened participation and indeed democratized the Church of God movement. And yet other developments belied this idea's influence. Shortly before Brown took office as editor the number of women ordained to the Church of God ministry began declining from a high of approximately one-third of all ordained ministers. He read this decline as a precursor to decreased spiritual vitality in the movement as a whole. Ever searching history for examples to make his point, he found there a correlation between declines in the number of women ministers and spiritual fervor.[44] Nevertheless the decline continued, as did the racial separation that had produced a separate African American camp meeting and the National Association. Until after 1960 the tent of spiritual democracy did not shelter many women or Black leaders in the Church of God movement.

The Influence of History on the Church of God

By the fall of 1933 some Church of God hearts were increasingly uneasy over the changes they saw creeping into the movement's life and thought. The old notion of charismatic leadership was under attack from, of all people, the editor of the Gospel Trumpet Publishing Company. C. E. Brown was giving away power, placing it in the hands of state assemblies and their credentials committees. At the same time other individuals had put the recently created bureaucratic structure to work endorsing enterprises such as liberal arts colleges, for which the New Testament gave little or no precedent. Worst of all, the "Anderson leadership"—especially at the college and the publishing house—did not endorse the apocalyptic vision of the church set down in the so-called standard literature of F. G. Smith. If the old verities were no longer affirmed, then changes in church practice were sure to follow. Signs of those changes were already manifest to some, as near as publication decisions at the Gospel Trumpet Company.

Calls for a standard literature did not cease with the demise of F. G. Smith's ill-fated resolution in the late twenties. Ministers in Ohio and elsewhere continued to refer to the movement's standard literature as if it formally existed. Smith may very well have encouraged such references. He and two other influential ministers, E. E. Byrum and H. M. Riggle, all three powerful members of the Publication Board of the Church of God, lobbied company leaders for the creation of just such a body of authoritative teaching.[45] In every case, the books proposed for the list had been published during the movement's first thirty years of existence, and they were regarded as the works of the founding generation. Against the proposal that some books be elevated to a higher status stood three men who were in position to squash it. Throughout his career as general manager, A. T. Rowe opposed a monolithic theology and encouraged new voices to speak in print. In this he was joined by Editor C. E. Brown, himself one of those new voices, and Book Editor Harold L. Phillips. Each man resolutely opposed proposals for the creation of a standard literature. The phrase may have remained on the tongues of those who wanted the movement's theological past to bear heavily on its present and future, but it never enjoyed the favor of the people who finally decided which books were to be published.

The source of the uneasiness of those who in the 1930s called for a return to the past should be attributed neither to self-serving interests nor paranoia. Better to locate that uneasiness in the perception that the movement had changed, and dramatically so. In fact, the Church of God movement had undergone enormous change since the bureaucratic revolution of 1917. The seeds of even greater changes were sown in 1930, but their fruit did not ripen until the end of the decade and afterward. The name of the plant that began growing in the Church of God garden in 1930 was *history.* Otto Linn applied the historical critical method to the study of the Bible. This was nothing new in the wider world of biblical scholarship, but in the smaller neighborhood of the Church of God Linn's work was revolutionary. If he and his contemporary but academic protégé Adam W. Miller were correct, then the exegetical and hermeneutical premise on which a standard literature rested was wrong. If the standard literature was wrong then so were the church practices associated with it, most importantly, comeoutism. After 1930 the ecclesiology of the standard literature began a steady decline at Church of God schools where the historical-critical method was taught. That literature did not disappear, but it found little favor in the places that could have given it institutional credibility—preeminently the movement's colleges but also the publishing house.

Although not formally trained as a church historian, widely read Charles E. Brown pushed the movement to consider itself in the full spectrum of church history. He was a practicing church historian whose research prompted new conclusions and practices in the Church of God movement even as it reinforced others. As in the case of Linn's biblical scholarship, Brown's historical research and many publications led him to the inescapable conclusion that Warner and others who read the Bible and church history through an apocalyptic lens had seriously misread the past. He set about correcting those mistakes in the first book he wrote after becoming editor. Tellingly, there the old apocalyptic language was loudly silent. Those who feared that something was amiss in the Church of God movement in 1933 were right to worry. If only in principle and with an effect that would not become clearly apparent for a decade or more, nevertheless history had triumphed over apocalyptic.

Notes

1. A. F. Gray, pastor of Park Place Church of God in Anderson, covered Byrum's courses for the 1929–1930 academic year as a temporary measure.

2. Perhaps the most significant name on the roster of Linn's students at Anderson is that of Adam W. Miller, who succeeded Linn as a professor of Bible at his alma mater and who continued teaching the historical-critical method as had his mentor. The use of the historical-critical method at Anderson during the 1930s must be among the earliest, if not the first, appearance of advanced forms of critical scholarship at any college or university sponsored by one of the holiness movement churches.

3. Cf. a photocopy of a letter from Smith to Linn dated February 7, 1934. Archives of the Church of God.

· 4. The *GT* serial was "Studies in the New Testament," and the commentary carried the same title. Cf. Otto F. Linn, *Studies in the New Testament,* 3 volumes. Vols 1 and 2 published under the Gospel Trumpet Company's new trade name, "The Warner Press," 1941 and 1942, respectively. Linn wrote two other commentaries: *The Gospel of John* (Anderson, Ind: Gospel Trumpet Company, 1942), and *The Gospel of Mark* (Anderson, Ind: Gospel Trumpet Company, 1944).

5. *GT* (December 9, 1939), 1.

6. *GT* (December 16, 1939), 5–6

7. Harold L. Phillips, Class Interview, March 1, 1982. School of Theology, Anderson University.

8. Harold Phillips, who succeeded Brown as editor of the Gospel Trumpet Company, voted with Gray and Martin to make the majority. Phillips, the youngster in a group of theological and church heavyweights, was made to feel every bit of his youth when, after the vote was taken, Smith looked him in the eye and said, "Well, we have a problem. But we wouldn't if one person would change his vote." Ibid.

9. *Copies of Studies in the New Testament,* Vol. III were sold in the company bookstore, but patrons had to request it by title.

10. Linn, *Studies in the New Testament,* Vol. III (hereafter SNT, III), 10.

11. Ibid.

12. Ibid.

13. Ibid., 79–83.

14. Ibid., 84.

15. Ibid., 105, 109.

16. Ibid., 108.

17. Ibid., 109–110.

18. Adam W. Miller, "The Interpretation of the Book of Revelation," unpublished M. A. thesis, Butler University, 1942. At Miller's request, his thesis was not to be copied, nor was a copy to be shelved in the Anderson College library.

19. Included in this faculty were Irene S. Caldwell, Ph. D. in Christian education from the University of Southern California and her husband, Mack M. Caldwell, Ph. D. in the sociology of religion from

Oregon State University. John W. V. Smith, Ph. D. from the University of Southern California, taught church history and Milo L. Chapman, Th. D. from Pacific School of Religion, taught Old Testament. Linn of course taught New Testament and Greek while A. F. Gray, himself the author of a recently published systematics, taught theology.

20. Brown's life and career is the subject of an academic thesis. Cf., Lee Dean Preston, *Charles E. Brown: His Life and Influence* (unpublished S. T. M. thesis, Iliff School of Theology, 1969).

21. J. A. Morrison, "College and Seminary Corner," *GT* (October 8, 1938), 13.

22. "Field Reports," *GT* (September 4, 1902), 6.

23. Morrison, Loc. cit.

24. "New Editor of the Gospel Trumpet," *GT* (July 3, 1930), 24.

25. Perhaps the clearest example of Brown's linguistic nimbleness is his description of himself as a fundamentalist. Some of his closest associates say that Brown did not mean by that term to connect himself to the Fundamentalist cause of the 1920s and '30s. Instead, Harold L. Phillips and the late Milo L. Chapman, who both knew Brown extremely well, say that Brown was certainly not a Fundamentalist but that by this term he meant his belief in the fundamental teachings of Christianity. It seems more than a little disingenuous of Brown to have thought that, at a time when the term was widely used in conservative Protestant circles, his listeners would not have assumed that he aligned himself with the Fundamentalists.

26. Prior to becoming editor, Brown had written on eschatology, *The Hope of His Coming* (Anderson, Ind: Gospel Trumpet Company, 1927), as well as three polemical works, *Can We Talk with the Dead?* (Anderson, Ind: Gospel Trumpet Company, n.d.), *Christian Science Unmasked* (Anderson, Ind: Gospel Trumpet Company,1919), and *Reds and Religion* (Anderson, Ind: Gospel Trumpet Company, n.d.).

27. (Anderson, Ind: Gospel Trumpet Company, 1931).

28. Brown, *A New Approach to Christian Unity*, 32.

29. Ibid., 47–48.

30. Ibid., 65.

31. Ibid., 63–67.

32. Other titles in his bibliography include: *The Way of Prayer* (Anderson, Ind: Gospel Trumpet Company, 1940); *Modern Religious Faiths* (Anderson, Ind: Gospel Trumpet Company, 1941); *The Way of Faith* (Anderson, Ind: Gospel Trumpet Company, 1943); *The Meaning of Salvation* (Anderson, Ind: Gospel Trumpet Company, 1944); *The Meaning of Sanctification* (Anderson, Ind: The Warner Press, 1945); and *Questions and Answers* (Anderson, Ind: Gospel Trumpet Company, 1949).

33. C. E. Brown, *The Apostolic Church* (Anderson, Ind: The Warner Press, 1947), vii.

34. Ibid., 31.

35. Ibid., 29.

36. Ibid., 31–32.

37. C. E. Brown, *When Souls Awaken* (Anderson, Ind: Gospel Trumpet Company, 1954), 112.

38. Ibid.

39. It is tempting to locate the origin of Brown's interpretation of the tension between the "leader principle" and spiritual democracy in international politics of the 1930s and after. After all, the man who was known simply as Germany's "leader" (*Fuehrer*) seized power in 1933, only three years after Brown became editor. (This is not to suggest that Brown thought that the early leaders of the Church of God were fascists.) He saw the expansion of democracy at work in the historic process. At best, all we can say about the relationship between some of Brown's ecclesiological views and politics is that the former were developing before the rise of the fascist dictatorships and totalitarian governments of the '30s, '40s, and '50s, but that the rise of such phenomenon reinforced Brown's conviction that democracy must win the day inside the church as well as out.

40. Ibid., 38–39.

41. Ibid., 39.

42. Harold Phillips recounts a moment that illustrated both the perception and the tension between those who saw the church with Smith's eyes versus those who saw it like Brown. In the early 1940s Editor Brown was invited to address a minister's meeting at Springfield, Ohio, a hotbed of support for Smith's vision of the church. Smith was also invited to make a presentation on the same topic. After

Brown, the second of the two to speak, finished, the floor was opened for questions. Immediately a minister commented that it appeared that Brown did not hold the same views as Smith and asked for an explanation as to how this could be so. The air was electric as the crowd kept one eye on Brown and the other on Smith, who was seated in the front pew. Brown, always ready to employ a metaphor, said, "Fred and I are like two traveling salesmen selling our goods in the same town. He works his side of the street; I work mine and we get along just fine." All eyes turned to Smith, who smiled and nodded in agreement, and the tension broke up in laughter. Interview (August 9, 2001).

43. The small case *c* in church of God in this sentence is not a typographical error. It became a convention in the Church of God movement to use an upper case *C* when referring to the movement, and a lower case *c* when referring to the church universal.

44. C. E. Brown, "Women Preachers," *GT* May 27, 1939, 5.

45. No formal list of titles proposed for inclusion on the standard literature list has survived. But Harold L. Phillips recalls that among the titles discussed were books written by advocates of the idea. According to Phillips, along with the works of D. S. Warner, the proposed list included Byrum's *The Secret of Salvation* and *Divine Healing of Soul and Body;* Riggle's, *The Christian Church—Its Rise and Progress;* and Smith's, *The Revelation Explained* and *What the Bible Teaches.*

Chapter 11
Experience, Part 1, "Liberalism"

In the theological lexicon of the Church of God, few words have been of greater importance than *experience.* By this term believers referred to and described conversion and sanctification. Penitent sinners did not simply come to faith; they were saved, and salvation was an experience to which they testified. Moreover, the experience of salvation was the doorway into the church. On the letterhead and signboards of hundreds of congregations across North America there appeared the slogan, "The Church Where a Christian Experience Makes You a Member." Salvation was the experience that determined church membership. Similarly, Church of God songwriters churned out scores of gospel songs that were collected in songbooks and hymnals in subsections with titles like "Experience and Rejoicing." Under the revivalist style of preaching featured throughout the movement, salvation started the new believer on an experiential journey through life. Thus a common request during Wednesday night prayer meetings took the form, "Tell us about your experience," and everyone in the room understood that exhortation to call for a testimony concerning what the believer had experienced of the Lord. Experience validated church teaching and new experiences sometimes required theological change. Church of God people never substituted experience for Scripture, but they did read the Bible through the lens of their experience and at certain points altered church teaching and doctrinal practice on that basis. By a variety of measures experience has been a crucial category in the theology of the Church of God movement.

The word *experience* can and has been applied theologically in ways that dramatically alter its meaning. When meaning changes alterations in practice are likely to follow. In the 1940s the meaning of the term *experience* began to lose some of its coherence in the Church of God. Reduced coherence or diminished uniformity are alternate ways of saying that the Church of God movement began investing crucial theological terms like _experience_ with a wider range of meaning. New ideas and forces began penetrating the movement, broadening and complicating theretofore simple definitions. An important avenue down which new ideas strode into the movement was graduate seminary education. Shortly before 1940 Church of God college graduates began enrolling in seminaries in significant numbers, and they tended to choose seminaries or graduate programs in religion that remained committed to one or another strain of theological liberalism. It would be too much to say that these Church of God seminarians imported liberal theology into the movement. But they were nonetheless influenced by important American liberal theologians such as Edgar J. Goodspeed, Shirley Jackson Case, and Walter Marshall Horton. These students acquired a vocabulary that included words and phrases that rang familiar in their ears, words that sounded familiar but were spoken with different theological accents. Through such educational experiences this rising generation of Church of God leaders was able to explore the wider world of theological scholarship while retaining, if in somewhat modified form, many of the doctrinal commitments and practices that they had brought with them to seminary.

Personal Experience: the Church of God and Pietism

Charles E. Brown was the first Church of God writer to connect the Church of God movement with seventeenth-century movement known as Pietism. He saw Pietists as the first of three phases of a post-reformation movement that Brown liked to call the "Great Revival." In none of its phases was the Great Revival sectarian, meaning that it was never in the custody of one denomination but was a broad movement among true Christians. Brown thought that each phase of the Great Revival emphasized a different aspect of Christian life and faith. The first era of the revival had emphasized regeneration, a favorite theme of Pietists. Sanctification or holiness was the special burden of the second phase, which Brown consistently associated with John and Charles Wesley. The theme of Christian unity characterized the revival's third phase, and Brown connected this principally to John Winebrenner. Each of these themes Brown represented as a torch, and the three torches, said Brown, had been combined in the hand of Daniel Sidney Warner.[1] Brown's reading of the history of post-Reformation Protestantism made the Church of God movement the heir of three parents, one of which was Pietist Christianity.

The Pietists, said Brown, were led by Philipp Jacob Spener,[2] whose message he characterized as "the Christian life is more than knowledge."[3] Spener, said Brown, emphasized life and experience over knowledge and doctrine, and Brown agreed: "This is the way true Christianity must show itself. In opposition to the dead formality and legalism which placed the essence of Christianity in forms and ceremonies, he [Spener] insisted on the absolute necessity of new birth."[4] Brown could have described D. S. Warner in much the same terms, but that would establish only a correlation between Warner and Pietism. To make a stronger historical connection Brown traced a genealogical line from Spener through such persons as August Hermann Francke, Georg Muller, Nicholas Zinzendorf, and the Wesleys to the holiness movement and Warner. This narrative linked the experientialist theology of the Church of God with the Pietist emphasis on experience.

Like seventeenth-century Pietists, early Church of God people balanced experience and Bible. Vital Christian living rested on two witnesses—the Word of Scripture and the Spirit who guided believers into all truth. It is certainly the case that "the word *Bible* was attached to all other important words in their theological vocabulary."[5] This linguistic habit confessed their belief in the sole authority of the Bible. Alongside this belief, it must be said, their equally strong conviction that religion is essentially experiential raised the category of experience to a status that made it confirmatory of the truths they read in the Bible. Thus early Church of God people sang, "I have read in the Bible what His favor doth impart; now, O glory, I have proved it. Now 'tis true within my heart."[6] Authority rested in the Bible, but Church of God people also believed that assurance came to believers through a personal knowledge of God, a knowledge that is experiential and thus mysterious rather than rational.

The idea that assurance lay in the witness of the Spirit illustrates the importance of unmediated experience in the Church of God movement. The direct prompting of the Spirit was often identified as the agent behind some important action. So, for example, it was the Spirit, said George T. Clayton, who gave him the idea to outfit a barge with a chapel that could be floated down the Ohio River, which barge became known as the *Floating Bethel.* Similarly the Spirit was said to prompt the first Church of God missionaries with a burden for a particular locale. Many saints prefaced their letters to the *Gospel Trumpet* by confessing that the Holy Spirit had led them to write a word of testimony. Until the work of Russell Byrum and Otto Linn, it was common for the prefaces of Gospel Trumpet Company books to carry testimonies from their authors as to how the Spirit had encouraged the work or illuminated its author's path. The language of unmediated experience worked itself deeply into the religious discourse of the Church of God movement.

The movement's experientialist approach to theology is underscored even more boldly by the absence of theological rationalism. The Church of God movement was not heavily invested in the Fundamentalist Controversy of the 1920s. The saints were quite aware of that debate, but they remained aloof for two reasons. First, they generally regarded it as an intramural struggle of denominational Christianity; as such it was merely a Babylonish squabble. Secondly and more important, however, there was nothing in the Church of God movement's teaching on biblical inspiration and authority that gave them reason to enter the Fundamentalist fray. While it is very difficult to state the convictions of the grassroots movement, it is quite clear that published writers such as H. C. Wickersham (1850–1916) and Russell Byrum, whose lives spanned a period from the first to third generations of movement leadership, both taught a doctrine of inspiration that focused on the Bible's writers before its words or even its ideas.[7] This doctrine of inspiration was quite consistent with the convictions of a people who regularly testified to the leading of the Spirit in their own lives and who insisted that the essence of religion was experiential.

Early movement writers made few explicit statements concerning the inspiration of the Bible. Its authority and inspiration were undisputed. Wickersham did offer a view of inspiration, and this statement diverged widely from Fundamentalist doctrine. Said Wickersham:

> The Bible is the only authentic source from which instruction can be derived, in relation to the knowledge of God; his various dispensations to mankind, and the duties required of men by their Creator. As it claims to be regarded as the book of God, a divine authority, so it claims to be the only authority. It is not *a* rule, it is *the* rule both of faith and practice. The Bible, therefore is the canon; that is the authoritative standard of salvation and morality.
>
> The different writers of the books of the Bible were inspired of God. It is not the words of the Bible that were inspired, it is not the thoughts of the Bible that were inspired; it is the men who wrote the Bible that were inspired. Inspiration acts not on the man's words, not on the man's thoughts, but on the man himself; so that he, by his own spontaneity, under the impulse of the Holy Ghost, conceives certain thoughts and gives utterance to them in certain words, both the words and the thoughts receiving the peculiar impress of the mind which conceived and uttered them.[8]

Wickersham's understanding of language undergirded his frank recognition of the diversity of the biblical writers. The Bible, said Wickersham, had been transmitted through human languages, which are incommensurable. "No human language has exactly one word and only one for each distinct idea. In every known language the same word is used to indicate different things, and different words are used to indicate the same thing. In every human language each word has more than one meaning, and each thing has generally more than one name."[9] This variability of meaning, coupled with the fact that the human mind is entirely capable of a wide variety of impressions from the same object (in this case, the text of Scripture), lends veracity to the complaint of Bible "objectors ... that the Bible can be made to mean everything and anything; all sects build upon it, the most diverse doctrines are derived from it...."[10] Given Wickersham's beliefs about language and perception, one should not be surprised that he held a dynamic view of inspiration. One then wants to ask how Wickersham determined the meaning of Scripture.

The answer to that question appears in Wickersham's assertion that the human mind "in its carnal state" is capable of a wide variety of impressions from the same object. In his view the proper approach to biblical interpretation lay not in a high view of inspiration but in a theory of interpretation that took account of the diversity of language and writer. "But this is no fault of the Bible. This is owing to the imperfections of the human language, and the fallen and depraved state of the human mind. The cause of division and sects is not in the Bible; but in the carnal mind of man, wresting the scriptures to his own destruction. Men need to have their understanding both opened and straightened out, that they may understand the scriptures."[11] Wickersham's nimble end-run around issues that posed major problems for other theories of inspiration began in beliefs common to other Church of God writers who asserted that the interpretation of the Bible rested on both the word of Scripture and the guiding illumination of the reader by the Holy Spirit.

Early Church of God writers certainly knew of the emergence of the higher criticism and its implicit challenge to traditional theories of biblical authority. Many of those writers were also aware of theories of biblical inspiration employed to repulse this challenge. Although they stated without reservation their belief in the Bible's authority, several Church of God writers took pains to reject the theory of the verbal inspiration of the Bible. D. O. Teasley argued:

> The spirits of the prophets are subject to the prophets (1 Cor 14:32). This scripture is conclusive evidence that the sacred writers did not lose their self-control. The inspired writers of the Bible were not, like the priests of heathen gods, thrown into a state of unconscious ecstasy in which their understand-

ings were inactive, while they gave utterance to words of which they knew not the import....

The Bible from beginning to end bears evidence of their calm, constant self-control. They spoke as they were moved by the Holy Spirit, but remained in full possession of their faculties and self-control; the human and divine mysteriously intermingled to give us a revelation worthy of God and suited to man.[12]

This line of reasoning led Teasley to state, "We hold the doctrine of plenary [or absolute] inspiration, not verbal inspiration, and believe that all the facts of Scripture are consistent with it...."[13]

Russell Byrum published an article in 1921 wherein he laid out the various theories of biblical inspiration, and their shortcomings as well as strengths.[14] No supporter of the higher criticism, Byrum labeled it destructive and the prompt for recent interest in theories of inspiration. He took a middle position between the "natural inspiration" advocated by "liberalists" and higher critics, on the one hand, and "absolute mechanical dictation" theories on the other. The former made the Bible a "mere human book" on a par with the Koran or the Vedas. The latter rendered the human role in the writing of Scripture no more than that of "passive instruments." Moreover, wrote Byrum, "The theory of dictation fails to account for the manifestly human element in the Scriptures, the peculiarities in style that characterize and distinguish the productions of each writer from those of the others; it is inconsistent with what we know of the interworking of the human and divine in our conversion, keeping, and so forth."[15]

The true theory of inspiration Byrum took to be one in which "God adapted his truth to ordinary human intelligence by shaping it in human molds."[16] According to Byrum, in this dynamic theory of inspiration,

The Scriptures are a result of the interworking of the human and divine, not of one without the other. This divine inspiration of the sacred writers was not, as an external force, acting upon them from without; but was from within and through their natural faculties, intellect, and personality. Upon what we can gather from the Scriptural teaching and from personal experience today as to the manner of the working of God's Spirit, we are safe in believing that these writers retained full use of every human faculty, but that the Holy Spirit exalted the exercise of those natural powers....[17]

Not all Church of God writers agreed with the ideas of biblical inspiration put forward by Wickersham, Teasley, and Russell Byrum. Some held theories nearer to Fundamentalism. However, there is no gainsaying that major theological authorities in the Church of God held theories of inspiration that diverged widely from Fundamentalist doctrine. It was the movement's experientialist epistemology that prevented it from making common cause with that camp.[18]

Early Church of God songwriters gave the movement songs that reinforced the importance of experience in the practices of church and Christian life. The Gospel Trumpet Company published numerous songbooks, but five could be termed major hymnals.[19] The topical indices of the latter four include sections under the topic of "experience" or "experience and rejoicing." Church of God people sang of their "joy unspeakable" at the experience of God's present reign in their hearts and that they did not have to wait for a millennial kingdom on earth. Perhaps no gospel song captured this sense of joyous experience any more than Barney E. Warren's beloved "A Child of God."

> Praise the Lord! my heart with his love is beaming,
> I am a child of God;
> Heaven's golden light over me is streaming,
> I am a child of God.
>
> Let the saints rejoice with my raptured spirit,
> I am a child of God;
> I will testify that the world may hear it,
> I am a child of God.
>
> Let a holy life tell the gospel story,
> I am a child of God;
> How he fills the soul with his grace and glory,
> I am a child of God.
>
> Saved from sin today, every band is riven,
> I am a child of God.
> Thro' the tests of life I have peace from heaven,
> I am a child of God.[20]

The cardinal tenets of orthodox Christian doctrine were never denied by the Church of God movement. Indeed they were fully embraced. But whenever and wherever they gathered, the saints sang their commitment to an experiential knowledge of the reality that lay behind the second order discourse of creeds and doctrinal summaries. In this, too, the movement's connections to Pietism are displayed. Pietists everywhere agreed that the assurance of salvation rested not on doctrines of infallibility, whether of pope, doctrinal formula, or Bible. Rather the locus of assurance was to be found in the personal identification of the believer with God, what Church of God people called (and sang) the witness of the Spirit.

The ongoing experience of believers was of such validating power that it occasionally led to doctrinal revision. In no case is this clearer than in the movement's teaching and practices associated with divine healing. E. E. Byrum's books and personal ministry made certain that the practice of divine healing would not be relegated to the doctrinal periphery. More than any other individual he helped the movement to accept divine healing as one of the marks of the true church; it was only there that sinners were saved, believers sanctified, and the sick divinely healed. Largely through his influence early saints did not consult physicians or use prescription medicines. But before Byrum's death in 1942 the movement had already begun revising the doctrinal practice of this central aspect of its life. Experience played a key role in that revision.

It did happen that the prayers for healing uttered in behalf of key individuals in the Church of God movement sometimes went unanswered. Better to say that those prayers were not answered in a manner consistent with the theological practice of healing then in force. Early in the twentieth century Clarence and Nora Hunter took their young family to the camp meeting at Yellow Creek Lake in northern Indiana. While there the Hunters' twin daughters, Mary and Martha, fell gravely ill. Despite the fervent prayers of the gathered saints the little girls died, one the day before and the other the day after their first birthday. The theology of healing then current made little room for such a tragic outcome. However, the Hunters were dedicated evangelists and their lives without moral taint. The faith of believers assembled around them was neither scarce nor weak, nevertheless the baby girls died. Clarence Hunter poured his grief into a gospel song that, despite its departure from the prevalent theology of healing, became a standard in subsequent Church of God hymnals. Hunter's song is titled "God's Way Is Best," and is noteworthy for a spirit of resignation utterly devoid of the insistence that God must repay faith with healing.[21]

Clarence Hunter collaborated on his song with a rising gospel worker, poet, and songwriter named Charles Wesley Naylor (1874–1950). Born in Athens County, Ohio, Naylor's early religious training was shaped by his family's Methodism. He joined the Gospel Trumpet Company in 1895, volunteering his services as a general worker. His musical and poetic gifts drew the attention of the *Trumpet* leadership, and he soon became an editorial

E. E. Byrum praying at a divine healing service late in his career. Even after revision in the movement's theology of healing, this special service remained a regular feature on Anderson Campmeeting program.

assistant. Only two years after he and Clarence Hunter produced "God's Way is Best" Naylor suffered very serious internal injuries when a heavy tent-post fell on him as the tent was being struck after a camp meeting in Florida. He returned to Anderson but did not recover. Some years later his injuries were exacerbated in an automobile accident, leaving Naylor almost a complete invalid. By this time he was widely known in Church of God circles for his fine gospel songs, many of which enjoyed enduring popularity. Nevertheless, there were whispers that God had not healed Naylor because he lacked sufficient faith or, even worse, that some unconfessed sin lurked within his heart. While such rumors circulated Naylor wrote devotional books that became quite popular, some of them running into several printings.[22] Naylor refused to heed the rumors concerning his alleged sin or weak faith even as he would not accept the theology of healing on which they were premised. Instead he challenged that theology with a new view of illness and suffering. Rather than follow the older view that found divine healing to be a corollary of the atonement and God's promise to the faithful, Naylor asserted that God was also present in and worked through suffering. "Pain," wrote Naylor, "is God's chisel, with which he carves his image in the heart."[23]

While Naylor offered the Church of God an alternate perspective on suffering, illness, and healing, others refused to countenance the rumors concerning him. His small house below the Anderson College campus became the goal of pilgrims who knew Naylor only through his songs or books and wanted to visit the man whose work had comforted them. College students also interrupted their days to walk down to Naylor's house. Some of Naylor's visitors knelt by his bedside to receive anointing and prayer for their afflictions. Meanwhile, others insisted that he was the worst thing that ever happened to the movement's theology of healing. But the experience of Naylor's continuing suffering combined with his spirituality to force further revisions in this doctrinal practice. It would be overstating the point to say that experiences such as the Hunters and Naylor endured were the singular cause of doctrinal revision. Rapid improvements in medical science also made physicians and medicines far more attractive. Such developments as the appearance of penicillin and other antibiotics that greatly reduced the mortality rate of illnesses such as pneumonia encouraged revisions in the practice of healing. The movement never abandoned the prayer and ritual of divine healing, but increasingly it practiced this aspect of doctrinal life alongside and even after visits to the doctor's office. Perhaps the clearest sign of theological change was that, before Naylor's death in 1950, the Church of God commissioned its first doctors and nurses as medical missionaries. The experiences of people and the movement's experience of them played a key role in this doctrinal development.

Church of God Students, Seminaries, and Graduate Study in Religion

Undergraduate study in Bible and religion stimulated a hunger for advanced theological study. In the late 1930s, but particularly after 1940, a growing number of college graduates, the great majority alumni of Anderson College, began pursuing graduate degrees, and many of these seminary graduates either already were or soon became important figures in the next generation of Church of God leadership. Otto Linn's example encouraged Adam Miller, Harold L. Phillips, and T. Franklin Miller to enroll in Butler University's School of Religion while Earl Martin earned an advanced degree at Northwestern University. Martin and Adam Miller both went on to long teaching careers at Anderson College. T. Franklin Miller held a succession of key national leadership posts in the movement, and Phillips succeeded Brown as editor in chief at the Gospel Trumpet Company. But it was Oberlin Seminary in Ohio that became the school of choice for a large majority of those men and women in the Church of God who earned seminary degrees before 1953. In the 1930s Anna Koglin, Dan Martin, and Gene Newberry were the earliest to pack their bags and set off for Oberlin. Koglin had already returned to Anderson College, where she taught German and Greek, but Martin and Newberry were quickly followed by Robert Reardon and Warren Edmondson. This group blazed a trail followed by more than a dozen others. Fifteen or sixteen seminary graduates may seem an insignificant number; measured against a Church of God ministry in which undergraduate degrees were rare, two dozen seminary alumni loomed large. Along with the Millers, Martin, and Phillips, several of the Oberlin students formed the nucleus of leadership in the rising generation of Church of God ministers.

Robert Reardon's ministerial career was defined by his twenty-five year presidency at Anderson College. Still another of the Oberlin group, Newberry, joined the fledgling School of Theology at Anderson College after earning a doctorate at Duke University. He taught systematic theology and ethics during a tenure that lasted for more than twenty-five years, most of it as the seminary's third dean. Not many years later John W. V. Smith also was appointed to the School of Theology faculty. Oberlin alumnus Hollis S. Pistole pastored Church of God congregations prior to being called to the Division of Church Service. He left the Board of Pensions to accept a faculty appointment in pastoral administration at the School of Theology. Delena Goodman became the head librarian at the School of Theology. Irene Smith Caldwell graduated from Oberlin and then enrolled at the University of Southern California School of Religion, where she earned a doctorate in Christian education. Caldwell worked for the movement's national Board of Christian Education and played a key role in the development of new church school curricula while she held successive faculty appointments at Warner Pacific College, the School of Theology, and Warner Southern College. Yet another Oberlin alumnus, Louis E. "Pete" Meyer, played an important role on the staff of the Board of Church Extension and Home Missions. No other seminary exerted so formative a theological influence on this generation of Church of God leaders and, through them, on the movement.[24]

During the years that Church of God men and women studied at Oberlin its leading intellectual lights were teachers like Clarence Tucker Craig, Herbert May, and, perhaps preeminently, Walter Marshall Horton. The Congregationalist church sponsored Oberlin, and Horton was widely respected both within and without his home denomination, serving on national committees and often charged with the responsibility of using his pen to represent Congregationalism. A graduate of Harvard and Union Theological Seminary, Horton also studied at the Sorbonne and the Universities of Strasbourg and Marburg before earning a Ph. D. in philosophy from Columbia. He was a prolific writer whose books covered a wide range of topics and who frequently contributed to journals such as *The Christian Century, The Journal of Religion,* and *Ecumenical Review* as well. In 1926 Horton was appointed Fairchild Professor of Systematic Theology at Oberlin, and by the time the Church of God students arrived he had already authored more than half a dozen books. Then in his mid-forties, he was in the prime of what was already a distinguished career.

Horton approached theology from the liberal side of the theological divide that widened during the 1920s in American Protestantism. He thought that the tension between the sciences and theology could be resolved through charitable, rational reflection. Thus one of his books attempted to "take stock of the assured results of the new psychology and, quite without dogmatic presuppositions, to see what theological conclusions they lead, and what theological adjustments they require."[25] His labor to bring ideas together from different intellectual disciplines was consistent with the great aim of his career, which was to unite Christians rather than see them divided. Horton was a dedicated participant in ecumenical endeavors as well as an advocate for improved dialogue between conservative and liberal Christians in the United States. His concern for such dialogue points up the fact that if it was the liberal side of the divide on which Horton stood, he was so near the watershed that he could easily see the other side, and across that divide he saw many ideas of which he approved.

The devastating consequences of World War I and subsequent social history combined to chasten Horton's liberalism. He read Barth and Brunner, and while he found in the former's work ideas to appreciate, he thought the latter offered more promise. He thought that the Anglo-Saxon world's strong commitment to the political liberalism of Locke, Mill, and Jefferson required of English-speaking theologians a corresponding theological liberalism.[26] From this position Horton regarded himself as a mediating figure who stood between "a liberal theology that is going out and a conservative theology that is coming in—something of a 'come-outer' from both points of view."[27]

Horton presented Church of God students at Oberlin with a compelling and attractive theology. In the first place he had an abiding respect for the church and insisted that theology be livable and practical. Secondly, he remained sufficiently a liberal to use the language of experience, the word that connoted so very much out of their previous religious training and reflection. By that term he meant something different than their Pietist usage, but there were nevertheless important overlaps. For example, Horton took a strong position on biblical revelation, stating that it was "classic and normative for Christian thought."[28] Thirdly, Horton's abiding concern for Christian unity also appealed to Church of God students who had grown to maturity in a movement that described itself as God's instrument to restore the lost unity of the church. To be sure, Horton's ecumenical involvement introduced them to a positive regard for ventures in world Christianity that were viewed askance by many of the folks back home. But their education at Anderson College, not to mention C. E. Brown's books, had already introduced these college graduates to a wider vision of Christianity. When they arrived at Oberlin they may not have been predisposed to Horton's ecumenism, but many of the Anderson alumni were at least ready to tolerate it. By means of his dynamic and wide-ranging intellect as well as his attractive personal spirituality, Walter Marshall Horton presented his Church of God students with an attractive theological option that resonated with many aspects of their theological inheritance.

In the 1940s and early 1950s men and women of the Church of God also studied at graduate institutions other than Oberlin. It attracted the largest number, but smaller numbers could be found at Butler University and, especially, the University of Southern California, which offered the doctoral program preferred by Church of God graduate students in the forties.[29] Like Oberlin, these two institutions also taught expressions of liberal theology. Insofar as these seminarians and graduate students espoused a theology that could be described as "liberal," what were its characteristics? Measured against most alternatives, their theology was hardly extreme. None denied the divinity of Christ and, under the tutelage of people like Horton, they left seminary with an understanding of the Bible enlarged by historical critical exegesis while simultaneously affirming that the Bible was God's personal

Gene W. Newberry, professor of systematic theology and third dean of the School of Theology at Anderson College

Word addressed to human beings. They still thought that Christian disciple-ship required the transformation worked through conversion, and their piety continued to be sustained by such practices as prayer and Bible study. The careers of two long-term professors at Anderson School of Theology illus-trate these characteristics as well as theological liberalism's influence.

Gene Wilson Newberry (1915–) and John W. V. Smith (1914–1985) joined the School of Theology faculty when the school was still in its infancy. Newberry received the school's first full-time appointment in 1950, its first year of operations, as a professor of theology although in his first years he taught a wide range of courses. Smith joined him in 1952 as professor of church history and the two became seminary mainstays until their simulta-neous retirements in 1980. Newberry was appointed dean in 1962 and Smith served as associate dean for many years. Both men were members of the group of Church of God students at Oberlin in the '40s and shortly afterward pursued doctoral studies, Newberry at Duke University and Smith at the University of Southern California School of Religion.

The appointments of both men represented the growing professionalism of college and seminary teaching in the Church of God. They were in the vanguard of a new generation of men and women defined primarily by academic careers. Both Newberry and Smith had served as pastors, but neither was shaped by that vocation to the degree that had stamped the previous generation of teachers. When Newberry and Smith succeeded Charles E. Brown at the fledgling School of Theology, something more than a simple change of personnel occurred. Brown and the others of his genera-tion had been defined first and fundamentally as pastors and evangelists who grew to be churchmen and churchwomen. Newberry and Smith were the first of the next generation who, while deeply committed to the church and who served in a wide range of national church assignments, nevertheless had been professionally formed by their seminary and graduate school experi-ence. The two were in no way unique in this. They were simply harbingers of things to come.

The formative experience of seminary and graduate school, especially the schools that they chose to attend, shaped Newberry and Smith in ways that prompted both men to rework certain elements of the doctrinal tradi-tion of the Church of God. Smith taught church history at the seminary, including the course on the history of the Church of God movement. He also worked out a new understanding of a key Church of God doctrine. For his doctoral dissertation Smith had written a comparative study of the approach of the Church of God and other groups to the subject of Christian unity. The doctrine and practice of Christian unity remained for him a lifelong pursuit.

John W. V. Smith, professor of church history at the School of Theology at Anderson College and a determined ecumenist who served in the Commission on Faith and Order (National Council of Churches of Christ, USA) for nearly thirty years.

Indeed, it would be fair to say that he practiced the doctrine of Christian unity far more than he wrote on the topic. Smith did not produce many written works during his long tenure at the School of Theology,[30] but he embodied a practice of Christian unity that was fairly new to the Church of God movement.

John Smith was a very collegial man who established friendships and working acquaintances with scholars and ecumenists from many different denominations. Born in Baca County, Colorado, he was the son of David P. Smith, a Church of God minister, and his wife, Nannie. Before entering Oberlin he had graduated Northwestern Oklahoma State College and taught high school for two years. Smith pastored in Vancouver, Washington before pursuing a doctorate in church history at the University of Southern California. His interest in ecumenical Christianity was kindled during his graduate studies when he served as an administrative assistant in the Church Federation of Los Angeles. Smith was an early and active member of the Conference on the Continuing Concept of the Believers' Church and, from 1957, a member of the Commission on Faith and Order of the National Council of Churches. He also attended meetings of the World Council of Churches as observer for the Church of God, on at least one occasion paying his own travel expenses. It was Smith's determined ecumenism that consti-tuted a reworked version of the Church of God movement's practice of Christian unity. Like many others he had no sympathy for the practice of come-outism, but he was nevertheless convinced that Christian unity was one of the movement's distinctive doctrines. In his view it was therefore necessary to develop new expressions of its historic teaching. Smith wove the movement's commitment to Christian unity with theological liberalism's interest in ecumenical Christianity to create a new understanding and prac-tice of that doctrine. To be sure, Smith's ecumenism put him on the left wing of the Church of God movement during a time when many of its constituents harbored suspicions of the National Council of Churches and other ecu-menical ventures. A comparatively small circle of like-minded individuals, some who were colleagues or former students and others who headed agencies in Anderson, shared his convictions. This group formed the core of a reworked practice of Christian unity in the movement.

Smith did not aggressively promote his understanding of Christian unity among his seminary students. He was not given to pushing agendas, but preferred to allow his students to reach their own conclusions. Even his course in the history of the Church of God was developed along the lines of a historical survey that did not explore the ongoing relevance of the move-ment's distinctive doctrines. It was in retirement that Smith became acutely concerned about a general lack of awareness in the movement of its key doctrinal distinctives.[31] While a seminary professor, Smith was more concerned that his students develop an appreciation for the connections between the Church of God movement and historic, mainstream Protestantism. Although he did not downplay the movement's origins in the holiness movement, for example, neither did he emphasize them. And he assigned his students comparative studies wherein they examined the doctrines of the Church of God in relation to other groups with similar commitments. Smith wanted seminarians to identify the general experience and common bonds that he thought the Church of God shared with other Christian bodies. In this approach one detects a vague connection to theological liberalism's appreciation for human experience as such and undetermined by concrete historical circumstance.

While John Smith taught church history his good friend Gene Newberry taught systematic theology and ethics in addition to presiding over the seminary for twelve years as its dean. Newberry was born and reared in southeast Ohio, but like Smith, his graduate experiences had introduced Newberry to a wider world of theological perspectives. For his doctoral dissertation he chose to research the epistemology of the nineteenth-century British poet Samuel Taylor Coleridge, an important source of American religious liberalism. Newberry balanced these broader theological and philosophical interests with long-term practical commitment to the national work of the Church of God and its congregational life. This commitment may have been Horton's greatest influence on Newberry. He served on numerous committees, task forces, and boards, including a twenty-year stint as president of the Board of Church Extension and Home Missions. Newberry also maintained a deep commitment to the work of the local church and consistently attempted to tie theology to its life. His first book, *A Primer for Young Christians,* is illustrative of his determination to make theology relevant and practical in the life of the local congregation. This commitment also manifested itself personally in Newberry's decades-long tenure as the teacher of the Pathways Sunday school class at Park Place Church of God.

It was perhaps due to Newberry's heavy administrative load that he did not produce a lengthy bibliography, and the books and occasional papers that he did write were in the main works for popular church consumption.[32] He did not write a systematic theology, but he did endeavor to rework aspects of the theological tradition of the Church of God and called upon others to follow that lead. He was certainly no doctrinaire theological liberal; on the contrary he was quite comfortable with the label *conservative*—as long as he could add the modifier *flexible*. Newberry's brand of conservatism appreciated traditional biblical meaning while it also saw in the gospel "a resiliency and contemporaneity that makes it applicable to ever new challenges."[33] He balanced a concern that the movement affirm some truths and pass them on to succeeding generations with a frank recognition that its teachers and preachers were obligated to restate the doctrines that they had inherited from the past. There is nothing in this that would indicate much liberal influence on Newberry until one inquires into the sources to which he referred.

Read through the work of Gene Newberry and one finds numerous references to religious writers such as Elton Trueblood, Leslie Newbigin, Robert Raines, and W. E. Sangster. None of these would be fairly categorized as a doctrinaire liberal. One will also find frequent references to current events and the wider world of Christianity. What one is less likely to find is specific mention of Church of God theological writers or their works. There is little question that Newberry was comfortable within and knew the theological tradition of the Church of God. He could summarize its main themes succinctly and with facility and insight.[34] He also critically assessed and appropriated some of those themes. For example, Newberry repudiated the "eradicationism" that emphasized what was taken out of a believer at sanctification. The deeper meaning of the doctrine, he emphasized, was explained better by what was put into the human personality. Thus, for Newberry and over against much Church of God preaching on this subject, "holiness turns more on the presence of love than the absence of sin."[35] There was no mistaking the importance of the doctrinal practice of holiness in Newberry's restated theology, just as there was no mistaking his break with much of previous holiness teaching.

> Holiness people face a deposit of difficult problems. We have had extremists stating the case. We have had the ethics of easy answers. We often attempt to overpower each other with a doctrinaire and arid theology and oratory. We judge and scold any who may not be in total agreement with our definition of holiness orthodoxy. Again, we may often have been our worst enemies.

> Holiness people often underestimate the complexity of the human predicament. We do not have the tough-minded facing of problems in this present world. We are guilty of promoting a position of cheap grace. It is impossible to define holiness negatively only. We cannot define the position by outlining how to avoid contamination. Sin is not a quantity, a thing.

Rather it is rebellion, an upside down relationship, a refusal of God's love. We do not always appreciate that the setting in which we live our life is the very real historical world.... Therefore, we must avoid asceticism, legalism, and social isolation as we state the holiness position. We are talking about a call to total commitment. We are talking about a quality of heart and life. We are talking about a penetration of love and power, just as St. Paul and Wesley did.[36]

Newberry looked beyond the doctrinal tradition of the Church of God for resources to support his modest efforts at theological restatement. Both situation and experience made him well suited to this task. Youthful friendships with boys who worshiped in denominational churches called come-outism into question. His study at Anderson gave him solid reasons for repudiating the practice. Seminary and graduate study had introduced him to a wider world of theological scholarship, and he applied his discoveries to the work of theological revision. However, he called on his seminary students to revise a tradition with which they were increasingly unfamiliar in the first place. Increasingly theology students entered seminary with little knowledge of the Church of God theological tradition. Although he assigned his students readings in Byrum's *Christian Theology,* Newberry also required them to read more outside the tradition than sources from within. It was appropriate, and desirable, that theology students read literature beyond their own church world. But it was equally important that they also know their own theological tradition. Newberry separated the Church of God movement from the emerging evangelical movement and celebrated the fact that a conservative group like the Church of God had "not been sucked into the vagaries of premillennialism and literalist eschatology as well as fundamentalist bickering."[37] That world was closed off to his students. But then it begs to be asked where these students were to turn for a fresh theological vision and the resources to do the kind of work as ministers to which Newberry called them. In many respects Gene Newberry was theologically quite conservative. But in addition to his own ecumenism and appreciation for the achievements of other Christian groups, one mark of liberal influence on him was the tendency to downplay the specificity of particular religious traditions in favor of more generalized notions of religious experience. Newberry's "liberalism," if it can be called that, was of the sort that opened students to a wider world without necessarily grounding them in the specific historical traditions of the Church of God.

The large majority of Church of God graduates of Oberlin as well as other seminaries and graduate schools did not follow a nineteenth-century theological program. They were receptive to new theological and historical sources. The first generation of seminarians retained important theological themes from the doctrinal heritage of the Church of God, but in characteristic liberal fashion they reworked those themes. Inevitably, the weight of sources from within the movement diminished in such a process. The "liberals" had been introduced to a larger world and they found much there to admire—especially in terms of scholarly sources. Correlative of this was a growing interest in and support for ecumenical Christianity. So it was that seminary graduates of this generation deeply admired world Christians like E. Stanley Jones, Albert Schweitzer, Frank Laubach, and Howard Thurman. These persons also appealed to this generation's ecumenical and internationalist instincts.

Concerning politics and social policy the first seminary generation repudiated isolationism. They also committed themselves to an internationalism that tended to align many in the group with the Democrat party, and several were quick to espouse the cause of civil rights when the movement emerged in the 1960s. They tended to oppose the death penalty and in later years also supported women's rights. They also influenced the educational direction taken by their students, who rarely chose an Evangelical or Fundamentalist seminary.[38] Some did, but they constituted a small minority, and for good reason. Liberalism's emphasis on experience sounded much more familiar to seminary-bound Church of God men and women than Evangelicalism's rationalist epistemology.

The first generation of seminary-trained ministers in the Church of God adopted a liberalism that, theologically speaking, would have been considered conservative by most standards. In the context of the Church of God, however, these men and women could be fairly described as occupying the movement's left wing. They were far more open to theological sources and ideas originating outside the Church of God. "Openness" may be the best description of their theological posture, one that they inherited from people like John Morrison, Russell Olt, and E. A. Reardon, who thought that the Church of God should be open to the truth toward which honest hearts were guided by the Holy Spirit. The seminary-trained generation was more receptive to approaches to Christian unity that were opposed by the movement's traditionalists, and they unanimously repudiated the remaining vestiges of come-outism. Their political and social views also stood in sharp contrast to the grassroots constituency of the Church of God—many of whom were Republican, isolationist, and suspicious of the United Nations, the National Council of Churches, and the Revised Standard Version of the Bible. Nevertheless, many of these seminarians took prominent positions of leadership in careers that extended from the 1950s into the early 1980s. They were well positioned to influence the generation following them in a genial liberalism that retained a warm affection for many aspects of the movement's piety and theology while it repudiated or reworked other elements of its teaching and practice. In this, these early seminarians remained within the Church of God movement theologically, but not in its mainstream. In fact, their leadership and the ideas that they brought with them made it more difficult to find the current in mainstream Church of God thought. The seminary graduates of the 1940s, and those who followed them in the 1950s, understood themselves as exponents of the theological tradition and practices of the Church of God. But they also reinterpreted and reworked elements of that tradition. Their experiences at Oberlin and theologically comparable seminaries and graduate schools had provided the anvil on which they had hammered out those reworked convictions.

Notes

1. Charles E. Brown, *The Apostolic Church: A Study in Historical Theology* (Anderson, Ind: The Warner Press, 1947), 249–256.

2. Brown's knowledge of Pietism apparently depended on English language sources, and the scope of those sources did not extend to Johannes Arndt, the early seventeenth-century Lutheran pastor who Spener regarded as the fountainhead of the Pietist movement.

3. Brown, *The Apostolic Church*, 249.

4. Ibid., 250.

5. John W. V. Smith, *The Quest for Holiness and Unity*, 84.

6. "It is True Within My Heart," *Select Hymns* (Anderson, Ind: Gospel Trumpet Company, 1911), No. 112.

7. Cf. Wickersham, *Holiness Bible Subjects*, 2nd edition (Grand Junction, Mich: Gospel Trumpet Publishing Company, 1894), 18–19; and Russell Byrum, *Christian Theology* (Anderson, Ind: Gospel Trumpet Company, 1925), 171–172.

8. Ibid.

9. Ibid., 16.

10. Ibid.

11. Ibid.

12. *The Bible and How to Interpret It*, 298.

13. Ibid., 308.

14. "How did God Inspire the Bible?", *GT* October 10, 1921.

15. Ibid.

16. Ibid.

17. Ibid.

18. For a fuller treatment of the doctrine of biblical inspiration in the Church of God, see Merle D. Strege, "The Peculiar Impress of the Mind: Biblical Inspiration and Interpretation in the Early Church of God (Anderson), unpublished paper (October, 1985). The most complete study of this doctrine is Stephen Wayne Stall, "The Inspiration and Authority of Scripture: The Views of Eight Historical and Twenty-One Current Doctrinal Teachers in the Church of God (Anderson, Indiana)," M. A. thesis, Anderson School of Theology, 1985.

19. *Select Hymns* (1911); *Hymns and Spiritual Songs* (1934?); *Hymnal of the Church of God* (1953); *Hymnal of the Church of God* (1971); and *Worship the Lord: Hymnal of the Church of God* (1989).

20. *Hymnal of the Church of God* (1971), No. 299.

21. "God's Way Is Best," Ibid., No. 376.

22. Naylor's five books in this category include, *Winning a Crown* (Anderson, Ind: Gospel Trumpet Company, 1919); *Heart Talks* (Anderson, Ind: Gospel Trumpet Company, 1922); *God's Will and How to Know It* (Anderson, Ind: Gospel Trumpet Company, 1925); *Secret of the Singing Heart* (Anderson, Ind: Gospel Trumpet Company, 1930); and *When Adversity Comes* (Anderson, Ind: Warner Press, 1944).

23. Naylor, *When Adversity Comes,* 48.

24. Other Church of God students who enrolled at Oberlin during this period include: Wendell Byrd, H. Revere Cook, Harry Dodge, Ed May, Warren Roark, and Edith Young.

25. Walter Marshall Horton, *A Psychological Approach to Theology* (New York: Harper and Brothers, 1931), 9–10.

26. Walter Marshall Horton, *Contemporary Continental Theology* (New York: Harper and Brothers, 1938), 226–228.

27. Walter Marshall Horton, *Theology in Transition* (New York: Harper and Brothers, 1931), xiv–xv.

28. Horton, *Contemporary Continental Theology,* 219. As Horton elaborated, "Before Barth, the Bible was to many liberal Protestants only a great piece of historical literature, behind which they were dimly aware of 'something like the thundering of ocean waves against thin dikes'; since Barth, there is a breach in those dikes, and the Bible has once more become to us what it was to our fathers, a personal Word from a living God, speaking directly to our personal state." Ibid.

29. Within a five-year period Irene S. Caldwell, A. Leland Forrest, John W. V. Smith, and Frederick v. Shoot earned Ph. D. degrees at USC's School of Religion, an institution sometimes described as the last outpost of theological liberalism in the United States.

30. His books include, *Heralds of a Brighter Day* (Anderson, Ind: Gospel Trumpet Company, 1955); *Truth Marches On* (Anderson, Ind: Gospel Trumpet Company, 1956); later revised as *A Brief History of the Church of God Movement* (Anderson, Ind: Warner Press, 1976); *I Will Build My Church* (Anderson, Ind: Warner Press, 1985); and his magnum opus, *The Quest for Holiness and Unity* (Anderson, Ind: Warner Press, 1980).

31. This concern led Smith to write the posthumously published *I Will Build My Church* (Anderson, Ind: Warner Press, 1985).

32. In addition to some collections of essays and sermons that he edited, Newberry wrote three books of his own, *A Primer for Young Christians* (Anderson, Ind: Warner Press, 1955); *Responding to God's Call* (Anderson, Ind: Warner Press, 1969); and *Soundings* (Anderson, Ind: Warner Press, 1972).

33. Gene W. Newberry, "The Dynamics of the Church," (unpublished paper: June 1961), 2.

34. As an example of this facility there is this quotation from an address that Newberry gave to a group of ministers in 1961: "We do not need a formal creed to have integrity in our theology. And we always are obligated to restate our doctrines for each generation. So we lift up again the primacy of the Bible, the supernaturalness of religion, the necessity of conversion, the church as the body of Christ, the call to ethical holiness, God's kingdom of love and power, the vision of unity, and the ministry of the Holy Spirit illuminating and energizing all we do." Ibid.

35. Gene W. Newberry, "The Ministry of the Holy Spirit," (unpublished paper: n.d.), 6.

36. Ibid., 8.

37. "The Dynamics of the Church," 2. Newberry added, "We never cease to thank God for this."

38. For example, in the 1950s Union Theological Seminary in New York was the seminary of choice for those Church of God men and women who did not select Anderson College's School of Theology. More than a dozen Church of God students enrolled at Union in that decade, and while Union did not favor liberal theological positions in those years, teachers like Reinhold Niebuhr would have been judged liberals by many Church of God folk.

Chapter 12
Doctors of the Church

By 1940 theological revolutionaries such as Otto Linn and C. E. Brown had overthrown the apocalyptic house that F. G. Smith had labored diligently both to build and defend. This is not to say that interest in the theology of the church in prophecy and history waned immediately on the publication of Linn's and Brown's books. Smith's work remained quite popular among a segment of the movement's ministers. In the wake of the publication of the third volume of Linn's *Studies in the New Testament,* chart-lecturers who were in decreasing demand at the close of the '30s suddenly began receiving more invitations. Renewed interest in Smith's work was but a holding action. The methods employed by Linn and Brown had taken up permanent residence in the colleges, first Anderson and then Pacific Bible College, with the corresponding result that their Bible and theology faculties did not consider the church-historical hermeneutic a valid form of biblical interpretation. If not the object of outright challenge, it was simply ignored. College students preparing for the ministry were taught newer forms of biblical study to the exclusion of the church-historical exegesis. It was left to an older generation of preachers with little or no college training to perpetuate that exegesis along with typological preaching and the apocalyptic ecclesiology. The future of college- and, after 1950, seminary-trained ministry belonged to Bible study that rested on historical-critical methodologies. At the same time, the study of church history placed the Church of God movement in a context that forced it to acknowledge the legitimacy of other Christian bodies.

The colleges and seminary shaped the theological future of the Church of God movement by training students in advanced methods of biblical study. However, through the work of key Bible and theology professors the colleges also reshaped the church of their own day. Through two decades, from roughly 1940 to 1960, four individuals, two at Anderson College and two at Pacific Bible College, made enormous contributions to the theological life of the Church of God movement. Earl Martin, Adam W. Miller, A. F. Gray, and, to a lesser extent, Otto Linn[1] were popular college professors who extended their scholarly work far beyond the confines of the classroom. Each of them published major books that translated their classroom work into an idiom available to much of the movement. All four were also popular on the preaching and conference circuits, and each wrote extensively for the adult Sunday school curriculum published by the Gospel Trumpet Company. They were theology and Bible teachers for the whole movement, and through their many and varied activities these men introduced new theological ideas into the thought-life of the Church of God.

Earl Martin, Pietist-Liberal Theologian

Earl L. Martin (1892–1961) was born in Steelville, Missouri to parents who were indifferent to religion. Despite the lack of parental encouragement Earl attended the services of a nearby Methodist church as a boy. He did not begin to attend school until he was nine years old but already had begun teaching himself to read by sounding out the words printed on the wallpaper that covered the walls of his family home; like other impoverished Ozark families, the Martins covered their walls with newspaper. After the death of his father, Earl's mother married a handsome widower named Tom Morrison—the father of John A. Morrison—and the two boys grew up as brothers. In his late teenage years Earl was converted in a Church of God revival meeting outside St. James. He had been teaching school for three years by then, but after his conversion the church occupied more and more of his attention. After a few years of part-time preaching he and his wife Blanche moved to Houston, Texas, where he assumed pastoral responsibilities and leadership of the missionary home located there.

While in Houston Martin was asked to write Sunday school curriculum for the Gospel Trumpet Company. He was just established as a curriculum writer when the search began for a principal for the Bible training school in Anderson. Because R. R. Byrum, then on the editorial staff, was reluctant to lose such a good writer, Martin lost out to his stepbrother Morrison for the appointment. Martin continued writing curriculum and contributed to the adult Sunday school quarterlies without interruption over a period of twenty-eight years. From 1928 to 1946 Martin himself wrote much of the material for the uniform lesson series published by the Gospel Trumpet Company.

The talented and industrious Martin quickly rose to national leadership in the church. He was elected a charter member of the Board of Church Extension and Home Missions. From 1922 to 1926 he worked in New

Earl L. Martin, minister, college and seminary administrator, professor, author, and long-term church leader.

England establishing new churches before moving his family to Anderson, where he enrolled in college that autumn. Martin's association with the Board of Church Extension continued from 1925 to 1953, and he served as president from 1929 to 1947. He also played an important role at the Gospel Trumpet Company, where he was a member of the Publication Board of the Church of God for forty years and was chair at the time of his death. Within the company structure he was a member of the editorial committee from 1929 to 1957 and a director from 1933 to 1957.

It is some measure of Martin's ability as well as the level of Anderson College's development—not to mention the fact that his stepbrother presided over the institution—that Martin was admitted without benefit of a bona fide high school education and invited to teach courses even before he graduated. Within two years he was a part-time teacher in the area of ministerial training; in his senior year he taught nearly as many credit hours as he carried as a student. Immediately upon graduation he became chair of the Division of Bible and Religion at Anderson, a post that he held until 1957. In 1936 he earned an M. A. from Northwestern University and in the same year was named vice president of the college. From 1930 his academic title was professor of applied theology, and he taught courses in systematic theology, pastoral theology, and Christian ethics. It was more bench than chair that Professor Martin held over the years. When Anderson College opened its graduate theological seminary in 1950, Earl Martin presided as the first dean. Declining health forced him to retire from the School of Theology in 1952. Although a stroke impaired his ability to teach and preach, Martin nevertheless taught for six months in 1957 at West Indies Bible Institute. In 1961 he served as acting president of Arlington Bible College in Long Beach, California.

A warm and friendly man, the avuncular, portly Martin and his wife were gracious hosts known for their hospitality to students and colleagues. His congeniality made him the person to whom others turned to arbitrate disputes, starting with the phrase, "Well, it all depends" as a means of forcing both parties to state their positions on the basis of fact.[2] At heart Martin was a preacher and deeply committed to evangelism. Although not possessed of a speaking voice easy on the ears of his listeners, the content of his sermons made him a popular preacher. At whatever post throughout his tenure at Anderson College, Martin remained a churchman with deep ties to the work of local congregations as well as the national boards of the Church of God.

Martin's first book, *What Should a Christian Believe?* was published in 1928. He also wrote books on the subjects of evangelism and local church organization as well as theological studies and a commentary on the Gospel

According to Luke. The book that Martin most hoped would gain wide acceptance was his *Toward Understanding God.*[3] Published in 1942, the book never achieved the interest for which Martin had hoped. While Martin's magnum opus may have proved too lengthy and technical for a popular audience of Church of God readers,[4] it does suggest the sources of Martin's theology. If he did not achieve the aim of teaching this theology through *Toward Understanding God,* he did reach the church through his many other books and Sunday school lessons.

Martin did not formally acknowledge any sources that may have influenced the content of *Toward Understanding God.* A few can be identified specifically, but there is no mistaking the influence of continental liberal theologians on Martin's work. For example, Martin began his book with a fundamental definition of religion that connected it to experience:

> Religion has to do with experience. It is life and a way of life. It is that which has to do with man's personal relationship to God. Religion may be conceived of as an adjustment to, harmony with, an experience of, support from, and service to that Power beyond oneself, which in the true religion is a Person, God. Religion becomes Christian when Christ is made the center of reference.[5]

While it cannot be stated with certainty that Martin read Schleiermacher, there is an affinity between the former's description of religion and the latter's theological starting point in the universal human feeling of absolute dependence. Like nineteenth-century German theological liberals, Martin thought that religious experience was primary and the stuff of which theology and doctrine were ultimately constructed.[6]

It would be an overstatement to say that Earl Martin was a theological liberal in the tradition of Schleiermacher, Ritschl, Hermann, or Harnack. In essence, Martin and nearly all Church of God theological writers were Pietists; they took it as axiomatic that knowing God took priority over knowing about God. Early German Pietists distinguished between scientific or rationalist theology and the true theology that rose out of experience and led to what they called *herzenreligion,* "heart religion." It was a distinction common among Church of God preachers and writers and, indeed, many in the holiness movement. After all, that movement could trace its theological genealogy from the Wesleys through the Moravian Brethren and Zinzendorf back to August Hermann Francke, P. J. Spener, and ultimately to Johannes Arndt, the fountainhead of this stream of the religion of the heart. Like their predecessors in this line, Church of God people thought that the essence of religion and the locus of religious assurance lay in the believer's personal experience of God rather than an infallible external authority. In the name of vital religious experience they also opposed what they often called "formalism," a misplaced regard for religious forms or rituals over that which they signified. Also, in the manner of Pietist Christianity, Church of God people were religious idealists. They insisted that followers of Jesus consecrate themselves for *entire* sanctification and reserved some of their sharpest rebukes for "nominal Christians," those who bore Christ's name but who had not "sold out completely to the Lord." Church of God people also resembled Pietists in their attitude toward the Bible. Certainly they thought that the Scriptures were to be both believed and trusted, but the saints thought of the Bible as the Book to be lived as much as the cornerstone of doctrine. That is a principle reason why many of those who wrote on the subject of biblical authority were so amenable to dynamic theories of inspiration. As Martin had put it, religion was a way of life, which is but to say that religion has first of all to do with ethics understood as a way of being rather than doctrine.[7] Thus Earl Martin was in good company with previous generations of Church of God preachers as well as Pietists of many times and places when he wrote, "We know God by personal experience, whether that experience be thought of in terms of intuitive knowledge, or of moral life wrought by God's saving grace, or as spiritual fellowship, which comes by trust and moral obedience. The highest knowledge comes through personal faith in a living and personal God."[8]

The significance placed on the category of experience linked Pietist Christianity in a general way with some theological liberals. Schleiermacher had been reared against a backdrop of Pietism in Germany as had Walter Rauschenbusch, the great Social Gospel reformer in the United States. Indeed, the latter never really abandoned this heritage; he never wavered in his affirmation of an experience of the risen Christ. The same could be said in even stronger terms of Earl Martin. Moreover, since he never doubted that experience, he could read and learn from theologians that fundamentalists and many other conservative American Christians shunned. It is beyond question, for example, that Martin had read Albert Schweitzer's *Quest of the Historical Jesus* and was so impressed with it that he paraphrased one of its most famous passages near the conclusion of *Toward Understanding God.*[9]

In 1945 the Gospel Trumpet Company published a quarter of elective lessons written by Martin under the title *Studies in Christian Doctrine.* Intended for youth and adults, Martin lifted the material for these lessons directly from *Toward Understanding God* and applied it as expositions of weekly Bible passages. Several years later he wrote his primer in Christian theology titled *This We Believe ... This We Proclaim.*[10] Originally published to augment leadership training for Church of God Sunday school teachers, this frequently reprinted book was widely employed as a kind of catechism. Through it Martin's theology reached perhaps its broadest and longest running audience in the movement.

This We Believe ... This We Proclaim blended Martin's Pietist Christianity and his interest in certain themes from theological liberalism. His discussion of revelation included the notion of humanity's intuitive knowledge of God and referred to the Bible not as the revelation of God but as the record of God's self-disclosure.[11] At the same time he made quite plain his view that the Bible is inspired. Martin also considered several different understandings of the Atonement, referring to all of them, from substitution to satisfaction to moral influence, as theories. The following extended quotation in which Martin summarized this consideration illustrates the manner in which his heart religion could underwrite conclusions that followed liberal lines of thought.

> Possibly the one theory which comes nearest to stating a philosophy of the atonement, and which can be so stated as to include the truth of the other theories is to be found in the "revelatory" theory. It seems to come nearest to expressing what the death of Christ was to accomplish. The cross was God's way of redeeming men, and out of its revelational value comes its redemptive value. The cross becomes the means of a personal revelation of a personal God in the person of his Son, to persons. This explanation puts the emphasis upon the personal, as over against the impersonal values of some of the other theories. This says most emphatically that redemption is personal, that Christ's death is a redemptive power made operative in human life through this expression of divine love and divine judgement, and that it is redemptively creative in that it makes personal that mystical union of God with the believer in such a way that Christ's poured-out life may be poured in, or imparted to, the believer. God redeems man by revealing his love and, paradoxical though it may be, reveals his love by redeeming."[12]

In Martin's various writings the warmth of experiential religion melted together elements of various and sometimes conflicting theological traditions, molding all into a theological perspective with a high degree of credibility among Church of God people. They trusted Earl Martin on the basis of his testimony and for the fact that his theological language bore the unmistakable sound of their religious idiom.

When he addressed the topic of ecclesiology Martin's work lost some of its certainty. He had no time for F. G. Smith's reading of Revelation, his apocalyptic ecclesiology, or come-outism as a practice of Christian unity. But when Martin considered the subjects of the church and unity he did so only in broad generalizations that offered few practical alternatives. Martin shared C. E. Brown's conviction that the church universal was composed of all those who genuinely belonged to Christ. That commitment vitiated the earlier practice of come-outism, but Martin replaced it with little that was new or even a restatement. All he offered was to repeat the view that if believers would agree to the idea that all true Christians already belong to the church universal that would be "a long step forward in bringing that unity for which Christ so sincerely prayed, as recorded in John 17."[13] Similarly, when his subject turned to practical steps toward cooperation, Martin spoke largely within the confines of the Church of God movement and offered no suggestions concerning greater cooperation among Christians in the denominations. Instead Martin only rehearsed the familiar appeals to move beyond the idea that Christian unity resided only in Christ and accept the fact that the New Testament insisted on a "functioning" as well as a spiritual unity.[14]

Adam Miller, Pietist Exponent of the Historical-Critical Method

Adam W. Miller (1896–1993) was born into a staunchly German Lutheran family in Baltimore, Maryland. As a boy he studied Luther's *Small Catechism* and at age thirteen was confirmed. Young Miller nevertheless was dissatisfied with Lutheranism and in 1916 experienced a spiritual awakening that led him to a small band of saints who met in Baltimore; later he was baptized during a camp meeting. To his parents this was nothing short of the rebirth of Anabaptism right in their very own house. Miller's commitment to the Church of God movement deepened, and a serious breach opened between him and his parents. Called to the ministry, Miller was ordained in the Church of God in 1918. He prepared himself for the pastorate by reading Gospel Trumpet Company publications, especially *Our Ministerial Letter.* After pastorates in Washington and Baltimore, Miller and his new wife, the former Grace Young, accepted an assignment as missionaries to Japan. He served as head of the Church of God mission there from 1922 to 1927.

For much of his life Adam Miller remained personally and institutionally involved in missionary work but also in other aspects of Church of God corporate life. Upon his return to the United States he was elected to the Missionary Board and continued to serve on it until 1957. After a six-year

Adam W. Miller's ministry was focused on foreign missions and higher education. Widely respected as a preacher and Bible professor, Miller served as the second dean of the School of Theology.

pastorate in Federalsburg, Maryland, Miller was named executive secretary of the Missionary Board and held that post from 1933 to 1948. Regarded highly among the ministry, during the 1950s Miller was the driving force on the Commission on Revision and Planning that was responsible for further translating C. E. Brown's concept of spiritual democracy into the church's corporate practice. Miller's work on that commission directly contributed to the bylaws and working practices of the reorganized Executive Council of the Church of God.

Miller's name came to be associated with Anderson College to the same degree that it was connected with Church of God missions. His academic life started later than many, for Miller was already in his mid-thirties when he enrolled as an undergraduate. During adolescence he had read widely and occasionally attended public lectures at Johns Hopkins University, but his formal, postsecondary education was postponed until the early 1930s, when he studied New Testament with Otto Linn at Anderson. Miller earned a baccalaureate degree in 1939, followed by an M. A. from Butler University in Indianapolis in 1941 where he wrote a thesis on the interpretation of the Book of Revelation. In 1946 and again in 1948 Miller spent his summers studying at Union Theological Seminary in New York. His teaching career began at Anderson in the thirties as a part-time instructor in Bible; like Martin, Miller was teaching at the college before he graduated. In 1945 he was appointed professor of New Testament. He succeeded Earl Martin as dean of the School of Theology in 1953 and served in that capacity until he retired in 1962.

Like his colleague Earl Martin, Adam Miller was very popular on the speaking circuit as an evangelist and teacher despite the fact that his public persona was not particularly warm. His frank, open, expository preaching was utterly devoid of histrionics, reflecting his no-nonsense German upbringing. A naturally reserved man, Miller could be distant and he was constantly on the go, perhaps consequences of the overflowing plate of responsibilities that he carried. His public presence was balanced by a pastoral side that always found room to encourage students who were struggling with difficult problems. Miller shared with Russell Olt a deep admiration for German models of higher education and the professoriate. Both men prized clear lines of organization and the order they conferred. Miller's belief in discipline made him a natural as dean of men at the college, and God help the lazy or indifferent student who strayed off the path only to find himself or herself in Miller's office. Adam Miller excelled in whatever assignment he was given—pastor, camp meeting and revival preacher, writer, missionary, board executive or college professor and administrator—and an unrivalled national stature in the Church of God was the consequence of the range and quality of his work.

In 1943 Miller published *An Introduction to the New Testament.*[15] He intended the book for use primarily among his students at Anderson College, and in fact the book was an outgrowth of his courses there. But Miller also designed his work for a broad range of church workers who had no opportunities for college work as well as Bible study classes in local congregations. As such this book, as well as the companion *Brief Introduction to the Old Testament* published more than twenty years later, afford ample opportunity to discover what Miller taught in his classroom and to the Church of God. The historical-critical method that he had first learned from Otto Linn was a presence in Miller's books and the use of literary criticism also made an appearance. He presented these methodologies and some of their conclusions from a generally neutral stance; sometimes he sided with more conservative viewpoints and on other issues he adopted a more liberal perspective. The positions he endorsed or rejected were focused narrowly on questions pertaining to the text of the Bible. Miller left to theologians such doctrinal issues as the authority and inspiration of the text.

If Miller did not offer liberal scholarship his wholesale endorsement, he nevertheless strengthened the credibility of some methodologies and conclusions of higher criticism among Church of God people. He employed these methods and presented their findings as legitimate theories to be taken seriously by careful Bible students. At certain points Miller, sometimes rather cagily, endorsed those findings. Two such topics were his presentations of the synoptic problem in his New Testament introduction and the documentary hypothesis in the Old.

"If a teacher should receive from three of his students papers which contained as much as two-thirds of identical material, with many of the statements or answers verbally identical, it is likely that teacher would conclude that there had been some copying."[16] From that everyday illustration Miller led his students on an inductive search toward the theory that multiple sources lay behind the canonical gospels. He offered statistical summaries that showed the preponderance of similarity between Matthew, Mark, and Luke. He called his students' and readers' attention to the differences between the gospels, with some blocks of material unique to Matthew and others to Luke. Such similarities and differences, said Miller, call for an explanation, and the theories that best explained the synoptics were those that worked from the presumption that there were multiple sources behind the canonical texts.[17] Miller did not necessarily share all the conclusions of literary criticism, but he accepted some on the basis of their utility for faith.

Thus he concluded, "Whatever may be the theories of the future, such theories ... carry the documentary source of our Gospel records back much closer to the lifetime of Jesus himself. Any research and investigation that takes us back nearer to the years of his life and ministry with suggested documents as sources of our present Gospels, can only confirm and increase our faith in the historical accuracy of these wonderful writings."[18] To those who found it difficult to accept the idea that the synoptic writers relied on written sources Miller offered Luke's prologue as evidence as well as the judgment that "the 'human element in the Gospels' is recognized by both Conservative and Liberal scholars."[19]

In his Old Testament introduction Miller was equally forthright in his endorsement of elements of the documentary theory. He placed traditional belief in Mosaic authorship alongside the theory that Yahwist, Elohist, Priestly, and Deuteronomistic literary traditions predated the composition of the Pentateuch. Miller resolved the dispute between the rival theories by relying on the work of the distinguished Old Testament scholar John Bright to conclude that Moses did indeed leave behind a significant record of the events of his life. However, "whether this record was written or in oral form we have no way of knowing now."[20] Miller qualified assertions that Moses' contribution formed the core of the Pentateuch: "it is not in the sense that he wrote it in its entirety, nor word for word, or even book for book."[21] He concluded by saying, "A study of the Pentateuch reveals the fact that the style, syntax, and vocabulary differ a great deal in different sections of the books, testifying to the existence of parallel sources. As a result the Pentateuch is believed to be the result of a long literary process begun and inspired by Moses and continued in his spirit."[22]

The adoption of the historical-critical method and the endorsement of some of its conclusions raised serious theological questions. Miller could not pretend otherwise. In his two introductions he studiously avoided the role of theologian, maintaining that such works as he had written were neither historical nor exegetical in nature. But he could not avoid the implications that they raised for such crucial theological issues as the nature of revelation, biblical inspiration, and authority. Both books addressed those issues and did so in the same manner. Miller simply handed off the football to a theologian, namely Russell Byrum, whose discussion of inspiration Miller quoted at length in both books:

> That the Scriptures are divinely given is shown by such texts as Second Timothy 3:16 and Second Peter 1:21. That they were written by men is equally clear from many texts, such as John 1:17; Romans 1:1; Galatians 6:11. God adapted his truth

to ordinary human intelligence by shaping it in human molds. The Scriptures are a result of the interworking of the human and the divine, not of one without the other. This divine inspiration of the sacred writers was not an external force, acting upon them from without; but from within and through their natural faculties, intellect, and personality. From what we can gather from the scriptural teaching and from personal experience today as to the manner of the working of God's Spirit, we are safe in believing that these writers retained the full use of every human faculty, but that the Holy Spirit exalted the exercise of those natural powers.[23]

Miller was content to let the movement's theologians, even one who had gone into a self-imposed internal exile, define inspiration. On the topic of revelation Miller followed the lead of teachers such as Earl Martin, defining revelation in what was the increasingly familiar idea that it was God's self-disclosure. That made the Bible the record of God's revelation.[24] On both issues Miller occupied the same solid, Pietist ground as his colleague Earl Martin. On that ground it was understood that men and women personally experience God, and from that testimony it was but a very short step to the view that God reveals himself in human experience. If that was so, then theories of multiple sources and authorship could not threaten a Christian's experience. As the results of valid scholarship, Miller could teach them without worrying that they would inevitably undermine the faith of students or readers. He may not have enthusiastically endorsed every aspect of the higher criticism of his day, and he nearly always offered his readers a conservative option. But there is no denying that Adam Miller also advanced the use of scholarly tools developed by theological liberalism. If they led their users closer to the Jesus whom Miller experienced as the risen Lord, then such tools were a precious gift.

In some respects Miller approached his published work with a degree of caution. His studies on the Book of Revelation make this point in one way but undo it in another. His Butler University thesis on the interpretation of Revelation had employed historical-critical methodology. Its bibliography included works by many leading liberal historical critics of that era, and in fact, Miller cited the works of some of the same scholars who had taught his mentor Otto Linn at the University of Chicago. Working independently of Linn, Miller took similar positions and reached many of the same conclusions as his former professor. But the two men differed temperamentally. Whereas Linn was quite willing to fight whatever battles were necessary to see his work into print, Miller, ever the pacifist, decided to keep his controversial work out of the church's eye. He stipulated that his thesis was not to leave the Butler library; neither was it to be mechanically reproduced in any fashion.

Scarcely a year after completing his thesis Miller published his introduction to the New Testament. Unlike the secrecy in which he attempted to cloak his thesis, Miller was quite willing to air his views on Revelation in his critical introduction. At points he tried to steer a middle course between Smith and Linn, listing the work of both men as suggestions for further reading. Miller also presented all the hermeneutical options in an evenhanded manner that betrayed no sympathies. However, in his concluding discussion Miller described the message of Revelation in terms that placed him much closer to Linn. Readers who searched *An Introduction to the New Testament* for Miller's endorsement of Smith looked in vain. He did not go out of his way to criticize Smith's methodology, but it was barely discussed—either in the pages of Miller's book or presumably in his classroom at Anderson College. His treatment of Smith's work was a case of damning by ignoring.

A. F. Gray, Churchman-Theologian

Albert F. Gray (1886–1969)[25] was born in the fertile Red River Valley of Dakota Territory to a family of pioneer farmers. His father died before Albert's second birthday, and his mother moved her six children to her father's farm in 1889. Two years later they relocated again, this time to Grand Forks. There young Albert was converted in a Salvation Army children's meeting in 1894. His sister had been converted in services there and went home to inform her younger brother that he would get saved the next day. Albert dutifully followed his sister's instructions and ever afterward marked the day as the beginning of his Christian pilgrimage. The Church of God movement had reached North Dakota in 1895, and Grand Forks became an important center of evangelistic activity. *Den Evangeliske Basun* Publishing Company, a Scandinavian language version of the Gospel Trumpet Company, briefly conducted operations at Grand Forks in 1902–1903 before moving to a more central location in St. Paul Park, Minnesota. Evangelists George W. Bailey and J. C. Peterman held services at the Gray home in Grand Forks, where Albert's mother and uncle, J. W. Baldwin, embraced the Church of God movement.

In 1902 Albert's mother moved her family once more, this time to Spokane, Washington. It was about a year later that Albert experienced sanctification in conjunction with a growing sense of ministerial calling. During meetings at Colfax, Washington in 1903 Gray accepted this call despite deep feelings of personal inadequacy. He told nobody about his decision but began

A. F. Gray. The central figure in the early history of higher education in the Church of God on the West Coast, Gray also held the respect of ministers and laypeople across the United States. He chaired the General Ministerial Assembly longer than any other person and served on numerous national committees and boards.

studying the Bible and reading all the doctrinal literature that he could find. His formal education extended only through the eighth grade, but Gray possessed a particularly apt mind. To prepare himself better for the ministry he enrolled in the Bible study correspondence course created at the New York Missionary Home by D. O. Teasley. That was virtually the full extent of Gray's education. In early 1905 he began his ministerial career under the tutelage of his uncle, J. W. Baldwin. The next ten years Gray spent as an itinerant minister, sometimes traveling by foot and other times by bicycle, preaching in small towns and open-air countryside meetings in western Idaho and eastern Washington, often within a fifty-mile radius of Lewiston, Idaho. In 1909 he was ordained and in that same year married Rosa Bannon.

The Grays were occupied in evangelistic and pastoral work through the first decade of their marriage. They started a new church in Clarkston, Washington in 1915 and built a solid congregation there over the next five years. In 1920 they moved to Boise, Idaho, where Gray's involvement with higher education began. For the five previous years he had served ably as a teacher in schools for gospel workers held in conjunction with state camp meetings or which Gray conducted on his own initiative. Meanwhile, in 1919 Church of God ministers in the Pacific Northwest assumed responsibility for the Spokane Bible Institute, one of the four Bible institutes founded by the Church of God during the decade from 1910 to 1920. On the basis of his previous efforts in behalf of ministerial education, Gray was asked to accept the assignment of president and principal in 1920 when the school was moved to Boise and renamed Pacific Bible Institute. In 1922 the school and its president relocated to the more populous Puget Sound region in an effort to bolster sagging enrollment, but to no avail. The ministerial governing board suspended operations in that same year. Gray returned to the pastorate, first in Walla Walla, then Yakima, Washington until he left the region in 1926 to accept a call to the prestigious Park Place Church of God in Anderson.

In the years prior to his call to the Park Place congregation, A. F. Gray was rising to national prominence in the Church of God ministry. In 1920 he had been ratified as one of the original members of the Board of Church Extension and Home Missions. This put him in association with such leaders as Earl Martin, A. T. Rowe, C. E. Brown, and R. R. Byrum. Although he served on this board for only one year when its membership was restructured, Gray had attracted favorable attention. In 1924 he was elected to the Missionary Board, a trusteeship he held for thirty-five years, and in 1927 board members elected him president. The same year he delivered the Baccalaureate discourse for Anderson College and was also elected to the Gospel Trumpet Company's publications committee. In 1926 he assumed the pulpit of one of the principal congregations of the Church of God movement. Only a year earlier Gray felt confident enough to take on the leadership question that had begun swirling about the most powerful man in the movement, F. G. Smith.

During Anderson Campmeeting in June 1926 Gray addressed the assembled ministers on the topic, "The Practical Workings of Divine Government in the Church."[26] He addressed questions that had arisen in the wake of the organizational boom that had begun in 1917. Gray argued that while all true saints were revolted by "man-rule" in the church, from that view it did not follow that ministers were led only through the unmediated guidance of the Holy Spirit. He made the point that the Spirit could and did govern by leading the hearts of board members and other forms of church organization. Gray also endorsed the notion of degrees of authority among the ministers, saying, "There are such men among us today whom we do well to recognize in the places where God has placed them."[27] At first blush this sounds like an endorsement of Smith and other leading ministers. But Gray went on to praise the virtues of more democratic procedures when it came to the all-important matter of discerning God's will for the church. Quoting the proverb, "In the multitude of counselors there is safety," Gray said, "Where men are practically equal in their gifts it is but natural to expect that the Spirit will express his will in some democratic way."[28] Gray did not endorse one form of polity over the other, but advised that God could work through either. Having remained squarely on the fence to this point, Gray concluded with two cautions. First, Church of God ministers must remember that authority is never vested in a position but solely depends on the gifts conferred by the Holy Spirit. In this he hearkened back to the old days of charismatic government and, like Smith, worried that the spate of recently created agency offices would tempt some to the erroneous view that office indeed sanctified officeholder. Gray's second caution was more ominous, if also somewhat oblique. He offered a word of warning to those "seeking preeminence who will grasp the idea that they are not a whit behind the chiefest apostles and seek to lord over the church. Such are false apostles and can be detected by their spirit."[29] Haughtiness was a sure sign of counterfeit leadership; the divinely authorized leader displayed the virtues that shone in Jesus—humility, mercy, and gentleness.

Gray's 1926 General Ministerial Assembly address marked his emergence as a leader and a theological voice in the Church of God movement. It was characteristic of his personality and his approach to theology that he did not take sides as the battle lines began to form over the issue of leadership authority in the church. As the new pastor of the church in Anderson attended by the vast majority of agency heads and staff people, Gray may have been declaring his own intention to steer a middle course. Then again, he was a mediator whether in terms of theology or church politics. Gray's moderate voice and refusal to take partisan positions engendered great confidence, and he was repeatedly reelected and appointed to a wide variety of national church responsibilities.

Gray served Park Place Church of God until 1933. During his tenure he was known primarily as a pastor. Parishioners responded to his steadiness, moderate theological views, consistency, and ready but gentle wit. The spotlight held no interest for him, and he was anything but flamboyant. People who remember A. F. Gray universally apply the word *integrity* to him. Possessed of a keen mind, Gray preferred to employ it asking questions that put him among the forward thinking ministers of his generation. Yet he posed those questions from a mediating position. His ministerial colleagues recognized this unusual combination of virtues and repeatedly reelected Gray chair of the General Ministerial Assembly, from 1934 to 1936, and then again from 1939 through 1954, the longest period of service in that post by any person. He served unusually long tenures in a wide variety of national assignments and committees until age slowed him after 1960.[30]

In 1933 Gray resigned the pulpit at Park Place and returned to Seattle, where he served the Woodland Park Church of God. He held this pastorate until 1938, when he resigned to devote all of his time and attention to presiding over a new Bible college in Spokane. The ambition to reopen a ministerial training institution had waxed and waned ever since the closing of Pacific Bible Institute. Finally, in 1936, a trustee board was elected and Pacific Bible College was incorporated. Courses were first offered in 1937. Gray taught theology as well as served as president. During the first academic year he continued to serve the Woodland Park church, commuting weekly across the breadth of Washington state. Gray saw the college through its early years of development and relocation to Portland, Oregon in 1942. His tenure as president lasted until 1957, but he occasionally taught courses in theology until 1963.

The book for which Gray was best known is also his largest, a two-volume systematics published, as was Russell Byrum's work, under the title, *Christian Theology*.[31]

Like Earl Martin and Adam Miller, A. F. Gray also spoke widely and wrote curriculum for adult and youth Sunday school classes. In 1953 the Gospel Trumpet Company published an elective curriculum titled *Studies in Christian Theology* as a sequel to Martin's previous study of the same title.[32] Gray's church writing closely conformed to his systematic theology. His

Sunday school lessons on topics such as the Bible's authority and inspiration made the same points and took the same positions found in his larger study. Gray covered the standard theories of inspiration, but without enthusiasm for either dictation or plenary verbal theories. In both book and curriculum Gray dismissed the idea that the words of the Bible were inspired. Instead he made a claim highly reminiscent of H. C. Wickersham. Both men insisted that inspiration came to the writer, differing only in degree from an inspired minister's delivery of last Sunday's sermon: "It is not the Bible, that is to say the book itself that was inspired but the writers. The inspiration of the Spirit of God had its direct contact with the mind and spirit of the writers.... It was in the minds of the prophets that the ideas of God were conceived and wrought into words."[33] Although this view exercised a controlling influence in Gray's theology of inspiration, he conceded that some elements of the Bible were likely inspired in a manner consistent with the other theories. But Gray could not resist criticizing the dictation theory for making skilled stenography the essential qualification for prophesy or writing: "God could have saved time and effort dictating directly to Tertius, Tychicus, Epaphroditus, and others who did Paul's writing for him."[34] Lecturing to undergraduate ministerial students, writing for those in the church constituency who read theological literature, and teaching the broad mass of youth and adults through his Sunday school lessons, Gray elevated theology with careful consistency and encouraged the Church of God movement to consider ideas that were novel—perhaps risky—in the minds of many.

No theological issue was of greater interest to the Church of God than the doctrine of the church. Here, too, Gray's writing consistently sounded the same themes regardless the audience. Theological commitments dear to Church of God hearts dotted his writing but with some important modifications. In his Sunday school curriculum, for example, Gray built his lesson on "Apostasy and Restoration" on the so-called little apocalypse in the Gospel of Matthew as well as some of Paul's letters. Only one point of the lesson rested on a text from Revelation. Gray treated the topic of apostasy as a long-term theme rather than a specific epoch of church history, a perspective he shared with Otto Linn, whose work on Revelation Gray had read fifteen years earlier. None of Gray's lessons on the church shows any affinity for F. G. Smith's ecclesiology or advocates Christian unity through the practice of come-outism.[35] On these points Gray agreed with C. E. Brown and taught the church that "the universal church consists in all those who have been born again."[36] On the subject of church organization Gray affirmed the traditional view that Christ governed the church through the gifts of the Spirit, but Gray spent little energy attacking denominations. His characterization of denominational Christianity was a description generally conceded by all Christians, and Gray stopped well short of condemning denominations as evil or the consequence of apostasy. Under his tutelage Church of God people learned that wherever they happened to find themselves, the converted were members of the church universal: "We are saved into the church, and this membership is good everywhere. One does not lose his membership by changing his residence. This fact gives him fellowship with the people of God wherever he may be, and the spiritual rights of a Christian belong to him wherever he is."[37]

Earl Martin, A. F. Gray, and Adam W. Miller flourished as academics, but they were never only professors. Each began his ministerial career as a pastor and gained national prominence in the movement as an agency leader and churchman. After they moved into academia, they remained deeply and directly committed to the health of the Church of God as a whole as well as the vitality of individual congregations. These "doctors of the church" reached across the breadth of the movement and deeply into the weekly lives of individuals in local churches to a degree unrivalled before or since. Neither Martin nor Miller nor Gray was a fundamentalist, although the latter was the most conservative of the three. So what terms could be used to describe the theology that they taught the Church of God movement in such a wide variety of venues?

Essentially each of these three men was a Pietist, although none was self-consciously so. Pietist Christianity had not yet become the subject of scholarly study in the United States. During the years that Martin, Miller, and Gray were teaching and writing the only extensive study of Pietism was that of Albrecht Ritschl, an unsympathetic account that had not been translated from its original German. Charles E. Brown was only beginning to connect the Church of God movement with Pietism, so there was little scholarship by which the three could interpret the Church of God movement and understand themselves theologically or historically. Instead they simply wrote out of their own rich personal experience, their experience in the church, and an experience of Christ in which they never doubted. Their accumulated years of service in a variety of public arenas gave Martin, Miller, and Gray enormous credibility among ministers and laypersons alike. The Church of God movement placed great confidence in these three teacher-ministers because they offered their work to the church in a religious idiom grounded in experience. The church understood that idiom as its own and prized it as the truth of Christian faith and discipleship.

Notes

1. Linn's work and influence is considered in chapter 10.

2. Dennis F. Boughton, "Earl Leslie Martin," unpublished paper, Anderson College School of Theology, May 16, 1975, n. File "Earl Leslie Martin," Archives of the Church of God.

3. Martin's books include, *So That the World May Know* (Anderson, Ind: Gospel Trumpet Company, n.d); *The Sin of Sectarianism* (Anderson, Ind: Gospel Trumpet Company, n.d); *What Should a Christian Believe?* (Anderson, Ind: Gospel Trumpet Company, 1928); *Toward Understanding God* (Anderson, Ind: Gospel Trumpet Company, 1942); *The Gospel of Luke* (Anderson, Ind: Gospel Trumpet Company, 1944); *You Can Believe* (Anderson, Ind: Gospel Trumpet Company, 1945); *You Can Be a Christian* (Anderson, Ind: Gospel Trumpet Company, 1946); *The Wondrous Cross* (Anderson, Ind: Gospel Trumpet Company, 1946); *We Must Evangelize* (Anderson, Ind: Gospel Trumpet Company, 1947); *Work and Organization of the Local Church* (Anderson, Ind: Gospel Trumpet Company, 1951); and *This We Believe, This We Proclaim* (Anderson, Ind: Gospel Trumpet Company, 1952).

4. Martin made no claim for his book as either systematic theology or a philosophy of religion. Nevertheless, *Toward Understanding God* made serious expectations of a church constituency unaccustomed to such literature.

5. Martin, *Toward Understanding God,* 13–14.

6. Martin ran out the relationship between experience, religion, and theology in a sequence illustrated in the following description. "It is good for us to keep in mind that when we write or talk about God there is no one-to-one correspondence between what we say and the reality about which we speak. To put it briefly, we might state it as follows: (1) God is the ultimate reality. (2) Religion is man's experience of God. (3) In experience, one never gets the total of that which is to be experienced. (4) One never gets in thought the total of what one has experienced. (5) One never gets in words the total of what one has thought. (6) Yet men do rationalize their experiences, and this gives rise to theology, or doctrine." Ibid., 16–17.

7. I have drawn on F. Ernest Stoeffler's seminal studies of pietism for these characteristics. Cf., *The Rise of Evangelical Pietism* (Leiden: T. J. Brill, 1965) and *German Pietism in the Eighteenth Century* (Leiden: T. J. Brill, 1973).

8. Martin, *Toward Understanding God,* 26–27.

9. Martin wrote, "God calls to us even above the tumult, and possibly at first the call is but faintly heard, as if it were the call of the unknown. He commands. He challenges. And as we respond to that call and obey that command, whoever we be, whether wise or simple, God reveals himself by responding, and we find him in the toils, the conflicts, the suffering, for he goes with us every day and every step of the way. As we enter into the fellowship of daily service, as an ineffable mystery, we shall in our own experience, come to know and understand God." *Toward Understanding God,* 248. Although Martin modified Schweitzer's text, in some respects altering its meaning, it is also clear that he lifted some exact phrases often enough to make the case that Martin was not simply paraphrasing.

10. (Anderson, Ind: Gospel Trumpet Company, 1952).

11. Ibid., 9–15. In the same discussion Martin limited the idea of biblical authority in a way never found among fundamentalists, for example: "The scope of the Bible's authority exactly coincides with the scope of the Bible's purpose, which is the redemption of man."

12. Ibid., 51. Martin quoted here from his previously published *The Wondrous Cross* (Anderson, Ind: Gospel Trumpet Company, 1946).

13. Ibid., 76.

14. Ibid., 84–86.

15. (Anderson, Ind: Warner Press, 1943). Miller's other books included *A Brief Introduction to the Old Testament* (Anderson, Ind: Warner Press, 1964), and *The Gospel According to Matthew* (Anderson, Ind: Warner Press, 1944).

16. Miller, *An Introduction to the New Testament,* 74.

17. Ibid., 83–84.

18. Ibid., 84.

19. Ibid., 77.

20. Miller, *A Brief Introduction to the Old Testament*, 30.

21. Ibid.

22. Ibid., 30–31.

23. Miller was quoting Byrum's *Christian Theology*, 171–172.

24. Miller, *Introduction to the Old Testament*, 5–7.

25. The principal source for information about Gray is his autobiography, *Time and Tides on the Western Shore* (Anderson, Ind: Gospel Trumpet Company, 1966). He is also the subject of numerous graduate student papers, collected in a biographical file in the Archives of the Church of God.

26. The text of Gray's address appears as an article in the *Gospel Trumpet* for July 8, 1926.

27. Gray, "The Practical Workings of Divine Government in the Church," loc. cit., 3.

28. Ibid.

29. Ibid., 4.

30. In addition to the long tenures that he served on the Missionary Board and as chair of the General Assembly, Gray also was a member of the Gospel Trumpet Company for more than twenty years, a member of the Executive Council of the General Assembly for twenty-two years, and for twenty-one years a trustee of Anderson College.

31. (Anderson, Ind: Warner Press, 1944). Gray's other books include, *The Menace of Mormonism* (Anderson, Ind: Gospel Trumpet Company, 1926); *How to Study the Bible* (Anderson, Ind: Gospel Trumpet Company, 1950); and *The Nature of the Church* (Anderson, Ind: Gospel Trumpet Company, 1960).

32. Gray wrote a two-quarter study on Christian doctrine that was followed in the series by Miller's study of the Old Testament.

33. Cf. *Studies in Christian Theology*, Vol. I (Anderson, Ind: Gospel Trumpet Company, n.d.), 13–17, and *Christian Theology*, Vol. I (Anderson, Ind: The Warner Press, 1944), 73–84.

34. Gray, *Studies in Christian Theology*, Vol. I, 15.

35. Gray, *Studies in Christian Theology*, Vol. II (Anderson, Ind: Gospel Trumpet Company, n.d.), 33–51.

36. Ibid., 36.

37. Ibid., 37. Cf., *Christian Theology*, Vol. II (Anderson, Ind: The Warner Press, 1946), 113–135, 167–189.

Chapter 13

The Watchman on the Wall

On December 7, 1941, the war that had spread across Europe and Asia engulfed the United States. American citizens mobilized for the war effort and anxiously searched their newspapers for news of battles on land and sea. Battlefields and exotic names such as Casablanca, Anzio, Coral Sea, and Iwo Jima etched themselves deeply into the nation's consciousness. A battle that erupted back home in Indiana in the Church of God during the war years paled in comparison, but for preachers and church leaders alike the "Slacum Controversy," as it came to be known, was no small matter. The national work of the Church of God movement had come under heavy attack. The targets were certain church practices and matters of church leadership. Joined to questions that concerned emerging organizational practice was the suspicion that movement leaders had "let down the standard" on the doctrinal practice of holiness. By 1944 this combination was ready to explode.

Earl Slacum and His Revolt

In the summer of 1944 I. K. Dawson published a small booklet under the disproportionately lengthy title *Working Together in an Enlarged Program of State Evangelism.* Dawson was secretary of evangelism for the Board of Church Extension and Home Missions, and his booklet was published under its auspices. While a minister in Illinois, he had put forward the idea that ministers in that state should create an office of "state evangelist." Dawson gave evangelism the widest possible application. He envisioned the office to include responsibility for planning efforts to plant new churches, developing training programs in personal evangelism, coordinating mission projects sponsored by local congregations, and, most significantly, counseling churches beset by problems or seeking pastoral leadership. Dawson's persuasive efforts proved successful, and he became the first occupant of the new office. His labors, particularly in the area of pastoral placement, earned him both admiration and resentment. Some churches and pastoral candidates appreciated his matchmaking skill. Others detected in such efforts a serious breach of customary theological practice. In a movement committed to church leadership by the direct influence and gifting of the Holy Spirit, such efforts as Dawson's could be read as meddling or, worse, the human usurpation of the Spirit's place as guide of the church.

Elver Adcock, executive secretary of the Board of Church Extension and Home Missions, harbored no suspicions of the office that Dawson and his fellow ministers had created. As a young man Adcock (1898–1989) had left Iowa for Anderson Bible Training School, where he earned a two-year certificate. Later he returned to complete requirements for the B. Th. In 1921 Adcock became assistant secretary to Russell Byrum at the newly created Board of Church Extension. Four years later he was elected executive secretary-treasurer and held that post for forty-one years. Adcock had a banker's conservative mentality, but he was also an inveterate opponent of narrow-minded thinking. As the forties drew to a close, Adock was a member of a small and very select circle of agency executives that included T. Franklin Miller, Steele Smith, John Morrison, and Adam Miller. These men presided over much of the business of the movement in much the same fashion as the old Gospel Trumpet Company. Adcock wanted nothing more than to bring system and order to the haphazard procedures that often characterized church management from the grassroots up through state ministerial assemblies and their work.[1]

From Adcock's point of view, Dawson's model for a state executive minister was an idea whose time had come. He invited Dawson to join the board and give his plan a national reach. Dawson's booklet put his idea in full view of the movement, and it quickly became known as the "Dawson Plan." In time, versions of the "state evangelist" model were adopted throughout the United States. When published, however, the Dawson Plan almost instantly sparked a major theological explosion. In nearby Muncie, Indiana, L. Earl Slacum, pastor of a newly planted church there, saw in Dawson's booklet only the latest and most brazen attempt by movement leaders to centralize control of the church. It was the proverbial straw that broke the camel's back.

Earl Slacum (1901–1987) was born in 1901 in Maryland and reared on his family's farm. At age seventeen he experienced conversion at Federalsburg, a famous meeting place with a long history in the movement. Almost immediately thereafter he experienced a call to the ministry and in 1923 enrolled in Anderson Bible Training School. He pastored churches in

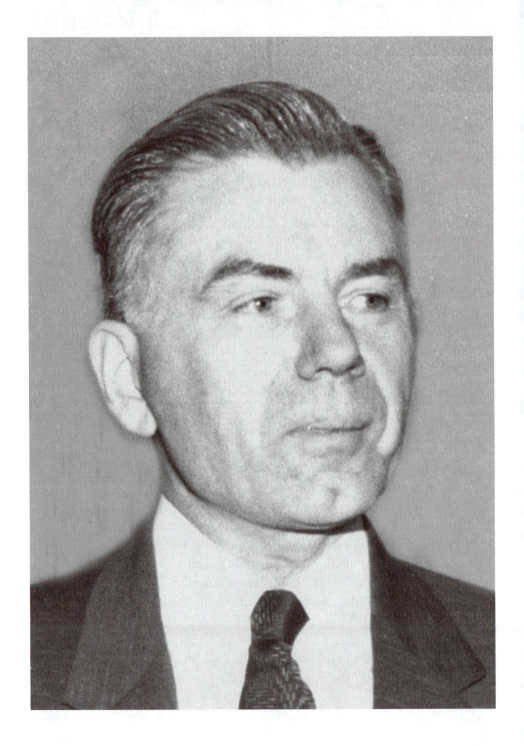

Elver A. Adcock. Long-term leader of the Board of Church Extension and Home Missions, Adcock was determined to bring orderly procedures and coherent planning to the work of state and local ministries.

Illinois and Ontario before returning to Anderson in 1935. One of several Church of God ministers intrigued with the possibilities offered by the medium of radio, Slacum had first developed a program in Ontario. At Anderson he launched a program called "The Bible Hour." In 1938 he moved to Muncie to assume responsibilities as the pastor of a new church. Slacum was aligned with the movement's theological conservatives and had a reputation as a "straight line" preacher, meaning that he hewed tightly to the views and practices that predated O. F. Linn, C. E. Brown, and Russell Byrum.

By early 1944 Slacum had become alarmed at what he considered the decline in "doctrinal preaching" in the Church of God. At the very center of his concern were the doctrinal practices of the church, especially those related to organization and Christian unity.[2] He worried about those in the movement who looked to its boards and agencies as "controlling systems." In Slacum's eyes this was a serious mistake that made more of these structures than originally intended. He thought of the Church of God movement primarily as "a group of people who have seen the vision of God's church, who have seen it standing out clear and distinct, free from every human system and man made organization."[3] Those who regarded the purpose of the boards and agencies as anything more than service to the movement threatened this ideal. Clear, straight preaching was needed to clarify the vision.

Slacum was also concerned about the movement's understanding and practice of Christian unity. In one sense Slacum was no sectarian. He agreed with the idea of Christian unity put forward by C. E. Brown, "that the church of God is composed of all of God's people everywhere" and recognized that denominations and "independent branches of Christendom" were filled with "outstanding leaders who are thoroughly Christian."[4] Such openness to Christians beyond the confines of the Church of God suggests that Slacum had strayed from the traditional categories of the apocalyptic ecclesiology. For him, however, there remained about the practice of Christian unity the unsolved mystery of how God would effect a solution to the problem of a divided Christendom "that will make practical the glorious ideal of Christian unity that is held out in the Bible."[5]

That the Church of God movement had lost its theological moorings to such important doctrinal practices Slacum attributed to three problems. First, he regarded the movement as so focused on contemporary methods and solutions that it was neglecting its theological heritage. A motorist must look in the rear-view mirror regularly in order to drive safely, as Slacum illustrated the point. If some denominations erred by staring in that mirror, he worried that there had arisen in the movement a "disrespect for the men, methods, and buildings which surrounded this work in its early days."[6]

Second, Slacum saw danger in the growing influence of theological notions external to the movement. The same airwaves that carried Slacum's weekly program also brought "unscriptural" ideas to the ears of the saints. In this regard he was especially concerned about the spread of premillennialism. Third, Slacum feared the introduction of new ideas by people within the Church of God. There were those during Slacum's ministry, he declared, "who have dared to advocate something that was contrary to the Bible."[7] Early in 1944 Slacum did not publicly name names, saying only that "not one of these men has remained in influence in the church."[8]

By the end of that summer Slacum's concern reached an alarmist stage and he turned up the rhetoric of his charges. In September the *Gospel Trumpet* published a new article by Slacum under the inflammatory title, "Is an Apostasy Emerging?" The saints were long accustomed to seeing such phrases applied to the denominational world. That Slacum used it with reference to the Church of God raised more than eyebrows, for the article's springboard was the text of 2 Thessalonians 2:7, "For the mystery of iniquity is already at work."[9] Ironically, a minister of the Church of God had used the communications medium of widest reach across the movement to throw darts at the movement's leadership.

Slacum detected signs of a growing apostasy in the Church of God. He believed that doctrinal declension had pushed the movement into this fall and blamed the movement's leadership for a general deemphasis on the historic teaching of the church. He also darkly hinted, "Men in high places begin to aim at other things beside that which is clearly taught in God's Word."[10] Still naming no names, Slacum ran through a catalogue of sins: the leader who tore apart the doctrines of the church in front of a group of ministers, churches that no longer held prayer meetings[11] or observed the ordinance of footwashing, laypeople, and ministers who frequented the movies but did not clearly state the doctrine of the church. "Is this apostasy?" Slacum asked. "You had just as well ask if this is winter when the thermometer hangs at twenty below zero and the ground is covered knee-deep in snow."[12]

According to John W. V. Smith, Slacum's fears were incited by the findings of a thesis written by Robert Reardon at Oberlin. The project's title was sure to attract the attention of people concerned about the state of church teaching: "The Doctrine of the Church and the Christian Life in the Church of God Movement."[13] Reardon's thesis documented the very thing that worried Slacum so deeply—changes in the movement's attitudes towards and teaching on the doctrines of unity and sanctification. He stated no concern about Reardon's work *per se*. However, that the younger minister had subsumed a discussion of sanctification under the larger category of the "Christian life" was just the sort of slippage to anger a man who frequently complained that Church of God people hadn't heard a sermon on sanctification in ten years. In the context of Reardon's Oberlin training in systematic theology, this terminological shift was quite proper, and his historically informed discussion was in step with the historical consciousness of people like Otto Linn, C. E. Brown, and Adam Miller. However, neither methodology nor terminology alarmed Slacum as much as Reardon's findings.

A key element in Reardon's research involved a questionnaire distributed to one hundred ministers of the Church of God across the United States. He took pains to insure that his survey reached the length and breadth of the church. At the time that he conducted this research, the number one hundred constituted one-sixteenth of the movement's ministers, so he apportioned his distribution according to that ratio but also made certain that states with small constituencies received at least one questionnaire.[14] Reardon surveyed this representative sample in search of answers to such questions as: (1) "Do you think that our movement should go back to the teachings of D. S. Warner?" (2) "Do you feel that our movement is in danger of becoming too liberal?" (3) "In your opinion, what is worldliness?" (5) "Do you feel that the term 'Last Reformation' should be applied to our movement?" and (6) "Do you favor membership in the Federal Council of Churches?"[15] Responses indicated that attitudes had moderated considerably from earlier views and practices. Even on the highly controversial issue of affiliation with the Federal Council of Churches, an amazing 55 percent of respondents favored the move. Even more telling were some of the respondents' comments quoted by Reardon. The spirit of these comments expressed the desire for a broader and more inclusive practice of Christian unity. Respondents also were impatient with what they regarded as an earlier generation's misguided preoccupation with the shibboleths of holiness rather than a focus on its substance—Christian love. The quotations that Reardon included also retreated from the movement's exclusivism, i. e. its self-description as the "Last Reformation," in favor of a position that said, in the words of one respondent, "We have grown away from the 'special people' consciousness to a more universal Christian attitude. Without surrendering loyalty to truth, we have come to respect the beliefs of others. As ministers we are willing to see our ideas tried and tested, and if they are found wanting to admit that they are wrong."[16]

Since their earliest days Church of God people had quoted the text of John 16:13, "Howbeit when he, the Spirit of truth is come, he will guide you into all truth," with an understanding that they needed to be open to new

I. K. Dawson developed a plan to coordinate various programs under the administrative authority of a state minister. Known as the "Dawson Plan," the model drew criticism from Church of God conservatives.

truths. That openness lived in tension with a separatism that declared the movement's vision of the church to be the truth. Slacum pushed the latter position further than most were willing to state in print. In his mind, vacillating attitudes had weakened doctrine. Early in his ministerial career, said Slacum, he had been told that the movement possessed all the truths essential to the restoration of the New Testament church, "all the truth that had been lost in the apostasy."[17] Later he had been taught—Slacum did not say by whom—that the movement did not possess all the truth. He wanted the movement to get off the theological fence. The "Last Reformation" of the church, as F. G. Smith and others had described the Church of God, must possess the truth—*all* the truth. "I have reached the conclusion," stated Slacum, "that we do have the *truth,* all of it that has been discovered from the pages of God's word. I now feel that when anyone says we do not have all the truth, a clear vision of what we do possess is slipping from the vision."[18]

All was not lost. Slacum saw hope in the fact that young ministers of clear doctrinal vision were still being called into the ministry. Their strong convictions and refusal to be silenced were positive signs for the movement's future. The great need of the hour was that older ministers and laypersons recover the old doctrines and embrace Slacum's attitude toward the truth. However, the ominous specter of spreading organization still overshadowed the movement's future. If that threat were to materialize, then, warned Slacum, "we will need a clear message again to come out of an apostatized movement that carries the name Church of God into a clear definite movement with the same name but with a different character."[19] The publication of I. K. Dawson's booklet on cooperative ministry, originating as it did from one of the national agencies, told Slacum that his worst fears had come to pass.

The Dawson Plan applied a bureaucratic model of organization to church work at the state level. It operated on the premise that stable and effective cooperation among local churches required organization if state programs such as Christian education, youth work, and the women's organization were to advance.[20] His booklet laid out the principles of this organization, offered a simple model, and included a sample of the bylaws under which it might be implemented. The plan was quite modest; Dawson did not propose an elaborate or complicated design. However, his booklet's title page carried the endorsements of the Gospel Trumpet Company and the executive committee of the movement's Commission on Evangelism. The cumulative effect of the plan and these endorsements led Slacum to believe that "Anderson" was extending its reach into the heart of the Church of God and controlling every aspect of the movement's life.

L. Earl Slacum, the "Watchman on the Wall."

At the Indiana State Ministers Meeting of September 1944 Earl Slacum declared war on the Church of God. This declaration took the form of a bombshell sermon entitled "Watchmen on the Walls." It was nothing short of a call to arms. As he later stated, his sermon "exposed and attacked" the Dawson Plan "as being contrary to the Word of God, ecclesiastical, dictatorial, binding upon church bodies, and heading toward unfair and unreasonable centralization of power."[21] He repeated his previous charges of doctrinal declension. That was the very core of Slacum's message. As a result of a deemphasis or, worse, alterations in, the movement's historic teaching, the important doctrinal practices of Christian unity, holiness, and the organization of the church had departed from the original standard. He pointed to the "liberalization" of the doctrine of Christian unity as having begun fifteen years earlier at a state ministers meeting. Although once again he mentioned no names, Slacum must have had in mind Russell Byrum's paper on Christian unity read to the Indiana ministers in 1929. Slacum did not offer any systematic criticism of Byrum's work, but used it simply as an example of the sinister declension that he saw everywhere. Similarly, concerning the practice of holiness, he attacked "those who represent us in the head-quarters" for frequenting the movies and he objected to the use of their salaries, originating as those monies did in local church offerings, for "jewelry, rouge, and lipstick."[22]

Slacum reserved his heaviest salvoes for the Dawson Plan. There was in that plan, said Slacum, "power enough ... to get a stranglehold on every department of the state work."[23] Dawson's proposed model of organization assigned responsibility for state activities to eight offices. Slacum seized on that number to say that an "ecclesiastical octopus" had grown up in the midst of the church. In case any of his readers missed the point, he added a dictionary definition: "an EIGHT-ARMED CUTTLE-FISH, A DEVIL FISH, an organization with many branches through which it maintains its hold on others."[24] Slacum saw in the Dawson Plan an extension into the state work of the kind of organization that had already wrapped its tentacles around the national ministry of the Church of God.

At bottom, Earl Slacum saw the Church of God movement slipping away from the teachings that he had heard as a youth and in the early days of his ministry, teachings on which he had always stood. He was unprepared to accept the theological and social developments that had been ongoing since the second decade of the century. He defended and sought the preservation of a doctrinal message that he summarized as:

> The doctrine of full salvation from sin, both the inherited
> and the acquired, that is dealt with in the two experiences:

justification, or a born again experience; sanctification, with the baptism of the Holy Ghost and fire; the doctrine of Divine Healing of soul and body as coming from Calvary, by the death of Christ on the cross. Let us emphasize the fact of the Church of God, as a Divine Institution, resulting from Calvary, according to Acts 20:28, which he purchased with his own blood. Let us see clearly that a great apostasy swept over the world, and the church was lost from view. But by a second process, known as the reformation, first of justification, second as sanctification, and then full restoration, that of restoring the church to her primitive purity and power. And that we believe that, according to the word of God that Babylon which represents God's people as in bondage and confusion, is fallen. And that God is now saying to the world, "Come out of her my people," and "as a shepherd seeketh out his sheep, so will I both seek out my sheep and search them out, from all the places where they have been scattered in the dark and cloudy days.[25]

Like D. S. Warner more than seventy years earlier, Earl Slacum went to Terre Haute with the intention of undoing a theologically objectionable organization constructed by others. In Slacum's case, however, the "others" were ministerial colleagues in his own church. Nevertheless, at the ministers meeting of 1944 he proposed an alternate and much simpler form of state organization based in the practice of the charismatic organization of the church. Indiana ministers rejected his proposal, but Slacum received enough expressions of sympathy to fan the spark of his rebellion into open flame. Those who voted against his proposal included not only pastors but also ministers who worked on the national agency staffs in Anderson, most of whom had little sympathy for the ideas of a man who had targeted them with both tongue and pen. For his part, Slacum read their opposition as but one more instance of bureaucratic maneuvering and ecclesiastical politicking, and this only increased his determination to call the church to action. He broadened his objective to include the national work of the Church of God.

Slacum's protest touched a nerve of discontent among more than a few Church of God ministers. There were those who shared his alarm at the growth of the national agency structure and who were just as uneasy that agency leaders and staff members had relaxed some aspects of the practice of holiness. Then, too, a certain resentment had developed among some who believed that a small circle of "big boys" was running the affairs of the entire church.[26] This resentment expressed itself any time someone sarcastically referred to Anderson as "Mecca" or the general offices located there as "headquarters." Casual use of that term might very well earn a sharp rebuke as well as the reminder that those were only "general offices" and that the true church's headquarters was in heaven. People also tended to think of the agencies as a very tightly knit group that conducted as one all the movement's business—as if the agencies shared a common mailbox at the U.S. Post Office in Anderson.

In point of fact there was a measure of truth to some of these suspicions and resentments. Prior to the development of the national boards and agencies, the ministers who were appointed and referred to as the "Gospel Trumpet Company" constituted a group who together functioned something like the national elders of the Church of God. Many of them had demonstrated their concern for the movement and its future by participating in such projects as *Our Ministerial Letter.* They were ministers who had earned the respect of their colleagues and most of the church. According to the doctrinal practice of charismatic church government, their considerable ministerial gifts had been recognized and their elevation to national prominence was understood to be the work of the Holy Spirit. However, as the number of boards and agencies grew, the charismatic government of the church increasingly resembled an "old boy" network.[27]

Only a cursory reading of the rosters of agency trustee boards during the 1930s and '40s will disclose the fact that the same names appear and reappear. To cite but one example out of many, in 1938 Earl Martin, then an Anderson College faculty member, trustee, and member of its executive committee, was not only a board member but a director at the Board of Church Extension and the Gospel Trumpet Company. Twelve years later Martin remained a trustee and vice-president of Anderson College and was still a board member at Church Extension and the Gospel Trumpet Company. When he attended agency board meetings in 1950 he would regularly have seen Oscar J. Flynt, who was also a member of the same three trustee boards. Ministers of the grassroots congregations that funded Church of God World Service and were the backbone of the Church of God movement could be forgiven for the perception that they were the "grunts" doing the work while a small cadre of big shots in Anderson piped the tune to which the movement danced.

The debate over Slacum's cause at the Indiana minister's meeting did not long remain on a lofty theological plane. The nature of his charges almost inevitably led to a discussion of personalities. However, this ugly side of the discussion did little to impede its spread, nor would Slacum retreat from any of his accusations. Over the next three years he continued to sound the alarm and in the process attracted a growing list of supporters among individual

ministers and entire congregations. Indeed, almost immediately after the
Indiana ministers' meeting of 1944 and on the basis of the support he
received there, Slacum took his case to the entire movement. He started a
small paper that initially carried the same title as his Terre Haute sermon.[28]
The paper's first issue was a printed version of "Watchmen on the Walls." To
this he appended demands for a clean sweep of all national offices, and he
invited every Church of God minister to join in the call for an open General
Ministerial Assembly. Slacum wanted an unfettered discussion of the issues
he had raised. Over time, issues retreated to the background as Slacum's
paper lobbed personal attacks at agency leaders. Much of his information
came from an anonymous source who regularly mailed Slacum typewritten
letters from Anderson.[29] His following grew and the Slacum agitation
continued for seven years. Over that period it attracted supporters not only
throughout the Church of God heartland of Michigan, Indiana, Illinois, and
Ohio but also reached as far as British East Africa.

Recovery and Reorganization

A year after Slacum's Terre Haute sermon, state and national organizations of the movement counter-attacked. The Agencies leaders chose to
respond to Slacum's allegations through regular organizational channels—
state and national ministerial assemblies—rather than directly and personally.
By a vote of eighty-two to thirty-nine the 1945 session of the Indiana
Ministerial Assembly adopted a resolution stating its disapproval of Slacum's
attacks and requesting their cessation. The resolution also distanced the
Indiana Assembly from Slacum, stating that at no time did it endorse him or
his program. The resolution made no effort to defend the church and its
leaders against Slacum's charges, but was based instead on concern over the
"unrest and lack of confidence in this great work" that they had prompted.[30]
Nevertheless, the *Watchman on the Walls* circulated widely through the
Church of God and touched several levels of discontent with the effect of
undermining confidence in the national agencies. It was incumbent on
church leaders to act to restore that confidence. One of their first steps was
to enlist the support of F. G. Smith.

After he left the Gospel Trumpet Company in 1930 Smith took the pastorate of the McKinley Avenue Church of God in Akron, Ohio. His dismissal
had done little to damage his credibility in the church. Smith and his wife,
Birdie, remained popular preachers—especially when, in the former's case, a
congregation or minister's group wanted more light on the church in prophesy and history. His books also remained very popular, so much so that the
plates for *The Revelation Explained* were no longer useable by the early

1940s. Smith's views on this subject had moderated somewhat over the years, and they appeared in the revised edition published in 1943. In the aftermath of Slacum's 1944 charges the rumor circulated that the publishing house refused to keep Smith's book in print unless he toned down some of his more extreme opinions. In fact, Smith had requested the opportunity to revise the book, but the rumors illustrated the declining regard in which even the venerable Gospel Trumpet Company was held. As a means of shoring up this eroding confidence, in 1946 company directors elected Smith president. The office was largely honorary; Smith's primary assignment was to direct and improve public—in this case, church—relations. Once deposed from the post that he loved and considered his divine calling, Smith nevertheless returned to Anderson and at age sixty-six immediately embarked on a grueling speaking schedule that criss-crossed the country. The effort proved too much for him, and Smith suffered a fatal heart attack in Anderson in the spring of 1947. Ironically, the stalwart warrior died at St John-Hickey Hospital in the care of the Sisters of the Holy Cross, daughters of the church that he had so often labeled a harlot.

The General Ministerial Assembly of the Church of God also responded to Slacum's assaults. He refused the Indiana Assembly's request to tone down his language, and his supporters refused to accept its judgment lying down. Instead they published a "Special Letter of Important Facts" that accused state assembly leaders and "Anderson people" of railroading the meeting. The persistence of Slacum's sympathizers led to the perception that the level of his support was rising, and this prompted General Ministerial Assembly officers to appoint a committee to investigate the entire affair. In 1946 a seven-member Committee on Research and Improvement was named. One year later their report exonerated agency leaders of the charge that they had let down the standard of holiness and found nothing in the agency structure and policies out of keeping with church practice. The General Ministerial Assembly responded to the report with a sweeping resolution that reaffirmed the ministerium's loyalty to the historic ideals and doctrines of the Church of God. The resolution also expressed confidence in the national agencies and brought down a ringing condemnation of the charges against them as false, deliberate, and "grossly unchristian."[31] Finally, the Assembly also resolved to call upon Earl Slacum and his supporters to repent, confess their errors, and make amends for the sake of the restoration of Christian fellowship and the unity of the church.

Slacum and his associates smelled a cover-up. Although he asked for the Assembly's forgiveness and apologized for any mistaken information or falsehood that his paper might have published, he refused to concede that his accusations were unfounded. Furthermore, Assembly and church leadership's refusal to admit any wrongdoing or errors in practice incensed Slacum, and he begged for official action to correct abuses that he continued to believe were accurately represented. The Assembly resolution gave credence neither to Slacum's beliefs nor his request for action. In the face of what amounted to public censure, Slacum and his followers had little choice but to leave the movement. Bent on reforming the Church of God reformation movement, they went into schism. A flurry of disfellowshipping actions followed, including one by which the Bessie, Oklahoma Church of God disfellowshipped the entire Church of God movement.[32] Slacum's new movement gathered support from local congregations in sympathy with his cause and went so far as to recruit Church of God field missionaries for service as missionaries under the auspices of their new and fully reformed movement. These actions only further angered state leaders in Indiana as well as national agency leaders. More years of agitation followed until Earl Slacum's credentials as a minister of the Church of God (Anderson, Indiana) finally were revoked in 1948.

While the issues pertaining to Slacum and his movement were coming to a head, a new special committee was commissioned to consider further some of the findings and suggestions made by the Committee on Research and Improvement. This new Committee on Revision and Planning, as it was named, was given a three- to five-year assignment charging it to study and make recommendations to improve relationships among the agencies and between the agencies and the General Ministerial Assembly. Among the new committee's findings were three desires among rank and file ministers: (1) greater privileges regarding agency trustee board nominations, (2) more direct ministerial control of the national agencies and their policies, and (3) a more representative national assembly.[33] In a way, one of the concerns growing out of the Slacum agitation finally but tacitly had been acknowledged. The Committee on Revision and Planning was at something of a loss at how to proceed and made no final recommendations during its term, except that at its end the committee recommended that it be given a second term. Reauthorized, the committee focused its attention on restructuring relationships among the national agencies. In 1954 the committee made its final report, one that recommended enlarging and reorganizing the Executive Council and assigning it broader responsibility for coordinating national agency work. The Council had been created more than thirty years earlier as the legal entity that conducted Assembly business when it was not in session. But the Council's responsibilities and authority were severely limited by agencies jealous of their own freedom to plan and act somewhat unilaterally. The 1954 reorganization restricted some of that freedom as it made the agencies part of the coordinated fund-raising and budgeting work of the Division of World Service. "More importantly, perhaps, than any other function, the Executive Council now provided a kind of neutral arena in which the various agencies could relate to each other without the competitive climate inherent in the previous 'fight-it-out-among-yourselves' system. Since elected members, including some laypersons, would always outnumber agency representatives, the power potential of 'Anderson' was considerably curtailed."[34]

Assessing Change

Once Earl Slacum's guns fell silent, C. E. Brown sallied forth to offer a theological and historical rebuttal. If the work of the Committee on Revision and Planning reflected changes in church practice in response to the Slacum agitation, it was *Gospel Trumpet* Editor Brown who addressed the theological and ethical issues. In 1951 he delivered a cycle of four lectures at the newly created School of Theology at Anderson College. Three years later these lectures were published under the title *When Souls Awaken: An Interpretation of Radical Christianity.* The latter two lectures addressed the practices of church organization and holiness matters not coincidentally at the heart of Slacum's earlier attacks. Brown marshaled his reply on historical ground that he had often trod in earlier books. In *When Souls Awaken,* however, he recast his historical interpretation of the Church of God as a subtle and somewhat oblique reply to those who had agitated the movement during much of the previous decade. Brown understood better than most the Watchman movement's fear of change, particularly at the point of doctrinal practices. His lectures addressed the issue of change by considering which aspects of those practices were permanent and which could appropriately be termed transient.

Brown reflected on the movement's doctrinal practice of holiness as an example of Christian asceticism. He was aware that such terminology was new to many of his readers. But through the use of such language Brown insisted that Church of God people reflect on the movement in historical categories. By this point in his career such usage was a well-entrenched theological habit. D. S. Warner had probably never used the phrase "ascetic discipline," but Brown did not take that to mean that Church of God people were bound to nineteenth-century forms of expression. His use of a proper theological and historical vocabulary may have been a side issue, but it was also one of his characteristic moves. He saw no reason to make a frontal attack on his opponents when they could be linguistically outflanked. Aside from subtly altering the movement's theological language, Brown was willing to say what few others were, in the face of Slacum's withering personal assaults: "there is an amazing amount of ignorance regarding the nature and meaning of ascetic discipline preached and practiced by Warner and his colleagues."[35] The Watchman movement had made icons of Warner and other pioneers, treating all of their ideas and practices as sacrosanct. Brown pointed out the fallacy of such icon-making by reporting his boyhood experience of being subjected to a two-hour camp meeting sermon by "one of our best educated ministers … on the subject of why we should avoid pepper."[36]

By redescribing the doctrinal practice of holiness under the category of ascetic discipline Brown prompted the Church of God to consider the purpose of a holy life. Ascetic practice, said Brown, aimed at the discipline of the Christian's life to the end that it be more effective in service to God, the church, and neighbor.[37] By thinking of holiness practices as forms of ascetic discipline, Brown shifted the lines of an argument that reached back to the days of C. E. Orr and the necktie controversy and of which the Slacum agitation was but the most recent installment. Church of God people erred, thought Brown, in the idea that sin was the only thing that God might call them to forsake. Even worse, this fallacy "immediately plunges us into a war of words regarding what is and what is not sin."[38] Forms of ascetic discipline were not badges of holiness, proof of a sinless life, but practices that aimed at enabling the Christian to be of greater service. Brown thought of the doctrinal practice of holiness as a means rather than the end. His criticism was apt but also carried risks. To drop traditional holiness shibboleths also made the practice of holiness more difficult to measure by the conventional standards—frivolous or prideful personal adornment, the use of caffeine or other stimulants, frequenting "movie palaces," and so forth. Moreover, the weakening of such practices also lowered one of the barriers that, sociologically speaking, separated the in-group from outsiders. When that wall was torn down, questions of group identity became more problematic.

From this recasting of holiness Brown cursorily reviewed the history of ascetic practices in the Church of God, situating that history in the broader narrative of the history of Christianity. His review started from the position that the principle of ascetic discipline was both valid and necessary to the life of the church but that this principle had often been misapplied. In 1951, the date of his lectures, Brown was one of the few remaining individuals, especially among agency leaders, who could be linked to the movement's earliest days in the twentieth century. He used his longevity to considerable effect, remembering when "even courtship was a pleasure denied the committed Christian. If you ask how we got married, I can only say that we believed in miracles."[39] Brown employed this review to legitimize holiness practice as a form of ascetic discipline while gently but firmly criticizing the movement for its excesses. He specifically referred to people like Orr and Slacum, but it is clear that in Brown's mind their myopic concern for neckties and movies had mistaken the intention behind the practice of holiness. Those in the movement who shared their convictions needed to rethink their position.

Brown also addressed the phenomenon of change as it regarded the doctrinal practice of the church and its organization, the second general area of concern in the Watchman movement. Even more so here than concerning the practices of holiness, Brown saw himself as a mediator between the movement's pioneers and a rising generation of leaders. He had personally known many in the pioneer generation and was familiar with its apparent confidence in doctrinal practices formed, as Brown said, "in an ironclad pattern of unchanging orthodoxy delivered by a complete and unchanging revelation which could suffer no change."[40] Reluctantly approaching retirement himself, he also watched a younger generation taking leadership positions and noted among it some who were ready to reject Warner's ideas concerning the organization and leadership of the church. Brown mediated these perspectives in two ways. First, he rehabilitated Warner and the movement's early leadership by indicating that the ablest of them did not really believe that the movement's message was incapable of change, although he conceded that the "theory of ironbound completeness" was an error into which some easily fell.[41] This description of the first generation gave Brown room to criticize its theology of the church—particularly at the point of its organization. Such criticism opened the way for the second element in Brown's mediating task. Even with his generous assessment of the founders, Brown still thought that at no point was the new generation more at odds with the pioneers than the one concerning the organization of the church. By pointing out the mistaken aspects of the pioneer's doctrinal practice on this issue, and by describing that generation as more open to change than was widely perceived, he attempted to bring the two closer together.

In the context of this discussion Brown analyzed the tension between two principles of church governance. He termed these the "leader principle" and "spiritual democracy." In Brown's view, Warner and the early generations of movement leadership had laid down and operated according to the leader principle. They understood the church to be governed ultimately by the Holy Spirit, who gifted men and women for leadership in the church. The Spirit had guided the church through the work of strong leaders like Warner, E. E. Byrum, and F. G. Smith. Little organization was necessary during most of the period of their stewardship, and the majority of people in the Church of God movement had accepted the doctrinal practice of church and its organization. As he read the movement's history Brown saw a new principle of leadership rising during Smith's editorial tenure, a principle of "spiritual democracy" that stood in tension with the leader principle.[42] The development and growth of the national agencies and other moves such as Brown's decision to shift responsibility for ministerial accreditation to state assemblies were examples of democracy as the principle of changing doctrinal practice. Such change inevitably produced tension.

Without his explicitly saying so—perhaps it was unnecessary in the context of that day—it seems clear that Brown regarded the recent Slacum controversy as an expression of the tension between the leader principle and spiritual democracy. For Earl Slacum the expanding work of state and national organizations encroached on what he considered the proper and simpler form of church governance that rested on the charismatic leadership model. Brown had some sympathy for Slacum, not for his preference for that model but because the national agency structure as it had evolved did not yet fairly represent spiritual democracy. The model of national church leadership was oligarchic rather than democratic; leadership in the movement had scarcely broadened on democratic lines. True enough, democratic voting procedures had been installed, but the same small circle of people kept winning the elections. Nevertheless, Brown did think that democracy in the church had been introduced in principle if not in ideal practice, and he regarded this introduction as the most portentous development in the movement's history. In his view it was the change from which all others flowed.[43]

Brown thought that the moment was long past when the practice of the church needed to conform to the democratic principle. The leader idea may have been necessary for the early decades of the movement's life, but that day was gone. Broad-based, democratically defined cooperation was the order of the day. Those in the movement who still feared modern methods of organization as the means to that end needed to change their attitude for, as Brown put it, "There can be very little cooperation among people who regard all organization as sin."[44] In case anyone missed his point, he stated for the record his belief that the movement's early insistence that the doctrine of charismatic governance of the church necessitated the elimination of all organization to be one of its most serious errors.[45]

Brown's book, published for the church, was originally a set of lectures delivered to seminary students—the next generation of leadership. For that generation Brown legitimized change and the alterations in church practice that were occurring even as he delivered and then subsequently published his lectures. He assessed change in the Church of God under the category of the transient and the permanent in the movement as well as Christianity at large.[46] It was a motif that saw in Christianity a central kernel of unchanging doctrine surrounded by a husk of secondary ideas that had been and could legitimately be altered according to new and different contexts. In Brown's view it was neither necessary nor advantageous to regard every aspect of pioneer teaching as set in concrete. A little humility was also in order: "when we have grown and developed to a point where we can fully understand God's guidance and God's plans we will be graduated to heaven."[47] Faith, not theology, was final. Brown underscored this assessment by describing D. S. Warner as a religious innovator and explorer. In Brown's eyes, after Warner received light on the church, "he spent the rest of his life trying to find ways, means, and methods of making that illumination fruitful in the restoration of the church both ideally and practically."[48] Such a view respected the achievement of Warner and the pioneer generation of the Church of God. Since Brown's perspective refused to grant the status of permanency to every aspect of that achievement, he freed the next generation of movement leadership from a slavish adherence to the past.

In 1951 Adam Miller, Gene Newberry, and Anderson College sociology professor Valorous B. Clear received word from Earl Slacum expressing his desire to be restored to the fellowship of the Church of God. Earlier that year he had brought an end to his schismatic movement when he resigned from all of its boards and committees, commenting that in five years the Watchman movement had created more organization than had the Church of God in a period five times longer. Two years later his credentials as a minister of the Church of God were restored, bringing to a formal end nearly a decade of unrest and open theological warfare. The acrimonious controversy had left many with deep scars. Some of these wounds, corporate as well as individual, did not heal easily or quickly. National church leaders did attempt to address organizationally some of the issues and attitudes that had spawned the Watchman movement. Others reinterpreted the pioneer generation's theological achievement in a positive light that nevertheless allowed room for change. Some regarded the Slacum controversy as a largely Midwestern battle. The majority of shells were fired at Indiana targets, but their explosions reverberated across the Church of God, rattling relationships across North America and beyond. As a result, the movement did not march immediately into the post-World War II era with a confident step. However, that stride began to quicken as the movement caught pace with a powerful interest in religion that swept America during the 1950s. The Church of God picked up the beat and during that decade and the one following entered the mainstream of American religious life.

Notes

1. This character sketch is indebted to Robert Reardon, "Movers and Shakers in the Church of God," n.p.

2. L. Earl Slacum, "Doctrinal Dangers Facing the Church of God," *GT* February 19, 1944), 9.

3. Ibid.

4. Ibid.

5. Ibid.

6. Ibid., 10.

7. Ibid.

8. Ibid.

9. L. Earl Slacum, "Is an Apostasy Emerging?", *GT* (September 16, 1944), 7. Perhaps the greater mystery is why Editor C. E. Brown decided to print Slacum's article.

10. Ibid.

11. Church of God people frequently cited the waning number and fervency of prayer meetings as a sign of decreasing spiritual fervor among their favorite target, the Methodists.

12. Ibid.

13. (Unpublished S. T. M. thesis, Oberlin Graduate School of Theology, 1943). A copy is shelved in the Archives of the Church of God.

14. An impressive 90 percent of recipients returned their responses. Ibid. Appendix I.

15. Ibid., 127. Reardon asked a total of sixteen questions.

16. Ibid., 112. Another respondent stated the issue more bluntly: "We are getting out of the little theological ditch which we were supposed to walk in and ask no questions."

17. Slacum, "Is an Apostasy Emerging?", 8.

18. Ibid. Slacum's emphases.

19. Ibid., 7.

20. I. K. Dawson, *Working Together in an Enlarged Program of State Evangelism* (Anderson, Ind: Board of Church Extension and Home Missions of the Church of God, n. d.), 14–15.

21. Slacum's supporters financed the publication of his sermon, which were distributed at no cost to any who wanted copies. He delivered the sermon on September 19, 1944, but the printed version lacks a date.

22. "Watchmen on the Walls," (Muncie, Ind: n.p.: n.d.), n.

23. Ibid.

24. Ibid. Slacum's emphases.

25. Ibid.

26. The phrase and the perception belong to John W. V. Smith, who analyzed these attitudes and their consequent development in *The Quest for Holiness and Unity*, 325–335.

27. Smith is even blunter in his assessment. "Before 1917 they had assumed leadership; after 1917 they were nominated and elected to leadership." *The Quest for Holiness and Unity*, 327.

28. The title later was changed to *Church of God Watchman*.

29. Smith, *The Quest for Holiness and Unity*, 330.

30. A copy of the resolution is housed in the Archives of the Church of God, File "Slacum Controversy."

31. The resolution is reprinted under the title "Faith in the Integrity of the National Work" in Callen, Ed., *Following the Light*, 169–171.

32. Copies of these resolutions can be found in the Archives of the Church of God, File "Slacum Controversy."

33. General Assembly Minutes, June 16, 1948.

34. Smith, *The Quest for Holiness and Unity*, 338.

35. *When Souls Awaken: An Interpretation of Radical Christianity* (Anderson, Ind: Gospel Trumpet Company, 1954), 69–70.

36. Ibid., 70.

37. Ibid., 71.

38. Ibid., 72.

39. Ibid., 75

40. Ibid., 101.

41. The question of the first generation's openness to change is highly debatable. Brown made Warner out to be a rather open and progressive individual. The real tests of openness came after his death and were the burden of E. E. Byrum, who was by nature and generation much more conservative than his predecessor. How Warner might have responded to the challenges that Byrum faced is an interesting matter for conjecture.

42. Brown's idea of spiritual democracy extended to a church practice is discussed earlier. See chapter 10.

43. Ibid., 105.

44. Ibid., 112.

45. Ibid.

46. Ibid., 106ff.

47. Ibid., 108.

48. Ibid., 111.

Chapter 14
Entering the Mainstream

The Slacum controversy coincided with the last years of World War II and the return to peacetime life for millions of GIs. However, the return of peace created a set of conditions that did not represent a return to normalcy in the Church of God. After the war, and particularly during the presidency of Dwight D. Eisenhower from 1952 to 1960, American churches and synagogues experienced unusually strong and steady growth. Americans of many persuasions understood religious commitment to be an important aspect of the American way of life as it was defined during Eisenhower's presidency. The Church of God movement also participated in this boom. In terms of both wealth and membership, the Church of God in the United States experienced unprecedented prosperity in the postwar era. Prosperity and alterations in attitudes and church practice indicated that the Church of God was moving toward the mainstream of American Protestantism.

Postwar Prosperity

Wartime rationing and restrictions on strategic materials effectively halted church construction during the years from 1940–1945. At the same time, wages were high, especially in the northern belt of heavy industrial states from western Pennsylvania to Illinois. Wartime production needs and the labor shortage created when millions of workers became GIs combined to drive up industrial wages in this region that was the Church of God heartland. Families had money, but many goods were scarce. The same was true for congregations. As members' incomes increased, so did giving to the local church. But the construction of new church buildings was next to impossible given the unavailability of construction materials co-opted by the war effort. The return of peace dramatically altered this situation. The combination of an available money surplus and the lifting of wartime rationing opened the floodgate that had held back pent-up demand for new church construction.

Local church property values increased by leaps and bounds in the Church of God after the conclusion of World War II. In 1940 the aggregate value of local church property was estimated at $4.6 million.[1] Ten years later that value was put at $21.6 million, an increase of approximately 450 percent.[2] The second half of the decade 1940–1950 witnessed an expansion of more than $14 million in local church property value, or 89 percent of the increase during the entire decade. Even more remarkable growth continued during the following decades. By 1960 the value of local church property had increased by a whopping $50 million,[3] and by 1970 the aggregate total had reached $125 million.[4] These figures do not include the value of corporately held properties such as the national offices of the Church of God or the campuses of Anderson College, Pacific Bible [later Warner Pacific] College, Gulf Coast Bible College, or Bay Ridge Christian College. Neither do they include the values of state held properties such as office buildings, campgrounds, nursing homes, and so forth. Altogether, the strong growth of property value demonstrates that the movement reached unprecedented levels of material prosperity during the postwar era.

Increased wealth marked only one route by which Church of God people moved toward the religious mainstream. A second is illustrated by the architecture of the new buildings constructed with increased contributions. The Baby Boom, and the revival of interest in religion combined to strain church building capacities. Once construction materials were available, congregations began replacing outmoded facilities that they had outgrown. However, building committees selected designs that expressed values beyond mere functionality. Postwar church architecture suggests that Church of God congregations were increasingly representative of the American middle class. The architectural histories of congregations in towns like New Albany, Indiana or St. Joseph and Lansing, Michigan make the point. In each case the congregation constructed a building during the postwar period, and the new edifices were a far cry from earlier buildings occupied by the congregations. One of the earlier buildings occupied by the New Albany congregation was a flat-roofed frame structure, known as the "Tabernacle," that more nearly resembled a warehouse than a house of worship. The church eventually constructed a brick structure of traditional American Protestant style, complete with split chancel. The new buildings at St. Joseph and Lansing were architectural twins. Constructed of hewn limestone, these traditional buildings could easily be taken for the home of a Presbyterian or Congregationalist church. They said "middle-class church" as loudly as any church building in America. In each case the congregation decided to construct a building that was beautiful as well as functional. Beautiful buildings

Pennway Church of God (formerly South State Street Church of God), Lansing, Michigan. The building was dedicated in 1955.

Photograph courtesy of the Pennway Church of God, Lansing, Michigan.

First Church of God, St. Joseph, Michigan, in 1952.

Photograph courtesy of the St. Joseph First Church of God, St. Joseph, Michigan.

The First Church of God, New Albany, Indiana, gathered in front of the Gospel Tabernacle, dedicated in 1931.

Photograph courtesy of the New Albany First Church of God, New Albany, Indiana.

First Church of God, New Albany, Indiana, dedicated in 1951.

Photograph courtesy of the New Albany First Church of God, New Albany, Indiana.

express something of the values and self-image of the congregations that contribute the money and time to build them. But these three examples painted a picture that was duplicated across the Church of God in the postwar era. Constructed of stone or brick in classic styles and located in handsome neighborhoods, new church construction combined with material prosperity to give the impression that the social location of the Church of God movement was shifting toward the mainstream of American Protestantism.

Another indication of this shift was the increased attention people began giving to the retirement of ministers. The care of elderly gospel workers had a lengthy history in the Church of God. The Gospel Trumpet Company built a home for aged *Trumpet* workers and saints shortly after its arrival in Anderson. About the same time Scandinavian-American Church of God folk at *Den Evangeliske Basun* Publishing Company founded the Church of God Old People's Home of the Northwest in St. Paul Park, Minnesota. The latter was not rebuilt after it was destroyed by fire, but the Anderson home housed residents into the 1950s—even after it had become an Anderson College dormitory. Undergraduates lived on the lower floor while the dwindling number of elderly lived out their days in upstairs rooms. But it was in the creation of the Pension Board of the Church of God that the movement expressed a systematic and long-term interest in the retirement of its elderly servants.

In the dark years of the Great Depression Elver F. Adcock had appealed to Church of God congregations and individuals to become regular contributors to the Minister's Benefit Association. This early effort created a fund to underwrite burial costs and provide limited assistance to permanently disabled and retired clergy that could offer scarcely more than minimal relief. But Adcock hoped for a larger financial program, and postwar prosperity enabled the realization of his dream. In 1948 the General Ministerial Assembly approved the creation of a voluntary retirement plan, with Lawrence Brooks named as executive secretary-treasurer. In its early years the Pension Fund of the Church of God enjoyed only limited participation. Some saints needed to be convinced that a pension fund did not demonstrate a lack of faith in God to provide for the material needs of the church's servants. At its inception the plan called for enrolled ministers to contribute 3 percent of their annual salaries matched by an 8 percent contribution from the congregation they served. In its first year the pension plan enrolled 267 members and achieved assets of slightly less than $130,000. To aid in capitalizing the fund, Church of God World Service, Warner Press, and the Woman's Missionary Society contributed slightly over $1 million, with the women's group providing more than half of that total. By the end of its first twenty-five years of operations the Pension Board held custody of assets totaling $15 million. The exponential growth of its ministerial pension program illustrates in yet another way the prosperity of the Church of God movement during the postwar period. But these years witnessed more than growing material prosperity. The movement's constituency also increased dramatically. Membership grew from 71,000 to 98,000 during the decade 1940–50, an increase of nearly 41 percent.[5] During the next decade membership grew another 32 percent to 129,000.[6] By 1970 membership had more than doubled since 1940, reaching a total of nearly 148,000 adherents.[7] Measured by membership growth or material prosperity, the period from 1945 to 1970 were salad years in the Church of God movement.

Changing Attitudes and Ethos

Scholarly studies completed by Church of God ministers early in this period indicate that attitudes in the movement were also undergoing significant change. A. Leland Forrest[8] and Valorous B. Clear[9] wrote doctoral dissertations that studied the Church of God movement through the lens of the sociology of religion. Coupled with Robert Reardon's Oberlin thesis these works document important attitudinal changes in the Church of God during the forties and early fifties. The Forrest and Clear dissertations were both indebted to the theories of the German theologian, Ernst Troeltsch. Troeltsch applied sociological theory to the study of theology and religion, and this work was mediated to an American audience through the applications of American scholars such as Liston Pope. Forrest depended on Pope's work, while Clear's dissertation was shaped by his reading of H. Richard Niebuhr. Together, their dissertations pointed to a maturation that had reached a level where the movement now produced ministers and scholars willing and able to study it within the theoretical framework of an academic discipline. What Otto Linn brought to biblical studies, Forrest and Clear brought to the study of the Church of God itself.

Leland Forrest's dissertation was the first large study of the Church of God undertaken according to a scholarly methodology. To be sure, C. E. Brown was widely read in church history and interpreted the Church of God in its light. As perceptive as Brown's work was, it remained for the next generation to apply techniques and theories of scholarly disciplines to the study of the movement. Forrest in particular studied changes in the movement as examples of a theory that interpreted the experience of religious communions as a transition from sectarian protest group to stable church. He was interested primarily in changes that had occurred in Church of God doctrine and institutions. The key element of his research involved a survey of four hundred Church of God ministers. His findings, based on the answers of one hundred ministers who returned his questionnaire, offer important insights into the changes that had occurred in the movement by 1940 and which accelerated in the postwar era.

Forrest considered the Church of God in the light of categories developed by Troeltsch and applied to American church groups by Liston Pope in such pathbreaking studies as *Millhands and Preachers,* the product of his research into religious attitudes and practices in a North Carolina milltown. Governed by his European setting Troeltsch had divided religious groups into two categories—church and sect. The former was the formal, state-sponsored, institutional church and the latter a voluntary community characterized by face-to-face relationships and often born in protest.[10] The American religious landscape offered no precise fit with Troeltsch's model; denominations were neither church nor sect. American sociologists of religion therefore often elaborated on these categories. Forrest's dissertation thus worked with a model that classified religious groups in one of four categories: sect, sect-type denomination, church-type denomination, and church. Especially in America it was understood that religious groups often start as sects but over time mature, in the process moving toward more institutionalized expressions of religion. Forrest wanted to identify the extent to which the Church of God movement had shifted along a continuum that began in "sect" and concluded in "church."

Forrest's study employed categories drawn from Pope's work to assess change in the Church of God on several lines. He wanted to locate the movement in transition from "sect" to "church" along each of five principal axes. (1) A key indicator of transition was property. Members of a "sect," in this view, were located on the margins of society, lacking in wealth and social power both individually and as a corporate body. (2) A second axis measured group change in terms of its attitudes toward other religious bodies. Sects typically held established churches up to ridicule at worst or refuse to co-operate with them at best. (3) An attitude of otherworldliness characterized the third axis. Sectarians' primary interest and emphasis is on the world to come; the present society can offer little of enduring value. (4) Sects making the transition toward a more churchly location also demonstrate that shift by moving from the fringes of their culture toward its center. The sectarian group yields some of its behavioral shibboleths in favor of general community norms. (5) The fifth axis by which Forrest measured change concerned worship. Whereas sectarian groups favored spontaneity and fervor, churchly groups worshiped in a more organized and restrained manner.[11]

Although Forrest noted several indicators that still identified the Church of God as a sectarian group, he found more reason to locate the movement in transition from sect-type denomination toward more churchly organization. In the years immediately following World War II respondents to his survey were well aware that the Church of God was enjoying increasing material prosperity. Not only were church property values rising; so were pastoral salaries. Church of God ministers, at least those who responded to Forrest's questionnaire, also exhibited a more cooperative attitude toward other religious groups. A full 96 percent of respondents said they participated in interfaith ministerial fellowships and/or the local council of churches. Nearly the same percentage reported that they preplanned their worship services, a far cry from the days when camp meeting preachers waited on the platform to see which of them the Spirit would lead to the pulpit. Church of God congregations were also moving nearer to the center of their local communities, as indicated by their members' and pastors' participation in service clubs and the adoption of local standards of dress and entertainment. Such factors indicated that the Church of God had achieved sufficient stability and organizational maturity to conclude that it was no longer a sectarian protest group. The movement was on the way toward becoming a middle class church.[12]

The Church of God and Ecumenical Christianity

Forrest's USC dissertation and Reardon's Oberlin thesis both reported a significant change in Church of God ministers' attitudes toward ecumenical organizations such as the Federal Council of Churches and other interfaith endeavors. Not all shared the new attitude of openness, and the division between ecumenically-minded ministers and those who opposed such connections deepened in the postwar period. Changing attitudes often flowed out of increased contact with non-Church of God ministers in local communities. Church of God pastors began joining local ministerial fellowships and/or service clubs. As fellow Rotarians or Kiwanians and at community ministers meetings, community-minded ministers encountered pastoral colleagues from the world of denominational Christianity and discovered them to be earnest Christians. It was but a short step from these encounters to participation in community-wide events such as local Thanksgiving and Good Friday services. The movement was shedding its old separatist posture and judgmentalism. Wider became the route by which the Church of God entered the religious mainstream of America.

Contacts between the Church of God and denominations as well as interfaith organizations increased corporately as well as individually. The movement had regularly sent observers to national and international ecumenical meetings as early as 1925. In August of that year C. J. Blewitt, of the New

York Missionary Home, and missionary to Sweden Carl Forsberg attended meetings of the Universal Conference on Life and Work in Stockholm. Blewitt kept an open mind toward the proceedings and was impressed by "so many great men and women showing such humility and earnestly seeking to get the world to understand the meaning of love in domestic and public relations."[13] Two years later the World Conference on Faith and Order convened in Lausanne. No saints represented the movement at this conference, but R. L. Berry took notice of it. He disapproved of an approach to Christian unity through federation. Besides, opined Berry, only the Holy Spirit could unite believers. However, even though he believed that the Devil would visit Lausanne, "God will also be there if any of his people are, and we cannot doubt that. So we believe God will be there to inspire his people to real unity such as the Bible demands and inspires."[14]

In some cases the commitments of individuals brought them into association with projects sponsored by ecumenical federations such as the National Council of Churches or its predecessor Federal Council. Such relationships were not always without controversy among the saints. As a graduate student at the University of Chicago Otto F. Linn had made a name for himself as a promising New Testament scholar. When the National Council's Bible translation project, the Revised Standard Version, got underway, Linn was invited to join the work and served on a translation subcommittee. Few in the Church of God were aware of Linn's connection with the RSV, but many people objected to its use in the movement's Sunday school curriculum and magazine.

Many fundamentalist and conservative Protestant groups were hostile toward the Revised Standard Version. There was a resentment that would have befallen any translation put forward to replace the beloved King James Bible. However, when the faithful read the RSV rendering of Isaiah 7:14 and its substitution of the word *virgin* with *young woman,* resentment erupted into anger. In the eye of many a believer, the organization that sponsored the project appeared to be attacking the doctrine of the virgin birth of Jesus. The militant anticommunist climate of America in the early 1950s led some conservatives to the suspicion that the RSV was part of a communist plot to undermine the faith of God-fearing Americans. Thus it was that some saints were appalled to find a favorable review of the hated translation in the pages of the *Gospel Trumpet.* Ministers like George Ramsey, Sr., later a Bible professor at Anderson College, made it their personal agenda to persuade the church of the RSV's merits, but to no avail. Editor Harold L. Phillips, who had succeeded C. E. Brown in 1952, had adopted a policy that permitted writers like Ramsey and others to cite the RSV in articles submitted for publication in the *Trumpet.* Angry letters demanded that the new editor drop the policy. Phillips had been installed in his office less than a year when he was visited by a prominent minister who insisted that Phillips refuse to allow RSV citations. However, he refused to be cowed, despite threats to cancel subscriptions.[15]

More telling than occasional individual forays into ecumenical cooperation is the lengthy history of Church of God agency involvement with program units of first the Federal, and then National Council of Churches. The Gospel Trumpet Company's connection with cooperative curriculum projects was but the earliest example of participation in cooperative Christian endeavors. The International Sunday School Outlines began publication in 1866, and from the twenties on the Board of Christian Education and the Gospel Trumpet Company used those outlines for the development of Sunday school curriculum. Later the Gospel Trumpet Company/Warner Press joined such organizations as the Protestant Owned Publishers Association and the Evangelical Publishers Association.

Other agencies and divisions also maintained long-term ecumenical relationships. The Church of God movement did not join either the Federal or the National Council, but their program units made concessions to the movement's organizational practices, accepting the participation of Church of God agency members on such terms as did not violate movement convictions. During his tenure as head of Church of God World Service C. W. Hatch, later the first executive secretary of the Executive Council, was for many years a member of the Federal Council of Churches' Commission on Stewardship. Hatch chaired the Commission at one point, and through this connection his booklet "Stewardship Enriches Life" was widely disseminated among mainline denominations. Later Directors of World Service Paul Tanner and James Williams continued the relationship that Hatch had inaugurated. Similar relationships existed between other agencies and ecumenical organizations. As early as 1918 the Missionary Board became a full member of the Foreign Missions Conference, and a decade later the Board of Christian Education joined the International Council of Christian Education. The most ecumenically active of the agencies, in 1935 the Board of Christian Education also joined committees that produced graded curricula and in 1943 the World Council of Christian Education. Youth programs, home missions, and the women's organization all had ties to co-operative associations reaching back as far as 1930.

After 1940 the doctrinal practice of Christian unity known as come-outism waned in the Church of God. Involvement with other church bodies, whether in local ministerial groups or cooperative community church projects, provided a viable alternative practice. For some Church of God leaders, involvement in various ecumenical projects or task forces seemed not only appropriate but right. Sometimes involvement resulted from the personal commitments of individuals like John W. V. Smith, who for decades served as a member of the National Council's Commission on Faith and Order. Largely through his active involvement, the Church of God has been the only nonmember of the National Council with uninterrupted Faith and Order participation, a record that stretches back to 1957.[16] In other cases the relationship between the Church of God and ecumenical Christianity developed as boards and agencies discovered the resources offered by the program units of the National Council. These affiliations made practical as well as theological sense to a generation of leadership that had developed a more cosmopolitan worldview. However, the movement's theological and political conservatism did not mix well with the National Council's reputation for social and political liberalism. That the movement's boards and agencies benefited from their associations with the National Council did not mollify those who thought that in them the movement was unequally yoked. Nevertheless, expanding interfaith relationships provide an important illustration of the manner in which elements of the Church of God movement made peace with American Christianity during World War II and the postwar era.

Altered Practices

During the postwar period significant church practices underwent dramatic changes that brought the Church of God closer to the mainstream of American Protestantism. In the movement's early days one could occasionally find people who abandoned medical careers to answer a call to ministry. S. G. Bryant and George Achor both left their medical practices to become flying messengers as the nineteenth-century turned into the twentieth. In a movement that urged its members to trust God for healing, a career in medicine lacked esteem. By the middle of the century that attitude had been nearly reversed. The Church of God had already commissioned physicians and nurses as medical missionaries to British East Africa, and Anderson College alumni were graduating from medical schools to open practices in the United States as well.

The practice of divine healing had been undergoing alteration almost since the moment of E. E. Byrum's death in 1942. He had long considered himself the recipient of a divine gift of spiritual healing, and after leaving the editor's office in 1916 he maintained a national ministry that specialized in prayer for the divine healing of the sick and afflicted.[17] Byrum's death nearly coincided with the development of penicillin, the antibiotic that revolutionized the treatment of bacterial infections. It was but the first in a wave of advances in therapies and techniques that only swelled through the 1940s, '50s, and beyond. Physicians might not have been able to cure the common cold, but by 1960 the resources of medical practice had advanced far beyond the days when Byrum first told D. S. Warner that God had gifted him for a healing ministry. It was inevitable that Church of God people would avail themselves of these resources. In this as in many other areas of American life, the experience of the men and women who served in the armed forces during World War II affected Church of God practice. Military doctors and their protocols certainly made no provision for the divine healing of the sick, and soldiers received the same standard treatment. Church of God constituents returned home after the war with a new attitude toward the wonders of modern medicine. As a consequence, some saints enthusiastically availed themselves of physicians and medicine while others remained true to the movement's original doctrinal practice. Still others prayed for healing, visited doctors, and suffered a guilty conscience. With no twinge of guilt a growing number prayed that God would guide the physician's hand.

By 1960 divine healing had lost its position as a core doctrinal practice in the Church of God movement. The divine healing service remained a mainstay of Anderson Camp meeting, but in the movement's early days the divine healing of the sick had been emphasized as one of the distinguishing marks of the true church. Yet, in 1960, R. Eugene Sterner's widely used introduction to the Church of God, *We Reach Our Hands in Fellowship*,[18] made no mention of divine healing in its list of the movement's distinctive teachings. In 1978 Sterner published *Healing and Wholeness*, the latest in a lengthy string of works on this subject published by the Gospel Trumpet Company/Warner Press. Sterner's book differed from its predecessors in that he wrote it in part to help the church recover a doctrinal practice that he feared was being lost. To be sure, he was eager to explore the practice in the light of recent medical and psychological advances. But Sterner also thought that it had fallen under neglect and that "our concepts need to be strengthened, deepened, and clarified."[19] Among those that needed clarification was the long-term idea that saw divine healing as part of the Atonement. Sterner made no comment on that view, preferring instead to consider the practice in relation to the healing character of God to which all creation testified. Furthermore, Sterner worked hard to disabuse readers of the old notion that sickness and disease were consequences of sin. Although he did connect sin to personal illness, Sterner made it quite clear that this cause-effect relationship did not hold in every case. Sin in the generic sense—the sinful condition of humanity—also had to be factored into the causes of illness, and therefore "it is wrong to condemn a sick person by assuming that there is some personal sin in his or her life."[20]

Sterner paid particular attention to developments in the field of psychology, specifically Freudian psychoanalysis. In this regard he extended the movement's discussion of divine healing in two directions. First, he established a strong connection between the mind and body. Secondly, and quite pointedly, he included mental illness and emotional disturbances under the umbrella of divine healing. In taking up this line of thought he followed the lead of the English clergyman and counselor Leslie Weatherhead, who combined a wholistic reading of the Bible and Christian faith with psychotherapeutic technique.[21] Sterner clearly thought that the movement's commitment to the doctrine of holiness had frustrated a better understanding of the relationship between physical illness and what he called our "deeper nature."

> We who have been taught holiness have been prone to pretend that we have no problems, that all our questions have been answered, all our doubts expunged, and all our temptations have been put in the past forever. There isn't much room left for confession, for real honesty about ourselves. We tend to "put our best foot forward," to wear a righteous mask and play a sanctimonious role, for if we open up and reveal our real needs we may be rejected. This must be challenged. Honesty and openness are necessary to healing. We may sometimes be seeking physical healing when the deep need, the real need, is for spiritual healing. Our sins may not always be the things we do.[22]

Sterner thought that the time had long passed when people of the Church of God should hammer away at biblical promises and demand of God the healing they offered. Given the powerful connection between mind and body that Sterner deeply appreciated, it was unthinkable to ignore the emotional and spiritual needs of people while expecting healing for their bodies. The "wisdom given by God" in the Bible required this admission.[23] Sterner's book maintained in principle the movement's historic commitment to its reading of the Bible's teaching on divine healing. At the same time, however, both in its stated concern that healing be given renewed emphasis and in its incorporation of psychological theory, his work illustrates significant changes in both theology and attitudes concerning this longstanding doctrinal practice.

Divine healing was not the only doctrinal practice undergoing alteration during the postwar period. Even during the war years Earl Slacum worried that leading ministers had lowered the standard of personal holiness. After the war signs abounded that people in the Church of God were modifying their understanding and practice of this central doctrine. In no area of concern were these signs greater than the traditional holiness shibboleths regarding entertainment. The journalist H. L. Mencken once famously but erroneously described Puritanism as the sneaking suspicion that somewhere somebody was having a good time. Mencken's description would have been better aimed at the churches of the holiness movement, the Church of God included, especially before World War II. During the postwar period the saints began revising their attitudes toward some forms of entertainment. In this they were led by the youth culture that itself became a social force during this era. In short, some of the saints began to have a little fun.

The churches of the Holiness Movement traditionally tried to control personal habits from the use of alcohol and tobacco to dress, as well as the forms of entertainment open to the saints. In this the Church of God resembled groups such as the Church of the Nazarene and the Wesleyan Methodists. Tobacco contaminated the body that was the temple of the Holy Spirit, and alcoholic beverages were associated with saloons and other locations of sin and vice. Like many other American Protestant groups, the Church of God from its very inception had been aligned with the prohibitionist movement. Little changed in Church of God attitudes towards alcohol and tobacco during the postwar years. But even in this area there were signs of moderation, in that it became more acceptable to patronize restaurants that served alcoholic beverages. They may not have imbibed, but saints, or perhaps their children, were not as insistent on shunning the very appearance of evil. The use of caffeine told a story of more rapid change in both attitude and practice. Early in its history the Church of God made little distinction between drinking coffee or alcohol. Coffee contained caffeine, a stimulant that saints were strongly discouraged from consuming. Even Scandinavians, whose coffee drinking reached legendary proportions, gave up their habit when they took their stand with the saints.[24] By the end of the postwar era, however, this aspect of holiness practice had been transformed to the point that coffee and doughnuts became standard fare in adult Sunday school classes across the United States and Canada.

The practice of holiness also relaxed in the area of personal entertainment. Nineteenth-century holiness preachers had condemned the theater and novel-reading, as well as ballroom dancing and other activities that mixed the sexes socially. Shooting pool and even bowling were condemned because of their association with drinking and gambling. These prohibitions remained in force during the early twentieth century, with the movie house added as an extension of the theater. However, English departments at Anderson College and Pacific Bible College rehabilitated the novel. Attitudes toward movies began changing in the 1940s, as Earl Slacum's fears document. Acceptance of movies accelerated during the '50s and '60s. Biblical epics like *The Robe* and the blockbusters *The Ten Commandments* and *Ben Hur* made movie-going appear less threatening to virtue and even a positively wholesome activity.

Young people in the Church of God, as adolescents everywhere in post-war America, were catalysts of change. Slowly but surely the teenage culture reshaped attitudes towards some forms of entertainment and with them the movement's practice of holiness. By the end of the era youth camp administrators—in the main ministers and local pastors—in many, but not all, regions of the country no longer segregated boys and girls during swimming time. The holiness prohibition of social dancing also eroded during the fifties, but more rapidly in the sixties and seventies, under the relentless pressure of the youth culture. By the end of the postwar era the Church of God doctrinal practice of holiness had considerably accommodated to mainstream American culture. Individuals and congregations in some regions were quicker to adapt than others. Ministers who were college or seminary graduates had been taught by their sociology professors that such changes were part of a process called cultural accommodation. That was far less threatening than what other pastors still referred to as "compromise with the world." By either description, less stringent holiness practices meant that the Church of God more nearly resembled other Protestant Christians in America.

Still another doctrinal practice to undergo change during the postwar era concerned the movement's commitment to pacifism. In this case it was World War II that fundamentally shifted a Church of God practice toward the Protestant mainstream. That the practice had been altered became apparent in the years following the war.[25] During the 1930s movement leaders repeatedly disavowed war as an instrument of national policy. The newly organized International Youth Convention repeatedly issued statements declaring its members' refusal to participate in any future war. In that same decade Adam Miller, Russell Olt, and F. G. Smith founded the Peace Fellowship of the Church of God. However, after the United States declared war on Japan and Germany the percentage of Church of God men who identified themselves as conscientious objectors was only fractionally larger than that for the general population.[26] In 1941 only twenty Church of God men resided in conscientious objector camps. Moreover, movement leadership's support of these men was never strong. The president of the Executive Council declared, "Our purpose is not to make conscientious objectors of our young men, but rather to give assistance to such as need assistance in obtaining this classification."[27] By 1945 the movement was $18,000 in arrears in its financial obligations to Civilian Public Service for the support of Church of God conscientious objectors living in its camps. Simultaneously, ministers availed themselves of the movement's new sponsorship of the military chaplaincy program. In 1941 nearly as many Church of God men were chaplains as resided in the CO camps.

Comment on the issue of war and peace during the postwar era demonstrates a further erosion of the movement's early pacifist commitments. Articles appeared in the *Gospel Trumpet* supporting Christians' participation in military service and hinting rather darkly that some students attended Anderson College only to escape the draft; such students were not regarded with good will. Only a few letters to the *Trumpet* editor spoke out in favor of pacifism. The most outspoken of these writers was Lansing pastor Robert Hazen, who described himself as one of "a very, very small minority in the Church of God who thinks with our Quaker and Friends [sic] brethren on the question of peace."[28] Hazen asked whether the "peace minority" had declined to such numbers that military service was no longer a controversial issue among Church of God people. He may very well have been correct. When Anderson College named its new library, it chose to honor Charles E. Wilson, former general manager of the Delco-Remy Division of General Motors in Anderson and—more to Hazen's point—secretary of defense in the first Eisenhower administration.

During the Vietnam War the majority of Anderson College students supported the presidency and policies of Richard Nixon, electing him in a mock election over rivals Eugene McCarthy and Robert Kennedy. A minority opposed the war, some so strongly as to prompt their participation in student demonstrations in Washington, DC. But the language and arguments they employed at no point connected their objections to the historic Christian pacifism of the early Church of God. Instead student opposition expressed itself in arguments and a rhetoric that could not be distinguished from the tone of student dissent on virtually any American college campus.[29] On the question of war and peace, students at the movement's largest college thought and sounded like many other anti-war protestors. Without a distinctively Christian narrative to support the movement's increasingly tenuous commitment to pacifism, the number of Church of God people committed to the doctrinal practice of pacifism melted.[30] The Church of God looked increasingly like a middle American Protestant denomination.

Pacifism was but one expression of what could be termed the social consciousness of the early Church of God. In its early decades the movement manifested its social concern in a variety of attitudes and measures. R. L. Berry expressed one such attitude when he opposed tithing because it discriminated against the poor.[31] Similarly, the saints who gathered in the New York missionary home under the leadership of Axchie Bolitho stated their belief that "race, color, and class are all contrary to the Christian spirit" just before declaring that "the profit motive in business must be replaced by a spirit of good will."[32] In the movement's earliest days the saints similarly expressed a concern for human need other than salvation. During the *Trumpet's* years in Grand Junction, Sebastian Michels enlarged his home for the children of the flying messengers, transforming it into an orphanage. In 1895 Mary Householder, of Danville, Illinois, started a home for unwed mothers. "Rescue work" was the subject of an issue of *Our Ministerial Letter* that explained the biblical foundation for caring for the sick and the needy, and issues of the *Gospel Trumpet* announced that the paper was free to the poor.[33] Although C. E. Brown expressed his personal sympathy with Walter Rauschenbusch's intention to Christianize the social order, it would be inaccurate to characterize the movement's early social concerns as an effort to remake the society according to the kingdom of God. The saints directed their attention and efforts toward the material problems of individuals.

Similar approaches to social needs continued after the institution-building of the twenties. In fact, the development of organizations enabled broader social ministry. After World War II a group led by Russell Olt and E. E. Perry became acutely concerned for the health and well-being of Europeans dislocated by the war. The Displaced Persons Act of 1950 provided for their relocation to the United States if sponsored by an American family. At the urging of Olt and Perry, the Church of God established a commission to coordinate this work. However, the commission was small and its financial resources too limited to allow for effective cooperation with the federal bureaucracies necessarily involved in bringing European immigrants to the United States. Therefore the Church of God commission cooperated with Church World Service, an agency of the National Council of Churches, which handled all of the clerical and administrative work involved in the process of relocating displaced Europeans. More Church of God families volunteered as sponsors than were needed to accommodate those saints among the millions of displaced Europeans, so Olt appealed to the church to sponsor Europeans of any creed or religion.[34]

The generation of Oberlin seminarians from the Church of God was a significant element that brought questions and issues of social justice to the attention of the Church of God in the postwar period. Oberlin Professor Clarence Tucker Craig had taught his students that the gospel could not be neatly separated into personal salvation or social action. To be a follower of Jesus embraced concern for human beings, body and soul.[35] John W. V. Smith articulated this ideal, as did Robert Reardon and Louis Meyer.

Aspects of the career of Robert Reardon (1919–) are illustrative of the social commitments of the Oberlin graduates who assumed leadership positions in the late fifties and sixties. Born in the Chicago missionary home, the younger son of E. A. and Pearl Reardon spent much of his boyhood in Anderson in the shadow of Park Place Church of God and the saints who regularly gathered there. E. A. Reardon twice served Park Place church as its pastor, and his son played with the children of the saints before later learning to listen to the adults conversing in the Reardon parlor about issues facing the movement.[36] Reardon graduated from Anderson College and joined the widening stream of alumni heading to Oberlin. In 1941 he married Geraldine Hurst, herself a rising young preacher. After earning the S.T.M., he served as pastor of the Church of God in Chester, Pennsylvania before returning to Anderson as assistant to John Morrison. Groomed for the assignment, in 1958 Reardon succeeded Morrison at the helm of Anderson College. Although covered by a velvet glove, his hand always held the tiller firmly in grasp. Urbane, articulate, and a consummate storyteller, Reardon presided over the college during two and a half decades of unparalleled expansion. First GIs, and then their baby-boom children enabled as well as forced the growth of programs and campus facilities.

No college program or campus event of consequence occurred without Reardon's blessing. In the early sixties new programs began catching the spirit of the Kennedy administration. A limited version of the Peace Corps, TRI-S (for Student Summer Service) was launched in 1964. During the same period Professor Marie Strong founded a service organization called Christianity in Action (and ironically nicknamed "CIA"). But such programs did not express the full measure of the college or Reardon's commitment to the emerging issues of social justice. As protestors marched across the South, Anderson College students, faculty, and administrators organized a rally supporting Blacks in Birmingham, Alabama. Southern parents expressed their unhappiness, but Reardon's support stood firm. On the other hand, he refused Black students permission to form a Black student organization on campus. It wasn't that he opposed Black consciousness. Rather, Reardon wanted to avoid polarizing the campus over a cause that he firmly believed should join Christians.

In 1968 Reardon drafted an Open Door resolution that was adopted by the General Assembly that June. The resolution culminated a decade of study that searched for improvement in race relationships in the Church of God and called every congregation to a practice that conformed to the following statement: "In accordance with the teaching Scriptures, this congregation of the Church of God welcomes fellow Christians without regard to race, color, or national origin, to participate fully and without reservation in its fellowship and work."[37] It was Reardon who brought the resolution before the Assembly, and not without some risk to the college with which he was closely identified. There was the distinct possibility that Southern parents angered by the resolution and similar activities on the Anderson campus would send their students elsewhere.

From 1957 on, church leaders tried to address race issues. Initially their record of achievement was checkered at best. The General Assembly adopted the Open Door resolution, but when Black ministers asked where Blacks were in the agencies they were told that the office building had a Black custodian.[38] It was in reaction to such attitudes that the climate and church policy began to change. In response to a joint call from the Executive Committee of the Executive Council and the National Association of the Church of God, in 1964 the General Ministerial Assembly adopted a resolution authorizing the creation of a permanent Commission on Social Concerns.[39] Race relations was only one in a list of social issues named in the enabling resolution. To the traditional holiness causes of temperance, gambling, and tobacco use were joined concerns for peace and world order. In the area of human relations, alongside race relations the resolution specified civil liberties, church-state relationships, and housing as matters under the new commission's purview.[40] In the ensuing years Assembly members also ratified or elected African American ministers to a growing number of national church offices. Robert Culp, of Toledo, Ohio and Samuel G. Hines, of Washington, DC, served multiple terms as chair of the General Assembly. Long-term Chicago pastor Marcus H. Morgan chaired the Executive Council from 1970 to 1981. In direct response to the call for a Black presence in national church leadership, Edward L. Foggs was elected and ratified as the first associate executive secretary of the Executive Council. And in 1976 the General Assembly ratified the appointment of James Earl Massey as speaker on the church's radio program, *Christian Brotherhood Hour.*

When combined with the actions and statements of several individuals, the steps taken by church leadership in the sixties and seventies point to changes in the movement's approach to social ministry. In its early days the saints attempted to address human need on an individual basis. The hungry were fed, orphans sheltered, and the poor given copies of the *Gospel Trumpet* in a spirit that followed Jesus' saying about the cup of water given in his name. By the end of the postwar period the church attempted to address the pressing social issues of the day through statements, strategies, and policy measures that resembled the discourse and actions of mainline Protestant denominations. Church of God social concern was always buttressed by appeal to the Bible, but both the subject of that concern and the actions that addressed it mirrored discussions in the larger society.

Hymnody provides one final measure of the extent to which the Church of God movement entered the mainstream of American Protestantism following World War II. In 1953 and again in 1971 new hymnals were published, the 1953 *Hymnal of the Church of God* being the first major hymnal to appear in two decades. Both were the product of a committee of musicians and ministers chaired by Robert Nicholson. In 1953 Nicholson was a faculty member at Anderson College and director of the college choir. Later he was appointed dean of the college. In both cases the committees asked ministers and church leaders to rate songs in the previously published hymnal then in use.[41]

The revision of a popular hymnal is a potentially controversial task. Church people will sooner purchase a new translation of the Bible than they will part with beloved hymns and gospel songs. Undaunted by this tendency, the 1953 and 1971 hymnal committees pursued their assignment in a manner that introduced the Church of God to a growing number of classic hymns of the Protestant tradition. Thus, to cite but one example, the 1971 hymnal included for the first time in a Church of God hymnal Harry Emerson Fosdick's "God of Grace and God of Glory." Of course, size limitations required the elimination of old songs in order to make room for the new. Several different criteria could be applied when deciding which songs were candidates for elimination, not all of the criteria directly concerning musicality or popularity. Thus, for example, the 1971 hymnal dropped the popular invitation song, "Whiter than Snow," out of respect for the church's African American community and others in the movement for whom the privileged use of the adjective *white* was objectionable.

Regardless the criteria employed for exclusion, the general tendency of hymnal revisions reduced the number of hymns and gospel songs written by Church of God songwriters. Church of God songbooks prior to the 1930 *Hymns and Spiritual Songs* featured the work of musicians and poets among the saints. The 1930 hymnal was the first to intentionally include musical literature from outside sources,[42] and this intention continued aggressively in the selection processes that produced the 1953 and 1971 hymnals. The net effect reduced the number of Church of God hymns and gospel songs in each successive edition of the movement's general hymnal. There is also this difference between the 1930 hymnal and its successors: later hymnals differed from the 1930 edition on another highly significant print. Although diminished from the movement's early days, the practice of songwriting remained alive and well in 1930 whereas by the postwar era it had effectively come to an end or dramatically changed form. Few new hymns or songs for the church were produced by Church of God songwriters after 1950. Replacing music for the church was an updated version of an old tradition in American Protestant music—the gospel song written for small ensembles and/or soloists. Throughout the fifties the "Christian Brothers" quartet sang this music on the *Christian Brotherhood Hour*. After 1960 it took a new turn in the hands of such songwriters as William "Bill" and Gloria Gaither, who were leaders in first wave of what came to be the burgeoning field of contemporary Christian music. A strong strain of musical creativity continued in the Church of God, but it was directed toward an audience much wider than the movement itself and as such did not often sound the theological themes distinctive to the Church of God. Whether in terms, then, of general hymnals published in the postwar period or in the new field of contemporary Christian music, the Church of God shifted toward, for some, the hymnody of mainstream American Protestantism and for others the popular songs of American Evangelicalism. In either case the direction of the shift was away from the theologically distinctive musical literature of the Church of God.

Moving Toward the Center

Various indicators strongly suggest that the Church of God movement shifted toward the center of American Protestantism during the period from the end of World War II through 1970. This is not to say that the entire movement experienced theological and social realignment. Movement leadership's changing commitments and relationships disturbed many in the Church of God, and in certain instances that leadership preferred that the grassroots church be kept largely in the dark about some of those relationships. However, measured by other indices many grassroots congregations were also shifting toward the center of American Protestantism.

The Church of God and its constituency participated in postwar prosperity and took a large stride toward the middle class. Measured against the well-established denominations of American Christianity, the Church of God movement may still have looked to be a poor cousin. Nevertheless, its real property assets jumped in value after the war in terms of local congregational holdings as well as the real property value of national agencies. Moreover, the upward social mobility of local church members was reflected in both the style and cost of their newly constructed church buildings. During the same period the movement undertook the creation of a ministerial pension fund. The first generation of Church of God ministers looked down on instruments of financial security such as life insurance because they were viewed as signs that people lacked faith in God to provide their material needs. That the movement created a ministerial pension fund signaled more than an increase in its corporate wealth; the Church of God was also shifting away from some of its early separatism.

A radical theological option presented itself to conservative American Protestants in the 1950s. Fundamentalism began developing the momentum that later made it a force with which to be reckoned in American society. Although Fundamentalism may have attracted isolated individuals in the Church of God, it is a fair question to ask why the bulk of the movement did not march to its beat. Three factors explain why there was little likelihood that the movement would make common cause with Fundamentalists. First, regardless whether they were accurate in their perception, Church of God people associated Fundamentalists with dispensational premillennialism. That eschatology was objectionable to Church of God conservatives because its reading of the apocalyptic literature of the Bible contradicted the work of F. G. Smith and others. More moderate voices in the Church of God rejected premillennialism on the basis of their historical-critical exegetical methods. Secondly, Fundamentalism also rested on a rationalist epistemology that seemed inevitably to insist on doctrinal statements as the foundation of fellowship. Indeed, some Fundamentalists defined a Christian on the basis of whether he or she would subscribe to a list of "fundamentals." To insist on a creed or doctrinal statement as the basis of Christian fellowship violated one of the very deepest theological commitments of the Church of God movement. Finally, Fundamentalists often aligned themselves with some of the most conservative elements in American politics. Some of the most militant antimodernists were also militant anticommunists and advocated American isolationism. These political views ran counter to those of Church of God leadership, colored as they were by internationalism and a concern for the rights of working people and others on the margins of American society. For all of these reasons the Church of God movement was never a very good candidate to join cause with Fundamentalism. In the 1950s, however, the Fundamentalist movement itself divided into a conservative wing who retained that title and a more progressive group that called themselves "neo-evangelical." Later the "neo" was dropped, and Evangelicals went on to become a potent force in American culture. In the 1950s, however, later Evangelical institutional mainstays such as Fuller Theological Seminary were in their infancy. Church of God leaders looked in other directions when it came to transdenominational associations.

Given the movement's commitment to Christian unity, it was likely that many Church of God leaders would be attracted to elements of ecumenical Christianity. Some of them had been trained at Oberlin, where they were influenced by the ecumenism of Walter Marshall Horton. Two additional and related factors also help to explain ecumenical Christianity's attraction for some Church of God people. In the first place the eclipse of come-outism as the movement's doctrinal practice of Christian unity left some thoughtful individuals searching for the means to express this key theological commitment. This search was given additional force, secondly, by the vacuum of new reflection on the church and Christian unity by Church of God theologians after 1940. The National Council of Churches' Commission on Faith and Order seemed a viable alternative for Church of God leaders like seminary professor John W. V. Smith who possessed an abiding theological commitment to the movement's vision of Christian unity. On the other hand, the Council's program units offered resources that agency executives such as C. W. Hatch and T. Franklin Miller found invaluable for their work,

The changing practice of Christian unity was but one of several doctrinal practices the alteration of which during the postwar period further indicated a shift toward the Protestant mainstream. By the end of the postwar era Church of God separatism and radicalism had markedly diminished, while the movement became more centrist in the practices of divine healing, pacifism, holiness, and social advocacy. Church of God people consulted physicians, entered the armed forces, and entertained themselves in ways that distinguished them less and less from their fellow American Protestants. By the conclusion of the postwar era, the Church of God movement could no longer be described as a sectarian protest movement. No longer a prophetic protest against the division of the body of Christ, the Church of God movement looked elsewhere for a reason for being and found it in the therapeutic church.

Notes

1. *1940 Yearbook of the Church of God.*
2. *1950 Yearbook of the Church of God.*
3. *1960 Yearbook of the Church of God.*
4. *1970 Yearbook of the Church of God.*
5. *1940 Yearbook of the Church of God, 1950 Yearbook of the Church of God.*
6. *1960 Yearbook of the Church of God.*
7. *1970 Yearbook of the Church of God.*
8. *A Study of the Development of the Basic Doctrines and Institutional Patterns in the Church of God* (Anderson, Indiana), unpublished doctoral dissertation, University of Southern California, 1948.
9. *The Church of God: A Study in Social Adaptation,* unpublished doctoral dissertation, University of Chicago, 1953. Clear later published his dissertation under the title *Where the Saints Have Trod: A Social History of the Church of God Movement* (Chesterfield, Ind: Midwest Publications), 1977.

10. The German language conveniently provided two very different words by which each group was easily distinguished from the other. Troeltsch used *Kirche* to refer to the state church while *Gemeinde* signified the sect. Hence the Church of God in Germany is known as *Die Gemeinde Gottes*.

11. Forrest, *A Study of the Development of the Basic Doctrines and Institutional Patterns of the Church of God*, 164–165.

12. Ibid.

13. "Stockholm Conference," *GT* (September 24, 1925), 4–5.

14. "Can Any Good Come Out of Lausanne?", *GT* (July 14, 1927), inside front cover.

15. Phillips, Letter to the author, July 20, 2001. Phillips estimated that the magazine lost 1,500 subscriptions over its continued openness to the RSV.

16. For a discussion of the ecumenical involvement of the Church of God, and an argument for the participation of other holiness churches as well, see Gilbert W. Stafford, "The Faith and Order Movement: Holiness Church Participation," *Wesleyan Theological Journal*, Vol. 32 No. 1 (Spring 1997), 143–156. An edited version of Stafford's article is reprinted in Callen, ed., *Following the Light*, 353–361.

17. Byrum's work enjoyed the widest reputation, but other ministers also wrote books and maintained ministries for healing. A partial list includes J. Grant Anderson, *Divine Healing* (Anderson, Ind: Gospel Trumpet Company, 1926); E. H. Ahrendt, *Healing for All* (Anderson, Ind: Gospel Trumpet Company, 1931); and O. L. Yerty, *Christ the Master of All Diseases* (Anderson, Ind: Gospel Trumpet Company, 1938).

18. (Anderson, Ind: Warner Press, 1960).

19. Ibid., 5.

20. Ibid., 20.

21. Cf. *Psychology, Religion, and Health* (Nashville, Tenn: Abingdon Press, 1952).

22. Sterner, *Healing and Wholeness*, 49–50.

23. Ibid., 51.

24. One man recalled visiting the Scandinavian camp meeting of the Church of God at St. Paul Park, Minnesota as a boy and hearing his mother remark that she had never seen so many Scandinavian people and not one coffee pot to be found in their midst. Carl Nelson, Interview, August 3, 1978.

25. For a more detailed discussion of the demise of pacifism in the Church of God see Merle D. Strege, "An Uncertain Voice for Peace: The Church of God (Anderson) and Pacifism" in Theron Schlabach and Richard Hughes, eds., *Proclaim Peace: Christian Pacifism from Unexpected Quarters* (Urbana, Ill: University of Illinois Press, 1997), 115–127.

26. Mitchell K. Hall, "A Withdrawal from Peace: The Historical Response to War of the Church of God (Anderson, Indiana)," *Journal of Church and State* 27, no. 2 (1985), 308, n. 26.

27. Minutes, Executive Council of the Church of God, January 6, 1941.

28. Robert J. Hazen, letter to the editor, *GT* (March 20, 1960), 16.

29. Cf. Strege, "An Uncertain Voice for Peace," 122–124.

30. The Peace Fellowship of the Church of God has continued its determined efforts to raise the movement's consciousness concerning Christian pacifism. Thanks to the generosity of Maurice and Dondeena Caldwell and others, Anderson University recently established an endowed peace studies fund to support the discussion of pacifism and peace-related issues.

31. See chapter 7.

32. Quoted in "Bless God for the Depression," in Merle D. Strege, *Tell Me the Tale: Reflections on the Church of God* (Anderson, Ind: Warner Press, 1991), 38.

33. John W. V. Smith summarized these activities in "Who Says We Have to Polarize?" *Colloquium*, Vol. 2. No. 8. (October, 1970), 1–2 ff.

34. Cf. "Big and Broad," Ibid., 10–13.

35. Gene Newberry and Robert Reardon both recall Tucker's dictum, "There is no social gospel; there is only the gospel with social implications."

36. Reardon's reminiscences of those years are published as *This is the Way it Was: Growing Up in the Church of God* (Anderson, Ind: Warner Press, 1991).

37. Cf. Barry L. Callen, ed., *Following the Light*, 244–246.

38. Letter, Reardon to the author, February 23, 2002.

39. The Commission served the church for thirty-four years until it was eliminated by a reorganization of national offices in 1998.

40. Ibid., 172–173.

41. The 1971 hymnal committee made much more extensive use of this process, inviting the comments of some seven hundred individuals as compared to the fifty who were asked to assist the 1953 hymnal committee.

42. "Foreword," *Hymns and Spiritual Songs* (Anderson, Ind: Gospel Trumpet Company, 1930), 3.

Chapter 15
Discordant Voices of Unity

Historian Morris Dickstein judged the decade of the 1960s as "likely to remain a permanent point of reference for the way we think and behave, just as the thirties were."[1] The sixties witnessed extraordinary events that shook American life. In the first years of the decade the optimism of John Kennedy's New Frontier unleashed pent-up forces that demanded changes beyond the newly elected president's range of vision. During the presidential primaries, signs of social change began emerging. Sit-ins occurred in the South, and that summer the radical organization known as Students for a Democratic Society was born. In 1963 Martin Luther King, Jr. led members of the Southern Christian Leadership Conference into Birmingham, Alabama in a dramatic demonstration against racial discrimination. Opposition to the civil rights movement also escalated; in the first five years of the decade some twenty-six civil rights workers lost their lives in the American South. The social and political radicalism of the sixties also contributed to the movement for "women's liberation." In 1963 Betty Friedan published *The Feminine Mystique,* a widely popular book that contributed significantly to the emerging feminist movement. Conservatives looked on with disapproval as protests and demonstrations demanded changes in the society that had seemed so tranquil throughout the Eisenhower years.

The call for social change fell on the ears of people in the Church of God movement during the 1960s and '70s. It empowered ethnic minorities and women to offer new interpretations of the movement's historic message of Christian unity. The unity of the church, said women, members of ethnic minorities, and White social liberals, was an ideal that had to address social concerns as well as the theological issues that divided Christians. Mirroring the larger society, the movement also was home to others who, in the name of a more traditional theology, resisted social change as well as the idea of the church as a change agent. Some in this group also espoused a view of the

Church of God movement that by 1970 had become largely passé. Those who clung to the old apocalyptic ecclesiology hearkened back to the theological vision of the Church of God that held sway before 1930 and organized themselves during the seventies to advocate the recovery of that vision. As in the larger American society, so also in the Church of God, many voices spoke up, each of them articulating an aspect of the life of the church that they believed demanded the attention of the movement as a whole.

African Americans and the Church of God

After 1917 the growing distance between White and Black constituencies had a paradoxical affect on African Americans in the Church of God. The National Association was left to its own resources. If Blacks were to hear the Church of God message, it would be delivered by Black ministers and gospel workers. Largely gone were the days when a Black preacher addressed a White meeting or where Whites addressed a Black congregation. As southern Blacks migrated to the industrial centers of the north, new churches formed and leaders developed to meet the challenges that accompanied this relocation. Interracial congregations had existed in northern cities for some time, but after 1910 these churches divided along racial lines. In New York, Chicago, and Detroit new African American congregations called Black pastors.[2] It was in this era that such people as Daniel F. Oden, J. D. Smoot, Raymond S. Jackson, and S. P. Dunn became prominent leaders of the African American church. Dunn (1881–1959) was a licensed minister in the African Methodist Episcopal Church before coming into contact with the *Gospel Trumpet.* He entered the Church of God ministry in 1907 and at first served churches in the South. Immediately following the 1920 Anderson Camp meeting, Dunn succeeded Smoot as pastor of Langley Avenue Church of God in Chicago. Over a thirty-nine year pastorate Dunn built Langley Avenue into a strong congregation and in the last years of his career was known as the "Radio Shepherd of Chicago" for his program on station WCFL. After the creation of the National Association, Black ministers continued to appear on the program at Anderson Campmeeting, and to be elected to agency trustee boards. For example, Dunn was a charter member of the Anderson College trustees and also a member of the Board of Church Extension and the Missionary Board. But this presence did not alter the fact that Blacks and Whites were largely separated. At last, in the racially charged environment of the sixties, Black ministers took up the question of the relationship of Blacks and Whites in the Church of God.

One of the first published signs of discontent among African Americans in the Church of God appeared as an article by James Marshall in an unofficial magazine published for a Church of God constituency. The son and grandson of Church of God ministers, Marshall taught part-time at Anderson College while he studied at the School of Theology. The first paragraph of Marshall's article none too subtly announced that it was time to reconsider the practice of Christian unity: "The Church of God manifests a glaring contradiction between its practice and the doctrine of Christian unity. Distinctions along the lines of creed, culture, and color continue to divide her membership. Any distinction between members contradicts the concept of Christian unity taught and practiced in the first-century church."[3] Marshall wrote out of his experience as a Black minister worshiping in White churches to point up differences in philosophy and patterns of worship. He refused to believe that such differences posed insuperable obstacles to integrated services. In time-honored Church of God hermeneutical style, Marshall cited the "New Testament church" as the norm for race relations in the contemporary church. The early church's "loyalty to Christ overshadowed and overpowered all objections and obstacles to fellowship."[4] Nevertheless, Marshall reiterated, so long as the Church of God remained unwilling to confront the racial segregation in its midst, "neither time nor truth is on our side."[5]

A decade and more of seething national unrest prompted the National Association to authorize a committee to assess relationships and issues of concern to African Americans. The Caucus of Black Churchmen in the Church of God met in Cleveland, Ohio April 16–17, 1970. Slightly more than ninety people attended these meeting convened for "the purpose of attempting both to share the burden of the Black church and to show the concerns it feels under God to be imperative if the church is to be the salt of the earth. It is out of this concern for the people of God faithfully to assume their role as Christians that those victimized by social indifference and religious irrelevance have come together to understand, listen, and then speak, 'thus saith the Lord.' "[6] The Caucus gave Black clergy the opportunity to:

> allow the victims of racial oppression affiliated with the Church of God to determine for themselves their assignment under God amid the Black revolution. [1] the historical suffering of Black men in America has revealed the necessity of power and the crime of failing to administer power justly. No person can adequately understand the history of the Black church in the Church of God unless he views that history against the background of attitudes and trends in the wider

community. Historically speaking, the Church of God has acquiesced to the prevailing social patterns in society.

Blacks cannot ignore the lessons of history within and beyond the Church of God. Blacks must not forget: (1) that power is seldom yielded apart from confrontation and conflict. (2) That the drive toward self-preservation often supercedes the claims of Christ when one's source of power is threatened. (3) That racism is so pervasive that only a radical surgery can remove its presence and influence. (4) That silence in the midst of a revolution is a sin. (5) That until all men are free no one is really free. (6) That the church is not detached from the world's predicament.[7]

The Caucus[8] produced a small collection of papers that was in effect both a defense of social activism among African American pastors as well as a declaration to the White church that business as usual was no longer acceptable. For Sethard P. Beverly, pastor of Third Street Church of God in Kansas City, Kansas, it was a question whether Black ministers could maintain their identity as Christians if they chose not to be involved in the suffering and oppression that characterized the daily lives of the sheep of their flocks. Moreover, said Beverly, the justice and righteousness of God put him on the side of the downtrodden in society. By implication, any minister interested in being on the Lord's side needed to follow a similar agenda.[9]

The social agenda of the Caucus of Black Churchmen inevitably raised questions regarding the peculiar racial modus vivendi between Blacks and Whites in the Church of God. Roughly 20 percent of the movement's constituency was African American, but a much smaller percentage of African American ministers held key leadership positions in national church offices. Many states had segregated ministerial assemblies. It seemed to be the case that the Black voice in the Church of God movement was relegated to a few seats on agency trustee boards. The work of the Caucus of Black Churchmen had the effect of bringing these issues to consciousness. It was painfully embarrassing for a movement committed to Christian unity, but White church leaders had to admit that the ideal of a church beyond division had not reached across the racial divide that ran through American society.

There were, of course, among White church leaders exceptional examples of people committed to a fully integrated church. The generation of seminary students trained at Oberlin in the forties had often heard Professor Clarence Tucker Craig say that there was no such thing in the New Testament as a social gospel, but there was a gospel with social implications.

Sensitized to social issues by Craig and others, many of the Oberlin graduates became staunch supporters of causes of social justice. It was this concern
that sponsored creation of the Commission on Social Concerns in 1964.[10]
One need not be a seminary graduate to champion the cause of African
Americans inside the Church of God or out. In 1960 Mississippi Governor
Ross Barnett had decided that Church of God minister Horace Germany
would either leave the state or die. He had come to Barnett's attention for his
warm relationships with Blacks and his desire to create a training school for
Black ministers. On a warm summer morning agents of the Mississippi State
Sovereignty Commission and members of the Ku Klux Klan savagely beat
Germany, leaving him for dead on the streets of Union, Mississippi.*
However, it was a Jamaican born minister, Samuel G. Hines, who focused the
movement's attention on racial division as a problem for its ideal of a church
beyond division.

Sam Hines (1929–1995) attended school in Savannah-la-Mar, Jamaica.
Called to the ministry as an adolescent, he subsequently graduated from
Jamaica Bible College. Later he studied at London School of Religion and
Tyndale College in Detroit. Ordained in 1952, Hines and his wife, the former
Dalineta Ellis, started an International Christian Fellowship in London a
year later. After pastoral service in Jamaica and Detroit, he took up the pulpit at Third Street Church of God in Washington, DC. Hines was fond of saying that the Church of God deserved an *A* for its message of Christian unity,
but an *F* for its practice. He was determined to weave the practice of racial
reconciliation into the movement's message of Christian unity. In point of
fact, he wanted the church to do its theology rather than simply affirm it as
a set of abstract beliefs.[11] Frequently asserting that "dogma divides, but ministry unites," Hines called the church to recover a practical understanding of
doctrine. Relatively late in his pastoral career, he and the Rev. Louis Evans,
Senior Pastor at Washington's National Presbyterian Church, and their
spouses entered into a covenant aimed at embodying racial reconciliation.
This personal covenant also involved their respective congregations in a program of cooperative activities. For Hines theology was a set of practices to be
employed in the life of the church. If the Church of God was to live out its
calling faithfully as a movement of Christian unity, then, said Hines, racial
reconciliation had to be a central practice of this lofty claim. He was as good
as his word. Hines worked tirelessly for the cause of racial reconciliation, not
only in the neighborhood surrounding his church, but also in international
travels that took him as far as South Africa. In his forceful but genial

---

*"Mississippi State Secrets." *History Undercover.* The History Channel. 28 February 2002.

Elsie Egermeier. The popularity of her Bible Storybook and its simple narrative approach to the Bible place her among the most influential theological writers in the history of the Church of God.

manner, Hines' insistence that the movement practice what it preached on Christian unity could not but emphasize the gap that had grown between beliefs and practice.

Women and the Church of God

In the movement's early decades, when theology was clearly expressed in and through doctrinal practice, women contributed significantly to the theological life of the Church of God. They did so as practitioners of the Galatians text that made no distinction between male and female. Practically oriented themselves, the saints read the Bible with an eye on the practices they found there. To them, St. Paul's habit of involving women like Phoebe, Priscilla, and others in the work of the church provided sufficient precedent for the practice of the restored New Testament church. In the minds of early Church of God people, Pauline practice seems to have outweighed his famous comments about women and speaking in the church. In any case, the ministers lists and yearbooks for the first half century of Church of God life carry the names of many significant women who were ordained ministers. Women like Allie Fisher, Sarah Smith, Mary Cole, and many others worked and preached alongside men as co-laborers. In some cases women, for example Nora Siens (later, Hunter) and Lena Shofner (later, Mattheson), formed their own evangelistic companies. Husbands and wives also formed some of the early evangelistic companies, but it was not always the husband who took the lead in these arrangements. When Clarence and Nora Hunter ran short of cash, it was Clarence who temporarily dropped out of gospel work to find a job, enabling Nora, the stronger preacher between them, to remain in ministry. Women contributed to the doctrinal practice of the church through their broad, enthusiastic, and influential ministries in a movement where it seemed not to matter whether ministers were male or female.

Women did write theology in the early Church of God movement. Jennie Carpenter Rutty published several books that addressed the theology and, especially, the ethics of young people. Rutty also frequently contributed articles to the *Gospel Trumpet* on a range of theological topics. But the most influential female theological writer in the Church of God wrote a single volume that may very well be the most influential book to shape theology across the movement's entire history. That volume was titled *Bible Storybook,* and its author was a diminutive woman named Elsie Egermeier. Born and raised on an Iowa farm, it was after her family moved to Oklahoma City that Egermeier (1890–1986) became acquainted with the Church of God. This introduction came through the ministry of Lena Shofner Mattheson. At age eighteen Egermeier joined the Gospel Trumpet Company in Anderson and was put to work editing children's literature. E. E. Byrum asked her to prepare a Bible storybook for children and in 1923 *Egermeier's Bible Story Book* was published. It became the all-time best seller among Gospel Trumpet Company/Warner Press publications; by 1953 the company sold its one millionth copy and by 1986 well beyond two million copies had been printed. Twice revised, Elsie Egermeier's book proved a reliable study pony ridden by many a theological student preparing for the Bible content exam at Anderson School of Theology. But its theological influence extends well beyond its enduring popularity and utility. More than any other book in the theological history of the Church of God, *Egermeier's Bible Story Book* reinforced the experientialist tendencies of the Church of God to a practice of Bible reading that was fundamentally narrative in nature.

"There is no more fundamental way to talk of God than in a story."[12] So says theologian Stanley Hauerwas, an observation endorsed in the work of biblical theologian Walter Brueggemann.[13] In Hauerwas's view the Bible is fundamentally a long narrative containing the stories of God, Israel, Jesus, and the church. The Bible is not first of all a book of doctrine or systematic theology but a narrative that, speaking broadly, testifies to the redemptive activity of God in the world of human affairs. Narrative is thus the Bible's first-order language. Christian groups like the Church of God instinctively read the Bible narratively, trained to see the Bible in this light by their experientialist epistemology. Out of its Pietist heritage the Church of God has regarded the experience of God as the primary means through which God is known. When through experience one comes to a knowledge of God, testimony becomes a primary form of theology. On Wednesday nights as well as other meetings Church of God people testified to God's presence in their lives and God's activity in their behalf. Such testimonies narrated experience. In the same way, Church of God people read the Bible as the narrative of the experience of the people of God, and it was Elsie Egermeier who trained them in this narrative reading style from the moment that their parents first opened her book to read to their children.

Though women have been influential both as practitioners and as theological writers, the status of women in the ministry of the Church of God declined after 1925. In that year women accounted for nearly one-third of all Church of God pastors, but from 1925 forward the percentage of women in the ministry declined sharply until 1985, when only two percent of Church of God congregations were served by a woman pastor.[14] There has also been a marked tendency to find women pastoring smaller congregations, typically of fewer than fifty members; the larger the church, the fewer the number of women actively involved in managing congregational affairs.[15] In 1976 the men serving on the trustee boards of national agencies of the Church of God outnumbered women in similar capacities by a ratio of nearly ten to one.[16] Moreover, the proverbial stained glass ceiling was not of recent construction but had been present since the first efforts at the bureaucratic organization of the church's work. In the 1920s, when women comprised a significant percentage of ordained ministers, few sat among the powerful ministers who made up the membership of the Gospel Trumpet Company and the agencies. In 1912 only one woman, Lena Shofner Mattheson, was in the group of ministers responsible for *Our Ministerial Letter*.

Three women in particular swam against the ebbing tide of women in the ministry after 1930, and each followed a different course to leadership. Along with others concerned for the cause of missions, Nora Siens Hunter (1873–1951) organized Church of God women into the National Woman's Home and Foreign Missionary Society of the Church of God. Founded in 1932, the "Woman's Missionary Society," as it was colloquially known for decades, pledged itself to the financial support of Church of God missionaries when the Great Depression threatened their recall. President of the society from its founding until 1948, the Reverend Mrs. Hunter criss-crossed the North American continent organizing local and state units. In the process she also demonstrated herself on more than one occasion to be a savvy negotiator when it came to wresting concessions from male-dominated ministerial bodies, in the process reaffirming her early work as a minister of national stature.

E. Marie Strong (1913–1995) pursued her ministerial calling as a successful and highly respected professor of New Testament at Anderson College. Women had served on religion faculties at Church of God colleges, but they tended to be placed in assignments often considered to be appropriate to women—namely Christian education. Not since Anna Koglin taught Greek had a woman held a post in biblical studies at Anderson or any other Church of God college. In 1953 Strong joined the Anderson faculty and remained for thirty-three years. She had studied New Testament with Adam Miller and then followed Otto Linn's example by pursuing graduate study at the University of Chicago. A very demanding and thorough teacher, Strong insisted that her students in the History and Literature of the New Testament learn the full range of critical scholarship, conservative to liberal, directed by a syllabus so large that the department required her to defray its duplicating costs by charging students a dime per copy. Strong stood in the historical-critical tradition of Linn and Miller, demonstrated by her small book on the interpretation of Revelation.[17] Her no nonsense classroom demeanor and use of advanced methods of critical scholarship were balanced by Strong's deep

Lillie S. McCutcheon, pastor, author, evangelist, and key figure in the founding of the Pastor's Fellowship.

personal piety. She was firmly committed to the principle that faith must have ethical consequences, especially where ethical action could meet human need. An evangelist and Nebraska pastor in her early ministry as well as a popular conference leader and speaker, Marie Strong represented something of a throwback to days when a divine call was understood to authorize both men and women to preach. Although she was not an outspoken advocate for the cause of women in ministry, she became a role model for young women who shared her sense of vocation.

From 1945 the pastor of the First Church of God in Newton Falls, Ohio was Lillie Sowers McCutcheon. During the years of F. G. Smith's pastorate in nearby Akron, McCutcheon (1921–1999) became his protégé in the area of church-historical exegesis. After his ouster from the Gospel Trumpet Company, Smith nevertheless remained the undisputed theological authority in much of Ohio and certainly in the northeastern quarter of the state. His interpretation of the Book of Revelation profoundly shaped McCutcheon's theology, so much so that the anti-Catholicism of Smith's apocalyptic ecclesiology became a feature of her preaching even in the heavily Catholic neighborhoods of Newton Falls.[18] Her message shaped by the separatism of the Church of God in northeast Ohio, and sharpened on the anvil of her own preaching, McCutcheon emerged as a combative advocate for old-line Church of God theology. She proved to be a shrewd and determined champion of that vision on the floor of the General Assembly. Prefacing one speech with the warning that there were two kinds of lilies—Easter and tiger—and that she aimed to represent the latter, the name stuck and she became known as "Tiger Lillie." Nora Hunter mobilized Church of God women into a highly effective national organization, while Marie Strong succeeded as an academic. By remaining in the pastorate Lillie McCutcheon faced perhaps the greatest challenge of the three, service to a local congregation in a movement that increasingly called men to fill church pulpits.

Prompted by the example of Marie Strong and others, a new generation of women called to ministry emerged in the sixties and seventies. Encouraged by some aspects of the feminist movement, members of this generation were determined to recover the historic role of women in the ministry of the Church of God. Their interest was not limited to celebrating a heritage. The new women in ministry called movement leaders to account for the great disparity between the number of women adherents in the Church of God versus the paucity involved in significant leadership roles. One of the dreams of this generation was realized when the Consultation on Women in Ministry and Missions of the Church of God reformation movement convened in Anderson in June 1989. Coordinated by Juanita Evans Leonard, associate professor of

Samuel G. Hines, longtime pastor of Third Street Church of God in Washington, DC, articulated the issue of racial reconciliation in the church by sermon and example.

church and society at Anderson University's School of Theology, the Consultation and the book prepared for it[19] called the Church of God to reclaim its heritage of women in ministry and challenged the movement to rethink its theology and mission in light of that reclamation. Among the several study papers and articles prepared for the consultation was an essay by Cheryl J. Sanders that focused on the issue of women in ministry as it exposed shortcomings in the movement's doctrinal practice of Christian unity.

Swarthmore and Harvard educated, Sanders taught on the faculty of Howard University Divinity School in Washington, DC where she also later succeeded the late Samuel Hines as pastor of Third Street Church of God. In her carefully crafted essay she drew on biblical and ethical motifs familiar to Church of God people to lay groundwork for her claim that an ethics for the people of God must advocate holiness and unity.[20] From this foundation Sanders then called into question "the privileged status of the White male in the Church of God"[21] and confronted movement leaders with a contradiction between the movement's message and its practice:

> A system that reserves the vast majority of pastoral and administrative leadership positions in the church for white men not only deviates from the principles of holiness and unity, but reveals a stubborn allegiance to sexism and racism. Such a system perpetuates itself by providing role models and support networks for white men who desire to serve, in effect excluding and discouraging those who are not white or male from aspiring to be trained and employed as leaders.[22]

As Sanders saw it, the problem ran much deeper than the national structures of the movement. Most local congregations were segregated by race and in them the roles and opportunities for women were effectively limited.

Sanders was a careful student of the sanctificationist tradition in the Black church in America. She applied her extensive knowledge of that tradition's theology to the situation she described in the Church of God. To find either sexism or racism, let alone both, in the Church of God movement was to accuse it of failing to live a life of holiness. But she also offered hope to the movement by connecting sanctification to social change. Where men and women were willing to follow Christ's call to holiness, said Sanders, "then the barriers of racial and sexual division can be dismantled, the needed healing and reconciliation can take place, and exciting new applications of the ethics of holiness and unity to the divine task of united ministry can begin to emerge."[23]

Sanders' call to a new practice of an ethics of holiness and unity, particularly as it related to women in ministry, was embodied in the work of Susie Stanley, at the time professor of church history and women's studies at Western Evangelical Seminary in Portland, Oregon. Like Sanders an ordained minister of the Church of God, Stanley and her husband John later accepted faculty appointments at Messiah College in Grantham, Pennsylvania. From the time she wrote her doctoral dissertation, Susie Stanley's academic research interests focused largely on the history of women in ministry. She not only contributed this historical perspective to the Consultation on Women in Ministry but also worked as an activist in the cause of women in ministry, especially where that cause concerned holiness denominations which, of course, nearly always had a strong heritage of women ministers. Stanley organized and remained one of the guiding spirits behind the Wesleyan/Holiness Women Clergy, an interdenominational organization aimed at empowering women called to ministry. The burden of Susie Stanley's work was to articulate a strong historical argument as well as a practice that validated the legitimacy of women's calling to ordained ministry.

From its very beginning the Church of God movement had regarded itself as a trumpet call heralding the restoration of the lost unity of the church. Until the sixties the movement regarded the wider church as a divided Christendom, and the problem, as the saints saw it, was the fragmentation and division of Christians into separate church bodies. The name for this organizational confusion was Babylon. In the wake of the social revolution unleashed in the sixties, groups within the Church of God began applying the movement's traditional rhetoric on unity to new and different problems. Overcoming denominational barriers was no longer the only way to think about Christian unity. African Americans and women in the Church of God translated the social crusades for civil rights and equal rights into a judgment on the movement itself. From their perspective, the divisive sins of racism and sexism within their own house had to be addressed if it wanted to fulfill its mission by being a "united church for a divided world."

Polarizing Theologies

Women and African Americans did not pursue their agendas utterly devoid of support from White males in the movement. In addition to the sympathetic ears of some agency staff members and executives, the new voices speaking up in the movement were joined by a group of largely younger ministers and graduate or seminary students who stood left of the movement's theological center. Several of these individuals met occasionally for fellowship and conversation in a group that was known informally as the

"Columbus Caucus" after their meeting place in Columbus, Ohio.[24] This group of ministers and students was gathered about a small, inexpensively published journal called *Colloquium.* Describing itself as "a publication of contemporary Christian comment," the first issue of *Colloquium* appeared in the autumn of 1969.[25] The late sixties were years of intense social ferment and rapid change when many college students sharply criticized the institutional church as hopelessly irrelevant to the crying needs of American society. Rather than drop out, as many of their generation did, the *Colloquium* circle hoped, in the magazine's words, "to give persons the opportunity to express creative and positive ways of interpreting and dealing with these pressures."[26]

From the outset *Colloquium* took the Church of God movement for its audience. The magazine situated itself squarely in the heritage of the movement, and insisted that its history and character provided the Church of God with a unique perspective from which to assess and comment on a wide range of issues. Social and political topics occupied the lion's share of the space in *Colloquium's* pages, but the magazine also addressed such topics as church growth, pastoral strategies, the need for a delegated General Assembly, the viability of church-related colleges, and why young people were forsaking the church. Its editorial policy, much in the theological vein of the times, determined to examine the pressing issues of the day in the light of Christian reflection. Less frequently did articles appear on more conventional theological topics, and never did the magazine treat its subjects as doctrine to be reasserted. When theological topics did come under consideration, it was for analysis and a search for restatement that could apply to a changed social setting. Indoctrination was not the magazine's aim; instead it intended to provide a forum for the free discussion of important issues facing the Church of God. The magazine used its small size and the flexibility it afforded to great advantage, publishing articles on topics that publications like *Vital Christianity* were either unwilling or unable to address. Less controversial topics included ministry in racially changing neighborhoods, pollution, and religion in telecommunications. But the magazine also frankly asked why young people were leaving the Church of God, criticized the Vietnam war, and in one issue featured an article by Jesse Jackson advocating family planning.[27]

Colloquium's final issue appeared in the first half of 1980. By that time only one of the original eight people associated with the magazine remained.[28] The Vietnam war was at its height when the magazine's first issue had appeared, and fifty American hostages were held in Iran at the time its last issue was published. In less than a year Ronald Reagan and a new conservative mood would sweep into the White House and the Congress, but *Colloquium* held its left of center course until its last breath. Its final number reprinted a *Sojourners* article by Evangelical Jim Wallis that took a position on the Iranian hostage crisis decidedly against the mood of the American public. Wallis wondered why Americans couldn't do what he thought was the Christian thing and ask Iranians to forgive the United States for its support of the Shah and his regime.[29] Wallis's article and *Colloquium's* editorial stance were swimming against the tide, but the magazine also touched a responsive chord among a sympathetic readership. These were Church of God people who regarded the magazine as "an antidote to middle America's blend of patriotism and religion."[30] Many of these subscribers appreciated the magazine's willingness to examine all sides of an issue and affirmed that such openness was a virtue needed by the Church of God. Some saw this openness as a necessary strategy for the movement, but worried that an affirmation of the movement's pluralism could turn "pathological when it produces ... spiritual-non-spiritual lables" [*sic*].[31]

Some who read *Colloquium* took the magazine as a hopeful sign of intellectual and theological vitality in the Church of God. Others regarded it as a deadly dagger pointed at the movement's very heart. The latter group considered the magazine and those who rallied around it to be a small but dangerous element pulling the Church of God "in a direction that has taken many a group down the road to destruction and a socialized version of the gospel."[32] In 1973 a group had begun rallying in opposition to what members perceived as the liberal drift of the movement's leadership and institutions, principally Anderson College. The resurgence of political conservatism that culminated in the Reagan Revolution provided the milieu surrounding these individuals. However, at their center were individuals intent on recalling the movement to the theological mindset of an earlier era. These individuals formed a movement that took the name "Pastor's Fellowship."

Rather like tactics employed by miners on the West Virginia and eastern Kentucky coalfields that were its point of origin, the Pastor's Fellowship could be likened to a wildcat strike. As Church of God liberals took *Colloquium* for their symbol, conservatives who comprised the Pastor's Fellowship also rallied around an unofficial publication, *The Reformation Witness,* which went into publication after the group's first meetings. The masthead of the *Witness* declared its editorial policy and theological stance: "earnestly contending for the faith which was once delivered to the saints." Evangelicals had leapt into prominence just prior to the 1980 general election. Sensing them to be kindred conservative spirits, the Pastor's Fellowship appropriated that word as part of their self-description. It was the case that theological issues prominent among conservative Evangelicals, namely the inerrancy of the Bible, did find their way onto the Pastor's Fellowship agenda. However, it was not so much American Evangelicalism that called the cadence to which the Pastor's Fellowship marched. Its deepest theological roots sank all the way down to the days of Schell, Riggle, F. G. Smith, and the apocalyptic ecclesiology. As the first issue of the *Witness* declared, "Our position and support will be from those who are Bible-believing, conservative, and evangelical. Further, we believe in the biblical concepts which brought the Church of God movement into existence."[33] Loyal to what it considered the authentic message of the Church of God, the Pastor's Fellowship was sharply critical of what it considered to be departures from that original standard and those people and institutions whose theological views were responsible for them. The Pastor's Fellowship sought a strategy and tactics that would galvanize the movement to reverse this drift, but until 1980 these efforts were only modestly successful.

A key theological idea at the core of the Pastor's Fellowship protest was the apocalyptic ecclesiology that had been articulated so well and for so long by F. G. Smith. However, by the 1970s it was no longer only Smith's interpretation that expressed this view. It had been rejuvenated through the preaching and writing of Lillie McCutcheon.

Other ministers of McCutcheon's generation and theological mindset also were involved in the organization of the Pastor's Fellowship. For example, O. L. Johnson of Springfield, Ohio and Harold Boyer, also of Springfield, were staunch conservatives given to the typological exegesis and exposition that had characterized preaching when they were up and coming ministers. Nor was it the case that only older ministers found common cause with Pastor's Fellowship. Other key leaders included Robert Lawrence, a contemporary of the *Colloquium* founders at the School of Theology in the late sixties. But it was McCutcheon who was the Fellowship's guiding spirit and who possessed its savviest and most articulate voice. She had made a name for herself not only as a camp meeting preacher, but also as the author of the latest version of the apocalyptic ecclesiology that hearkened back to the 1890s. In 1964 she published these views in an exposition of Revelation titled *The Symbols Speak*.[34] Significantly, Warner Press did not publish McCutcheon's book, but of equal significance was its endorsement by Harold Boyer, longtime and influential chair of the General Ministerial Assembly. Her exegesis may not have enjoyed the approval of Harold Phillips, editor in chief at the publishing house, but that did not mean she lacked for platform or influential friends. She would not have welcomed the thought that she was herself a polarizing figure, nevertheless McCutcheon was closely identified with the emergence of the Pastor's Fellowship, its causes, and the theology on which they rested.

Much of the contents of *The Symbols Speak* reiterated the findings of F. G. Smith and the church-historical exegesis of Revelation that was first articulated in the work of W. G. Schell. As with those earlier works, McCutcheon's book also read the history of Christianity as having begun in a golden age that was followed by apostasy and a partial restoration succeeded by the final renewal of the church. McCutcheon stopped short of identifying the Church of God as the last reformation, but she did say that the movement had "dedicated its energies, strength, and spiritual power to make this contribution of spiritual truth [the doctrine that only Christ can be the head of the church] to world Christianity."[35] In her view, and in that of Pastor's Fellowship members, this truth was the genius of the Church of God movement. Fellowship leaders believed that it rested on the foundation built by Schell, Riggle, Smith, and now McCutcheon. The movement's identity hinged on this truth and the foundation on which it was built. The Pastor's Fellowship read the decades since 1930 as a history of decline in the movement's confidence and a loss of identity brought on by the abandonment of the apocalyptic ecclesiology. It was the agency leadership and Anderson College, principally its Bible and theology professors, that the Fellowship held responsible for this decline.

Anderson College and the "Open Letter."

Events in the spring of 1980 made Anderson College the lightning rod for conservative discontent in the Church of God. Ironically, during the previous four or five years, key liberal members of the faculty had concluded that institutional administrators were shifting the college to toward mainstream Evangelicalism and began leaving the institution.[36] Any apparent move in that direction was overshadowed by the appearance of the Rev. Jesse Jackson as campus guest and preacher in undergraduate chapel. One of Jackson's principal aids was Frank Watkins, a former pastor of an inner city Chicago Church of God congregation and one of the founders of *Colloquium.* That *Vital Christianity* interviewed Jackson and gave him additional favorable attention only increased the suspicions of conservatives that the college and church leadership had drifted dangerously toward the political and theological left. Jackson's chapel address was the latest in a string of speakers that included comedian turned anti-war critic Dick Gregory and University of Notre Dame President Theodore Hesburgh. Church of God conservatives were especially incensed that the college administration had invited Catholic Hesburgh to deliver the address at Anderson College Commencement, for it simultaneously served as the beginning of Anderson Camp meeting. Jackson's visit cemented conservatives' belief that the college was disregarding the historic positions of the church. Nowhere was that suspicion stated any more clearly than in another unofficial magazine, *Crossroads,* which began publication in 1979.

What *Colloquium* was to Church of God moderates and liberals *Crossroads* represented to the church's conservatives. Its coeditors were Hope Harrington, an alumna of the School of Theology who was working as a secretary at Warner Press, and Jerry Kolb, an accountant and part-time associate pastor who had recently enrolled in the School of Theology.[37] *Crossroads* appealed to the interests of traditional conservatives, but it did not identify closely with the apocalyptic ecclesiology that was the hallmark of true Church of God conservatism. Instead the magazine's editorial policy was shaped by several issues that were calling American Evangelicals to arms. *Crossroads* focused its attention on issues like abortion, feminism, the Equal Rights Amendment, homosexuality, and biblical inerrancy. In a prepublication announcement the magazine's editors described its importance in these terms:

> For a long time, conservative Christians said, 'Preach the word and leave politics alone,' and the only ones in the arena were the liberals. During that time, the moral decay cultivated by socialistic humanism has eaten away the very foundations of civilization, until today the whole western world stands on the brink of destruction.... No one who is aware of today's problems can deny that we are 'at the crossroads' as never before.... [*Crossroads* was needed] because so often the only information we get on these issues is from a liberal viewpoint. It's not easy to stay well informed. You are extremely busy and can't spend all your time delving into current issues, our own church literature, projects, and so forth. That's where the *Crossroads* staff wants to help.[38]

The help provided by the *Crossroads* staff was not always fair-minded. For example, in its first issue the magazine printed an argumentative article sharply critical of a pamphlet recently published by members of the School of Theology faculty. Titled *We Believe,* the pamphlet was a "statement of conviction" that summarized key doctrines of the Church of God on the occasion of the church's centennial. Kolb portrayed the pamphlet in a sinister light, criticizing it for theological minimalism. In his view the pamphlet's affirmation that the Bible is the inspired Word of God masked a creeping liberalism because neither the words inerrant nor infallible appeared.[39] Other *Crossroads* articles were similarly energized by the social and political views stemming from groups like the Moral Majority and other elements of the Evangelical Right. *Crossroads* saw signs of liberalism on the campus of Anderson University and in the hallways of the national agency offices. The magazine took for itself the role of a watchdog to bring to the attention of the Church of God indications of the liberalism it found. In fairness, the magazine was not solely responsible for creating the rising level of conservative mistrust. However, *Crossroads* also fed conservative suspicions of "Anderson" that had been latent in the church for two generations, always ready, as in the case of the Slacum controversy, to spring to life.

Conservatives' worst fears were realized in the spring of 1980 when the Church of God was rocked by the publication of an "Open Letter." Written to Robert H. Reardon by Leroy Oesch, pastor of First Church of God in Camden, South Carolina and previously a faculty member at both Warner Pacific College and Gulf Coast Bible College, the broadside alleged that "liberalism" had taken root in the college. Its signs were manifested especially in a sociology course on human sexuality, Bible courses that did not presume the doctrine of biblical inerrancy, and a general slippage in the student body regarding standards of holiness. Oesch attached several exhibits to his letter, mailed to every minister listed in the Church of God *Yearbook.* These exhibits included samples of objectionable language taken from campus theatrical productions and quotations from the student newspaper, the *Andersonian.* But the most inflammatory elements of Oesch's letter were candid comments drawn from an interview with LaVern Norris, professor of sociology and the instructor in a course on human sexuality, alongside sexually explicit drawings from one of the course textbooks. Many ministers made no distinction between the explicit illustrations and pornography. Oesch's letter and its allegations stormed to the front and center of attention. The entire movement seemed up in arms. College supporters rushed to its defense in the name of reason and enlightened toleration. Opponents attacked it for its departure from the truth and descended on Anderson for the annual convention demanding to know what was going on at the college.

Unusually large crowds attended Anderson Camp meeting in June of 1980 for it was planned as the celebration of the Church of God centennial. In anticipation of a larger than typical attendance at the General Assembly, the meeting location was shifted from Park Place Church of God to O. C. Lewis Gymnasium on the college campus. The site of hotly contested athletic events proved an appropriate venue for one of the most fractious and emotionally charged Assembly sessions in memory. Not since the camp meeting of 1934 and the ratification of John Morrison had the movement faced a moment laden with the potential for such hostility. The controversy that erupted about Anderson College revealed the deepening theological polarities threatening to divide the Church of God, and Chairman Paul Hart was unable to keep a lid on the pot boiling furiously on the Assembly floor. Reardon and the college were repeatedly attacked in the harshest terms, and the matter was only resolved, and that temporarily, by the appointment of a committee[40] charged to inquire into Oesch's allegations and bring back its report the following year.

The committee began its work almost immediately after camp meeting adjourned. However, the movement did not leave members to conduct their inquiry in a detached atmosphere. Letters flew back and forth from one side of the debate to the other. State assemblies drew up resolutions of no confidence in the college and its administration and sent copies to the committee, which was also treated to an ongoing correspondence between Oesch and Norris, each claiming the moral high ground in the cause between them. During its meetings in August 1980 the committee recommended that, pending further review, the college administration remove Norris as the instructor of the human sexuality course and another textbook be found. Some years later he retired, having never again taught the course that was his academic and professional specialization.

The 1980–81 academic year understandably proved to be unusually uncomfortable on the Anderson College campus. Seminarians and undergraduates allied with the Pastor's Fellowship and conservative opposition to the college listened carefully for any indications of heresy in their professors' lectures, ready to pass along what they had heard to others ready to turn ideas into ammunition. Some church people, clergy and lay, gave up on the college and church leadership as lost causes. Privately printed broadsides exhorted their readers to abandon the college and those who identified with it. The most extreme of these sentiments came from a completely polarized right wing of the movement:

> Forget that Anderson even exists (except to pray for, and witness to, those involved). After all, the true church of God has no more to do with Anderson, Indiana, than it has to do with the Vatican. Don't take the spiritual energy that you could be using to win souls, and waste it on the attempt to purge a sprawling institutional monster which has no Biblical reason for existence in the first place, and which grows more top heavy every day. Instead of looking to the worldly wisdom included in Anderson literature, look to the Bible and the guidance of the Holy Spirit for direction.[41]

When the 1981 camp meeting arrived, tempers had cooled considerably. Nevertheless, critics of the college and church leaders who identified with it[42] were determined that the committee not whitewash the case. Thus college opponents successfully moved to amend the Assembly agenda to bring the adoption of the World Service budget to the floor after the Select Committee's report. It was a thinly veiled threat as well as an indication of the low level of trust. Along with the other agencies of the church, the college was a line item in the budget, and World Service support ran to several hundred thousand dollars. The change in agenda suggested that college critics would amend the budget to the college's loss if its report was unsatisfactory.

Chairman Hart and the Anderson College trustees had jointly appointed the Select Committee, but its findings and recommendations were made as a report from the College trustee board. The report replied to five areas stemming from Oesch's charges: (1) the relationship between the college and the church; (2) the integration of faith and academic subject matter; (3) personnel policies; (4) the relationship between the trustees and the college administration; and, most specifically, (5) the human sexuality course. In the course of its report Anderson College explicitly stated that it did not subscribe to secular humanism, but sought instead "to approach the human condition in the light of God's revelation of himself and his will in Jesus Christ."[43]

Three specific items stood out in the report. First, the Oesch letter and *Crossroads* had made biblical authority at Anderson College and the School of Theology a critical issue and attempted to tie the authority of the Bible to the doctrine of biblical inerrancy. The trustees' report affirmed the centrality of the Bible to the heritage of the Church of God but refused to accept inerrancy language as the norm for the church's understanding on biblical authority, at the same time urging that a "body of qualified persons" explore that theological issue. In the spring of 1981 the faculty of the School of Theology preemptively devoted an issue of *Centering on Ministry* to the topic of biblical inspiration and authority. The journal was a publication of the seminary's Center for Pastoral Studies. Edited by Jerry C. Grubbs, professor of Christian education, the carefully worded issue offered historical and theological analyses of several doctrines of biblical authority, but with special reference to the Church of God. The articles eschewed inerrancy as a category out of harmony with the church's theological heritage while affirming the Bible's authority in matters of faith and morals. Editor Grubbs summarized, "Is it not time to shake hands on the fundamental conviction that the Bible is the inspired and authoritative Word of God? If we don't, we may find ourselves glaring across a battlefield at each other while the rest of the world is lost in its sin."[44]

Scholars at other Church of God colleges might not have given Grubbs the answer his rhetorical question assumed. A graduate student at the School of Theology, Steven W. Stall, surveyed the opinions of twenty-one Bible and/or theology professors at Church of God colleges and the seminary regarding statements on the inspiration and authority of the Bible. Stall found the views of seventeen respondents to be fairly equally distributed along a continuum stretching from an inerrantist position to a view that regarded the Bible as "the primary source and guideline for doctrine. The Bible is a unique testimony to God's self-disclosure."[45] The majority of professors were clustered between the extreme poles of the continuum. A few exceptions notwithstanding, Stall's work tended to confirm the School of Theology faculty's view that biblical inerrancy was not a doctrine supported by many academics in the Church of God. In the face of his research, the assertion that Bible and theology professors at Anderson were the only non-inerrantists in the Church of God could not be sustained.

Secondly, the report responded to a demand that a creed or doctrinal test be imposed on college faculty members as a condition of employment. Here the trustees stood firmly on the rock of anticreedalism to which Church of God preachers all the way back to Warner had anchored themselves. The position of the trustee board was that "the historic opposition of the Church of God reformation movement to standardizing and legislating formal creedal statements has been wise and should be maintained. The intended unity among Christians is not based on the achievement of full agreement on all theological questions."[46] Some Assembly members refused to accept the trustees' position and brought to the floor a motion to require members of the college faculty and agency staffs to subscribe to a doctrinal statement. A broad coalition of traditional conservatives, moderates and liberals combined to send this motion, and others of a similar bent, to defeat by margins of approximately fourteen to one. The noncreedal nature of Church of God doctrine was resoundingly affirmed.

Thirdly, college trustees addressed the relationship between the Church of God and its colleges. Characterizing this relationship as "largely informal and undefined," the report stated that no widespread understanding existed to define a responsible relationship between church and academic institutions. In an effort to speak to that need the report offered exhibits intended to allay conservative suspicions. The college revised its application for employment to include a statement of the institution's mission and employment standards. One element of that statement was the college's stated intention to employ persons who subscribed to that mission and whose lives reflected "a belief in and commitment to Jesus Christ and the Christian faith as these are interpreted through the historic witness of the Bible and the contemporary witness of the Holy Spirit."[47] Such measures did not satisfy the editors of *Crossroads*.[48] Nevertheless, the indications were that Anderson College had heard the criticism leveled against it and responded by shifting by some degrees to the theological right. In addition to changes in employment practices, the college trustees also affirmed "the historic position of the Church of God refusing to condone the practice of homosexuality as an alternative Christian lifestyle."[49] While they maintained the importance of freedom of thought to the work of a Christian liberal arts college, the trustees also continued the decision that had removed Professor Norris from his course. However, they refused to yield to demands for a new textbook for the course, noting instead that several Evangelical colleges employed the same text.[50] In an effort to mollify conservatives, the trustees reported that a supplemental text of a clearly Christian perspective had been added to the course curriculum, once again appealing to the new text's use in Evangelical institutions. These steps further indicated that Anderson College was willing to follow a more Evangelical intellectual agenda. That willingness expanded as the eighties gave way to the nineties.

When the Open Letter controversy broke, Robert Reardon knew immediately that he and the college were locked in a very serious battle. At stake were more than issues of liberal or conservative dispute. First a churchman and then a college president, Reardon regarded the controversy as the crucible in which the theological future of the Church of God was at stake. He saw the church in much more moderate terms than either *Crossroads* or the *Reformation Witness*. He did not attempt to make the church into something it was not, but he also believed that a determined, highly politicized minority had seized control of the 1980 Assembly. In his view this minority had stampeded a large block of moderates who were justifiably alarmed by some of the Oesch letter's allegations, not to mention the rumors and innuendo in the correspondence and resolutions that piled up during the spring and summer of 1980. Reardon also believed that these theological moderates would see according to the light of reason once the issues were placed fairly before them. That the Assembly accepted the College's report a year after the controversy's eruption proved him correct.[51] Nevertheless, during that year the church had been more polarized than during the Slacum controversy and nearly to the degree of the struggle between John Morrison and F. G. Smith.

Christian Unity?

Those who addressed the issues of racism or sexism and those who struggled through the polarizing theological debate of the Open Letter controversy were not the only theological voices raised during the sixties and seventies. Several of the movement's elder statesmen and scholars spoke to the topic of Christian unity along more conventional lines. They were determined that the Church of God movement keep in sight what they considered one of its most central and distinctive contributions to American Christianity. They were equally determined to prevent further theological polarization while they also encouraged the movement to rethink its historic message. The ecumenical movement had radically altered the ecclesiastical landscape since the days of Warner, Riggle, and F. G. Smith. These statesmen and theologians wanted Church of God people to take stock of this altered landscape, evaluating it for the good that had been achieved and not condemning it out of hand, in order to determine a new course of action regarding the cause of Christian unity. For some of these distinguished churchmen the issues that women and Blacks were raising did not go unnoticed, but they nevertheless persisted in thinking of Christian unity as first and foremost a theological issue confronting churches.

At the West Coast Ministers Meeting that convened the spring of 1968 Adam W. Miller, dean emeritus of the School of Theology, delivered four conference papers on the topic of Christian unity and ecumenical trends.[52] The program committee had requested Miller to address the topic, for, as he said, a feeling of uncertainty permeated the entire movement regarding its position among the churches of Christendom. Miller traced the history of fraternal conversations that had developed between the Church of God and several other similar groups: the Churches of God of North America and later the Church of the Brethren, and the Brethren Church. Four-way conversations were held between the groups in the spring and, again, in the fall of 1964. Four years later bi-lateral conversations began with the Evangelical Covenant Church at its initiation. Miller carefully described the limits of both sets of conversations, explaining that formal unions were never contemplated. In keeping with the ecumenical spirit of the day, Miller celebrated the fact that such conversations had occurred at all. While he sympathized with those who wondered what such conversations might mean for the future of the Church of God, he also took a flourishing ecumenical spirit as a clear imperative for honest searching.

Another topic of concern that Miller addressed dealt with the movement's self image. He carefully reviewed key elements of the theological heritage of the Church of God but made a very clear point concerning the

341

relationship of a church's heritage to its present and future. Heritage was not something to be sealed changeless and delivered to future generations. On the contrary, said Miller, "What we have received from the past may have to be refined and the meaning extended. We have to restate the heritage in terms of the peculiar needs of this age...."[53] Out of his review, and in an effort to restate the movement's heritage of thought concerning Christian unity, Miller identified three problems and hindrances to clearer self-understanding. While he thought that the Church of God had left the practice of come-outism behind, Miller also thought that the nature of the unity subsequently sought by the Church of God was unclear. Was there a unity to be sought beyond spiritual unity? Was there more to Christian unity than cooperative efforts in Christian education or stewardship programs? Such questions "underline for us the need to face the problem of a more satisfactory definition of the nature of the unity we seek."[54] Then Miller added, tellingly and somewhat presciently in 1968, "Perhaps the failure to follow through on this is due to a lack of theological consensus among us as a fellowship."[55]

Only a few years after Adam Miller delivered his paper another careful student of the Church of God published his concern over the threat of growing theological polarization. From his vantage as historian of the Church of God, John W. V. Smith read the movement's history in such a way as to believe that polarization, although part of the movement's past, was avoidable.[56] In Smith's view, amid many possibilities the polarization that most threatened the Church of God was "the conflict between those on the one hand who maintain that the primary task of the church is to proclaim the 'good news' ... and those on the other hand who see the church ... as a primary force in ministry to human need, eliminating injustice and humanizing the structures of society.... In the common idioms, the 'conservative evangelicals' are lined up against the 'social gospelers.' "[57] He argued that alongside the early movement's strong emphases on personal salvation and holiness other more socially directed concerns could also be detected.[58] Smith built up several examples of early compassion for the disenfranchised, poor, and destitute to make a case for a view of the nature of the gospel and the role of the church in the world that encompassed both traditional evangelism and social concern. Historical precedent served as an example to the contemporary church: "The pioneers saw no real conflict between the two emphases. They made both important. There may not have been complete agreement, but they did not allow polarized positions to disrupt their fellowship or hinder their witness spiritually or socially."[59] Like Adam Miller, so also John W. V. Smith thought that the key to a healthy future and a vital unified witness to the churches of Christendom, lay in the responsible adaptation of the theological heritage of the Church of God to the circumstances of the present.

T. Franklin Miller (1910–), president of Warner Press from 1965, surveyed the past before looking to the decade standing between him and the centennial celebration of the Church of God. A veteran of more than thirty-five years of service to the national work of the Church of God, in his first assignment Miller built the Board of Christian Education into a nationally recognized ministry. He cultivated face-to-face relationships with ministers and laypersons alike; across the United States countless Church of God people referred to workshops and leadership development meetings conducted by "T. Franklin." Educated at Anderson College and Butler School of Religion, Miller was well read and precise in debates whether oral or written, and he could be a very determined adversary. His preparation was meticulous, and he expected a similar attention to detail in his associates. His penchant for detail made him particularly effective in discussions that were conducted behind the scenes. These qualities, combined with his many years of service, earned Miller appointments on several national committees and task forces.[60]

Miller reflected on the future of the Church of God and identified several important categories, one of which, again, was Christian unity. In the late sixties and early seventies movement leaders were searching for an answer to a critical aspect of the theological heritage of the church that had become something of a question mark. Polarities of opinion did not unduly alarm Franklin Miller; he regarded them as perpetual features of the movement's common life. Likewise he took it as a positive sign that many voices in the constituency—young and old, clergy and laity, men and women—were articulating their concerns. Miller preferred what he regarded as a broadening, more democratic, participation over the more authoritarian and oligarchic governance of the past.[61]

The impending centennial celebration prompted Franklin Miller to ask questions about the movement and its future. In light of the movement's historic interest in the doctrine of Christian unity, what was to be its identity among the churches of Christendom and its reason for being in the next century of its existence? He saw an occasion for rejoicing in the near universal acceptance of the importance of Christians unified in a redemptive fellowship. But, said Miller, echoing Adam Miller's assessment, "One of the really big and serious aspects of our celebration of one hundred years ought to be at this point of coming to understand ourselves as a movement, the nature of the Church and the unity to which God calls his people."[62] Franklin Miller thought that the achievement of such an understanding would come through vigorous and healthy discussions on doctrine in the General Assembly. Frank and honestly debated conversations emulated the first century church and, on his view, face-to-face discussions were indispensable to a "renewed searching for the mind of God for our reason for being as a movement, and our mission, as well as our relationship with other bodies."[63] In 1971 Miller was optimistic that the Church of God would be able to restate its self-understanding, but to this appraisal he added a word of criticism concerning Christian unity in the face of the racial tension that was a part of daily American life. Adeptness at "the numbers game" could not be permitted to replace matters of social justice on the movement's agenda. Miller was critical of the movement's past performance in "the areas where the Christian witness is so crucial—arenas of racial tension, poverty, exploitation, ignorance, violence, war, hatred, [and] intolerance."[64] For Franklin Miller, the theological health of the Church of God, its identity, and its doctrine of Christian unity depended on the answers that it gave to such pressing social questions.

On the eve of the Church of God centennial, and at the moment when theological polarities were soon to inflame ministerial passions, one of the movement's most distinguished and widely respected ministers published one of the centerpiece volumes in Warner Press's "Doctrinal Library." James Earl Massey (1930–) published the volume on Christian unity.[65] About a half generation behind the first group of Oberlin seminarians, Massey had also enrolled there before achieving national prominence as a preacher serving Metropolitan Church of God in Detroit. While pastor of this prominent African American congregation he also served as president of Jamaica Bible College and, later, campus minister at Anderson College. The author of numerous books and articles, Massey's distinguished career later included assignments as dean of the chapel at Tuskegee University and dean of the School of Theology at Anderson University.[66] At the time that he wrote his volume for the Doctrinal Library, Massey held the post of speaker on the Church of God syndicated radio program, *Christian Brotherhood Hour.*

In his study paper for the Consultation on Doctrine, Massey had introduced the idea of "psychic unity" as a necessity if the Church of God were to mature into effective service as an example of Christian unity. Psychic unity was not to be understood as unanimity of thought and action. On the other hand, Massey characterized as doomed those who were willing to live in polarized isolation. Rather, he sought a unity of Christians manifested as a "willed movement toward each other."[67] Differences among Christians could not be overlooked or denied; they had to be squarely faced with the intention of learning from one another. Psychic unity aimed at achieving a quality of relationship that could only be described by the word *agape.*

James Earl Massey. Author, preacher, radio minister, and educator.

The subtitle of his book in the Doctrinal Library, *A Study of the Relational Imperative of Agape Love,* placed Massey squarely in the theological tradition of D. S. Warner, connecting Christian unity to the sanctifying work of the Holy Spirit. Uncharacteristic of the movement's approach to theology, Massey separated doctrine from practice in an effort to emphasize the latter when it came to Christian unity:

> The doctrine of unity is one thing, and the spirit of unity is another. The doctrine of unity points to a life in fellowship and highlights the relationships generated and governed by Christian love. The spirit of unity involves that love itself, and it enables the believer to break free from patterns of selfish individualism and experience the fellowship that a common faith allows and shapes. This relational imperative of love always works against fragmentation, anonymity, coldness, distance, and divisiveness. It generates openness to share and be in community. Christian unity is a gift from God through the Spirit, but it is experienced only as we open ourselves to be in community with other believers.[68]

In keeping with long established Church of God exegesis, Massey took as his starting point New Testament example. On this footing he gave unity the broadest possible application. Christian unity transcended differences in economic and social class as well as theology. The unity of Christian fellowship also needed to discipline natural human preferences for individualism, location, age, and "human groupings" that tend to divide the church.[69] In language that reflected an early appreciation for cultural diversity, Massey did not insist that Christian unity required the elimination of the differences that mark one culture or ethnic group from another. Instead he took the view that the church was the place where, in the spirit of agape, the distinctives of each human grouping could contribute to the life of the whole. Moreover, warned Massey, it was wrong to remain exclusively within the confines of one's own group. "Groupings can aid us, but they can also cripple us if the mindset and lifestyle they promote are influenced by prejudices and pride. As Christians, we must be willing to be led beyond our own familiar group so that we can touch those who are in other settings."[70] At the end of a decade and more of marked polarities in the theological life of the Church of God, another of the movement's senior statesmen thus attempted to articulate the doctrine of Christian unity in traditional reference to other Christian bodies, but also with respect to the racial and gender, the social and political, tensions that had stretched the fabric of the Church of God movement to the point of tearing.

A United Church for a Divided World?

As it moved into the eighties, the Church of God movement was showing the wear and tear of more than a decade of polarized opinion and fractious theological debate. Deep differences within the movement undercut its theology of Christian unity, forcing it to come to terms with the changing landscape of an American society searching for ways to give larger and more significant voices to women and members of ethnic minorities. African Americans, in particular, and women in the Church of God took up the causes that were part of the larger society's debate, articulating them for and to the Church of God. In the process they forced the movement to enlarge its doctrinal practice of Christian unity, one of its salient theological ideas. The church responded to this criticism with policies that were more inclusive at the national level. African Americans and members of other ethnic minorities were voted on to trustee boards to an extent greater than had previously been the case. In 1974 the Executive Council created a new position, associate executive secretary, with the understanding that a Black person would be the first to occupy the office. The following year Edward L. Foggs was elected to this post. In following years additional African Americans assumed positions as staff members of several national agencies of the Church of God, but Hispanics and women did not fare as well.

Opinion continued to be divided over such matters as the nature of the church and its mission. Throughout the seventies theological conservatives insisted that the mission of the church was to save the lost. The Commission on Social Concerns tended to draw conservatives' ire, even though it was not always deserved. The existence of the commission itself symbolized for some conservatives the misguided policies and attention of social liberals in the movement who were deflecting it from its evangelistic mission. Polarized theologies paralleled divided opinions on the issue of church and society. Those who read and supported *Colloquium* tended to line up against the emergent Pastor's Fellowship and also, for its brief career, *Crossroads.* Meanwhile the movement's elder statesmen and long-time students of its history sought ways to overcome the increasing polarization of the seventies. They looked to the past and found there examples where a spirit of dialogue overcame polarities that some believed were inherent in the movement. Several often discordant voices competed for the solo part in a chorus of voices calling for doctrinal renewal or restatement, and the decade ended with one of the most divisive episodes in the movement's one-hundred-year history.

The Open Letter controversy of 1980–81 settled some issues but left others unresolved. Faced with proposals to employ doctrinal tests as a condition of employment in the national agencies, some movement conservatives joined forces with moderates and liberals to send such proposals to resounding defeat. In this the Church of God held fast to one of its most deeply held and longstanding doctrinal practices. In the wake of the controversy Anderson College, soon to become Anderson University, moved steadily away from some of the more liberal stances it had taken in the sixties and seventies. In the eighties the university embraced a more Evangelical posture through formal association with such organizations as the Coalition for Christian Colleges and Universities. The Pastor's Fellowship remained concerned that both undergraduate and seminary Bible professors refused to teach the church-historical exegesis that Fellowship members insisted was the authentic teaching of the movement. As the eighties wore on toward the nineties, the polarities of the sixties and seventies gave way to a new set of issues concerning the doctrinal practice of the church. New or altered practice drew inspiration from a culture dominated by the values of the market and the therapist. Coupled with the fractious debates of the early eighties, these new conceptions of the church raised questions whether the movement as a whole could any longer sustain a common vision of itself as an agent of Christian unity.

Notes

1. Quoted in James T. Patterson, *Grand Expectations: The United States, 1945–1974* (New York: Oxford University Press, 1996), 443.
2. Cf. James Earl Massey, "The Church of God and the Negro," in *The National Association of the Church of God Historical Report, 1917–1974* (West Middlesex, Penn: National Association of the Church of God, 1974), 9. See also Massey, *An Introduction to the Negro Churches in the Church of God Reformation Movement*, 17–24.
3. "One Lord, One Faith, One Baptism, Two Churches," *Colloquium* (Vol. 1 No. 1) (October 1969), 1.
4. Ibid., 2–3.
5. Ibid., 3.
6. *The Church of God in Black Perspective* (n.p.: n.d.), i.
7. Ibid., i–iii.
8. The Caucus was directed by a steering committee composed of Leonard Roache, George Suddeth, Ronald Fowler, Robert Hill, Sethard Beverly, and Marcus Morgan.
9. Ibid., 23.
10. The text of the resolution authorizing the commission's creation is reprinted in Barry L. Callen, editor, *Following the Light* (Anderson, Ind: Warner Press, 2000), 172–173.
11. Samuel G. Hines, with Joe Allison, *Experience the Power* (Anderson, Ind: Warner Press, 1993), 2. Sam Hines' personal papers were posthumously gathered into a book co-authored with Curtiss Paul DeYoung titled, *Beyond Rhetoric: Reconciliation as a Way of Life* (Valley Forge: Judson Press, 2000).
12. Stanley Hauerwas, *The Peaceable Kingdom: A Primer in Christian Ethics* (Notre Dame: University of Notre Dame Press, 1983), 25.
13. Cf. *Theology of the Old Testament* (Minneapolis: Fortress Press, 1997), 43–44, n. 126.
14. Juanita Evans Leonard, Ed., *Called to Minister, Empowered to Serve: Women in Ministry* (Anderson, Ind: Warner Press, 1989), 175.
15. Ibid., 173.
16. Ibid.

17. *Basic Messages from Revelation* (Anderson, Ind: Women of the Church of God, 1985).

18. For a full account of Lillie McCutcheon's life see Barry L. Callen, *She Came Preaching: The Life and Ministry of Lillie S. McCutcheon* (Anderson, Ind: Warner Press), 1992.

19. *Called to Minister, Empowered to Serve*, see above, note 14.

20. Sanders, "Ethics of Holiness and Unity in the Church of God," in *Called to Minister, Empowered to Serve*, 131–137.

21. Ibid., 142.

22. Ibid.

23. Ibid., 145.

24. The Caucus met from 1971 to 1973. Members included, among others, Raymond Brennan, Richard Harp, Roger Hatch, Bruce Kelly, John Stanley, and Frank Watkins.

25. *Colloquium's* editorial board was comprised of four recent students at Anderson School of Theology. James Marshall was still a student in 1969, but Raymond Brennan, Roger Hatch, and Frank Watkins had graduated. Hatch was a doctoral student at the University of Chicago. Brennan was a pastor in Pittsburgh, and Watkins served an inner-city Chicago church before he eventually became a key member of Jesse Jackson's staff. The editorial board was supported by a staff that included Arlene Callen, James Cook, David Liverett, and Henry M. Williams.

26. "Editorial," *Colloquium* Vol. 1 No. 1 (October, 1969), 2.

27. *Colloquium* Vol. 5, No. 4 (May 1973). Jackson discussed but did not advocate abortion. In fact he criticized abortion policy as a tool of politicians who did not want to spend money in programs to feed, clothe, and educate the poor.

28. James Cook, in 1980 pastor of the Church of God in Corona, California, was now one of three editors. He was joined by John Stanley, pastor in Detroit, and his wife, Susie. Fred Shively, pastor of the Church of God in Woodburn, Oregon, and his wife, Kay, were contributing editors. Staff members were H. Richard Harp, M. Bruce Kelly, and Kurt L. Burgess.

29. Jim Wallis, "We Could Just Ask Them To Forgive Us," *Colloquium* (Vol. 12. No. 1) January/May 1980, 1.

30. "Forum," *Colloquium* Vol. 11, No. 6 (November/December 1979), 8.

31. "Forum," *Colloquium* Vol. 12, No. 1 (January/May 1980), 8.

32. "Forum," *Colloquium* Vol. 11. No. 5 (September/October 1979), 8.

33. Masthead, *The Reformation Witness*, 1979.

34. (Newton Falls: n.p.)

35. Ibid., 105.

36. Important departures in the mid-seventies included Carl Williams, a professor in the sociology department, and professor of philosophy Delwin Brown. Brown was already acquiring a national reputation as a leading exponent of process theology.

37. The magazine also listed Mrs. Joan Hart of Lebanon, Missouri and Dr. William S. Anderson, a physician and former medical missionary who had recently opened a practice in Anderson.

38. The flyer carrying this announcement is part of the file, "Crossroads," Archives of the Church of God.

39. Jerry E. Kolb, "We Believe A Giant Step?" *Crossroads* (November 1979), 6. Kolb concluded his article with the kind of innuendo that often appeared in the magazine: "Few major changes in the movement, good or bad, have ever slapped us in the face. They have occurred gradually, usually in limited steps. It is at first tolerated; then it subtly begins to be accepted, and finally it is endorsed and actively promoted. This Statement, if allowed to, may break the 'shock barrier' against man-made creedal statements. Will the Church of God soon have an 'official' creed? The present Statement of Conviction may be a giant step in that direction." Ibid., Kolb's emphasis.

40. Members of the committee included G. David Cox, Chairman, James Burchett, David Grubbs, Samuel Hines, Kenneth Jones, Fred Menchinger, Wilma Perry, Harold Phillips, Kenneth Schemmer, and Willard Wilcox.

41. Hilton Hinderliter, "An Urgent Message to the Church of God: About the Centennial, Anderson College, and More," (n. d.). Hinderliter's letter was distributed by the Franklin Avenue Church of God in Vandergrift, Pennsylvania, where David Bailey was pastor.

42. Almost unnoticed in the controversy surrounding Anderson College in the summer of 1980, W. E. Reed retired as executive secretary of the Executive Council and took a special assignment with the college aimed at repairing its damaged relationship with the movement.

43. Report of the Anderson College Board of Trustees to the General Assembly of the Church of God, June 16, 1981, 7. The most complete file of materials related to the Open Letter Controversy are two boxes in the collected papers of Robert Reardon, Archives of the Church of God.

44. "The Inspiration and Authority of the Bible," *Centering on Ministry* Vol. 6 No. 3 (Spring, 1981), 2.

45. Stall, "The Inspiration and Authority of Scripture," Loc. cit., 79.

46. Ibid., 8.

47. Ibid., 18.

48. Cf the issue of *Crossroads* for Spring 1981.

49. Anderson College Trustees Report, June 16, 1981.

50. One of the colleges that employed the textbook was Anderson's sister institution, Warner Pacific College. That the Open Letter controversy was in part a continuation of a multi-generational discontent with Anderson College is born out in that neither Oesch nor other critics of Anderson appeared interested in including Warner Pacific under some of the same charges. Despite its use of the controversial text, Warner Pacific was untouched by the controversy.

51. Reardon offered his assessment in a letter to the college trustees dated July 1, 1980. Reardon papers, Archives of the Church of God.

52. At the recommendation of the Committee on Christian Unity, edited versions of Miller's papers were published by the Executive Council of the Church of God. Given internal references in Miller's papers, their edited version had to have been prepared in the fall of 1968, some six months after they were first delivered.

53. Adam W. Miller, "Our Self-Image as a Movement," in *Christian Unity and Ecumenical Trends* (Anderson, Ind: Executive Council of the Church of God, n.d.), 9.

54. Ibid., 13.

55. Ibid.

56. "Who Says We Have to Polarize?" *Colloquium* Vol. 2 No. 8 (October 1970), 1ff.

57. Ibid.

58. Ibid., 2.

59. Ibid., 6.

60. This sketch is partially indebted to Robert Reardon, "Movers and Shakers in the Church of God."

61. T. Franklin Miller, "Projections for the '70s of the Church of God," mimeographed ms, Anderson College Alumni Lecture, November 5, 1971), 2. Archives of the Church of God.

62. Ibid.

63. Ibid., 4.

64. Ibid., 4–5.

65. *Concerning Christian Unity* (Anderson, Ind: Warner Press, 1979).

66. Massey's autobiography, *Aspects of My Pilgrimage* (Anderson, Ind: Anderson University Press, 2002), was unavailable at the time of this study.

67. James Earl Massey, "The Unity of the Church," in *Consultation on Doctrine* (Anderson, Ind: Executive Council of the Church of God, n.d.), 28.

68. Ibid., 7–8.

69. Ibid., 49–61. Massey employed the phrase "human groupings" as a synonym for race or ethnic ground.

70. Ibid., 55.

Chapter 16

Experience, Part 2, The Therapeutic Church

The Church of God movement's theological reliance on experience as a way of knowing made certain elements of Protestant Liberal theology attractive to a rising generation of ministers in the 1930s but more widely in the '40s. The use of the historical critical method in biblical studies, an interest in the ecumenical movement, a heightened regard for social issues, and an internationalist posture all became characteristic of the generation of leaders who had been introduced to theological liberalism at seminaries and graduate schools. But the importance attached to experience also opened the movement theologically to ideas and values originating in different quarters. In the second half of the twentieth century Americans felt the full influence of what came to be termed the "therapeutic culture." People in the Church of God were no more immune than others to the values of this culture. Indeed, with its emphasis on feeling and personal experience, aspects of the culture of therapy made good sense to people who validated their theological commitments experientially. After 1970 the Church of God movement opened itself up to and followed the therapeutic culture along either of two routes. Some of the movement's theological leaders reshaped the concept of the church along therapeutic lines, while at the same time many local congregations were led by church-growth oriented pastors to adapt strategies and techniques of the consumer culture—itself deeply indebted to therapeutic language—to local church life. By either route the Church of God movement's ecclesiological practice was recast in the shape of a therapeutic church.

Calls for Renewal: The Era of Consultations

In 1963 the Church of God entered an eleven-year period when movement leaders intensely reassessed church thought and practice. The vehicle through which these reassessments were conducted was a series of congresses and consultations, nearly always with nationwide participation. These meetings attempted to direct the movement's attention toward the future on such matters as social concerns, the calling and preparation of ministers, and the doctrine of the church. The first of these meetings occurred in Anderson in the spring of 1963 under the title, "All Board Congress and Planning Council." The title indicates the largest single element of its attendees: board members of all the agencies under the umbrella of the General Ministerial Assembly. Agency staff members also attended the congress, as did full-time state coordinators and one additional designated representative from each state. Some 260 people participated in the All Board Congress. The meeting had been called because of a "longfelt need for a reappraisal of our work, and for a dynamic new sense of mission and purpose."[1] Congress participants were dissatisfied with a perceived stagnancy in "the promulgation of our doctrinal position," and called for perpetual reevaluation of the movement's teachings.[2] While calling for a clearer and more relevant expression of the movement's "theological foundations," the Congress also wanted to avoid "a dry and arid creedalism which would undermine individuals whose faith is growing in an atmosphere of Christian fellowship and freedom under God."[3]

The All Board Congress called for theological reassessment because its participants believed that church doctrine was the foundation on which rested the movement's sense of identity and purpose. Distinctiveness itself was not a goal sought by the Congress participants, but they did believe that the message of the Church of God, i. e. "a genuine demonstration of Christian unity and of vital personal experience," could contribute to the larger world of Christendom:

> We feel that our openness toward fellow Christians and to the truth, our conception of membership by salvation, the absence of creedalism, and our emphasis upon the dynamic nature of living relationships in Christ offer us some opportunity for Christian witness. It may be that our combination of teachings is significant, unity being possible only on the basis of truth and experience emphasized in this movement across the years.[4]

While committed to the idea of a distinctive message, the Congress also thought that real danger lay in the possibility that the Church of God movement could become preoccupied with itself. Some in the movement might be tempted to "live on the memory of a few strong personalities who were able to rally a good force about them." But, declared the final report, it would be a mistake to take "their concepts of truth and [attempt] to confront today's situations with them."[5] Congress participants wanted the people of the movement to avoid the temptation to unite on the basis of history and theology rather than testify to a unity based in their common participation in Christ.

The All Board Congress tied the church's doctrine tightly to practice. Great ideas left unimplemented were not likely to stir the church. New goals for the movement were to be clearly identified and stated, and a structure that could implement them was regarded as essential. The Congress called for a sweeping study of national, state, and local organizational structures with an eye toward coordinating the work of the church. In addition to these goals, the Congress also expressed its concerns regarding three additional areas of church life: the need for spiritual renewal, the need of a strong evangelistic outreach, and the need to be more deeply aware of the social forces and issues then swirling through American society. Few areas of church life escaped the attention of the All Board Congress and Planning Council.

Seven years after the All Board Congress had issued its call to the church, the Consultation of the Church of God convened in 1970. Some two hundred men and women from the United States and Canada met to deliberate the state of the church in light of the findings of the All Board Congress and the events that had rent American society during the intervening years. Social unrest as illustrated by student protest of the Vietnam War and the race riots in Detroit and Los Angeles was deeply etched in the minds of the people who gathered in Anderson early in 1970. Their agenda was determined only in part by the questions of identity and doctrine that had been so important to the All Board Congress. In 1970 the practices of evangelism, missions, leadership development, and lay ministry garnered the lion's share of the church's attention. However, it could not turn its face from the pressing social issues of the day. As far as doctrine was concerned, the 1970 consultation restricted itself to discussions concerning the doctrine of Christian unity. But in the face of the unrest tearing the fabric of American society, consultation participants also reworked the movement's doctrine of the unity of all Christians in ways that considered barriers to that unity beyond the old bugaboo of denominationalism.

By 1970 "internal unity" had become a problem for the Church of God. The 1970 consultation deliberated what members regarded as two sets of polarities that had developed within the movement. The first set divided the movement doctrinally. Consultation participants recognized divisions between subgroups within the movement who thought of the church as either an inclusive or exclusive fellowship; those who clung to come-outism versus those who sought more cooperative practices of unity; those who insisted on a broad uniformity within the movement versus those who welcomed diversity; or those who located the movement's unity in a core of clearly stated doctrines versus those who were more comfortable with the idea of a living doctrinal tradition. The second set of polarities featured divisions on the matter of race and racism's threat to the internal unity of the Church of God. But the question of race and the divisions between African American and Anglo church members was understood to have ramifications extending beyond the realm of social justice. The Church of God movement's historic commitment to the unity of all Christians was also at stake. As consultation participants posed the issue: "How can the church minister effectively in missions, evangelism, and unity, without seriously undertaking to bring reconciliation and equality within its ranks?"[6] Later that year the Caucus of Black Churchmen addressed that question as well.[7]

The 1970 consultation essentially set the agenda for the Church of God movement throughout the balance of the '70s.[8] Given the attention directed to problems of Christian unity and practice within the movement, it was perhaps inevitable that additional consultations were contemplated. In 1974 a Consultation on Ministry convened along with another consultation the focus of which was to be on doctrine, specifically the doctrine of the church. Unlike the previous consultations and congresses, the Consultation on Doctrine did not include a large, centrally gathered meeting. In 1971 the General Assembly authorized the Executive Council's Division of General Service to conduct this churchwide discussion. The Assembly appropriated no funds for the project, not even for the committee charged with responsibility for its conduct. If one's treasure follows the heart, one wants to ask whether the Assembly's heart was really in a discussion of Church of God teaching on the church. The work of the thirty-member design committee, as well as the consultation itself, had to be conducted by mail. Undaunted, the committee pursued its task under these severe restrictions. The central document of the consultation was a booklet containing study papers written by five widely known Church of God ministers. Church Historian John W. V. Smith prepared a historical overview of the development of corporate procedures in the movement. Keith Huttenlocker, pastor in New Albany, Indiana, wrote an essay on the nature of the church. A third paper on the mission of the church was written by R. Eugene Sterner, formerly head of the Division of Church Service but since 1967 speaker on the *Christian Brotherhood Hour*. Arlo F. Newell, pastor in St. Louis and chair of the General Assembly, wrote an essay on the polity of the church. The final essay in the booklet was written by James Earl Massey, pastor of the Metropolitan Church of God in Detroit and a widely respected African American church leader inside the Church of God movement and out.[9]

The papers directly bearing on the discussion at hand are those by Huttenlocker and Sterner.[10] Despite repeated calls for the restatement of key doctrines in language more relevant to the times, Huttenlocker's essay on the nature of the church added little to the movement's historical discussion of the topic. Thus he moved through familiar considerations of the church's nature as subject to the lordship of Christ and comprised only of the converted. He also perpetuated the movement's historical practice of come-outism, but with a new slant. Following in the steps of C. E. Brown, Huttenlocker argued that the church was made up of the converted, who by definition were those whose lives have been reoriented from evil to good; God did not call Christians out of the denominational system but from the world. Thus, wrote Huttenlocker, "the church is the product of God's regenerative work in society."[11] Because salvation was so closely connected to the formation of the church, Huttenlocker also brought under discussion the practice of holiness alongside the doctrine of Christian unity. Giving ecclesiological application to a theorem from geometry, he contended that "things reconciled to the same thing are reconciled to each other."[12] However, holiness and unity Huttenlocker treated as separate characteristics of the true church. Unlike Warner and the stream of traditional Church of God doctrine, Huttenlocker did not treat holiness as the means by which the church is made one. Instead he regarded it as a characteristic of the church inherent in the belief that the church is composed of all who are saved in Christ.

If Huttenlocker's essay stood in some connection to the doctrinal past of the Church of God, R. Eugene Sterner's paper on the church's mission moved in a direction that departed from that earlier tradition. In the first place, Sterner chose to emphasize the mission of the whole church rather than any distinctive purpose of the Church of God movement. He saw ecumenism as having had the effect of blurring the movement's vision of its mission, leaving people confused and uncertain as to how to proceed. But confusion need not obscure another truth concerning the movement's reason for being. As he put his and the movement's task, "Rather than look for some *unique* mission, should we not seek to fulfill the basic mission God has given his people?... We proceed with the understanding that the intention of this movement is to address itself to the wholeness of the church's mission over against the fragmentation which has characterized much of Protestantism."[13] Sterner's conception of the mission of the church was one that had already been accepted by many in the Church of God movement and which became increasingly familiar in subsequent years. In this view, any special mission or purpose for the Church of God receded into the background while the conception of its mission could scarcely be distinguished from that of any other Christian body. Broadly stated, for Sterner the mission of the Church of God was to be, through teaching, witnessing, serving, and in its very being, the caring community of Christian love. In his words, "We cherish, rather, the ideal of a people moved upon by the Holy Spirit and outgoing in loving service. Our ideal is that of a dynamic fellowship, flexible and imaginative as it encounters people in various strata and segments of society. We envision the fellowship as loving enough to rise above class, culture, and race, and to be God's object lesson in human brotherhood."[14] Sterner's emphasis on the church as a caring fellowship presaged important changes in the movement's doctrinal practice of the church over the ensuing decades.

The Church and the Therapeutic Culture

Philosopher Alasdair MacIntyre identifies three dominant characters of twentieth century American culture—the aesthete, the manager, and the therapist.[15] As MacIntyre defined them, characters are moral representatives of their culture in the sense that they provide that culture with a moral ideal and, thus, "the character morally legitimates a mode of social existence."[16] Dominant characters provide a culture with many of its personal and social norms. By way of illustration, the manager as a cultural character has become so pervasive in American culture that its terminology is now applied to organizations where such language once would have been thought rather odd. Thus, for example, American voters in the 2000 presidential campaign were asked to decide between two candidates, each of whom presented himself as the better manager of the executive branch of government, a self-description that would not have occurred to Abraham Lincoln or Woodrow Wilson. Similarly, the term *CEO* came to be applied to an ever-widening circle of organizations irrespective of the fact that their origins lay far afield of the business corporation; church pastors and denominational executives could be heard referring to themselves by this term. The cultural characters of manager and therapist came to have profound impacts on the doctrinal practice of the church in the Church of God movement during the last quarter of the twentieth century. In the case of the cultural character of the therapist, the effect of that impact was to reshape the way in which Church of God people thought about the church and, correlatively, its doctrinal practices. In effect, this reshaping led to the development of what can be called a "therapeutic church."

Philip Rieff studied the influence of the ideas and applications of psychotherapy on American culture from Freud through Jung and Reich to David Herbert Lawrence. Rieff concluded that there had emerged the "triumph of the therapeutic," a cultural revolution in which "psychological man" was in the process of replacing "religious man."[17] This replacement would result in a very different set of cultural institutions reinforcing an equally different set of cultural values. Thus, said Rieff:

> Where family and nation once stood, or Church and Party, there will be hospital and theater too, the normative institutions of the next culture. Trained to be incapable of sustaining sectarian satisfactions, psychological man cannot be susceptible to sectarian control. Religious man was born to be saved; psychological man is born to be pleased. The difference was established long ago, when "I believe," the cry of the ascetic, lost precedence to "one feels," the caveat of the therapeutic. And if the therapeutic is to win out, then surely the psychotherapist will be his secular spiritual guide.[18]

Throughout the course of the twentieth century the "therapeutic" won triumphs in American Protestantism to the extent that the pastor-as-counselor came to influence a conception of the ministry that previously had been shaped by the role of the pastor-as-evangelist or pastor-as-administrator. Many Protestant seminaries applied the "therapeutic" to the study of pastoral care and counseling, requiring a semester or more of Clinical Pastoral Education of all students preparing for the ministry.[19] Given the ministry's historic commitment to the cure of souls it was not difficult to extend this role in the direction of the therapist. However, the triumph of the therapeutic in American culture was even more complete in areas yet further from its original domain, and the new therapeutically inclined shape of these areas in turn began to reshape the Church of God movement's conception of the church. These new areas were advertising and entertainment, and together they played important roles in the creation of the late twentieth-century consumer culture that profoundly influenced many aspects of American life, the church included.

Historians of advertising point to a seismic shift in the strategies of American advertisers after the turn of the twentieth century. Previously consumers had read or listened to advertisements expecting to learn information about products; advertising strategy aimed at the goal of informing purchasers. By the early 1900s, however, advertising agencies had begun considering the psychology of their efforts, and this resulted in a fundamental strategic reorientation. Advertisers became less interested in informing prospective customers and more concerned that they associate feelings of well-being with the products advertised. This shift was a crucial moment in the history of American culture, for it signified a change from a "Protestant ethos ordered to the conception of salvation through self-denial to a therapeutic ethos stressing self-realization in this world—an ethic characterized by an almost obsessive concern with psychic and physical health defined in sweeping terms."[20] As the century progressed, pleasure and well-being became increasingly important criteria for Americans, not only in respect of their consumer choices but as determinants in an ever-widening circle of decisions. This growing influence was powerfully reinforced by the new medium of television in the second half of the century. Television proved to be a remarkably powerful form of entertainment. In fact, cultural historian and critic Neil Postman argued that television's extraordinary power as entertainment transformed televised forms of public discourse—news reporting, political debates, education, religion, and so forth—into shows that viewers assessed on the basis of their ability to entertain. As in advertising, information was replaced by a particular set of feelings where pleasure took center stage. Conditioned by television, Americans came to require that public discourse be entertaining, in a word, pleasurable.[21]

The Church of God proved quite susceptible to the consumer-therapeutic culture of late twentieth-century America. The movement was certainly not alone in this susceptibility, but its stress on the epistemological importance of experience rendered the Church of God especially vulnerable to the surrounding therapeutic and consumer culture. Among Church of God people experience had a long history of validating belief, and commonly such experience was unmediated. Part of its legacy as a child of Pietist Christianity was the importance that the Church of God movement placed on experience as the locus of true theology and the means, along with Scripture, of validating religious truth. Thus Church of God people had sung that the biblical truth was proved in their hearts. Of course, feelings are an important aspect of experience. Even as the language of experience had opened the door to liberal theology in the 1940s, the consumer-therapeutic culture's version of the language of experience—the language of pleasurable feeling— also sounded right to Church of God people, steeped as they were in the importance of experience. That such language had the ring of truth about it manifested itself in different ways in the movement's doctrinal practice of the church.

The Therapeutic Church

The All Board Congress and the consultations of the early '70s had each in its own way called for a reassessment and fresh statement of the core doctrines of the Church of God movement. This call was answered in an important way by Warner Press's decision to publish the "Church of God Doctrinal Library." Eight volumes comprised the Library, each assigned to a different writer and all to be published in time for the 1980–81 centennial anniversary of the Church of God movement. Somewhat curiously, few of the movement's theologians received assignments. Gilbert W. Stafford of the School of Theology at Anderson College, and Kenneth L. Jones, a professor at Mid-America Bible College were the only two theologians of advanced theological training to write books for the series. The other six writers were either pastors or members past or present of the national agency leadership.[22] That so few trained theologians were part of the overall project may be attributed to the democratizing process that had been at work in the movement since C. E. Brown had assumed the editorial reins at the Gospel Trumpet Company. In 1971 that process had taken its most aggressive step toward eliminating the "interlocking directorates" of the '40s and '50s when a bylaws change was adopted prohibiting any agency or Executive Council employee from membership on the council or any of its constituent members. This move definitely broadened participation by grassroots churches and pastors. But it also disqualified some of the movement's most highly educated ministers. In one way this perpetuated a long-standing rift in the movement. On one side stood the movement's educators and educational institutions while on the other could be found some of its most influential pastors. The fear that "Anderson" might exercise too much control in the church was a lingering residue of the Slacum agitation. This fear served to keep open the rift, despite the activity of individual professors as conference leaders and speakers, since it was Anderson College that many theologians called home. An informal Warner Press editorial policy also limited the number of writers from Anderson to be assigned to a given project for fear that the grassroots church would react negatively to the presence of too many "Anderson people."

Given that the doctrinal practice of the church had been the centerpiece of the movement's theological writing since the days of D. S. Warner, the volume on the church might have been considered the most important in the series. Extraordinary meetings over the past decade and a half had been calling for a fresh theological statement on the church. Considered in this light, the volume on the church was the plum assignment of the Doctrinal Library. However, when the person originally assigned to this task failed to complete a manuscript Warner Press turned to R. Eugene Sterner, a stalwart figure whether as pastor, agency leader, radio minister, or state coordinator. But Sterner had already contributed a volume to the series, *Healing and Wholeness.* In an emergency step necessitated by Warner Press's desire to have the library completed in time for the centennial, Sterner was asked to revise his previously published book, *Being the Community of Christian Love*.[23] Revised, some chapters altering little other than titles, the book appeared as *God's Caring People* in 1981.

R. Eugene Sterner (1912–) was representative of the generation who rose to positions of church leadership in the 1950s and who led the Church of God through the '60s and '70s. He was born and raised on his family's farm near Turnip Hole, Pennsylvania. In his teenage years Sterner's parents were converted in a revival meeting and within a year, so was their son. It was then that a man named Forrest Kilgore from the nearby town of Callensburg traveled to the Sterner home to explain to this family of new converts the Church of God revealed in the pages of Scripture. In the heart of the Great Depression, Sterner enrolled at Anderson College. He stayed for only two years, long enough to become impressed with Russell Olt's insights into psychology and marry the former Mildred Rabberman. Sterner left Anderson for the Church of God in Elwood City, Pennsylvania, the first of four successful pastorates through the '30s and '40s. He remained committed to advancing his education, completing undergraduate study while serving the Ruston, Louisiana church, pursuing graduate study in psychology while pastor of the Church of God at Lanette, Alabama, and theological study at Bonebrake Theological Seminary at Dayton, Ohio during his pastorate there. A self-described independent thinker, Sterner made it a point to join the local ministerial fellowship in every community where he served, and he found satisfying friendships among the ministers of churches that many Church of God preachers still described as "denominational Babylon."[24]

In the 1940s Sterner took the first of a series of assignments in the national work of the Church of God. After the retirement of Irene S. Caldwell he served as interim secretary of the Board of Christian Education. This assignment was followed by his Dayton pastorate, but in 1953 the Sterner returned to Anderson as executive director of the Radio and Television Commission of the Church of God until 1961. Widely respected as a preacher and evangelist, Sterner played a key role on the Commission for Revision and Planning and the creation of the Division of Church Service, which he subsequently headed from 1955 to 1967. In 1968 he succeeded W. Dale Oldham as speaker on the Church of God movement's nationally syndicated radio program, *The Christian Brotherhood Hour*.

Sterner's early life had left him emotionally wounded and with unresolved feelings of resentment. The tough, no-nonsense Pennsylvania Dutch culture of his childhood was devoid of warm, caring relationships. A harsh, critical and often judgmental spirit at the local church only added to

Sterner's hunger for nurturing relationships. The demands of the life of holiness as practiced by his church taught him that no sanctified person ever felt anger or resentment, so as a teenager and young adult Sterner learned to repress these feelings. When he began his college study Sterner found the unhealthiness of his childhood and church background confirmed in psychological theory. He learned to complement psychology with theology and then found freedom from what he called the "sins of the spirit"—anger, animosity, resentment—by forgiving and asking for forgiveness.[25]

Sterner's approach to the doctrine and practice of the church was heavily indebted to the discourse and values of the therapeutic culture. This culture was given a decidedly Christian cast for Sterner through his friendship with E. Stanley Jones, a well-known Methodist missionary and minister who influenced a wide circle of leaders in Sterner's generation.[26] Jones had acquired a reputation as a world Christian and for his "Christian ashrams" or retreat centers, an adaptation from his encounter with Hinduism as a missionary in India. In the early 1960s Sterner met Jones and participated in his first ashram, and this experience began a decade of association with Jones as friend and ashram staff member. It was here that Sterner discovered the meaning of Christian love in a liberating experience where he was able to honestly speak his heart and mind. There he learned what was for him the full meaning of the New Testament word *koinonia,* a fellowship that is the sharing of life.

The books that Sterner wrote and revised between 1971 and 1981 all employ therapeutic language and values. To be sure, Sterner did not abandon traditional theological discourse, but he tended to therapeutic descriptions of the human predicament and offered the church as the community whose loving care overcame certain aspects of that predicament. Thus, for example, Sterner began his discussion of the church with a description of loneliness as a pervasive feeling stemming from the "lack of relatedness, the feeling of standing alone, isolated, without any genuine companionship or understanding. It is the bottled up feeling of never being able to unburden yourself to another, the feeling that no one has the time or inclination to listen and to hear you through and that, even if someone did hear you, the result would be rejection."[27] Sterner analyzed the false steps often made to remedy the problem of loneliness as symptoms of inauthentic existence: "People wear masks to hide who and what they really are, probably not because they wish to be dishonest, but because they are afraid to be known."[28] Furthermore, said Sterner, in loneliness and inauthentic existence humans often deny their real feelings to themselves and in the process reach a point where an honest, realistic self-understanding becomes impossible.

God's forgiveness and love provided the remedy for the loneliness and inauthentic existence that Sterner described, and in his view the church became an important mediator of that loving forgiveness. Christians needed to "understand and appreciate the genius of the gospel and the healing power of genuine Christian fellowship. God's love, mediated through the deep relatedness of Christian friends who know the meaning of forgiveness can work wonders of healing."[29]

Therapeutic language may have permeated Sterner's writing, but he also reiterated the movement's traditional doctrine concerning the nature of the church. C. E. Brown's version of Church of God restorationism informed Sterner's portrayal of a church that had fallen away from New Testament standards of membership, leadership, and mission. Nevertheless he saw signs of a recovery of the church's true nature wherever Christians refused to see it in terms of institutions, buildings, or creeds. Like first-century Christians, the true church in the twentieth century was dynamic, not static—the people of God on mission.[30] Sterner thus saw the diminishing distinction between clergy and laity as a recovery of the New Testament principle that all Christians are called to ministry. "More and more," said Sterner, "we are seeing the Church in the light of the New Testament, but many laypersons are reluctant to accept the involvement and responsibility that rightfully belong to them. Closely related to this point is the fact that the early Christians were known as a servant people."[31] Whether in the first century or the twentieth, all believers were called to be a servant people that Sterner described as a "loving fellowship," and it was in this phrase that he wedded traditional Church of God discourse on the church to the language of the therapeutic culture:

> The unique characteristic of this fellowship was that it was more than mere togetherness. It was unity in the Spirit of Christ and in the love that is shed abroad in our hearts by the Holy Spirit. People outside the Body could not help but see a new kind of relationship among Christians and a new quality of life in them.
>
> Loving fellowship was quite basic in the New Testament church, and it is still vital today. Probably no single aspect is more important to those who seek a church home than the quality of the fellowship to be found. Two things stand out as the most basic criteria in a church. People want to be part of a fellowship that is warm and caring, and they want to hear the Word of God responsibly taught. Let organization and

program serve this end. The church is that body of believers who are in right relationship (fellowship) with God and fellow Christians.[32]

The idea of the church as a caring fellowship was a long-term theme in Sterner's ecclesiology. As early as 1957 he had published work in which he described the church in these terms. Already then Sterner believed that Christians needed to emphasize, and that American society needed, a church that defined itself in terms of fellowship. This emphasis signaled a subtle change from conventional Church of God ecclesiology, a change apparent in a comparison of Sterner's book with A. F. Gray's *The Nature of the Church,*[33] a small volume published about the same time. Gray approached his subject out of the, by then quite familiar, perspective that described the New Testament era as the church's golden age followed by institutionalization, division, and decline. Without resorting to F. G. Smith's apocalyptic restorationism Gray nevertheless insisted that the recovery of the lost unity of the church depended on Christian hearts and minds being fully in accord with Christ.[34] Furthermore, Gray was suspicious of the word "fellowship" when applied too broadly as a description of the relationship among Christians. Fellowship had to be understood as possible only among those who had "like empathy with Christ."[35] As such, fellowship for Gray was far more than friendship, good will, or toleration.

Sterner would not have disputed Gray's insistence on believers' common experience in Christ as the basis of Christian fellowship. What distinguishes his approach from Gray's is the different starting points of their respective discussions. The latter began and framed his discussion in the "biblical-theological" approach that was the hallmark of his generation of Church of God writers. Sterner respected and somewhat followed this approach, but he also tempered it by paying greater heed to the world to which he insisted the church was called the minister. In a limited sense of the term Sterner was more "existentialist" than historical theologian. He was informed more by the present than he was interested in traversing the historical road by which church and world had reached their present states. For Sterner the world's brokenness and division were illnesses that only the gospel of Christ could heal. To be sure, sin was the root cause of the world's misery; on that point Sterner insisted. But the consequences of sin he typically described not in legal or quasi-legal terminology but in the language of sickness and disease. Sterner would not have disputed the sinner's need to be justified before a righteous God, but he also displayed a marked preference for the language of sickness and healing—in a word, a therapeutic model of the gospel.

The themes of salvation as a healing experience and the church as the redemptive fellowship instrumental in that healing ran through Sterner's theology. They show themselves, for example, in one of the important Church of God books of the '60s, Sterner's *We Reach Our Hands in Fellowship*.[36] Intended as an introduction to the Church of God for new constituents and religious seekers, the book expresses something of the self-understanding of the Church of God as the postwar period drew to an end. The manner in which Sterner approached his subject, for instance, suggests that the movement's understanding of itself as an advocate of Christian unity had not died. He rehearsed in terms familiar to movement readers the narrative of a New Testament church as the standard from which the medieval church departed and which had subsequently been regained in the Church of God movement. Sterner wanted new converts to appreciate this element. Thus in joining fellowship with the Church of God they were making common cause with a group that had a particular identity even if new developments in the cause of Christian unity had clouded its sense of purpose. However he also modified this understanding in two important ways. In the first place he muted the old triumphalism inherent in the Church of God's claim to be the restored church of the New Testament. Thus he did not claim for the movement exclusive title to that restoration.[37] Furthermore, Sterner portrayed both the New Testament church and the Church of God movement in less glowing terms than had previous generations of writers. He stopped short of saying that all of the virtues of the former were restored in the latter; in fact, Sterner said that they were not. Furthermore, he expressly stated that the first-century church was not without its faults, nor was the Church of God.[38]

Secondly, Sterner modified the movement's self-understanding through description of the characteristics of the true church and the importance assigned to one in particular. Early Church of God writers had described the true church as the place where sinners were saved, believers were sanctified, and the sick were divinely healed. Ironically, given his therapeutic vision of the church, divine healing did not come under discussion in *We Reach Our Hands in Fellowship;* the new birth and life in the Holy Spirit, however, remained crucial topics. Practice was not so indebted to the therapeutic culture that the church had lost sight of "religious man's" need for salvation. Sterner considered these topics under a set of basic qualities that he found both in the church of the New Testament era and in the Church of God movement: fellowship, simplicity, freedom, and equality.[39] It was the church's characteristic as a loving and redemptive fellowship that Sterner emphasized. Thus, for example, when Sterner described the medieval church it was no longer "popery" *per se* that was the problem, but that "church ceased to be characterized by warm, loving fellowship of growing persons and became dominated by an ecclesiastical machine with some men ruling over other men."[40] The practice of fellowship was, in Sterner's view, crucial to the spiritual life of the church corporately and individually. Indeed, the church as a community of loving fellowship, he said, was the "channel of [God's] redemptive plan—the body in which he lives and carries out his divine plan."[41] Sterner made loving and redemptive fellowship the hinge on which a vital church turned:

> Any pastor or evangelist will testify that the salvation of souls in any group depends pretty largely upon the quality of fellowship in that group. This sense of deep relatedness among Christian people is contagious. Simply to be in a group of people who are deeply united in fellowship is a quickening, awakening experience. The effectiveness of our testimony and witness depends to a considerable degree on the quality of the fellowship we enjoy.[42]

It would be too much to say that Eugene Sterner's career as a speaker and writer, influential though it was, was in itself the cause of a shift in Church of God ecclesiology. But his work is emblematic of a major change in the way in which many in the movement described and thought about the church after 1960. The language of therapy prevalent in American culture contributed significantly to this change. Church of God people referred to the church less and less in apocalyptic terms and also less and less in terms of Brown's historical understanding. Ministers and laypersons alike described the church as a healing refuge and caring fellowship, the antidote for souls battered and wounded by the alienation of modern life. The culture of therapy pushed the movement's ideas about the church in this direction, but in Sterner's work the church remained the community whose caring fellowship was instrumental in the salvation of individual souls. In other words, it was necessary for the individual to become a member of the body. Accordingly, a new doctrinal practice of fellowship became crucial to the Church of God understanding of the church.

In the wake of the growing influence of the consumer culture on the church's life, people began to lose sight of the link that Sterner had forged. The church became increasingly a place sought out by individuals who came, or departed, on the basis of perceptions concerning the satisfaction of their individual needs. In return, many congregations began to develop plans for ministry in ways that resembled a business's approach to marketing its products. Correlatively, the church's worship also began to take on a new set of values.

Church in an Entertainment Culture

The notion of American religion as a marketplace in which churches competed with each other for the interest and commitment of individuals was not a new development in late twentieth-century American culture. The federal constitution guaranteed religious freedom and in the process separated all religious organizations, primarily churches in late eighteenth-century America, from the government as their revenue source and as the authority on which they could rely to enforce religious rules and regulations. The constitutional separation of church and state, in Martin Marty's memorable phrase, "threw religion into the marketplace."[43] Competition between churches, if not direct, nevertheless became the new word of the day. Ministers and church leaders were forced to learn new ways of communicating their message in language that would attract and hold the allegiance of people who were no longer forced by law either to attend or financially support churches. Some denominations adapted to the new situation better than others. Those that proved successful in their adaptation often were so because they either came into being during or emphasized the values of, the popular democratic culture of nineteenth-century America.[44] Methodist and the restorationist churches of the Stone-Campbell movement—the Christian Church—proved to be remarkably successful as "people's churches" in the early nineteenth-century. The Church of God and the other Holiness Movement churches, among others, arose as popular religious movements toward the century's conclusion.

From its very beginning the Church of God movement was a "people's church," an heir to the plain spoken, democratic tradition of the popular denominations of nineteenth-century America. Often of the people themselves, early Church of God preachers took no pride in the titles and degrees of conventional ministerial preparation. Learning and the social status that it conferred could not compare with the "unction of the Spirit" when it came to validating a man or woman's call to the ministry. That so many women were recognized and ordained to the Church of God ministry in its early decades is further testimony to the movement's character as a "democracy of the Spirit." Arising out of the people, preachers delivered sermons in popular language and idiom. As with their early nineteenth-century antecedents, so also for the Church of God the popular idiomatic expression of the gospel proved to be of great strength in attracting new constituents through most of the twentieth-century. However, as that century unfolded, the language of therapy and the consumer culture reshaped popular culture. At a moment when the Church of God had been shorn of a dominant self-description, (i. e., the apocalyptic ecclesiology and its understanding of the movement as the "Last Reformation,") and when key practices were undergoing alteration, the movement's connection to the popular culture became a double-edged sword. As the language of the people came to be dominated by the ideas and values of the therapeutic-consumer culture, churches that employed this cultural idiom sometimes experienced high growth rates. However, this often at the expense of a weakened theological discipline and doctrinal practice. In this situation, ministers and congregational leaders needed to be especially watchful lest the use of a powerful cultural idiom become the means by which the church was recast as a religious shopping mall. As such, the desires of parishioners determined the content and shape of congregational worship and ministries.

In no aspect of church life were these developments more openly or controversially displayed than in the practice of worship and music. Gospel songwriting and singing had been of extraordinary importance throughout the life of the Church of God movement. Historically, Church of God people sang their faith. That practice altered significantly, at least in terms of song-writing, in the 1960s. In the process, the theology written into its hymnody disappeared insofar as new songs were concerned. At the same time, tastes changed so that the music idiom of many standard Church of God gospel songs began to sound quaintly old-fashioned to late twentieth-century ears— particularly those born after 1960. In response to the desires and tastes of a rising generation, after 1970, music and worship styles steadily adopted expressions of the popular musical culture in ways that, to an unprecedented degree, introduced into worship values that could be described as "entertainment." The entrance of the entertainment culture into the church worked a transformation that, for the non-creedal Church of God was portentous.

The rapidly expanding use of praise choruses and contemporary gospel music in worship dramatically altered the style and conduct of worship in many American church communions after 1980. These alterations have had a particularly telling effect on the self-understanding of the Church of God movement, for "where creeds are sung more than said the mutations of music are prime indicators of transformations of faith."[45] Early songbooks carried the movement's theology and conveyed it through song. The practice of singing their faith connected people to each other and to the movement's mission. For regular attenders that meant that the message of holiness and unity, divine healing, and the kingdom, could be reinforced through song twice on Sundays and again in Wednesday night prayer meeting. The 1953 and 1971 hymnals enlarged the faith of Church of God people by including more hymns that were part of general Protestantism. Especially by 1971, Church of God people had generally accepted C. E. Brown's idea that all Christians were members of God's church. There was a certain symmetry between this idea and the practice of including and singing the great hymns of the wider church. Nevertheless, in the face of altered doctrinal practices and without the use of creeds to serve as theological norms for the movement, the use of a more inclusive hymnal also could not but diminish worshipers' understanding of and identification with the movement's reason for being. One cannot identify with what one knows only vaguely, or knows not at all.

After 1980 the use of hymnals themselves increasingly became a controversial issue in the Church of God as it did elsewhere. During World War II and into the postwar era Church of God people became more open to the music of the popular culture. That growing receptivity, the burgeoning gospel music business, and the rise of a new musical genre, the praise chorus, combined to change the musical tastes of many people in the movement, especially the younger generations. In the late 1980s Warner Press was able to take advantage of the Gaither Music Corporation's network of relationships to publish a new hymnal, *Worship the Lord*,[46] that included songs and choruses of the new Christian music. The new hymnal retained much of the traditional Protestant hymnody and the songs of the Church of God movement. However, it was certainly a telling feature of the changed situation that editors felt obligated to identify with a special symbol what had become known as Church of God "heritage hymns." That Church of God people had to have their own songs identified for them was a sure sign of a weakening sense of identity.

For some Church of God congregations, particularly those that described themselves as "community" churches or otherwise minimized the historic name "Church of God," even the 1989 hymnal rather quickly became passé. The ephemeral nature of praise choruses gave and took away popularity with a rapidity that no hymnal could keep up with. The application of advanced technology in worship, whether overhead or power point projectors, also tended to keep hymnals in their pew racks gathering dust. Praise choruses and contemporary gospel music were written by Christians who tended to downplay specific church affiliations for the sake of more generalized Christian consumption. That these songs were sung with greater frequency in Church of God worship settings may very well have strengthened the bonds of Christian unity between people of the movement and others who sang generic praise choruses. An argument could be made that it was through such common elements of worship that Christians, especially those who identified with American Evangelicalism, were coming together. Given the fact that this musical literature was also nearly devoid of the theological combination of holiness and unity on which the movement's theology rested, Church of God congregations who felt a sense of unity with other Christians had little theological understanding of the basis of Christian unity; they just knew they felt good being together with other Christians. Critics of this unreflected sense of unity could point out that it is no virtue accidentally to do the right thing. In order to be virtuous, one must do the right thing for the reasons that virtuous people do so. For some in the Church of God this objection made little impression, but they were nevertheless forced to confront the possibility that a more generalized practice of singing contributed to the movement's diminished understanding of what it was and why it existed.

Critics of the new Christian music also pointed to the manner in which its use had altered worship itself in ways that paralleled the value of entertainment in popular culture. In the movement's early days, as part of its legacy in camp meeting revivalism, worship typically was exuberant and marked by fervor. During World War II and in the postwar era worship lost something of the flavor of the camp meeting as the Church of God shifted toward mainstream Protestantism. But stalwart movement loyalists still had Anderson Camp Meeting to which they could annually return in order to experience, as many of them said, the real Church of God. In the '70s and '80s, as the popularity of gospel and contemporary Christian music exploded, Church of God people found a medium through which to experience the depth of feeling in worship that had been characteristic of the movement in the early days. The updated melodies and harmonies of the new Christian music paralleled those in much of popular music, so that musically there was little to distinguish it from the larger culture. Church of God teenagers of the '50s could appreciate the musical difference between the songs that they sang in church and those they listened to on the radio—whether sung by Elvis Presley, Pat Boone, or Ray Charles. The gap between pop music and Christian music closed during the ensuing decades.

During this same period the Church of God movement slowly but surely made peace with an increasing number of elements in American culture, especially those related to entertainment. Like other holiness churches, the movement began with an attitude that might be described, in H. Richard Niebuhr's classic terms, as "Christ against culture."[47] Early Church of God people were highly suspicious of the world; to "compromise with the world" was to give in to the allurements of the values, which is to say the temptations, that it seductively offered. In 1900 the saints' list of temptations was appreciably longer than one that would have been written in 1980. Church of God people dropped their early opposition to the purchase of insurance policies and created a ministers' pension fund. In 1900 the saints refrained from consulting physicians, a practice that was almost completely reversed as the twentieth century marched on. The early movement closely monitored social activities and relationships between the sexes. *Trumpet* family members had divided their weekend afternoon volleyball games according to sex, and when the men were finished they were not permitted to remain outside to watch the women play. Even in the 1950s many state youth camps had segregated the swimming hour, boys during one half and girls the other, and social dancing was forbidden on the campuses of Church of God colleges. In the wake of the youth revolution of the '60s much of this segregation went by the boards.[48] In the 1940s Earl Slacum had charged Anderson agency leaders with the sin of going to the movies; as the postwar era unfolded fewer and fewer people of the movement any longer believed that movies were sinful, nor did they worry about the matter. The explicit portrayal of sex and violence in film and television was a concern, but opposition was aimed at these themes rather than television and motion pictures in general.

The movement's growing receptivity to elements of the entertainment culture also appeared in changing worship styles. The issue at stake here was not, of course, the tawdry elements of that culture, but entertainment itself. Even as television trained viewers to expect that what they watched should be absorbing and exciting, so worshippers came to have the same expectations of worship. Now worship increasingly needed to be enthusiastic and exciting. The style of worship, in many cases, also changed from the formality of an ordered program to one that was increasingly casual and informal. The sermon also changed; classic expository preaching gave way to a more relational style that closed the gap between preacher and audience. Under the burgeoning influence of the church growth movement, congregations also attempted to change their language. "Church language" came to be seen as a stumbling block to the "unchurched," and therefore it was incumbent on evangelistically-minded congregations to adopt a less churchly form of discourse. For example, some ministers and their congregations dropped the use of the term *sanctuary,* replacing it with "auditorium." In this case language also seemed to shape the physical reality occupied by the church, for new church buildings often resembled auditoriums more than conventional sanctuaries. In all of these ways some congregations of the movement, including many who came to be regarded as models of contemporary church life and evangelism, illustrated the movement's adaptation to and adoption of some of the values of the culture of therapy and entertainment.

Less a Movement, More a Church Where Needs Are Met

The model of the therapeutic church captured a large segment of the Church of God movement after 1970. What was the consequence for the theology and doctrinal practice of the Church of God, particularly when that question is posed against the movement's historic mission as an agent of Christian unity? In a word, this capture accelerated the transition that the Church of God had been making from sect-type to church-type denomination. As the Church of God moved through the 1960s, '70s, and on, its adherents were less and less conscious of having affiliated with a movement on a particular mission. Narrower, more individualistic concerns replaced the cause of Christian unity as motivation to join or remain in congregations of the Church of God.

In the early decades of the movement's history, people who joined the ranks of the Church of God commonly testified that they had "seen the church." They made common cause with the movement because they saw it to be the realized fellowship of a New Testament ideal where Christians dwell together in unity and peace. On their testimonies, frequently printed in the pages of the *Gospel Trumpet,* many of these early saints hungered for such a church. They "took their stand" with the Church of God because participation in the movement and its self-consciously stated mission of Christian unity satisfied that hunger. In this sense, one can describe the early Church of God as a special interest movement centered on the realization of Christian unity through the experience and practice of holiness. That these early saints were expected to "come out" of Babylon in order to join this movement seemed a contradiction only to outsiders. Those inside the movement understood its logic and the necessity of forsaking the world of denominationalism.

The logic of come-outism was powerfully reinforced by the apocalyptic ecclesiology of W. G. Schell, H. M. Riggle, Lillie S. McCutcheon, but above all F. G. Smith. The influence of the *Gospel Trumpet* and the many publications of the Gospel Trumpet Publishing Company combined to give this ecclesiology a broad influence throughout the Church of God. Combined with the fact that the movement's leadership was in these decades little more than an oligarchy shaping thought and doctrinal practices, the apocalyptic ecclesiology gave Church of God people even stronger reason to affiliate with the movement. It was in their view the embodiment of the true church into which God was calling all faithful Christians at the end of history. To be sure, there were those who never accepted the apocalyptic ecclesiology or who came to repudiate it. New forms of biblical scholarship and a new historical consciousness combined to challenge the earlier apocalypticism. These dissident voices nevertheless remained loyal to the idea that the Church of God had a mission connected to Christian unity. But the theologians among them were hard-pressed to articulate a new vision of that unity. In the wake of the Slacum controversy that vision continued to wane, especially because no new doctrinal practice had replaced the older practice of come-outism. Church of God people committed to Christian unity began to cast about in different directions for practices or affiliations wherein their commitment to this cause might be expressed, but they were part of a dwindling minority.

The cause and practice of Christian unity among Church of God people was overtaken by a simpler idea of evangelism. The movement had always been concerned for the salvation of souls. However, the doctrinal practice of come-outism was predicated on the belief that participation in denominational Christianity was sinful, and people needed to flee those associations with every bit the same determination as they would shun any other sin. The practical outcome of this nexus was, in Valorous Clear's phrase, "guerrilla evangelism," proselytizing Christians from the denominations. As the doctrinal practice of come-outism waned Church of God ministers and evangelists had to rethink evangelism. The movement's original theological insight that the experience of salvation was the doorway into the church remained intact, but now it was severed from the theology and practice of Christian unity. Men and women continued to enter the fellowship of Church of God congregations, but less and less with the conviction that they were joining a movement committed to a cause. Instead people joined congregations on the basis of the way they portrayed themselves—warm, caring fellowships where people could find their needs met. The consumer culture taught Americans that it was not the provider but customers who determined their own needs and how they were to be filled. The therapeutic church that emerged after 1970 was indeed a warm, caring fellowship that responded to the deep needs of men and women. However, this new understanding of the church also meant that now each person was free to determine the degree to which the church met those needs. This dynamic gives moral authority over to the individual who, as customer, is always right when it comes to answering the question whether needs are being satisfied. In this new situation congregational discipline became highly problematic. The new phenomenon of the therapeutic church also reinforced the centrifugal force inherent in congregationalist polities. No longer bound together, if it ever was entirely, as a movement disciplined by the ideal and doctrinal practices of Christian unity, the Church of God found itself becoming a loose association of congregations who related to the larger fellowship much in much the same spirit as individual members related to them. Participation in the life of the Church of God movement came to be determined on the basis of whether or not needs were being met, and increasingly it was left to each congregation to answer that question.

Notes

1. R. Eugene Sterner, quoted in John W. V. Smith, *The Quest for Holiness and Unity*, 376.

2. An excerpted version of the report of the Findings Committee, chaired by Sterner, is printed in Barry L. Callen, ed., *Following the Light*, "All Board Congress and Planning Council," 281–285. The quotation is found on 282.

3. Ibid., 281–282, *passim.*

4. Ibid, 282.

5. Ibid.

6. "Consultation of the Church of God (June 1970)," in Callen, Ed., *Following the Light*, 285.

7. See chapter 15.

8. *Quest for Holiness and Unity*, 400.

9. The study papers were printed and distributed in a booklet titled *Consultation on Doctrine* (Anderson, Ind: Executive Council of the Church of God, 1973).

10. Massey's discussion of Christian unity appears in chapter 15.

11. "The Nature of the Church," Ibid., 9.

12. Ibid., 10.

13. "The Mission of the Church," Sterner's emphases. Ibid., 14.

14. Ibid.

15. Cf. *After Virtue*, 2nd edition (Notre Dame, Ind: University of Notre Dame Press, 1984), 23–35.

16. Ibid., 29.

17. Philip Rieff, *The Triumph of the Therapeutic* (New York: Harper and Row, 1966), 1–27.

18. Ibid., 24–25.

19. For an overview of changing conceptions of the ministry and especially the emergence of the minister-as-counselor see H. Richard Niebuhr and Daniel Day Williams, *The Ministry in Historical Perspective*, revised edition (New York: Harper and Row, 1956).

20. T. J. Jackson Lears and Richard Wightman Fox, "From Salvation to Self-Realization: Advertising and the Therapeutic Roots of the Consumer Culture, 1880–1930," in Richard Wightmen Fox and T. J. Jackson Lears, eds., *The Culture of Consumption* (New York: Pantheon Books, 1983), 3–38.

21. Neil Postman, *Amusing Ourselves to Death: Public Discourse in the Age of Show Business* (New York: Penguin Books, 1985), 83–98.

22. The entire list of books and their respective authors is as follows: Dwight L. Dye, *A Kingdom of Servants*; Keith Huttenlocker, *God, Can I Get to Know You?*; Kenneth L. Jones, *The Word of God*; James Earl Massey, *Concerning Christian Unity*; Arlo F. Newell, *Receive the Holy Spirit*; Gilbert W. Stafford, *The Life of Salvation*; R. Eugene Sterner, *God's Caring People*; and Sterner, *Healing and Wholeness*.

23. (Anderson, Ind: Warner Press, 1971).

24. Sterner was fond of saying, "When everybody is thinking alike, nobody is thinking very much."

25. The analysis is Sterner's personal recollection. R. Eugene Sterner, Interview, December 3, 2001, Anderson, Indiana.

26. Jones spoke in chapel services at Warner Pacific College as well as Anderson College and was also at services of the International Youth Convention of the Church of God.

27. Sterner, *God's Caring People* (Anderson, Ind: Warner Press, 1981), 5; Cf. Sterner, *Being the Community of Christian Love*, 9.

28. Sterner, *God's Caring People*, 5.

29. Ibid., 6.

30. Ibid., 26.

31. Ibid., 29.

32. Ibid., 30.

33. (Anderson, Ind: Warner Press, 1960).

34. Ibid., 60.

35. Ibid.

36. (Anderson, Ind: Warner Press, 1960).

37. Ibid., 28.

38. Ibid., 22.

39. Ibid.

40. Ibid., 14.

41. Ibid., 38.

42. Ibid.

43. Martin E. Marty, *Righteous Empire* (New York: The Dial Press, 1970). See his discussion from 35–77.

44. This aspect of early nineteenth-century American religious life had been illuminated with great insight by Nathan Hatch in his *The Democratization of American Christianity* (New Haven and London: Yale University Press, 1989).

45. David Martin, "Whatever Happened to Methodism?", *Books and Culture* (May/June 2001), 15.

46. (Anderson, Ind: Warner Press, 1989).

47. H. Richard Niebuhr, *Christ and Culture* (New York: Harper and Row, 1951).

48. As of this writing social dancing is still not permitted on the campuses of Church of God colleges, despite the fact that the large majority of students—including those of the Church of God—no longer understand or appreciate the reasons for this policy. As a compromise, Anderson University endorses dances off-campus, but only when a recognized campus group applies to the Department of Student Life to act as sponsor for the event.

Epilogue

At the conclusion of his centennial history of the Church of God John W. V. Smith pointed to three items of unfinished business on the movement's agenda. *Organization, relationships to other Christian bodies, and a new sense of mission* were matters that Smith thought needed the focused attention of the movement's best thinkers as it entered its second century.[1] Twenty years into that century, church leaders had given very determined attention to the first item on Smith's agenda, much more so than to either mission or relationships. All three items are related to the question of identity that had nagged the movement since the 1940s. As the movement entered the new millennium a growing number of its constituents asked, "What is the Church of God?" and it seemed that as many as asked also provided their own answers to that question.

In the late 1980s the General Assembly established a Task Force on Governance and Polity to study the movement's national organization. Under the leadership of Robert Nicholson the task force undertook a zero-sum analysis of the movement's organizational structures and relationships. The study began with the grassroots church and proceeded through state offices to the national agencies. The analysis and the recommendations stemming from it hoped to strengthen mission and ministry.[2] Effective planning and more cooperative relationships between planning units were the goals of the recommendations announced by the task force in 1992. However, church leadership turned away from two intriguing proposals. Task force members wanted to strengthen local church participation in the movement's national life. Some believed that a traveling convention would increase the attendance of those adherents for whom the distance to Anderson was a barrier. Accordingly, the task force recommended a study of the possibility of holding the annual convention of the Church of God and the meetings of the General Assembly at a location other than Anderson. However, nothing ever came of this recommendation. The second proposal addressed a growing perception that the General Assembly was no longer a body wherein matters of theology and vision could be debated. Many Assembly members had recoiled in disgust from the fractious session of 1980. Assembly officers and Executive Council staff members worked hard to avoid a repeat of those meetings. In the process, Assembly sessions often became largely procedural affairs, with the most important agenda item being the adoption of the annual Church of God World Service budget. The task force recommended the establishment of a triennial meeting for the purpose of discussing theologically substantive issues, but this proposal was the single one of nine that the Executive Council did not approve.

The work of the Task Force on Governance and Polity did not answer the discontent that continued to simmer in the grassroots church. There local pastors and some laypersons continued to be troubled by the feeling that they were only remotely connected to "Anderson," and that their voices were largely unheard in matters of national church policy. In an effort to address the feeling of disconnectedness in the local church, General Secretary of the Leadership Council[3] Edward L. Foggs led the development of a complete restructuring of the national agencies. In 1996 the General Assembly over-whelmingly adopted in principle a plan for restructuring the national work of the Church of God in the hope that a new organization would enable the national ministries of the church "to function with maximum responsiveness to congregational needs."[4] In 1998 the Assembly was asked to formalize a restructuring plan adopted in principle two years earlier. Some voices spoke in favor of the restructuring plan in the stated belief that the movement's future depended on its adoption. It was difficult not to avoid the irony; the future of a movement begun in protest against the organization of the church now was said to depend on a savior called restructuring. Grassroots church people hungered for closer connections to the national ministries of the church. In the Assembly's rush to satisfy this legitimate need, it also over-looked the fact that, despite General Secretary Foggs' claim, new structures do not necessarily entail a new vision of the church and its ministry.[5] Foggs had apparently confused a vision for the church with the means of achieving it. The latter are what may be described as "goods of efficiency"; they are the tools groups employ to accomplish their purpose. There is no guarantee that improved organization will generate or even enhance a vision of the group's reason for being. Those who looked to organizational restructuring to cure the movement's ills had not sufficiently attended to the historical and theo-logical questions that concerned changes in the movement's identity which had lingered over a half century.

Secondly, John Smith thought that the movement's mission remained an item of unfinished business. The mission of the church received considerable attention in the eighties and nineties, culminating in a 1988 Mission Statement for the movement. Much of this attention was focused on evangel-ism, and in 1991 the church launched a vigorous program of evangelism called "Vision-2-Grow." Throughout the decade three different Vision-2-Grow directors, Rolland Daniels, Oral Withrow, and Joseph Cookston, guided what certainly appeared to be a highly successful program. Average attendance in Sunday morning worship increased by nearly 18 percent during the period 1988–1999. As General Secretary Foggs reported, the program included efforts to improve the vitality of congregational life, offered continuing education opportunities to pastors, and strengthened pastoral relationships and family life.[6] Others credited the program's enthusiasm and innovating spirit for contributing to the climate that led to the restructuring of the national ministries. If numerical growth was not the exclusive target of Vision-2-Grow, the statistical growth of many congregations and the movement as a whole nevertheless was the primary indicator of the program's success.

Historically speaking, evangelism had never been the exclusive mission of the Church of God movement. In the minds of the first two generations, the goal of restoring the lost unity of the church stood close by evangelism as the movement's twin purposes, and these twins were identical rather than fraternal. In fact, it would be appropriate to view Christian unity and evangelism as the movement's Siamese twins. The early Church of God named as sin a believer's participation in the Babylonian world of denominational Christianity. "Come-outers" were saints who shunned that world as surely as if they had repented a life of crime. It was the opinion of early Church of God people that denominational Christians needed salvation just as much as any "unchurched" sinner who knelt at an altar and asked God's forgiveness. In this view the tactics aimed at persuading believers to abandon denominational Christianity constituted evangelism. Come-outism was the principal doctrinal practice of Christian unity in the early Church of God, but it was also a key evangelistic tactic. Christian unity and evangelism could scarcely be distinguished as the reason for being in the early Church of God. Correlatively, but without the benefit of a published mission statement, the movement held its identity and therefore its mission clearly in view.

The triumph of historical methods of scholarship in the 1930s effectively separated the Siamese twins bonded together in come-outism. In the process both were weakened, one of them mortally. C. E. Brown taught the movement that all the saved in Christ were members of the true church, regardless of denominational affiliation. Come-outism as the doctrinal practice of Christian unity progressively weakened over the ensuing decades and eventually died, a vestigial practice among splinter groups and a warmly regarded memory of the most conservative of Church of God people. The death of come-outism, however, also weakened the movement's revivalism. Evangelism in the Church of God had been essentially limited to the annual fall or spring revival. In the wake of come-outism's demise, and after the

1960s, enthusiasm for revivals and even the venerable institution of camp meeting waned. It was no longer clear what strategy for evangelism the movement would take. Postwar prosperity masked the problem, but in terms of its original mission the movement had begun limping. The Vision-2-Grow program brought a new strategy and tactics for evangelism. However, taken over from the church growth movement of Evangelicalism, some of these tactics encouraged pastors to play to some of the values of the consumer and entertainment culture. In the process they also minimized history and tradition, the locations of the theological distinctiveness in which a sense of identity and mission is to be found. Christian unity, the other twin in the movement's historic reason for being, did not receive the same determined attention that Vision-2-Grow gave to evangelism. Movement leadership did not invest the goal of Christian unity with the same level of energy and resources. Despite mention as the last item of the 1988 Mission Statement, Christian unity effectively disappeared as an element of Church of God identity and mission; evangelism had become the movement's reason for being.

"Relationships" constituted the third item of unfinished business on John Smith's agenda for the Church of God. Ever since the 1940s and the emergence of a vigorous ecumenical movement in the fifties, the practice of Christian unity had been something of a problem for the movement. By relationships Smith referred to the manner in which the Church of God did or did not interact with other Christian bodies bilaterally as well as in movements of interdenominational cooperation. Come-outism isolated the Church of God until 1930. From about that time, in some cases slightly earlier, several agencies and special committees established formal relationships with ecumenical church councils and their program units. These relationships were never hidden from the church, but neither were they well advertised. They did not grow out of a well-articulated theology of Christian unity but were instead motivated largely by a legitimate if more pragmatic concern. In the main, boards and agencies that joined interdenominational councils were searching for resources that would enable them to perform their tasks more effectively.

It was not until 1965, some eighty-four years after it began, that the Church of God got around to formally signaling its responsibility as a Christian unity movement among the churches of Christendom. In that year the General Assembly established a Committee on Christian Unity. John Smith, himself an enthusiastic and determined ecumenist, saw in the creation of this committee a sign of the church's maturation. "No longer do we just preach unity and wait for the Holy Spirit to bring it about; we now accept the possibility that the Holy Spirit may be seeking to lead other

Christians along those same lines, and we are willing to join them in the quest."[7] The better part of wisdom would have cautioned Smith to guard his optimism. In the eighties and nineties the Church of God as a whole demonstrated only a lukewarm interest in forging or strengthening relationships with interdenominational bodies or other church groups.

The conciliar movement posed a particular problem for the Church of God. Here were Christians expressly interested in improving relationships among Christian bodies, whether in the United States or around the world. Ecumenists seemed to be stealing Church of God thunder, but under the lingering influence of come-outism the movement dared not endorse national or world council initiatives. A significant number of agency leaders, staff members, college professors, and church leaders were sympathetic to ecumenical Christianity and found ways of participating in its life. Some, like Adam Miller and R. Eugene Sterner, publicly endorsed this participation.[8] But such endorsements were seasoned with caution. The Church of God would not join the National Council of Churches, the National Association of Evangelicals, or any other cooperative association of church bodies. It was not only that the very polity of the church prevented such a move, although that was certainly a factor.[9] Church of God people have been very wary of the kind of unity envisioned by interdenominational cooperative ventures, insisting that denominational mergers and church federations can never substitute for the unity of the Spirit in the bond of peace. That concern was held by all, but conservatives and the grassroots church were more vocal in their expressions and their reluctance to forge such relationships. In 1985 the Committee on Long Range Planning offered a resolution, subsequently endorsed by the General Assembly, that encouraged efforts "to seek intentional interchurch relationships through which its own ministries are enriched and which provide opportunity for the Church of God reformation movement to live out its message of Christian unity through enriching the entire Body of Christ."[10] Two years later the National Council of Churches and the World Council were sharply criticized on the floor of the same General Assembly, and questions were raised about the propriety of agency involvement with either body. In 1988 a special committee reported back to the Assembly a list of guidelines qualifying the participation of all Church of God agencies in interchurch cooperative relationships. The committee report evidenced an attitude that, on the one hand, wanted to avoid a posture that would in effect make a denomination of the Church of God while, on the other hand, recognize the movement's longstanding conviction that organizational affiliation was not a desirable practice of Christian unity.[11]

Its relationships to conciliar ecumenism aside, during the eighties and nineties the Church of God did pursue dialogical relationships with one interdenominational organization and one church body. In 1967 there had convened in Louisville the first of what proved to be an enduring series of meetings under the title, "The Conferences on the Concept of the Believers' Church." Harold L. Phillips and John W. V. Smith were early participants in this series of meetings that brought together representatives of the Believers' Churches. In 1984 the seventh meeting convened in Anderson largely through the efforts of Smith and Gilbert Stafford. However, it has been largely through the participation of individuals that the Church of God has remained connected to such conferences. The mid-eighties climate of hostility toward interchurch cooperation made officials at Warner Press and Anderson University reluctant to sponsor the publication of the conference papers from the conference.[12]

Bilateral conversations between the Church of God and the Independent Christian Churches/Churches of Christ offered grounds for greater optimism. In the latter eighties conversations began between representatives of the two groups and developed into a series of "Open Forum" meetings, the first in 1989 at Trader's Point Christian Church in Indianapolis, where members of both groups gathered for worship and discussions of issues common to all.[13] This series of meetings did enjoy the support of Executive Council staff members, but it was still largely the project of a handful of individuals deeply supportive of the cause of Christian unity. No person in the Church of God was more committed to that cause throughout the eighties and nineties than Gilbert W. Stafford, professor of Christian theology at the School of Theology at Anderson University. It is also fair to say that, above all others, Stafford had worked out a theological foundation for continuing efforts at interchurch cooperation.[14] Following John W. V. Smith's death in 1984, Stafford assumed his seat on the Commission on Faith and Order of the National Council of Churches. There as well as in the Believers' Church conferences and the bilateral conversations with the Independent Christian Churches/Churches of Christ, Stafford carried the torch of Christian unity as a theological expression of the mission of the Church of God.

Perhaps in other church bodies as well, but acutely in the Church of God, the items of unfinished business on John Smith's agenda—organization, mission, and relationships—extend from the church's self-understanding, its sense of identity. From 1940 on a sense of identity was in question in the Church of God. The search for identity underlies Gilbert Stafford's *Church of God at the Crossroads,* the book that touched a sensitive nerve in the church and which began the discussion of the preceding pages. From the forties through the mid-nineties the church's theologians did not offer much in the way of published work that directly guided that search, nor did they provide many fruitful leads. Until the publication of the Church of God Doctrinal Library in the 1970s, the two most useful works on ecclesiology were brief studies by R. Eugene Sterner and A. F. Gray. But had there been a flood of theological reassessments, no assurance could be given that the constituency, clergy or lay, would welcome them. There once was a day when common doctrinal practices and the *Gospel Trumpet* provided the glue that held the Church of God movement together. Common practices served to knit the movement into a common church culture that shaped a generally consistent theological vision among the constituency. The absence of strong organizational structures placed a heavy burden on the *Gospel Trumpet/Vital Christianity* to play a role as a polity for the Church of God. However, after a run of more than a century, the final number of the church paper was published in September 1996. The number of subscribers may have dwindled, but when the magazine died the church still had lost an important symbol around which it could identify. The factionalizing tendencies of radical congregationalist polity also manifested themselves by the increasing willingness of individual congregations to purchase goods and services from suppliers other than the Anderson-based agencies. For whatever their reasons, and some were certainly legitimate, as churches purchased Sunday school curriculum from independent publishers or negotiated building loans wherever the best deal was available, the ties that bound congregations to each other and to the Church of God as a whole weakened. Without fresh theological reassessment and shorn of important symbolic connections, internal relationships turned out to be an important item of unfinished business in ways that John Smith had not foreseen.

The celebration of the Church of God centennial stimulated something of a renaissance in theological and historical reflection on the church. The question of identity still lingered, but not for lack of fresh perspectives or books that helped the church to consider its heritage and mission in the light of historical understanding and theological understanding. The publication of John W. V. Smith's *The Quest for Holiness and Unity* in 1980 was a highlight among several books published on the history of the Church of God. Also worthy of mention are Barry L. Callen's collections of largely primary sources, a two-volume compilation titled *The First Century* (1979) and, more recently, *Following the Light* (2000). In commemoration of the centennial Editor Arlo F. Newell committed Warner Press to a series of nontechnical works called the "Church of God Doctrinal Library." The eight-volume series included studies of a range of doctrinal subjects from God to healing, the

Holy Spirit to the church, and the kingdom of God to the Christian life, all written to instruct and inform the theological perspective of the Church of God. Finally, Gilbert Stafford's *Theology for Disciples* (1996) offered the church a volume that filled the need for fresh theological restatement by and for people of the Church of God.

The renaissance of theological writing would be of greater benefit to the church as a whole were there formal opportunities for discussions on the question of identity. In the early nineties the Executive Council had quashed proposals for a churchwide triennial discussion group. However, organizational restructuring provided for a triennial visioning conference. A vehicle was now in place to prompt informed discussions concerning mission, relationships and organization and thus begin to articulate a new identity for the Church of God. The issue was now whether conference planners would organize "futuring" sessions predicated on an understanding of the movement's historic theological commitments and practices.

In the late nineteenth and early twentieth centuries the earliest adherents of the Church of God did not take their stand with the saints to have their wants or even their needs met. They made common cause with the movement on the basis of a shared view of a church beyond division, to which realization they were willing to devote themselves. In this the movement's first self-understanding was born. Doctrinal practices articulated that self-understanding, enabling others to see the church. In time, new intellectual currents forced revisions in that self-understanding. Internal struggles combined with unprecedented prosperity postponed the long-needed theological reassessment. In the early twenty-first century resources and mechanisms were available to articulate a fresh new perspective that might once again prove attractive to those who hungered for a greater unity of fellowship among Christians and who also wished to say that they had seen the church.

As the millenium turned, the Church of God stood at one of those decisive moments that occur in the history of religious groups. Different voices beckoned the movement to follow down any one of several paths that led from the crossroads where the church found itself. Some voices called the movement to recover its traditional practices convinced that it would regain a lost identity in the process. Other voices encouraged the church to adopt new strategies of church growth that gave the appearance of abandoning much of the movement's historic teaching. Still others spoke as the somewhat chastened heirs of a cosmopolitan tradition sympathetic to calls for social justice that resonated with the larger society. Thus the Church of God stood at a junction where it earnestly sought a path that would faithfully express its understanding of the people they believed God called them to be.

Given their rich and unique theological history, one would hope that twenty-first century saints would allow their forefathers and foremothers a vote in the determination of that answer, and thus be willingly shaped by the living faith of the dead.

Notes

1. Cf. *The Quest for Holiness and Unity*, 436–447.
2. "Recommendations: Task Force on Governance and Polity [June 1992]," in Callen, *Following the Light*, 190–191.
3. He who was formerly known as executive secretary had his title changed from "executive" to "general," and those who formerly belonged to the Executive Council now became members of the Leadership Council.
4. "Restructuring the National Ministries," in Callen, *Following the Light*, 196.
5. In his final report as general secretary, Foggs enthusiastically supported the proposed reorganization, saying, "We stand prepared to enter the twenty-first century with new vision, fresh perspective, and gifted leadership as Church of God Ministries, Inc. [the new corporate name for the national ministries of the Church of God] sets the pace for an ever-expanding reach in the church's mission and ministry." Ibid.
6. "Vision-2-Grow," in Callen, *Following the Light*, 280.
7. "Establishment of the Committee on Christian Unity," in Callen, *Following the Light*, 174. The original resolution establishing the committee called for a membership composed of five appointed members representing the School of Theology, the Editorial Division of Warner Press, the Divisions of General Service and Church Service, and the Missionary Board. The executive secretary of the Executive Council was also a member. Four additional members, elected by the General Assembly completed the committee's membership.
8. Cf., for example, Miller's collection of conference papers, *Christian Unity and Ecumenical Trends*, or Sterner, *Toward a Christian Fellowship* (Anderson, Ind: Warner Press, 1957), 30–34.
9. The bylaws of the General Assembly have long maintained that it is not an "ecclesiastical body."
10. "Acceptable Inter-Church Cooperation," in Callen, *Following the Light*, 187.
11. Ibid., 188–189.
12. Eventually a publisher was found. Cf. Merle D. Strege, editor, Introduction by John Howard Yoder, *Baptism and Church: A Believers' Church Vision* (Grand Rapids, Mich: Sagamore Books, 1986).
13. For a volume that documents the traditions and mutual work of these two groups cf. Barry Callen and James North, *Coming Together in Christ* (Joplin, Mo: College Press Publishing Company, 1997).
14. For a sample of Stafford's thought in this regard see, "The Faith and Order Movement: Holiness Church Participation," in Callen, *Following the Light*, 353–361, and especially Gilbert W. Stafford, *Theology for Disciples*, Foreword by James Earl Massey (Anderson, Ind: Warner Press, 1996), 221–246.

Glossary of Terms

Asceticism—the practice of renouncing the use of or participation in things generally believed to be good for the sake of a higher, spiritual good. Fasting during Lent as spiritual preparation for Easter is one form of asceticism.

Charismatic government—the Church of God doctrinal practice based on the belief that God organized the true church through the agency of the Holy Spirit, who chose people for service in the church by conferring upon them the gifts ("charisms," from the Greek *charisma*) necessary for the position. To be gifted was also to be divinely appointed to a particular calling.

Christian primitivism—the desire to return to the original condition of Christianity as it is believed to exist in the New Testament era. In the specific case of the Church of God, primitivism focused on the ideal of the "New Testament church," the conditions and life of which, it was believed, needed to be restored. In this sense, primitivism can be considered generally as a synonym for "restorationism" and "restitutionism."

Church-historical exegesis—see page 95, footnote.

Dispensational premillennialism—Premillennialism is the belief that Christ will return and afterward establish a one thousand year reign on earth. Dispensationalism is a category of premillennialism commonly associated with Charles Nelson Darby and popularized by the Scofield Reference Bible. In this system of interpretation, God's plan for world history is ordered according to a series of dispensations.

Documentary hypothesis—a theory concerning the authorship of the first five books of the Old Testament. Applying the insights of the so-called higher criticism, scholars compared these books and identified four major literary traditions. Followers of the theory concluded that the anonymous authors of these four sources (code-named *J, E, P,* and *D,* and not Moses) wrote the bulk of the material from which the first five books—the Pentateuch—were written.

Ecclesiology—the field of theology that deals with biblical and historical teaching on the aspects, nature, and understanding of the church. "Apocalyptic" ecclesiology here refers to the understanding of the church worked out principally by F. G. Smith whereby that understanding rested heavily on the apocalyptic books of the Bible, Daniel and the Revelation. Similarly, "radical" ecclesiology refers to the belief in the Church of God that the true church needed to conform to New Testament ideal of the church as the source. In this sense "radical" comes from the Latin *radix,* "root."

Epistemology—from the Greek word *episteme* meaning "knowledge," epistemology is the field of philosophy that deals with theories of knowing and asks such questions as: "On what bases do human beings come to knowledge?" "Do humans know primarily through the processes of the mind or through experience?" "How is knowing shaped by the particular communities of which humans are members?"

Evangelicalism—a broad term capable of several different applications, but in the context of twentieth-century American Protestantism, Evangelicals are typically characterized by (a) belief in the authority of the Bible, (b) the necessity of personal conversion, and (c), the mandate to evangelize the entire world. Evangelicals also tend to stress the importance of rational belief in core doctrines of Christianity.

Exegesis—the reporting, description, or explanation of a text. Exegesis is closely related to hermeneutics, as the discipline of interpretation, especially here, biblical interpretation. Modern exegesis includes study of the Bible in its original languages and an analysis of the historical context of the material under consideration. Other, more advanced methods of analysis may also be applied.

Hermeneutics—the science of interpretation, including the rules or principles that guide the interpretation of a text, specifically here, the text of Scripture.

Historical-critical method—see page 204, footnote.

Liberalism—sometimes also referred to as "modernism." Originating mainly in Germany before spreading to England and North America in the nineteenth- and twentieth-centuries, Protestant liberalism attempted to adapt traditional Christian teaching to the intellectual and scientific currents that developed in the wake of the European Enlightenment. Liberals tended to reject supernaturalistic explanations in favor of the view that God was at work in the world through the processes of history and the natural order. Divine transcendence was replaced by the notion of God's immanence.

Ontological—from "ontology," the branch of philosophy concerned with the consideration of being. Ontology considers the sheer existence or being of things.

Pietist/Pietism—a spiritual movement originating in Germany in the early seventeenth-century through the work of the Lutheran pastor, Johann Arndt. Pietists protested a rationalist approach to theology that emphasized assent to sound doctrine to the near exclusion of a concern for godly living. Pietist writers became masters of the devotional life and laid great stress on the experiential knowledge of God. They also emphasized the ethical component of Christianity, insisting that good works followed from and were evidence of justification.

Preterist—an interpretive approach to the Book of Revelation that works primarily from an understanding of its message to the first-century church. Preterists do not read Revelation as a prediction of the future, whether of world history or the history of the church.

Restorationism—see above, "Christian Primitivism."

Revivalism—one of the key characteristics of a broad segment of nineteenth- and twentieth-century American Protestantism, its origins lay in the seventeenth-century Great Awakening made famous by preachers such as George Whitefield and Jonathan Edwards. Early revivals were spontaneous, but by the mid-nineteenth-century had become a routine feature of much of Protestant spirituality, emphasizing periods of focused spiritual intensity during which the unconverted were invited to repent and lax believers were encouraged to greater vitality and recommitment. The revivalist style of preaching, in which the sermon's goal was more to persuade than instruct and exemplified in nationally known figures such as Charles G. Finney and D. L. Moody, was regarded in many quarters as the essential if not definitive form of the sermon.

Synoptic problem—from a compound of Greek terms meaning "to see together," the phrase refers to the special study of the relationship between the gospels of Mark, Matthew, and Luke, specifically the extensive simi-larities as well as the differences between them. These relationships fostered critical theories concerning the composition and authorship of the three gospels that pushed well beyond the traditional view that they were written by the people whose names they carry.

Typology—a form of biblical interpretation that sees relationships between events or people in an earlier period with those of a later point in time. For example, early Church of God writers regarded the Israelite tabernacle as a type of New Testament salvation read in Wesleyan terms. The tabernacle's Holy Place was thus interpreted as a foreshadowing of justification while the Most Holy Place anticipated the experience of entire sanctification.

I Saw *the* Church

People

Achor, George, 302
Adcock, Elver, 271
Anderson J. Grant, 61, 68-70, 74, 91-92, 315
Anderson, William S., 349
Arndt, Johannes, 246, 252
Bailey, George W., 261
Baldwin, J. W., 261, 263
Barth, Karl, 236, 247
Bass, Dorothy, 18
Berry, R. L., 92, 144-145, 160-161, 300, 308
Beverly, Sethard P., 320
Blaney, J. C., 144
Blewitt, C. J., 113-114, 299-300
Boland, J. M., 16
Bolitho, Axchie, 308
Boone, Pat, 369
Boyer, Harold, 333
Brennan, Raymond, 349
Brooks, Clara M., 58
Brooks, Lawrence, 296
Brown, Carrie Becker, 212
Brown, Charles E., 13, 61, 82, 135, 162, 195, 205, 210, 221, 223, 226, 239, 246, 267
Brown, Delwin, 349
Brown, Willis M., 210
Brueggemann, Walter, 324
Bruffet, Fred, 199
Brunner, Emil, 236
Bryant, S. G., 302
Bunch, Willis D., 210
Burchett, James, 349
Burgess, Kurt L., 349
Byers, A. L., 5, 11-12, 38,42, 58,60, 70, 115-116, 131-132, 162
Byers, Jacob W., 125, 128
Byers, Jennie, 80
Byers, Mrs. C. E., 116, 200
Byrd, Wendell, 247
Byrum, Eli, 63

Byrum, Enoch E., 40, 63-64
Byrum, Lucinda, 63
Byrum, Noah, 87, 92
Byrum, Robert, 154
Byrum, Russell, 110, 128, 154-155, 164
Byrum, Bessie Hittle, 156
Caldwell, Irene S., 222, 247, 360
Caldwell, Mack M., 222
Callen, Barry L., 11, 31, 133, 162, 164, 199, 315, 348-349, 373, 381
Callen, Arlene, 349
Carver, E. I., 167
Case, Jackson Shirley, 204, 226
Chapman, Milo L., 223
Charles, Lottie, 58
Charles, Ray, 369
Clayton, G. T., 165, 227
Clear, Valorous B., 12, 289, 297
Cole, George, 87, 183, 199
Cole, Mary, 68-69, 90, 115, 131-132, 323
Cole, Jeremiah, 39, 74, 115
Coleridge, Samuel Taylor, 242
Cook, H. Revere, 247
Cook, James, 349
Cookston, Joseph, 377
Cox, David G., 349
Cox, G. David, 349
Craig, Clarence Tucker, 236, 308, 320
Critchell, B. P., 37
Culp, Robert, 310
Cyprian of Carthage, 102
D'Aubigne, Merle, 97
Daniels, Rolland, 377
Darby, John Nelson, 167
Davis, Alice, 40
Dawson, I. K., 270-271, 276-277, 279, 290
Dickstein, Morris, 317
Dodge, Harry, 247
Dowie, Alexander, 122
Dunbar, C. R., 5-7
Dunn, S. P., 318

394

Dykstra, Craig, 18
Ebeling, F. J., 168, 180
Edmondson, Warren, 235
Edwards, Jonathan, 167, 386
Eisenhower, Dwight D., 292
Elliott, Benjamin F., 82
Farrow, Lucy, 122-123
Finney, Charles Grandison, 2, 77
Fisher, Allie, 39, 50, 115, 323
Fisher, Joseph C., 22, 39-41
Flynt, Oscar J., 281
Foggs, Edward L., 310, 347, 376
Forrest, A. Leland, 247
Forrest, J. E., 92, 128, 247
Forsberg, Carl, 113, 300
Fosdick, Harry Emerson, 311
Fowler, Orson Squire, 68
Fowler, Ronald, 348
Francke, August Hermann, 227, 252
Friedan, Betty, 317
Gaither, Gloria, 312
Gaither, William, 312
Gaulke, Max, 167, 176, 178-179, 181
Germany, Horace, 321
Goodman, Delena, 235
Goodspeed, Edgar J., 204, 226
Gray, A. F., 164, 200, 206, 210, 219,
    222-223, 249, 261-267, 363, 381
Gray, Rosa Bannon, 263
Gregory, Dick, 334
Grubbs, David, 349
Harp, H. Richard, 349
Harrington, Hope, 335
Hart, Joan, 349
Hatch, C. W., 301, 314
Hatch, Roger, 349
Haynes, W. A., 41
Hazen, Robert, 307
Heffren, H. C., 167, 179, 181
Heinly, Floyd W., 147, 187
Henry, W. J., 41, 68, 83
Hesburgh, Theodore, 334
Hill, Robert, 348

Hines, Dalineta Ellis, 321
Hines, Samuel G., 163, 310, 321, 328-
    329, 348-349
Hodge, A. A., 167
Hoffman, Heinrich, 89
Horton, Thomas, 39
Horton, Walter Marshall, 226, 236-
    237, 247, 314
Householder, Mary, 308
Howard, J. N., 49, 383
Hunter, Clarence, 232, 234
Hunter, Martha, 232
Hunter, Mary, 232
Hunter, Nora Siens, 232, 325
Hurst, Geraldine, 309
Husted, Mary, 153
Huttenlocker, Keith, 354, 373
Inskip, John S., 5
Jackson, Jesse, 331, 334, 349
Jackson, Raymond S., 318
Johnson, D. D., 33
Johnson, L. H., 35-36
Johnson, O. L., 333
Jones, E. Stanley, 245, 361
Jones, Kenneth L., 359, 373
Joplin, Scott, 47
Keagy, Rhoda, 39
Keller, Sarah, 4, 6, 33-34, 36, 52
Kelly, M. Bruce, 349
Kennedy, John, 317
Kennedy, Robert, 307
Kerr, Tamzen Ann, 4
Khan, A. D., 54, 81, 92, 169, 180,
    185, 187
Kilgore, Forest, 360
Kilpatrick, A. J., 30, 49, 165
King, Martin Luther, Jr., 317
Kirkpatrick, Celia, 39
Knapp, Martin Wells, 122
Koglin, Anna, 235, 325
Kolb, Jerry, 335
Latourette, Kenneth, 215
Laubach, Frank, 245

Location